THE
Black Arts

The Goat of the Witches' Sabbath, or Goat of Mendes,
after Eliphas Levi

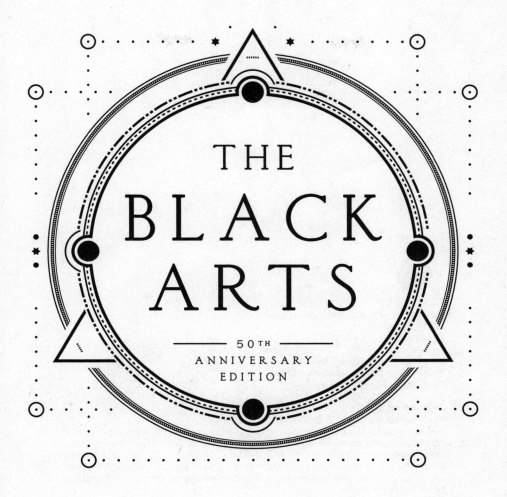

THE
BLACK
ARTS

50TH
ANNIVERSARY
EDITION

— RICHARD CAVENDISH —

INTRODUCTION BY MITCH HOROWITZ

A TarcherPerigee Book

tarcherperigee

An imprint of Penguin Random House LLC
375 Hudson Street
New York, New York 10014

First Capricorn edition 1967
First Perigee trade paperback edition 1983
First TarcherPerigee edition 2017

TarcherPerigee with tp colophon is a registered trademark of Penguin Random House LLC.

Most TarcherPerigee books are available at special quantity discounts for bulk purchase for sales promotions, premiums, fund-raising, and educational needs. Special books or book excerpts also can be created to fit specific needs. For details, write: SpecialMarkets@penguinrandomhouse.com.

Library of Congress card catalog number: 67-10950

Printed in the United States of America
67th Printing

Contents

Diagrams

Introduction

The Black Arts
After Fifty Years

by Mitch Horowitz

The year of publication commemorated by this fiftieth anniversary volume of *The Black Arts*—1967—could be seen as a banner moment for the rebirth of occult and esoteric spirituality in the modern West.

In 1967, the toy giant Parker Brothers relaunched the Ouija board, having bought rights the prior year from descendants of manufacturer William Fuld, and sold a record two million talking boards, surpassing sales of its leading game, Monopoly, and installing the mediumistic device into playrooms across America.

As governor-elect of California, Ronald Reagan in January 1967 raised eyebrows by scheduling his inauguration at the perplexing hour of 12:10 a.m., prompting persistent questions—which ran throughout his presidency—over the extent of his and his wife's dedication to astrology. Reagan would admit only that "Nancy and I enjoy glancing at the daily astrology charts in our morning paper." At that time, about 1,250 out of 1,750 daily papers featured daily horoscope columns, a postwar high.

In 1967, The Beatles learned Transcendental Meditation (TM) from the Maharishi Mahesh Yogi, indelibly marrying the youth culture to the pursuit of

Eastern and esoteric wisdom. The following year, The Beatles' famous sojourn to the Maharishi's northern Indian ashram in Rishikesh resurrected the ideal of the Westerner seeking wisdom in the Far East, a template laid in the late 1870s by Russian-born occult explorer Madame H. P. Blavatsky, who left behind the relatively cushy environs of New York City to move to India, a place then as alien to most Westerners as the surface of another planet.

Also in 1967, the bestselling biography *Edgar Cayce: The Sleeping Prophet*, by tabloid journalist Jess Stearn, brought renewed attention to the early twentieth-century medical clairvoyant. Cayce's popularity was followed by a wave of "channeled" literature—Cayce first used the term "channel" in the mystical sense—under the names of such other-dimensional entities as Seth, Ramtha, and Abraham.

This ferment of occult and mystical enthusiasm soon exploded across the culture as Americans were urged to "be here now," try psychedelics to "tune in" to higher energies, use new practices in yoga and Zen, rediscover native shamanism (or variants of it) in the books of Carlos Castaneda, and shiver over evils, new and ancient, with the shock of the Manson murders and the popularity of movies like *The Exorcist* and *Rosemary's Baby*.

Into this atmosphere, British historian Richard Cavendish (1930–2016) launched his enduring and influential study of occult history and practice, *The Black Arts*. The book won immediate popularity, gaining the affections of Mick Jagger, author Isaac Bashevis Singer, and, well, me, when I first began seriously studying the occult about twenty years ago. I discovered the book on the backlist of the publisher for which I now work, and was immediately enchanted with the green-blue-black psychedelic-goth graphics of the original cover art. At a later date, the book was redesigned in the more ordinary style of a heavy-metal album cover, which hyped up the sinister (serpents coiling from eye sockets of skulls) and played down the mysterious, alluring, and mature. With this fiftieth anniversary edition, TarcherPerigee restores the mood of the original, and returns a few missing images to the interior. Mercury, rejoice.

In the minds of many modern people, the occult stands for the sinister and Satanic. This is a mistake, historically and spiritually. The term "occult" comes from *occultus*, Latin for "hidden." Classically speaking, occult philosophy posits the existence of an unseen dimension of life whose forces are felt on and through us. In the late ancient world, when the temple orders of Egypt, Greece, and Rome, and the folk beliefs and nature-based religions of Europe, were losing appeal to Christianity, the church fathers did what we as humans have always done: labeled the other side, i.e., the historical and theological losers, in terminology of our own liking, in this case as demon worshippers and purveyors of dark sorcery, a characterization that pre-Christians and pagans had never claimed for themselves. Indeed, for readers who were or are put off by Cavendish's malevolent-sounding term "black arts" in the title, he quickly explained his choice: "No one is a black magician in his own eyes, and modern occultists, whatever their beliefs and practices, think of themselves as high-minded white magicians"—yet they are driven, as we all are, by the "titanic attempt to exalt the stature of man . . . this gives it [magic] a certain magnificence."

Isaac Bashevis Singer, in a shrewd and admiring critical essay on *The Black Arts* in *Book Week* on April 9, 1967, agreed with Cavendish, noting: "We are all black magicians in our dreams, in our fantasies, perversions, and phobias."

And, to this I would add, in the pursuit of our highest ideals. As Cavendish and Singer detected, we are not very different from the classical magician when we strive, morally and materially, to carry forth our plans in the world—to ensure the betterment of ourselves and our loved ones; to heal sickness; to create, sustain, and, above all, to *generate things* that bear our markings, ideals, and likenesses. All of this is the expenditure of power, the striving to physically establish our inner drives and images.

I do not view the search for individual power, including through supernatural means, as necessarily maleficent, and neither, I think, did Cavendish. Historically and psychologically, it is a fundamental human trait to evaluate, adopt, or avoid an idea based upon whether it builds or depletes our sense of personal agency. "A living thing," Nietzsche wrote in *Beyond Good and Evil*, "seeks above all to *discharge* its strength—life itself is *will to power.*" The difficulty is in making our choices wisely.

We sometimes deny or overlook this power-seeking impulse in ourselves, associating it with the tragic fate of Faust or Lady Macbeth. It can be argued, however, that all of our neuroses and feelings of chronic despair, aside from those with identifiably biological causes, grow from the frustrated expression of personal power. We may spend a lifetime (and countless therapy sessions) ascribing our problems to other, more secondary phenomena—without realizing that, as naturally as a bird is drawn to the dips and flows of air currents, we are in the perpetual act of trying to forge, create, and sustain, much like the ancient alchemist or wizard.

The ultimate frustration of life is that, while we seem to be granted godlike powers—giving birth, creating beauty, spanning space and time, devising machines of incredible might—we are bound to physical forms that quickly decay. "Ye are gods," wrote the psalmist, adding, "but yet shall die as princes." Immortality and the reversal of bodily decline is the one magic no one has ever mastered. The wish to surpass the boundaries of our physicality is behind some of our most haunting myths and parables, from the Trojan prince Tithonus, to whom the gods granted immortality but trapped in a shell of misery and decay for failing to request eternal youth, to the doomed scientist Victor Frankenstein, who sought the ultimate alchemy of creating life only to bring destruction on everyone around him.

In *The Black Arts*, Cavendish captures the human striving and universality behind the magical search. He also demonstrates virtuosity for explaining ancient and more recent rituals, rites, and esoteric philosophies with splendid clarity. Although he casts a critical eye toward some of the customs he explores, Cavendish never places himself above or in opposition to them. The historian realizes that these practices, whether they are to his or your private liking, reflect a basic human need. Nor does the author evaluate his facts from a distant remove. Cavendish, as Singer noted, "does discreetly hint that there may be a kernel of truth in the magicians' fantastic assertions."

First appearing in 1967, *The Black Arts* narrowly predated (and helped foresee) the explosion of mainstream interest in New Age and spiritual-therapeutic philosophies. The book also arrived just as the modern world was experiencing the rebirth of Wicca, or witchcraft, a nature-based religion now officially recognized within the U.S. military (whose service members and veterans may select the pentagram from among more than sixty-five "emblems of belief"). By many accounts, Wicca is one of the fastest-growing religions in the Western world today. It is not difficult to imagine a cohort of aspiring teen witches among Cavendish's earliest readers (some of whom probably graduated to his magisterial twenty-four-volume encyclopedia *Man, Myth & Magic*, which he edited in 1970).

To learn more about the current occult scene, in its popular and esoteric variants, you can select among dozens of twenty-first-century books. Indeed, you will get much more from recent books for having read Cavendish's. But make no mistake: *The Black Arts* is much more than a well-timed period piece. It stands nearly alone as a simultaneously comprehensive and inviting guide to the world of premodern esoterica. Cavendish performed an epic feat of distillation in this well-sifted compendium. He created vivid descriptions of philosophies that many writers botch, such as Kabbalah (an area where Singer felt the book displayed distinction), European spell casting, and the messy topic of Satan worship, which is not exactly a tradition so much as a patchwork of historical experiments, foibles, and, not infrequently, frauds.

Cavendish's descriptions are so clear that the intrepid reader can use his book, as I admittedly once did, not only as a historical work but also as a guide to practice. If you are bold enough (and I hope it's boldness and not fickleness or venom), you can try your hand at variants of numerology, astrology, and divination. I believe strongly that to understand the meaning and ideas behind any faith or spiritual practice (by spiritual I mean belief in extra-physicality), a participatory approach is necessary, even if only temporarily. Whether you view the occult critically or sympathetically, and there are grounds for both responses, you will never understand the pull of the religious or occult appeal without getting involved in it. Messy hands are the fee of entry.

Soon after Cavendish published his study, another writer and journalist, Lewis Lapham, followed The Beatles to the Rishikesh ashram for a firsthand view of their encounter with the Maharishi. Lapham was a progenitor of the "New Journalism" (not a term he claimed for himself), an approach to report-age that included an expressly participatory element. In this vein, Lapham took measure of the charismatic, bearded guru's influence on The Beatles in a two-part 1968 article for the *Saturday Evening Post*, "There Once Was a Guru from Rishikesh." The journalist viewed the Maharishi and his flowered aco-lytes with immediate suspicion, and regarded them from a sardonic and even caustic remove. Yet it never occurred to Lapham, who sat in on rap sessions, group meals, and other events, to use the easiest and plainest means available to test his instinct that there was something fishy about the robed man selling bliss: namely, placing his bottom on a cushion and trying the TM technique. A mantra, if you desire one, is about as easily attained as a learner's permit to drive—and, indeed, at that particular time and place was much easier.

In 2017, almost fifty years after his visit, I asked Lapham, a gentlemanly and approachable man, whether he had learned TM in Rishikesh or another time. His reply: "Even in Rishikesh I didn't practice Transcendental Medita-tion. The Maharishi furnished me with a mantra, but I failed to employ it as a stairway to the stars." There was no discernible curiosity toward the thing being judged. This is the opposite of Cavendish's approach. That intellectual quality in Cavendish—to place his hands (and yours) on the driver's wheel—is what has given his book its posterity, and won it unlikely dedication from both mainstream literary voices and contemporary occult seekers.

As I have written in *Occult America* and elsewhere, occult philosophy is the kernel that gave rise to most of today's modes of therapeutic and self-help spirituality. Indeed, the idea of an individual spiritual search now seems like a birthright. This was not always so. During the Renaissance, when occult forms of worship and magic were being rediscovered, translators, artists, and religious scholars began to enunciate the first modern conception of a personal spiritual search, located beyond the parameters of any one congregation or faith. That impulse pulled Thoreau into the woods, set Blavatsky on her globe-spanning search, drew The Beatles to Rishikesh—and lured many readers to this book.

In the closing pages of *Occult America*, I identified five spiritual principles with which most modern people agree, even those who are disinclined toward religion. These beliefs came into vogue—and have grown only stronger—in the years of occult ferment immediately following Cavendish. As you will see in his pages, these principles found their earliest sounding in Western life through occult and mystical practices. They are:

1. Belief in the therapeutic value of spiritual and religious ideas.
2. Belief in a mind-body connection in health.
3. Belief that human consciousness is evolving to higher stages.
4. Belief that thoughts, to some greater or lesser measure, determine reality.
5. Belief that spiritual understanding is available without allegiance to any specific religion or doctrine.

The encounter between modern people and occultism, including many of the practices explored in this book, resulted in a vast morphing and reframing of arcane beliefs from the Old World into the new, boundary-free spiritual culture of our own era. This new spiritual culture is often called the New Age—a term critics use derisively but I use with respect. New Age spirituality is, quite simply, therapeutic spirituality, and the seeking of self-potential through metaphysical understanding. The New Age extols religious egalitarianism and has, in my view, responded more fully than any other movement in history to the inner needs and personal search of the individual.

In reading *The Black Arts* you will discover much more than magical systems from the past; you will also discover ideas that have shaped us as a culture—and that likely reflect aspects of your interior life.

Mitch Horowitz is the PEN Award–winning author of books including *Occult America*; *One Simple Idea: How Positive Thinking Reshaped Modern Life*; and *Mind As Builder: The Positive-Mind Metaphysics of Edgar Cayce.* He is vice president and executive editor at TarcherPerigee. Follow him @MitchHorowitz.

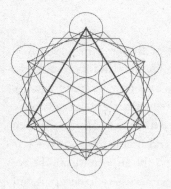

CHAPTER ONE

The World of the Black Magician

THE driving force behind black magic is hunger for power. Its ultimate aim was stated, appropriately enough, by the serpent in the Garden of Eden. Adam and Eve were afraid that if they ate the fruit of the Tree of Knowledge of Good and Evil they would die. But the serpent said 'Ye shall not surely die: for God doth know that in the day ye eat thereof, then your eyes shall be opened and *ye shall be as gods*, knowing good and evil'.[1] In occultism the serpent is a symbol of wisdom, and for centuries magicians have devoted themselves to the search for the forbidden fruit which would bring fulfilment of the serpent's promise. Carried to its furthest extreme, the black magician's ambition is to wield supreme power over the entire universe, to make himself a god.

Black magic is rooted in the darkest levels of the mind, and this is a large part of its attraction, but it is much more than a product of the love of evil or a liking for mysterious mumbo-jumbo. It is a titanic attempt to exalt the stature of man, to put man in the place which religious thought reserves for God. In spite of its crudities and squalors this gives it a certain magnificence.

*The numbers refer to the notes at the end of the book. These notes contain references only.

The great fascination of magic is in the type of thought on which it is based. Magical thinking is not random, it has its own laws and its own logic, but it is poetic rather than rational. It leaps to conclusions which are usually scientifically unwarranted, but which often seem poetically right. It is a type of thinking which has been prevalent all through the history of Europe, which lies behind huge areas of our religion, philosophy and literature, and which is a major guide-post to the regions of the spiritual and the supernatural, the regions of which science has nothing to say. There is no necessity to accept it, but it rings many a far-away, summoning bell in the depths of the mind.

It is natural to think of magic as a thing of the past, which must have withered to dust under the hard light of modern science and scepticism, but, in fact, this is not the case. Magical thinking is still deeply embedded in the human mentality. Magic has been practised throughout European history, down to and including the present day, and it has attracted more interest and support in the last hundred years than at any time since the Renaissance.

No one is a black magician in his own eyes, and modern occultists, whatever their beliefs and practices, think of themselves as high-minded white magicians, not as sinister Brothers of the Left-hand Path. In October 1964 the Los Angeles police arrested thirty-nine gipsies on charges of fortune-telling. The gipsies immediately accused the police of violating their religious freedom. They were not telling fortunes, but giving 'spiritual readings'. 'Gipsies are born with the power to look into the future. It's part of our religion. We are members of the Palmistry Church.' About a year earlier the British witch covens celebrated one of their great annual festivals, All-Hallows Eve, with rites involving the magic circle, the magic knife, incantations, nudity and frenzied dances. One of the St. Albans witches, naked except for a string of beads, is reported as saying, 'We are not anti-Christian. We just have other means of spiritual satisfaction.'

The most notorious and most brilliantly gifted of modern magicians, Aleister Crowley, was regarded as a black sorcerer by many other occultists, and his rituals are saturated with sex and blood to an extent which, to put it mildly, scarcely fits the normal conception of white magic. But he himself professed nothing but contempt for black magicians. Among them he included Christian Scientists and Spiritualists, as well as those of his fellow occultists who disapproved of him.

In the same way, the writers of the old grimoires, or magical textbooks, which instruct the reader in methods of calling up evil spirits, killing people, causing hatred and destruction or forcing women to submit to him in love, did not think of themselves as black magicians. On the contrary, the grimoires are packed with prayers to God and the angels, fastings and self-mortifications and ostentatious piety. The principal process in the *Grimoire of Honorius*, which is usually considered the most diabolical of them all, overflows with impassioned and perfectly sincere appeals to God and devout sayings of Mass. It also involves tearing out the eyes of a black cock and slaughtering a lamb, and its purpose is to summon up the Devil.

It is not merely that people are naturally disinclined to pin nasty labels on themselves and that the human mind can always find excellent reasons for evoking the Devil or killing an enemy or causing harm and destruction. The magician sets out to conquer the universe. To succeed he must make himself master of everything in it—evil as well as good, cruelty as well as mercy, pain as well as pleasure. Deep at the heart of the magical outlook is the pagan but not ignoble conviction that everything has its place and function in the order of the universe and that all types of experience are potentially rewarding. The complete man, which is what the magician attempts to be, is the man who has experienced and mastered all things. This conviction is closely related to the magical theory of the relationship between God, man and the universe.

1. The Magician's Universe

'The soul goes round upon a wheel of stars and all things return. . . . Good and evil go round in a wheel that is one thing and not many. Do you not realise in your heart, do you not believe behind all your beliefs, that there is but one reality and we are its shadows; and that all things are but aspects of one thing; a centre where men melt into Man and Man into God?'

'No,' said Father Brown.

G. K. CHESTERTON *The Dagger with Wings*

'Man is made in the image of God' and it has often been sardonically observed that 'God is made in the image of man'. Both statements are accepted as true in magic. Man can make himself God because he has the divine spark within him. He is a miniature image of God and God is man writ large. Aleister Crowley defined God as 'the Ideal Identity of a man's inmost nature. Something ourselves [I erase Arnold's imbecile and guilty 'not'] that makes for righteousness' and 'the Great Work is the raising of the whole man in perfect balance to the power of Infinity', at which point he becomes God. Another notorious sorcerer, the great Renaissance magician Cornelius Agrippa, writing about 1510, asked how it was possible for a man to wield magical powers and answered, 'No one has such powers but he who has cohabited with the elements, vanquished nature, mounted higher than the heavens, elevating himself above the angels to the archetype itself, with whom he then becomes co-operator and can do all things.'[2]

This 'Ideal Identity' or 'archetype' is the fundamental unity which magicians see behind all the apparently diverse and disorderly phenomena of the universe. The world we live in may seem to be a rag-bag of odd, fortuitously assembled bits and pieces, but magicians believe that it is really a whole—like a design or a machine—and that all its parts are necessarily connected together in a certain way. Human beings are wholes of this kind. A man is made of many different things—his body and appearance, his mental and spiritual characteristics, his moods, his humour, his different ways of expressing himself at different times and in different circumstances—but these are all linked together into one organism with one underlying personality. In magic the universe is a human organism on a colossal scale. Just as all the facets of a man's character and behavior are aspects of a single personality, so all the phenomena of the universe are aspects of some one thing which underlies and connects them. This one thing is a being, a force, a substance, a principle, or something which it is not possible to describe in words at all. It is the One, or God.

The Universe and everything in it constitutes God. The universe is a gigantic human organism and man is a tiny image of it, a toy replica of God. Because he is a miniature of the universe, by a process of spiritual expansion a man can mystically extend his own being to cover the entire world and subject it to his will. It is because all things are aspects of one thing that all things are grist to the magician's mill. The complete man, who has experienced and mastered all things, has vanquished Nature and mounted higher than the heavens. He has reached the centre where man becomes God. The achievement of this is the Great Work, the supreme magical operation, which may take a lifetime or many lifetimes to complete.

In this unified magical universe mysterious forces are at work, moving beneath the external fabric of things like the invisible currents of the sea. Their effects are all around us, but most of us do not recognise their true nature. The universe is man on a huge scale and the impulses which move man—love, hate, lust, pity, the urge to survive, the urge to dominate—are found on a much greater scale in the universe. For instance, all things contain a greater or lesser amount of 'life-force', an immensely powerful drive which impels life to continue. It shows itself in the instinct of self-preservation, in the urge to survive— the struggle of everything in Nature to cling to life even in cruel and hopeless conditions—and in the universal urge to procreate, to ensure life's continuation by reproducing one's own kind. Magicians also see a force of violent destructive energy in the universe, which is a greater counterpart of man's destructive impulses and lies behind every form of savagery, bloodshed, warfare and havoc. These forces are named for gods and planets. The life-force is called the force of the sun, because the sun's light and heat are necessary for the existence of all life on earth. The violent destructive force is named for Mars, the Roman god of war.

The great moving forces of the universe are described and classified in various ways. Magicians who follow the theory of a mysterious body of doctrines called the Cabala list ten of them. Until fairly recent times astrologers believed in seven major forces, which they connected with the sun, the moon and five planets. They now have nine or ten, adding Uranus and Neptune and sometimes Pluto. Numerologists list nine forces, which they connect with the numbers from 1 to 9.

The magician masters these forces by experiencing them, by absorbing them into his own being and subjecting them to his will. He can do this because the forces are inside him as well as outside him. They are his own impulses magnified. The channel between his inner impulses and the forces outside him is his imagination, and a powerful imagination is his most important single piece of equipment. His powers of concentration are also vitally important. He must be able to focus the whole force of his being on a single aim, a single idea. He trains his powers of imagination and concentration to an abnormal pitch of efficiency by various techniques. The importance of concentration in magic is reflected in the old belief that you can recognise a magician by the fixed stare of his eyeballs.

If a magician wants to turn the current of destructive energy associated with Mars against an enemy, he sets his imagination to work to construct an intensely vivid mental picture of the force. Everything available to him which will contribute to this picture is used—gestures and dancing, drink, drugs, sex. He chants incantations which state the nature and attributes of the force of Mars. He fills his mind with images of blood and torment, rage and ruin and pain. If he is thoroughgoing the mimicry will extend to actual bloodshed and the torture of an animal or another human being. He unleashes all his own inner tides of hatred and violence and the ceremony gradually works up to a frenzy of savagery in which the force takes possession of the magician's entire being, in which he himself becomes the force, controls it by his will and hurls it against his victim.

Magicians believe that this ceremony, properly performed, will have crushing and scarifying effects on the victim. The theory is that any strong emotion of feeling carries a charge of force which is likely to affect the person at whom it is directed. The effect will vary with the strength of the feeling and the sensitivity of the target. When you sense an emotion radiating from another person and, as often happens, you seem to understand immediately what that person is feeling, you are reacting to a current of force whose nature you recognise instinctively, as if you were a kind of radar receiver registering invisible waves in the atmosphere. In magic a wave of powerful emotion is projected with calculated intent by someone who has developed his powers to an abnormal pitch, and according to occultists the results can be far-reaching. An exceptionally gifted and powerful magician may be able to kill by the sheer force of concentrated hatred, especially if his victim is someone of unusual sensitivity.

We recognise that in ordinary life someone who has a strong personality can make himself obeyed by the force of his will. The same thing is considered true in magic, but to a much greater degree. Man is potentially God and the human will, wielded by a magician who has learned how to concentrate and project it, has potentially the limitless power of God. As the nineteenth-century French magician Eliphas Levi put it, 'To affirm and will what ought to be is to create; to affirm and will what ought not to be is to destroy.'[3]

The great forces cannot be described as either good or evil. They have a good side and an evil side, or in occultists' terms a positive and a negative aspect. The evil side is the province of powerful evil beings called 'demons'. (The good side, correspondingly, is the province of the 'angels' or beneficent spirits, but the black magicians are much more interested in the demons.) The magical universe is like an ocean. The great tides move through it invisibly and men are swept about by them, but are sometimes strong enough and clever enough to master and use them. And in the cold black currents which come up from the deeps there are strange and sinister creatures lurking—evil intelligences which tempt and corrupt and destroy, malignant elementals, astral corpses, zombies, nightmare things which the malice of sorcerers has created, the 'shells' or 'husks' which are the waste products of the universal organism. This is a development of the belief held by many primitive peoples that diseases are evil spirits. The demons are the universe's parallel to the viruses, impurities and waste products of the human body. Or from the psychological point of view, they are the universal equivalents of the dark, cruel, animal depths of the human mind.

Belief in the existence of evil supernatural beings seems to be instinctive. In all known societies down to modern times people have believed in demons and ghosts. The fear of something which lies in wait and pounces has a particularly long-lasting hold on humanity. The seven terrible Babylonian devils called *maskim*, which were the evil counterparts of the gods of the planets (just as in modern theory the demons are the evil side of the great occult forces), were beings which lurked in ambush. The Arab *ghul* sets traps and waits in hiding, ready to spring. The well-known verses of Psalm 91 probably refer to demons—'Thou shalt not be afraid for the terror by night; nor for the arrow that flieth by day; nor for the pestilence that walketh in darkness; nor for the destruction that wasteth at noonday.' (This passage was believed to be a powerful charm against evil spirits.) The Egyptian *Book of the Dead* mentions sinister beings which set snares and work nets and are fishers. Their leader is the god whose face is behind him, which finds an echo hundreds of years later in the Devil of the witches' sabbath who has a face before and behind. Even today, in an atmosphere of general scepticism about such things, there are probably very few of us who have not felt the presence of the terror by night.

Occultists do not believe that demons can be dismissed as products of overactive human imaginations (nor do Roman Catholic theologians). There are two streams of magical tradition about the Devil and his angels. In one tradition the Devil is the magician's god, as in witchcraft, and his favour is won by worshipping him and doing his will. In the other, the demons are evil intelligences which have great power but which can be dominated by a magician who is sufficiently strong and daring. Demons are subdued by the force of the magician's will in rituals of blood and sacrifice, perfumes, symbols and curses. These operations are said to be extremely dangerous.

Fear of the dead is another old terror and graveyards are still not widely regarded as pleasant places at night. Prehistoric burials have been discovered in which it is clear that the corpse was tied up in a cramped, foetus-like position soon after death. When modern primitives do this it is usually to prevent the dead from coming back to attack the living. The same motive may lie behind prehistoric burials of bodies in jars or under heavy stones: to stop something from getting out. The Sumerians and their successors in Mesopotamia, the Babylonians and Assyrians, believed that if a corpse was not properly buried with the appropriate ceremonies and gifts it would come back and stalk the streets, attacking the living and trying to suck their blood. The Greeks thought that offerings must be made at the graves of dead relatives, whose ghosts would take revenge if they were neglected.

The art of controlling the spirits of the dead is necromancy, which is also extremely dangerous. Modern occultism brings in the notion of the astral corpse. When a man dies his body remains on earth, but in his 'body of light'—a replica of the earthly body made of finer and subtler material'—he goes to a mysterious, ethereal plane of existence which is called the astral plane. His soul eventually mounts to still higher planes, leaving the body of light in the astral plane as an astral corpse. Just as the earthly body retains enough innate life-force to grow its nails and hair for a time after death, the astral corpse retains a faint spark of life. It has an intense desire to live again, like the Mesopotamian vampire-corpses which would suck people's blood to recover life, and it can be attracted back into the normal world, either consciously by necromancy or sometimes unconsciously. It can then absorb enough life-energy from living creatures to prolong its shadowy existence almost indefinitely. Some occultists believe that Spirtualist seances really summon not 'spirits' but astral corpses.

Another important magical theory about the universe is the doctrine of opposites. The early Greek philosophers were impressed by the existence of pairs of opposites in Nature. They saw that the life of the universe seems to move in pendulum swings. Day gives way to night and summer to winter, calm follows storm, what is born must eventually die and what grows strong will in time grow weak. But they did not think that the universe could be entirely explained in these terms. They believed that there was something more fundamental than the opposites, something which held them in balance so that the pendulum swung regularly to and fro, from day to night and back to day, something of which the opposites were themselves a part.

The magician's search is for this 'something' which underlies and connects the opposites, the mysterious One which reconciles all diversity in unity. The path to the One lies through the reconciliation of opposites. To experience and master all things is to experience and reconcile opposites—good and evil, the spiritual and the material, freedom and necessity, reason and passion, laughter and tears. In magic, as in the Hegelian dialectic, progress comes through the reconciliation of opposites, thesis and antithesis, in a synthesis which transcends them.

The Greeks called a perfect balance between opposites 'justice', and magicians have a correspondingly high regard for exact balance and equilibrium. To achieve a reconciliation of opposites there must be a perfect balance between them. I cannot reconcile the forces of love and hate in my own nature unless I have brought them both to an equal pitch. Otherwise one will outweigh the other and no true synthesis will be obtained. The magician tries to bring all the forces of his being into a proper balance. He must not, for instance, devote himself to reason and intelligence at the expense of his instinctive drives, his passions and emotions.

Many magical ceremonies are deliberately designed to summon up and unleash the animal driving forces from the deeps of human nature. The *whole* man is to be raised to the power of infinity, not man as civilised thinker or man as ravening beast, but man as a combination of both.

One of the occult applications of this theory of opposites and balance is in the area of sex. The stock occultist's example of progress through the reconciliation of opposites is the union of male and female (the two opposites) which results in the creation of new life—a child. Eliphas Levi remarked that 'Generation is in fact a work of the human androgyne; in their division man and woman remain sterile.'[4] It is not merely that man and woman are physically sterile if kept apart. In magical theory they are also spiritually sterile.

There is an old tradition that man was originally bisexual. A Jewish legend says that Adam was a man on his right side and a woman on his left, and God separated the two halves. In another version Adam and Eve were originally joined at the shoulders, back to back, and God split them with an axe. These stories were intended to reconcile the existence of two sexes with the belief that man was made in the image of God. God, or the One, cannot be described as either masculine or feminine. The One links all the opposites together in unity and it combines male and female. If man was made in God's image he must originally have been bisexual.

The magician cannot become the One unless he becomes bisexual. One step towards this is for the male magician to cultivate the female side of his nature, but without impairing his masculinity, and the female magician vice versa (carried to the point of deliberate homosexual activity in some cases). Another method is copulation. In a sense the beast with two backs is a bisexual creature, a human androgyne, and copulation in which man and woman are joined into one being can therefore be a mystical approach to the One.

This idea should not be written off as merely an ingenious justification for sex orgies. The feeling that sex is sinful, dirty and utterly unworthy of the realm of the spirit and the divine is entirely foreign to magic, as it was foreign to the pagan world in which magic has its roots. On the contrary, in antiquity it was thought that just as in man new life is the result of copulation so all life in the universe is the result of the sexual activity of the gods. There are numerous myths which describe the creation of the world as the result of a copulation between gods. Aeschylus in the *Danaids* saw the life of Nature as the offspring of the union of earth and sky. 'Holy sky passionately longs to penetrate the earth and desire takes hold of her to achieve this union. Rain from her bed-fellow sky falls and impregnates the earth and she brings forth for mortals pasturage for flocks and Demeter's livelihood.'[5] Among the Sumerians 4,000 years ago the king went through a rite of sacred copulation each year with a priestess who represented Inanna, the goddess of procreation, to ensure that the land of Sumer and its people would be fruitful and prosperous in the coming year. The same rite is found in many other societies.

When sexuality is admitted into the world of the divine it is possible to think of union with the divine in sexual terms (and many Christian mystics have spoken of union with God in these terms). In the pagan mystery religions union with the god was often achieved symbolically by sexual intercourse. An essential element of witchcraft is sexual union with the god (the Devil). Among the witches of the primitive Ozark hill country in the United States initiation as a witch involves intercourse with the Devil's representative, a man who is already a member of the cult. A woman who decides to become a witch goes to her family burying-ground at midnight in the dark of the moon. There she formally renounces the Christian faith and offers herself body and soul to the Devil. She strips naked and copulates with the man who is responsible for teaching her the secrets of the cult. Both of them repeat certain words which are believed to attract demons and ghosts of the evil dead, and the ceremony ends with the recitation of the Lord's Prayer backwards. It is repeated for three nights in succession and must be witnessed by at least two other initiates who are also naked. The ceremony is far from being merely a sex orgy. Vance Randolph, who investigated the Ozark witches, was told by women who had experienced both that 'the witch's initiation is a much more moving spiritual crisis than that which the Christians call conversion'.[6]

Magical ceremonies designed to release the driving forces from the depths of man's being naturally tend to be heavily spiced with sex. The sex-drive is a powerful force in man, and correspondingly in the universe, which the magician must experienced and control. Inhibitions and repressions are obstacles to the development of the complete man and must be swept away. Magic takes a pagan delight in the pleasures of the senses, but magical theory insists that sensual indulgence for its own sake will not serve the magician's purpose (and it is interesting that many witches said that intercourse with the Devil was extremely painful). If the magician lets himself be carried away on the tides of desire he has failed to achieve the perfect balance of opposites from which magical progress comes.

One of the most deeply reverenced of magical documents is the Emerald Table of Hermes Trismegistus. Magicians, who deal in mysteries, are always enthralled by anything which is exceptionally mysterious, and the Emerald Table is impenetrable in the extreme. It is said to have been a tablet of emerald, engraved with writing in Phoenician characters, which was discovered by Sarah, the wife of Abraham (or alternatively by Alexander the Great), in a cave-tomb where it was clutched in the fingers of the corpse of Hermes Trismegistus. Hermes was the Greek god of wisdom and patron of magic. Hermes Trismegistus—thrice-greatest—was supposedly a grandson of Adam, a sage of surpassing wisdom and the builder of the pyramids.

A Latin version of the Emerald Table was in existence by 1200 and earlier Arabic versions have been discovered. No two translations of it agree and none of them make very much sense, but for magical purposes the important part of it is the opening sentence of the Latin version—*quod superius est sicut quod inferius et quod inferius est sicut quod superius ad perpetranda miracula rei unius*, 'that which is above is like that which is below and that which is below is like that which is above, to achieve the wonders of the one thing'. This is the great magical doctrine of 'as above, so below', which is the foundation of the art of astrology. It is one way of putting the theory that man is the earthly counterpart of God: as God is in heaven so man is on earth. It is also a statement of the old belief that events on earth parallel the doings of the gods in heaven.

Events on earth run parallel to events in heaven because both depend on the workings of the same force ('the one thing' which reconciles the opposites of 'above' and 'below'), like two wheels turned by the same cog-wheel. Astrology developed originally in Mesopotamia, where each city-state had its own patron god and every change in the balance of power between the city-states was seen as the direct reflection of a change in the relationship of the gods. Modern astrology is built on this same belief, with the planets substituted for the old gods, because the Babylonians and Assyrians connected their principal gods with the planets.

For example, a conjunction of Jupiter (the planet of health) with the two malevolent planets Saturn and Mars is a portent of plague. In the fourteenth century it was thought that the terrible Black Death of 1348 had been signalled by one of these conjunctions in 1345. It was later accepted that another conjunction of the three planets heralded the arrival of syphilis in Europe. Modern astrologers say that a man who is born when Venus is close to the sun in the zodiac is likely to be effeminate—femininity (Venus) affects his personality (the sun)—and if Saturn is opposite the sun in the sky he will catch cold with unusual frequency, because Saturn is the coldest planet, the one furthest from the warmth of the sun (or it was until the discovery of Uranus, Neptune and Pluto). Napoleon's tendency to overeat could have been predicted from the fact that Venus was in the sign of Cancer when he was born. Venus stands for love and Cancer rules the stomach, so Napoleon was naturally afflicted with undue love of his stomach and its pleasures.

These are cases of 'as above, so below' reasoning, but the converse—'as below, so above'—is also important. Events in the sky are signals of events on earth, but it is equally true that occurrences on earth are evidence of conditions in heaven. By inspecting the markings on a sheep's liver I can discover whether the gods or the stars are favourable for any enterprise which I have in mind.

This is the basis of many highly eccentric methods of predicting the future, because any event, however trivial and apparently meaningless it may be, can give a clue to the direction in which the universe as a whole is moving. The ancients drew omens from the internal organs of animals, dreams, lots, the shapes taken by oil or flour dropped on the surface of water, unusual events like monstrous births, and the movements of animals and birds. Agnes Sampson, a famous Scottish witch who was executed in 1590, used to predict whether sick people would recover or not by watching the behaviour of a large black dog. Plutarch, who lived at the turn of the first and second centuries A.D., said that the Egyptians drew omens from the chance remarks of children. The thirteenth-century astrologer and magician Michael Scot believed that sneezes are portents of the future. If you sneeze twice or four times when you are involved in some business venture and you immediately get up and walk about, the venture will be successful. When a contract has been drawn up, if you sneeze once it will be kept, but if you sneeze three times it will be broken. Sneezing twice in the night for three successive nights is a sign of death in the house.[7]

Modern methods of fortune-telling are just as odd, if not odder, and depend on the same theory of the universe. Books which tell you how to interpret dreams, palms, playing-cards or tea leaves can be found in many bookshops and public libraries. A curious technique is moleosophy—divination by moles on the body. If you have a mole on the right side of your forehead you are talented and likely to succeed, but if it is on the left side you are stubborn, extravagant and dissipated. A mole on the right knee means a happy marriage, on the left knee bad temper, on the right hand success in business, on the left hand the curse of an artistic temperament. These rules come from a book published in the United States, with perfect seriousness, in 1945.[8]

All these methods, which seem to involve random events—the chance remarks of children, a sneeze or two, a mole on the body—depend on the belief that the events are not random at all. The universe is a whole, a great design. Any event which occurs is part of the design and can be used to predict events in the future because they are also parts of the design.

The principle of 'as below, so above' is not limited to fortune-telling. Events 'above' and 'below' run in parallel courses. By manipulating events here 'below' I can affect the course of events 'above'. At Rome in 1628 Pope Urban VIII employed a magician called Tommaso Campanella, an ex-Dominican friar who had earlier been imprisoned for heresy, to ward off an eclipse which the Pope feared would be the signal for his death. Campanella and the Pope sealed off a room against the outside air and draped it in white hangings. They used two lamps to stand for the sun and moon and five torches for the planets. They assembled jewels, plants and colours connected with the benevolent planets Jupiter, Venus and the sun, drank liquor which had been distilled under the influence of Jupiter and Venus, and played 'Jovial and Venereal' music. They were trying to create their own little favourable sky in the sealed room in place of the hostile real sky outside, either to prevent the eclipse from occurring at all or at least to guard the Pope, who was in the sealed room, against its effects. Their efforts were evidently successful, as Urban VIII did not die until 1644.[9]

2. Imitative Magic and the Magical Link

Superstitions are instinctive, and all that is instinctive is founded in the very nature of things, to which fact the sceptics of all times have given insufficient attention.

ELIPHAS LEVI *The Doctrine and Ritual of Magic*

Magic depends heavily on mimicry. Campanella and Urban VIII constructed an imitation sky in their sealed room. The magician tortures or kills an animal in a ceremony of hatred as an imitation of the action of the force he is trying to arouse. When a magician musters the full power of his will and acts in a certain way, he believes that he causes the forces of the universe outside him to act in the same way. This is an extension of the rule of 'as below, so above'. As the magician behaves 'below' so will the forces of the universe behave 'above'.

Knots are very sinister things, much used by witches, because to tie a knot is magically to tie and impede the person who is the target of the spell. An example is the terrible death talisman of the string with nine knots, sometimes called 'the witches' ladder'. The string is tied with a fierce concentration of hatred against an enemy and hidden somewhere close to him. The knots slowly throttle the life out of him and he dies. The only cure is to find the string in time and untie the knots.

Witches sometimes tied knots to stop cows from giving milk, but their main use in witchcraft was to prevent a couple from enjoying the pleasures of the bed. Jean Bodin, the political philosopher who was also an authority on witchcraft, was told by a witch at Poitiers in 1567 that there were more than fifty ways of tying a knot for this purpose. The knot could impede the man alone or the woman alone for a day or a year or a lifetime. It could make one love the other, but be hated in return, or it could make the pair tear each other with their nails in love-making. Different types of knot would prevent inter-course or procreation or urination.[10]

In the second *Idyll* of Theocritus, written about 275 B.C., the witch Simaetha tries to draw her faithless lover Delphis back to her by another type of imita-tive magic. She lights a fire and throws grain on to it, saying that the grain represents her lover's bones. She burns bay-leaves—'Delphis racks me; I burn him in these bays. . . . So waste his flesh to powder on the fire.' She heats wax over the fire, chanting that as it melts so may Delphis be melted with love. She has stolen part of his robe and she shreds it and drops it on the flames. She believes that as the ingredients of the charm burn in the fire so Delphis will 'burn' with love for her. In a similar scene in Virgil's eighth *Eclogue* the witch twines threads around a small figure of her lover, made of clay and wax, to 'entwine' him in her love.

Mimicry alone is not enough. Imitating the action of a force arouses it to act in the way which is imitated, but to direct it at a particular victim there must be a link between the spell and the victim, otherwise the force will not hit the intended target. The link may be created simply by words, by saying that the grain is the victim's bones and the bay-leaves his flesh, or by making a doll which is a miniature replica of him, or by working on a part of his body or his clothes or something which has been closely connected to him.

A grim Scottish method of finding out whether someone who is ill will recover or not establishes a magical link by the force of words alone. Dig two holes in the ground. Call one 'the living grave' and the other 'the dead grave'. Fetch the sick man and put him on the ground between the holes, without telling him which is which. If he turns his face to the living grave he will re-cover, if to the dead grave he will die. The sensation of the sick man who be-lieves in this test can be imagined. It may have worked efficiently in many cases because of the psychological effect on the patient who discovered that he was bound to get well or doomed to die.

Once the link has been made the effects of the spell follow the principle of imitative magic, the law of 'like to like'. In 1597 Isobel Ritchie of Aberdeen was accused of murdering Thomas Forbes. She took two pillows to his house and weighed them against each other and then, in the words of the accusation, 'in thy inchanting manner appointed the one pillow to be the said Thomas and the other Elspet Forbes, his daughter, and because the said Thomas his pillow was the lightest, by thy witchcraft he died'.[11] The heavier pillow stood for the plumpness of life and health, the lighter for the shrunkenness of starvation and death. The force of the words said in an 'inchanting manner' created a link between Thomas Forbes and the lighter pillow, and so he died.

Physical contact or nearness also establishes a link. A singularly unpleasant cure for a child's whooping cough is to tie a nest of mice round the child's neck in a bag. This links the mice with the cough in the child's throat and as the mice starve to death in the bag the cough will gradually disappear. Writing in 1944, Christina Hole said that in the last five years in Cheshire she had known women who rubbed their children's warts with a snail and impaled the snail on a thorn, convinced that as it lingeringly died the warts would dwindle away to nothing.[12] In December 1962 a woman was arrested in a suburb of San Francisco and accused of charging $70 to cure stomach pains by rolling an egg to and fro on the sufferer's stomach and then smashing the egg on the floor.

Another kind of link is provided by the magical law that anything which has once been part of a man's body or in close contact with him retain its connection with his body even after it has been physically separated from him. This is the basis of the well-known primitive fear of allowing your cut hair or nails to fall into anyone else's hands because they can be used against you. They are still magically linked with your body and whatever is done to them will effect you. In a famous case at York, Pennsylvania, in 1929, John H. Blymyer was sentenced to life imprisonment for the murder of Nelson Rehmyer. Rehmyer, who was notorious in the area as a black magician, was killed in a struggle to get a lock of his hair, which was to be buried as part of a charm against him. Aleister Crowley, who had much to fear from certain rival magicians, was always careful to see that no one could get hold of his hair, nail clippings, excreta or other bodily products.

The best-known type of imitative magic relies on creating a link with its victim by making an image of him in wax, clay, rags or whatever material is to hand, usually including his hair or nail clippings, blood or sweat, which retain their connection with him. The image is pierced with a nail or a needle, broken in pieces, twisted and tortured, burned or sunk in water, and because it is a replica of the victim, linked to him through its appearance and the products of his body, whatever is done to it is done to him.

Image magic has been practised in every part of the world and in all periods of history. In some prehistoric cave paintings animals are shown pierced with arrows, probably as a magical aid to hunting them. A recent example is the discovery in February 1964 of the figure of a naked woman, six inches long and made of modelling clay, near Sandringham in Norfolk. It was stuck through the heart with a sharp sliver of hawthorn and near it were a black candle and a sheep's heart.

This figure may have been meant either to kill or to seduce. Piercing the image's heart can be intended to pierce the victim's breast with love. A fifteenth-century book, written in a mixture of Hebrew and Yiddish, says that to seduce a girl you should make a female figure of wax, with the sex organs clearly shown. The face should be as good a likeness as possible. Across the breast of the figure write her name, '___, daughter of ___ (father's name) and daughter of ___ (mother's name).' Write the same thing on the back between the shoulders. Then say over it, 'May it be Thy will, O Lord, that N. daughter of N. burn with a mighty passion for me.' Bury the figure carefully so that its limbs are not broken and leave it for twenty-four hours (probably near the girl's house or a path which she often takes, to create a link with her by physical nearness, but the charm does not say this). Dig the figure up again and wash it three times in water, doing this once in the name of the Archangel Michael, once in the name of Gabriel, once in the name of Raphael. Then dip it in urine (presumably your own, to create a link between the girl and you) and afterwards dry it. When you want to arouse passion in the girl pierce the figure's heart with a brand-new needle. This entire charm appears in the book written backwards.[13]

In 1329, Pierre Recordi, a Carmelite friar, was sentenced to imprisonment for life for invoking demons and making wax images to win the love of women. He moulded the wax with his own blood and spittle (magically mingling his own body with the woman's body represented by the image). Then he buried the image under the woman's threshold. He said he had seduced three women in this way and had given thanks to Satan with sacrifices afterwards.

In January 1960, while the office building of the Hereford Rural District Council was being repaired, a small figure of a woman was found in the cellar. Tucked into its skirt was a piece of paper worn and dirty with age, on which was written the name Mary Ann Wand and the words—'I act this spell upon you from my whole heart, wishing you to never rest nor eat nor sleep the restern part of your life. I hope your flesh will waste away and I hope you will never spend another penny I ought to have. Wishing this from my whole heart.'[14]

Almost three centuries before, at Salem in 1692, images were found in another cellar with much more serious consequences. According to Cotton

Mather's account of the trial of Bridget Bishop, in his *Wonders of the Invisible World*, John Bly and William Bly gave evidence that when they knocked down the cellar wall of the old house she used to live in 'they did in the holes of the said old Wall find several *Poppets*, made up of Rags and Hogs-bristles with headless Pins in them, the Points being outward; whereof she could give no account unto the Court that was reasonable or tolerable'. There were several other charges of witchcraft against Bridget Bishop. She was hanged from the branches of an oak-tree eight days later.

In 1560 a wax image of Queen Elizabeth I with a pin jabbed through its breast was found in Lincoln's Inn Fields, to the horror of the court. The witches of North Berwick tried to kill James VI of Scotland (afterwards James I of England) with a wax image. Agnes Sampson and nine others met near Prestonpans, the Devil their master being with them. The image, wrapped in a linen cloth, was shown to the Devil. After he had approved it, the image was passed from hand to hand, all saying, 'This is King James the Sixth, ordained to be consumed at the instance of a nobleman, Francis, Earl Bothwell.' The image was to be roasted to kill the king. Many writers have suggested that the 'Devil' in this case was the Earl of Bothwell himself.

Here, as in many other cases, the link between the victim and the image is strengthened by formally giving the image the victim's name. 'This is King James the Sixth. . . .' In 1315, Hugh Geraud, Bishop of Cahors, and two other bishops who were fanatical enemies of Pope John XXII were accused of plotting the Pope's death by poison and sorcery. They first tested the efficiency of their magic by killing the Pope's favourite nephew with a wax image and then went on to the main task. Three wax images were baptised in full form with the names of the Pope and two leading members of his court. They were hidden in loaves of bread and sent to the papal court at Avignon. The messengers were searched at the gates of Avignon. The loaves and images were found in their baggage with a whole battery of sorcerer's equipment—poisons and herbs, arsenic, quicksilver, rats' tails, spiders, toads and lizards, marjoram, mint, vervain and the hair of a criminal who had been hanged. Hugh Geraud was found guilty, flayed alive and burned in 1317.

The American journalist William Seabrook came across two cases of image magic near St. Remy in southern France in 1932.[15] A friend of his fell on a tangled path down a hillside and lost the use of his legs, although there was nothing physically the matter with him. Seabrook discovered that his friend had been bewitched, went to the witch's house and found in the cellar a jumbled mass of thorns and brambles, in which was a doll with a china head. It wore a man's costume and its eyes were covered with a black cloth. Its legs and feet were tangled in a criss-cross network of thorns. 'It slumped, sagging there at an ugly angle, neither upright nor fallen, grotesquely sinister, like the body of a soldier caught in barbed wire.' An altar stood against one wall of the cellar and above it was written INRI, with the letters distorted into obscene shapes. Above this again was a pair of horns.

INRI was written above the head of Jesus at the Crucifixion, the letters standing for 'Jesus of Nazareth, the King of the Jews'. The horns belong to the great Goat of the witches' sabbath. Horns and all forked or two-pointed objects are symbols of the Devil. They deny the One, which is God, and assert the Two, God and the Enemy.

In the other case Seabrook found an image which was intended to do murder. The doll was stuck through with pins and smeared with toad's blood. (Toads have long been popularly believed to be poisonous.) Near it was a Bible and on the Bible an inverted crucifix from which hung a toad, crucified head downwards.

If the image is accidentally damaged, the victim is not harmed. The image created the necessary link with the victim, but what injures him is the fierce current of deliberate hatred for which the image provides a focusing point. The torture of the image is often accompanied by rites designed to work the magician's malicious fury up to a pitch of frenzy—appeals to the Devil and acts of sacrilege (the obscene distortion of INRI, the toad crucified upside down), the burning of materials like henbane or black hellebore which give off intoxicating fumes, slaughtering an animal near the image or drenching it with poison. The powerful psychological 'kick' which the magician derives from these rites strengthens the waves of destructive violence which he projects at the image. In this way he attempts to charge the image with a malevolent force which will obsess the victim's mind and destroy him. 'All these rites', a modern occultist explains, 'can play their part in causing an image—especially one already associated with destruction—to spring into a black, abounding vitality which can burn itself into the conscious and subconscious, especially during sleep. . . .'[16]

3. Analogies and Correspondences

How are we to explain the strength and grip of superstition? Certainly in its origin and development sinister non-human demoniac influences play a great role. . . .

PHILIPP SCHMIDT S.J. *Superstition and Magic*

Magic is sometimes said to be a primitive form of science, but it is very much nearer to poetry than to even the most rudimentary science and, like poetry, it relies extensively on the use of analogy. The whole magical universe itself is built on the analogy of the human body. Imitative magic, which depends on the principle of analogy, the law of like to like, is only one more example of this tendency. Magic makes use of all kinds of associations and connections between things whose relationship to each other is a matter of similarities and parallels. For instance, things which are backwards or upside down—an inverted crucifix or saying the Lord's Prayer backwards—are linked with evil and the Devil because they reverse the normal and proper order of things and the Devil is the arch-rebel who seeks to overturn the order established by God.

This is a natural parallel for the mind to draw, but in occult theory the connection between evil and things which are reversed is not merely symbolic but real. Man is a tiny replica of the universe. If two things are naturally associated together in the human mind, which is an image of the 'mind' of the universe, this is evidence of a real connection between the two things in the universe. Many of the important magical analogies and connections are not natural to most people's minds today, but have been handed down by tradition from the remote past. This enhances their value for occultists, who believe that humanity was a great deal wiser in these matters in the remote past than it is now.

An example is the magical use of salt to ward off demons. All devils are supposed to detest it and no salt should be used in ceremonies designed to attract them. Salt is anti-demonic because it is a preservative. Demons are creatures which corrupt and destroy. Anything that has preservative qualities is contrary to their nature, and disagreeable to them. Iron can also be employed against demons, because men discovered and used meteoric iron long before they found iron ore in the earth. Since it first came from the sky, iron is 'heavenly' and devils fear it.

On the other hand, the left is associated with evil. Black magic is 'the Left-hand Path'. Moving to the left in magic is done with evil intent and attracts evil influences. Some spells will only work if you move to the left while repeating them. The tendency to connect the left with evil is very old. When the Babylonians drew omens they usually considered the left side bad and the right side good. In Homer birds flying to the right are a favourable omen, but birds which fly to the left are unfavourable. 'Sinister' was the Latin word for both left and evil and has kept the double meaning in English (it still means left in heraldry).

The probable explanation of this general disapproval of the left is the fact that the right hand is normally the stronger and the left hand the weaker. The word 'left' comes from the Anglo-Saxon word *lyft*, which meant weak. To be left-handed is peculiar and suspect, a reversal of the proper order of things, and so the left is associated with the powers of evil which rebel against God. Some modern psychologists say that left-handedness is often a characteristic of men who are sexually abnormal—homosexual or perverted. A stock example is the Emperor Tiberius, a notorious pervert who was left-handed.

A more obvious but equally ancient connection is the link between blood and life. Primitive people who observed that as a man loses blood he weakens and eventually dies came naturally to the conclusion that his blood contains his life. But the magical connection is not merely the physical one. A man's life includes all his experiences, characteristics and qualities, and these are contained in his blood. A classical cure for epilepsy is to drink the blood of a slaughtered gladiator, which conveys his strength and healthy vitality into the epileptic's body. The gladiator should be freshly killed, because the energy in his blood will dissipate quite quickly. Pliny's *Natural History* says that some epileptics found it most effective to reach the gladiator before he was actually dead and gulp the invigorating blood down as it came warm and bubbling from the dying man's wounds.

The sadistic Hungarian Countess Elizabeth Bathory bathed regularly in human blood to preserve her looks. Her supplies came from peasant girls who were kept in chains in the cellars of her castle and whose fresh young blood was expected to give the Countess's skin a youthful bloom. When she was arrested in 1610 the dead bodies of about fifty of these girls were found. She once wrote to her husband, 'Thorko has taught me a lovely new one. Catch a black hen and beat it to death with a white cane. Keep the blood and smear a little of it on your enemy. If you get no chance to smear it on his body, obtain one of his garments and smear it.' The magical theory behind this is that the hen's life, which was characterised by an agonised death, has been transferred to the enemy in the hen's blood. His death in the same agony will follow. Beating the black hen to death with a white cane is an interesting example of a reconciliation of opposites.[17]

The blood of an executed criminal is a strong protection against disease and misfortune, because it carries the vigorous energy of a man cut off in full health and the powerful force of his resentment and fury at the fact. Spectators at executions, including those of Charles I of England and Louis XVI of France, struggled to dip cloths and handkerchiefs in the dead man's blood. When John Dillinger, the notorious gunman and bank robber, was shot down and killed by F.B.I. agents in Chicago in 1934, people gathered round and soaked their handkerchiefs or pieces of paper in a pool of his blood on the sidewalk. Some of the women dipped the hems of their skirts in it. The blood was quickly used up, but enterprising local tradesmen sold large quantities of fake Dillinger blood.

A sidelight on the belief that you can absorb a man's qualities by drinking his blood or eating part of his body is provided by recent experiments with flatworms at the University of Michigan. The worms are conditioned to respond to lights and to negotiate a maze. A conditioned worm is then killed and fed to an untaught worm. In some cases the untaught worm acquires the conditioned worm's ability to respond to the lights and the maze simply by eating it. The tentative explanation is that the conditioned worm's memory is connected with a chemical, possibly ribonucleic acid, in its body, but other experimenters have not obtained the same results.

Most of us do not associate the colour green, copper, the number 7, the dove, the sparrow, and the swan together in our minds, but in magical theory these things are linked because they are all connected with the force of Venus, the universal current of love. These connections are part of what is called a 'system of correspondences'. From the earliest times men tried to understand the way in which the world is constructed by classifying all the features of the universe in terms of the gods who controlled them. Magicians have followed suit, substituting the great driving forces of the universe for the gods. Everything is classified in terms of the force with which it is connected.

The system is extremely detailed, but the oldest and most important part of it is the set of links between planets, metals and colours.

Planets	Metals	Colours
Sun	Gold	Gold, yellow
Moon	Silver	White
Mercury	Quicksilver	Grey, neutral
Venus	Copper	Green
Mars	Iron	Red
Jupiter	Tin	Blue
Saturn	Lead	Black

These correspondences are vitally important in magic because magicians use them in their attempts to control the great occult forces. In a ceremony of hatred and destruction the magician uses things which are red or made of iron. He drapes the room in which he is working in crimson hangings. He wears a scarlet robe and a ruby in a ring on his finger. The ring is made of iron and he uses a magic wand made of iron. The number 5 also corresponds to Mars and the magician lights five candles and has pentagrams (five-pointed stars) drawn or embroidered on his robe. These things arouse and control the force of Mars because they are connected with it in the universe, as if it was an animal on the end of a chain made of red, iron and 5.

The reasons for linking these particular things together are hidden far back in antiquity, but the logic behind most of the connections seems clear. Gold and yellow go with the sun because the sun is golden or yellow in colour. For the same reason silver and white belong to the moon. In the ancient world the sun and moon were believed to be the most important of the heavenly bodies and were distinguished from the others. They were the two which gave light and were therefore the most valuable to men, and it was natural to connect them with the two most important metals, gold and silver.

Blue is the colour of Jupiter because it is the colour of the sky, and Jupiter, the ruler of the gods, was lord of the sky. Tin may belong to Jupiter because the planet has a silvery appearance like tin. This link seems to be very old. The Sumerian term for tin was 'metal of heaven', which suggests that they already connected it with the ruler of the sky and possibly they thought the sky was made of tin. Quicksilver belongs to Mercury (and is called mercury) because it is the most mobile of the metals and Mercury is a particularly fast-moving planet, which shoots across the sky at great speed, as is suitable for the god who carried the other god's messages.

Lead, the darkest and heaviest of the metals, was naturally assigned to Saturn, the dimmest and slowest-moving planet, which trudges heavily through its slow path round the sun. In the old cosmology Saturn is the farthest planet from the sun, the ruler of life, and is the lord of death. The analogy between death and night was drawn very early. Black is the colour of night and the colour invariably associated with death in Western countries.

Copper is the metal of Venus, probably because Aphrodite, the Greek Venus, was closely associated with Cyprus and Cyprus was the classical world's chief source of copper. The cult of Aphrodite ('the Cyprian') seems to have spread to Greece from the Near East through Cyprus, from which copper was also imported, and one of her principal shrines was at Paphos in western Cyprus, where she had been born from the sea. Venus is not only the ruler of love but also the mistress of Nature and the characteristic colour of Nature is green. In most languages the word for green is connected with words for plants, leaves and grass. Our 'green' comes from the Germanic root *gro*, which probably meant 'to grow' and also appears in 'grow' and 'grass'.

The most interesting of the correspondences is the link between Mars, iron and red. Iron became the metal of Mars when the superiority of iron weapons over bronze weapons was discovered. The Hittites were the first people to develop the use of iron weapons. (They were also noted for the use of horses in battle and the horse is a beast of Mars in magic as a result.) The Assyrian army was equipped with iron weapons by 800 B.C. and dominated the Near East for two hundred years. The Dorians brought the Iron Age to Europe when they invaded Greece and defeated the bronze-wielding Achaeans.

Red is connected with Mars through several chains of association. The planet has a reddish look and the Egyptians called it 'the red star'. Red is the colour of blood and Mars was the god of bloodshed and war. The war-chiefs of

Rome in early times painted themselves bright red with vermilion and the same custom has been found among other primitive peoples. Red is the colour of energy and vitality and in astrology Mars rules all forms of violent energy and activity.

The word for red in most languages is based on the fact that red is the colour of blood. Our 'red', Greek *eruthros* and Latin *ruber* and *rufus* are all akin to Sanskrit *rudhira*, 'blood'. In primitive belief, the blood contains the body's life and so red becomes the colour of vigour and vitality. This is probably the explanation of the prehistoric custom of colouring corpses in red. In a prehistoric graveyard near Nördlingen in Bavaria thirty-three human skulls were found embedded in red ochre (and all facing west, where the sun 'dies' in the evening). Finds at Grimaldi in Italy included a boy's skeleton stained red with peroxide of iron, three bodies in a grave lined with red ochre and the scarlet skeleton of a man whose bones had been covered with powdered haematite. The intention was probably to keep the body in a usable condition in case its owner might need it again, by painting it with the colour of life and vitality.[18]

The connection with blood and death gives red some sinister overtones. An ancient Egyptian papyrus contains a prayer to the goddess Isis—'O Isis, thou great magician, heal me and save me from all wicked, frightful and red things.' The Egyptians had the curious custom of jeering at red-headed men on certain religious occasions. They connected red with Typhon, a demonic dragon and evil power. In Scotland and Ulster until fairly recent times a fisherman who met a red-headed woman on the way to his boat would turn back because he would have no luck with his fishing that day. If a woman with red hair came into a house where the milk was being churned it was thought that her presence would spoil the butter.

Because it carries a current of energy and vigour red can be used to make a particular powerful poison. In 1580 an epidemic broke out at Aix in France and an English doctor named Thomas Flud said it was caused by Jews who had gone about rubbing poison on the town's door-knockers. The poison was snake venom, but it was made peculiarly virulent by being strained through people with red hair. Flud said that the Jews kidnapped a red-haired man and tied him to a cross, keeping his mouth open with a wedge of wood. Then they stung him with adders and collected the poison froth from his mouth. Others stripped a red-headed woman, buried her in the ground up to her middle, stung her breasts with adders and drained the slaver from her lips.[19]

People's reactions to colours today seem to match their traditional occult significance remarkably neatly, whether because colours really do have their own innate force or simply as the result of the association of the same ideas with them for centuries. Green, which is traditionally the colour of Venus, the force of love, peace and harmony, does exert a peaceful, pleasant, tranquilising influence. Blue has a subduing effect which is an appropriate reaction to the colour of Jupiter, the ruler of all things. Red, the colour of energy and vitality, has a highly stimulating and exciting influence. B. J. Kouwer found that the ideas which people tend to associate with red are passion, emotion, temperament, action, rebelliousness, force, sexuality, tension, love, spontaneity, victory, shame. Most of these fit very well with the magical and astrological character of red as the colour of Mars, the planet of force, battle, action, energy, vitality, with connotations of violent emotion, passion and sexual vigour. Ovid in his *Fasti* called Priapus, the god of the phallus, 'red Priapus', and it is the red light which marks the brothel. Similarly, Kouwer found that the ideas generally associated with black, the colour of the grim and ominous Saturn, are death, night, murder, anxiety, misery, defeat.[20]

4. The Modern Magicians

To attain the *sanctum regnum*, in other words, the knowledge and power of the magi, there are four indispensable conditions—an intelligence illuminated by study, an intrepidity which nothing can check, a will which nothing can break, and a discretion which nothing can corrupt and nothing intoxicate. TO KNOW, TO DARE, TO WILL, TO KEEP SILENCE—such are the four words of the magus . . .

ELIPHAS LEVI *The Doctrine and Ritual of Magic*

Perhaps as a result of the widening gulf which has increasingly tended to separate the ordinary educated person from both Christianity and science in the last hundred years interest in occultism and magic seems to have been on the increase. The practice of magic has also flourished and magicians of the nineteenth and twentieth centuries—especially Eliphas Levi, MacGregor Mathers and Aleister Crowley—hold a high place in magical history.

Eliphas Levi, whose real name was Alphonse Louis Constant, was born in Paris about 1810. His father was a shoemaker and the family were poor, but the boy was precociously clever and was educated for the priesthood. He was expelled from the seminary for holding peculiar and heretical opinions and never became a priest. The conflict between his orthodox Catholic education and his fascination with magic runs through all his books and although he tried hard to reconcile the two warring tendencies in his thinking he was never really successful.

His expulsion from the seminary suggests that Levi was attracted to occultism at an early age. As a magician he undoubtedly followed his own instructions to know, to dare and to will, but fortunately he did not keep entirely silent. In 1855-6 he published the two volumes of *Le Dogme et Rituel de la Haute*

Magie, his most brilliant book. Wildly and woollily romantic, vague and verbose, often abstruse and sometimes patently absurd, it is written with zest and imagination, considerable evocative power, and a depth of insight into the theory and practice of magic which make it well worth reading over a century afterwards. His later books are less interesting, including his *History of Magic* (1860) and *The Key of the Mysteries* (1861), which he himself translated into English when he was reincarnated as Aleister Crowley.

Levi made very little money from his books. He earned a pinched living by giving lessons in occultism to aspiring students, an imposing figure with a great spade beard, rather dirty personal habits and a gluttonous appetite. He was reconciled to Catholicism by 1860 and died in 1875, comforted by the last rites of the Church.

The learned English occultist A. E. Waite, who was not a reincarnation of Levi, but succeeded in translating the *Doctrine and Ritual* all the same, said that in it Levi revealed the secrets of an occult society into which he had been initiated, and was expelled from the society for doing so. Waite does not say whether this was the English occult group headed by Bulwer Lytton, the novelist, but Levi apparently was a member of this group in the early 1850s. He was always more interested in theorising about magic than in actually practising it, and the only magical operation he is known to have performed was one of necromancy, though of an unusually pure and elevated kind, the evocation of the ghost of the pagan philosopher and magician Apollonius of Tyana. This happened in 1854 in London.

Levi's description of this operation is strikingly simple and straightforward when compared to his usual high, rhapsodical style. He was persuaded to attempt it by a mysterious woman in black who said she was a friend of 'Sir B___ L___'. He prepared himself by fasting and abstinence for twenty-one days beforehand. (3 and 7 are both magically powerful numbers and $21 = 3 \times 7$.) The ceremony was conducted by Levi alone, without witnesses, in a room with four concave mirrors and an altar resting on a new white lambskin. The sign of the pentagram (a five-pointed star) was carved in the white marble top of the altar, around which was a magic circle—a chain of magnetised iron—as a barrier against evil forces. On the altar was a small copper chafing-dish with charred laurel and alder wood in it. Another chafing-dish stood at one side on a tripod. Levi wore a white robe—the prevalence of white was to show the purity of his intentions and appeal to beneficient influences—and on his head a wreath of vervain leaves entwined in a golden chain. Traditionally, vervain has the power to ward off demons. He held a brand-new sword in one hand and a copy of the ritual for the ceremony in the other.

Levi lit fires in the two chafing-dishes, so that the smoke would provide material from which the ghost could make itself a visible body, and chanted a long and mysterious incantation to summon the ghost from the world of shades. 'In unity the demons chant the praises of God; they lose their malice and fury. . . . Cereberus opens his triple jaw, and fire chants the praises of God with the three tongues of the lightning . . . the soul revisits the tombs, the magical lamps are lighted. . . .' He chanted in a low voice, gradually rising higher in pitch. The smoke eddied and floated about the altar. It seemed as though the earth began to shake and Levi's heart beat more quickly, He heaped more twigs on the fires and as the flames sprang up he saw in front of the altar the figure of a man, which dissolved and vanished away.

Levi repeated the incantation. Something seemed to brighten in the depths of the mirror behind the altar and in it he saw a figure moving towards him. Closing his eyes, he three times summoned the ghost to appear. 'When I again looked forth there was a man in front of me, wrapped from head to foot in a species of shroud, which seemed more gray than white; he was lean, melancholy and beardless.'

Levi was frightened. His body felt abnormally cold and when he tried to speak he found that he could not articulate properly. He put one hand on the pentagram for protection and pointed his sword at the apparition, mentally ordering it to obey him. The figure became shadowy and disappeared. He commanded it to return. Something touched his sword-arm, which went numb to the elbow. He turned the point of the sword downwards. The figure immediately reappeared, but Levi felt a sensation of intense weakness and evidently fainted.

Levi's arm was numb and painful for several days afterwards. The figure had not spoken, but the two questions he had meant to ask it seemed to have answered themselves in his mind. The answers were 'death' and 'dead'. He did not believe that the figure was the ghost of Apollonius and he says that the preparation for the ceremony and the ceremony itself had the effect on his mind of 'an actual drunkenness of the imagination', which might have caused hallucination, but he was convinced that he had seen and touched something real. 'I do not explain the physical laws by which I saw and touched; I affirm solely that I did see and that I did touch, that I saw clearly and distinctly, apart from dreaming, and this is sufficient to establish the real efficacy of magical ceremonies. . . . I commend the greatest caution to those who propose devoting themselves to similar experiences; their result is intense exhaustion, and frequently a shock sufficient to occasion illness.'[21]

Another French magician, a few years older than Levi, was Pierre Vintras, who announced that he was a reincarnation of Elijah with a mission to prepare the way for Christ's Coming in Glory. He founded a mysterious sect called the Work of Mercy which prided itself on a large collection of communion wafers, miraculously marked with blood. Levi examined the marks on three of these bloody hosts and diagnosed them as devilish. The first was the sinister sign of the reversed pentagram—a five-pointed star with two points upwards—which is a symbol of Satan, the two upper points representing the horns of the sabbatic goat. 'It is the goat of lust attacking the Heavens with its horns. It is a sign execrated by initiates of a superior rank, even at the Sabbath.' The second was a reversed caduceus, with the heads and tails of the intertwined snakes pointing outwards instead of inwards, and above the snakes' heads was a V. Like all reversed symbols and symbols of Two, these are emblems of evil. The third host was marked with the Hebrew letters of Jehovah upside down. This is again a symbol of the Devil, signifying the reversal of the right order of things—'Fatality alone exists, God and the Spirit are not. Matter is all, and spirit is only a fiction of this matter demented.'[22]

When Vintras died in 1875 the leadership of the Work of Mercy passed to a defrocked Catholic priest, the Abbé Boullan, and this set the stage for the great 'battle of bewitchment' of the 1880s and '90s. Boullan was born in 1824. After he had taken orders he became the spiritual director of a nun called Adele Chevalier, who heard supernatural voices and claimed to have been miraculously healed of a disease by the Virgin Mary. Boullan and Adele Chevalier became lovers. In 1859 they founded the Society for the Reparation of Souls which in spite of its high-sounding name was devoted to sex-magic and on at least one occasion to ritual murder. On December 8, 1860, Boullan ceremoniously sacrificed a child, born to him by Adele Chevalier, as the high point of a Mass. Boullan, who had a pentagram tattooed at the corner of his left eye (the left side being the side of evil) and celebrated Mass in vestments on which an inverted crucifix was embroidered, specialised in exorcism—the casting out of evil spirits. He recommended consecrated hosts mixed with faeces (which as a fertiliser contains powerful life-energy) as a cure for nuns who complained that they were tormented by devils. He also taught them how to hypnotise themselves into thinking that they were copulating with Christ and the saints and how to enjoy sexual intercourse with his own astral body.[23]

In 1875 Boullan announced that he was a reincarnation of John the Baptist and the new leader of the Work of Mercy. Some members of the sect refused to accept him, but he gathered a group of followers around him at Lyons. Late in 1886 they were visited by the young Marquis Stanislas de Guaita, a morphine addict who later founded the Kabbalistic Order of the Rose-Cross in Paris. Guaita had read Eliphas Levi the year before and was enthusiastically immersed in the study and practice of magic. He stayed two weeks at Lyons and came away disgusted. Boullan believed that humanity's path to God lay through the sex act. He encouraged intercourse with supernatural beings and with other mortals, and the group performed ceremonious Unions of Life, or ritual copulations. Guaita said that the practical result of Boullan's teaching was unlimited promiscuity with adultery, incest, bestiality and masturbation practised as solemn acts of worship.

A month later a follower of Boullan's called Oswald Wirth also left Lyons in disgust. Guaita and Wirth joined forces. In May 1887 they wrote to Boullan announcing that they had judged him and had condemned him. They explained afterwards that all they meant by this was that they would show him up in public as a scoundrel, but Boullan was convinced, perhaps rightly, that they intended to kill him by black magic. He took the necessary measures to defend himself and the great battle of bewitchment began.

The story of this magical contest is irresistibly comic now, but it was not at all humorous for those who were involved in it at the time. It is not clear whether the Guaita faction were actually casting spells against Boullan at all, but Boullan was convinced of it and in terror of his life launched appalling anathemas, conjurations and incantations against the foe. He was assisted by his housekeeper, Julie Thibault, who was clairvoyant. One of Boullan's supporters, Jules Bois, describing the scene at Lyons, said that Boullan asked Julie Thibault if she could discern what the workers of iniquity were doing. She said they were putting a portrait of Boullan into a coffin (to kill him by imitative magic). Next she announced that they were saying a Black Mass against him. Boullan retaliated with a ceremony called the Sacrifice of Glory of Melchisidek, in which 'the feminine rite allied to the masculine rite, red wine mingled with white, created . . . a victorious ferment, by which the impious altars were overthrown and the hierophants of Satanism struck dead'. Unfortunately, it turned out that the Satanic hierophants had been only temporarily discommoded, as on a later occasion mysterious thumping noises, like the blows of a fist on flesh, were heard. Lumps appeared on Boullan's face and with a loud cry he tore open his robe to show a bleeding wound on his chest.[24]

Another of Boullan's partisans, from 1890 on, was the novelist J-K. Huysmans, who dabbled extensively in the occult and whose novel *La Bas* contains one of the most famous descriptions of a Black Mass. Huysmans was with Boullan at Lyons in 1891. By this time Boullan had enlisted another clairvoyant girl besides Julie Thibault. Boullan's party were convinced that Guaita had tried to poison the girl. They believed that he could volatalise poisons and project them through space. (He was also supposed to own a familiar spirit, which was kept locked in a cupboard when not needed.) However, the girl had retaliated. Writing to a friend, Huysmans said that Guaita 'ought now to be in bed, and the arm he usually injects with morphine should be looking like a balloon. . . .' Boullan was 'flinging himself about all over the place. I'm told that de Guaita poisoned the little clairvoyante, who promptly counterattacked by virtue of the law of return. So that it would be interesting to know whether, in fact, de Guaita had been laid low. The two women here see him in bed.' The law of return is the principle that the force of the spell which fails rebounds on the head of the sorcerer.

In another letter Huysmans said, 'Boullan jumps about like a tiger-cat, clutching one of his hosts and invoking aid of St. Michael and the eternal justiciaries of eternal justice: then standing at his altar he cries out "Strike down Peladan, s.d.P., s.d.P." And Maman Thibault, her hands folded on her belly, announces, "it is done." ' (Peladan was one of Guaita's group.)[25]

Huysmans became convinced that he himself was one of the targets of Guaita's sorcery. He felt the presence of an invisible force all about him and something cold moving across his face. At bedtime what he called 'fluidic fisticuffs' were aimed at him. His cat seemed to be suffering from the same symptoms. He appealed to Boullan for help. Boullan sent him one of the blood-marked hosts from the Vintras collection and a paste made of myrrh, incense, camphor and cloves which would keep evil influences at bay if burned in the fireplace. (Like salt, spices have power against demons because they are preservatives.) On one occasion Boullan warned Huysmans not to go to his office next day. Huysmans stayed at home and in his absence a heavy mirror fell down and smashed on his desk. Anyone sitting at the desk would probably have been killed.

The battle reached its climax at the beginning of 1893. On January 3rd Boullan wrote to Huysmans, saying that the new year was one of ill omen. 'The figures 8-9-3 form a combination which foreshadows bad news' (probably because 8+9+3 = 20 and 2+0 = 2, which is the number of evil and the Devil). During the previous night Julie Thibault dreamed of Guaita and in the early hours of the morning 'a black bird of death cried out. It was herald of the attack.' Boullan woke at 3 a.m., feeling that he was suffocating. He lost consciousness for half an hour, but by four o'clock he believed that the danger was past. He was mistaken. He died the next day, January 4th.[26]

Both Huysmans and Jules Bois were convinced that Boullan had been killed by sorcery. After Bois had published violent attacks on Guaita, in which he accused him of being a black magician, Bois and Guaita fought a duel with pistols. As the day of the duel approached it was believed that both sides were filling the atmosphere with frantic spells and conjurations. On the way to the duel one of the horses pulling the carriage Bois was in stopped dead in its tracks and began to tremble and then to stagger as if it had seen the Devil himself. This trembling fit lasted for twenty minutes. At the duel itself each man fired once and neither was hit. Afterwards it was found that a bullet was stuck in the barrel of one of the pistols. The Bois supporters were convinced that his gun had fired and that they had magically prevented Guaita's bullet from leaving his pistol. Three days later Bois fought a duel with one of Guaita's friends, an occultist who called himself 'Papus' and wrote one of the standard books on the Tarot cards. On the way to this duel Bois again had to cope with what seemed to be occult interference with the horses. The horse drawing his first carriage collapsed. He took another, but this horse fell and the carriage overturned. Bois arrived battered and bleeding at the duel, which was fought with swords. Neither man was injured.

While these fearsome events were taking place in France an important occult society, the Order of the Golden Dawn, had been founded in England. At its peak the Golden Dawn had one hundred members and lodges in London, Paris, Edinburgh, Bradford and Weston-super-Mare. Members included W. B. Yeats, two writers of occult thrillers, Algernon Blackwood and Arthur Machen, the Astronomer Royal of Scotland, and an elderly clergyman who had succeeded in making the elixir of life thirty years before, but had always been frightened to drink it. Now that he really needed it, it had evaporated. Another member was the eccentric Allan Bennett, who eventually became a Buddhist monk. He had been brought up a Roman Catholic, but renounced this faith at the age of 16 when he discovered the mechanism of childbirth. According to Aleister Crowley, Bennett's reaction was, 'Did the omnipotent God, whom he had been taught to worship, devise so revolting and degrading a method of perpetuating the species? Then this God must be a Devil, delighting in loathsomeness.' Bennett carried a glass 'lustre' or candlestick about with him and once used to blast a Theosophist who had dared to doubt its powers. 'It took fourteen hours to restore the incredulous individual to the use of his mind and muscles.'[27]

The Golden Dawn's most precious possession was a mysterious manuscript written in code, which had been discovered on a London bookstall in 1884 by a clergyman, Dr. Woodman. Woodman showed it to William Wynn Westcott, a doctor who was an authority on the Cabala and became both London Coroner and Supreme Magus of the Rosicrucian Society in England. Neither of them could make very much of it. They consulted Samuel Liddell Mathers.

Mathers was in his early forties at this time. Apart from the fact that he had been to Bedford Grammar School, where he distinguished himself as a runner, very little is known of his early life. With the help of his wife, who was clairvoyant, he deciphered the mysterious manuscript, which turned out to deal with certain problems of the Cabala and the Tarot. Once installed in the Golden Dawn, Mathers began to churn about like an infant cuckoo in the nest until he had forced out the founders and could take command of the society himself. He claimed to have a magical link with three Secret Chiefs in Paris who confirmed him as Visible Head of the Order. Westcott finally resigned in 1897 (and in this year the Marquis Stanislas de Guaita died, aged 36, of an overdose of drugs).

According to Mrs. Mathers, in her introduction to the 1938 edition of her husband's *Kabbalah Unveiled*, the Golden Dawn studied 'the intelligent forces behind Nature, the Constitution of man and his relation to God' with the good magical objective that man 'may ultimately regain union with the Divine Man latent in himself. . . '. In spite of this high aim the Order was soon disrupted by personal quarrels, especially after Aleister Crowley became a member and attempted to seize the leadership from Mathers. Many of the members complained that Mathers had absurdly high pretensions—he announced that he was spiritually directed from the Temple of the Holy Spirit—and the society broke up in quarrelling and confusion. It was later revived and reconstituted under the respectable leadership of A. E. Waite.

Mathers and his wife Moina, the sister of the philosopher Henri Bergson, lived in Paris. (Mathers tried to convert Bergson to magic, but without success.) Their house was decorated as an Egyptian temple and they celebrated 'Egyptian Masses', invoking the goddess Isis. Mathers officiated in a long white robe, a metal belt engraved with the signs of the zodiac, bracelets round his wrists and ankles, and a leopard-skin slung across his shoulders. He was convinced that he was descended from the Scottish clan MacGregor and took to calling himself MacGregor Mathers, Chevalier MacGregor and Comte de Glenstrae. W. B. Yeats, whose magical name in the Golden Dawn was *Daemon est Deus Inversus* (The Devil is God Reversed), was a frequent visitor to the Mathers household in Paris. In the evenings they used to play a peculiar form of chess for four players. Yeats and Mrs. Mathers played against Mathers and a spirit. Before moving his spirit-partner's piece Mathers would shade his eyes and stare earnestly at the spirit's empty chair at the other side of the board.[28]

Mathers edited and translated important magical textbooks—the famous *Key of Solomon*, which he unfortunately bowdlerised, the *Sacred Magic of Abramelin the Mage* and the *Kabbalah Unveiled*, which is largely either unintelligible or tedious, but which has a valuable introduction by Mathers. He also worked out a far-reaching system of magical correspondences (described in Chapter 3) which was taken over and developed by Aleister Crowley. Mathers and Crowley were bitter enemies. When Mathers died in 1918 many of his friends were convinced that Crowley had murdered him by black magic.

Aleister Crowley—poet, painter, mountaineer, traveller, chess player, brilliant talker when in the mood, asthmatic, heroin addict, satyriac and master magician—was born in 1875, the year of Eliphas Levi's death. He later became convinced that he was a reincarnation of Levi. (In earlier lives he had been Cagliostro and Alexander VI, the Borgia Pope.) His father, a brewer, left Crowley a fortune which he spent with astonishing rapidity. His parents were Plymouth Brethren and he was brought up in a strictly puritanical atmosphere. He was educated at Malvern, Tonbridge and Trinity College, Cambridge, where he acquired a chess blue, a homosexual love affair, and the beginnings of a highly sinister reputation. He enjoyed mountain-climbing and as a young man made creditable assaults on K2 and Kangchenjunga. In 1903 he married Rose Kelly, sister of the painter Gerald Kelly, who was afterwards President of the Royal Academy. She had clairvoyant powers and it was through her that a spirit named Aiwass dictated Crowley's first important magical work, the *Book of the Law*, in Cairo in 1904. She took to drink and Crowley eventually divorced her.

Crowley joined the Order of the Golden Dawn in 1898, taking the magical name of Brother Perdurabo (I shall endure). In a brilliant biography of Crowley, *The Great Beast*, John Symonds describes how Crowley attempted to oust Mathers and take over the leadership. Mathers, outraged, sent a vampire to attack him, but Crowley 'smote her with her own current of evil' and defeated her. The struggle was waged hotly on both sides. Mathers succeeded in striking Crowley's entire pack of bloodhounds dead at one blow and caused Crowley's servant to go mad and try to kill Mrs. Crowley. The servant had to be overpowered with a salmon gaff. In reply, Crowley summoned up the demon Beelzebub and forty-nine attendant devils and sent them off to chastise Mathers in Paris.

Expelled from the Golden Dawn, Crowley founded his own society, the A ∴ A ∴ (*Argentinum Astrum*—Silver Star), but its membership was never as numerous or as distinguished as the Golden Dawn's. By 1914 it had thirty-eight members. In 1910 Mathers obtained a court order to stop Crowley from publishing the Golden Dawn's secrets in his magazine, *The Equinox*. Crowley appealed against this order, and, rather impertinently, used a talisman from the *Sacred Magic of Abramelin*, which Mathers had translated, the one recommended for 'gaining the affection of a judge'. The talisman was effective and Crowley's appeal was successful. This talisman consists of the following letters, written on parchment:

```
A L M A N A H
L
M A R E
A A L B E H A
N
A R E H A I L
H           A
```

Sexuality runs all through Crowley's poetry and magical writings. He had a remarkable appetite for women and was apparently very attractive to them. He wore a special Perfume of Immortality, made of one part ambergris, two parts musk and three parts civet, which gave him a peculiar odour, but which he said attracted women and also horses, which always whinnied after him in the streets.[29] In 1912 the leaders of a German occult society specialising in sex-magic, the Order of Templars of the Orient, were alarmed by the fact that

Crowley was publishing their Order's secrets in *The Equinox*. They approached him in London, found that he had discovered these secrets independently through his own researches, and invited him to join the Order. He became British head of the O.T.O. with the title of Supreme and Holy King of Ireland, Iona and all the Britains that are in the Sanctuary of the Gnosis.

Crowley spent the First World War in the United States, writing anti-British propaganda for the Germans. Blood and iron always appealed to him. In 1916, living in Bristol, New Hampshire, he ascended to the high magical grade of Magus, going through a ceremony of his own invention in which he baptised a toad as Jesus Christ and crucified it.

In 1920 he went to Cefalu in Sicily and set up his Sacred Abbey of Thelema ('the will' in Greek), with his current mistresses, the Scarlet Woman and Sister Cypris (a name of Aphrodite). Very few disciples arrived and very little money. Crowley was in urgent need of both for most of his life. Rumours of abominable rites and orgies, some of them well founded, floated out from the abbey, and Mussolini's Government expelled Crowley in 1923. He was later expelled from France as well and wandered forlornly from England to Germany and Portugal and back again, much in the eye of the popular Press, which called him 'the wickedest man in the world'. He himself preferred the title 'The Great Beast'.

Crowley's numerous magical writings appeared in obscure magazines or were published in limited editions at his own expense. The clearest and most accessible of his books are his brilliant occult thriller *Moonchild* and his masterpiece *Magick in Theory and Practice*, published in 1929. Although he had the usual occultist's love of obscurity for its own sake, Crowley had great gifts as a writer, with a pleasingly sardonic sense of humour and, when he chose to use it, a talent for clarity. His *Magick in Theory and Practice* is probably the best single book ever written on the subject.

Crowley died at Hastings in 1947. His orgiastic 'Hymn to Pan' was recited during his extremely odd funeral service in the chapel of the crematorium at Brighton, to the scandal and annoyance of the local authorities. The last few lines show him as he liked to think of himself.

> . . . I am thy mate, I am thy man,
> Goat of thy flock, I am gold, I am god,
> Flesh to thy bone, flower to thy rod.
> With hoofs of steel I race on the rocks

Through solstice stubborn to equinox.
And I rave; and I rape and I rip and I rend
Everlasting, world without end,
Mannikin, maiden, maenad, man,
In the might of Pan.
Io Pan ! Io Pan Pan ! Pan ! Io Pan !

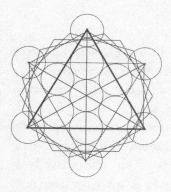

CHAPTER TWO

Names and Numbers

THE conviction that the name of a thing contains the essence of its being is one of the oldest and most fundamental of magical beliefs. Names are used to identify things. Instead of reciting a long and detailed description of the characteristics of an animal, it is more convenient to say, this is a 'frog'. But to distinguish between the name of the frog and the creature itself is a modern and sophisticated habit of mind. For the magical thinker the name sums up all the characteristics which make the animal what it is, and so the name is the animal's identity. If it did not have this name but some other—'toad' perhaps—it would not be what it is, but something different.

This is the root of the magical theory that the name of a thing is a miniature image of it, which can be used as a substitute for the thing itself. A man can be injured as effectively by working on this miniature image of himself, his name, as by working on a figure of him in clay or wax; and when a wax image is used it is often baptised with the name of the victim it represents. A classical method of killing or injuring an enemy is to write his name on a piece of lead, wax or pottery, add an appropriate curse and bury it. Many of these curses have been found in tombs and temples in Greece, Asia Minor and Italy. 'As the lead grows cold' one says, 'so grow he cold.' Sometimes a nail was driven through the name, to pierce the enemy. 'I nail his name, that is, himself.' Some of the curses were connected with lawsuits. The name of an opponent in the courts was buried to stifle his slippery tongue. Others were intended to strike the victim with disease. 'I put quartan fever on Aristion to the death.'[1]

An early outgrowth of the magical theory of names was the concept of the 'real' name. If any man can be subjected to magical influence simply by using his name, life becomes altogether too dangerous and it must also have been observed that knowing a thing's name did not actually give a magician power over it. This was explained by saying that the ordinary names of things are merely convenient labels. The name which enshrines the essence of a creature's identity is its 'real' name, which is secret.

In many primitive societies a man has two names. One is for ordinary, everyday use and the other, his real name, is kept secret. It may be so secret that the man himself does not know it—it was whispered into his ear by his mother when he was a baby. If a sorcerer discovers the real name he can destroy the man, for instance by magically enticing the name into leaves or straw which he burns or scatters. As the name is turned to ashes in the fire or blown away on the wind, the victim weakens and dies. He real name is his identity and as it disintegrates so does he.

The real names of gods, angels and demons were also kept secret, for the same reason. Plutarch said that in early times the name of the guardian deity of Rome was carefully concealed. It was forbidden to ask this god's name or anything else about it, even whether it was male or female, probably because the Romans were afraid that enemies could nullify the god's power or even charm the god away from them if its name was known. In the Bible the rider on a white horse of Revelation who is called Faithful and True has another, secret name. 'His eyes were as a flame of fire and on his head were many crowns; and he had a name written, that no man knew but he himself.' The angel who visited Manoah, the father of Samson, refused to reveal his name—'Why askest thou thus after my name, seeing it is secret?' The angel who wrestled with Jacob also refused to tell his name, presumably because he thought Jacob could use it to defeat him. Jewish commentators believed that this angel's real name was Sammael. He was the terrible angel of death and poison, whose name means Venom of God.[2]

The belief that the name of the thing *is* the thing lies behind the biblical habit of using 'God's name' to mean 'God'. God says 'he shall build a house for my name', meaning 'for me', and tells Moses to obey the angel who goes before the Israelites because 'my name is in him', meaning 'I am in him'. St. Paul says that God raised Christ 'above every name that is named', meaning 'above every being that exists'.[3]

An Egyptian legend describes how the goddess Isis tried to capture the power of the sun-god Ra and reign supreme over all the world. To do this, she had to discover his real name. Ra was old and he dribbled and slobbered. Isis collected some of his dropped spittle (which magically retained its connection with his body) and mixed it with earth to make a venomous snake. The snake stung Ra and the god was in agony. When every remedy had been tried without success he agreed that Isis should take his name. 'I consent that Isis shall search into me and that my name shall pass from me into her.' In taking his name, Isis was really taking his identity. By herself becoming Ra she could exercise his supreme power.[4]

There are many survivals of the old belief in the magical significance of names. Parents take trouble about choosing a name for a child, often with the underlying feeling that the name will affect the child's character. To help them choose, books and magazines list the 'meanings' of names. In Jewish tradition, still frequently observed, a child should never be named for a relative who is alive, because the relative will die if his name is taken for the child. People who enter religious orders take new names to show that as new men and women they are beginning a new life: so do people who join occult societies, and witches sometimes took new names on entering the Devil's service. Beyond this, most of us still tend to make the deep-rooted magical assumption that words have meaning independently of the way in which they are used and that terms like 'beauty' or 'democracy' are the *names* of things whose characteristics are independent of our opinions about them. It is only in recent times that this assumption has been questioned by philosophers.

One of the most interesting survivals of the magical theory of names is modern numerology. A respectable numerologist would not attempt to destroy you by means of your name, but he does believe that your name contains the essence of *you*. If it analysed according to a set of traditional rules, it reveals your character and your destiny.

The fact that your name distinguishes you from other people is the basis of the numerologist's conviction that it enshrines your individuality. But anyone who sets out to discover the true meanings of names runs into the difficulty that the multitudes of different people in the world have multitudes of different names. The task of analysing all these names is hopeless unless they can be reduced to a reasonably small number of types. This is done by turning all names into numbers. Only the numbers from 1 to 9 are used (sometimes with 11 and 22 added) and this gives the numerologists a manageable quantity of categories to work on.

1. Fortunes by Numbers

The power which the student may sometimes draw into himself when trying to realise the inner meaning of these great names and powers is sometimes so great as to cause physical breakdown . . . In extreme cases the end is insanity. In milder cases a slight mental trouble may easily result.

LEONARD BOSMAN *The Meaning and Philosophy of Numbers*

To find the number of your name you start by turning each letter of the name into a number. Unfortunately, numerologists do not agree about the number value to be given each letter. There are two main systems. In the first, the 'modern' system, the numbers from 1 to 9 are written down and the letters of the alphabet are written underneath in their normal order.

1	2	3	4	5	6	7	8	9
A	B	C	D	E	F	G	H	I
J	K	L	M	N	O	P	Q	R
S	T	U	V	W	X	Y	Z	

The second system, the 'Hebrew' system, which is based on the Hebrew alphabet with assistance from the Greek, does not use the figure 9 and does not list the alphabet in the normal order.

1	2	3	4	5	6	7	8
A	B	C	D	E	U	O	F
I	K	G	M	H	V	Z	P
Q	R	L	T	N	W		
J		S			X		
Y							

Less than half the letters have the same values in both systems and numerologists will often give different interpretations of the same name, because they are using different number systems. All the following examples use the Hebrew system, which is based on two alphabets in which the letters were used as numbers, where our ABC has never been used this way. In Hebrew there were no purely numerical symbols—like our, 1, 2, 3—and the letters of the alphabet also stood for numbers. The same thing is true of classical Greek, in which all the letters did double duty as numbers, and of Latin, in which some of the letters stood for numbers and some did not.

Using the Hebrew alphabet, numbers can be assigned to most of the letters of our alphabet. A is 1 because the Hebrew A (*aleph*) stood for 1. Similarly, B (*beth*) is 2 and G (*gimel*) is 3. Zeros are disregarded, so that L (*lamed*—30) is 3 and T (*tau*—400) is 4. Number equivalents for letters like J and X which do not exist in Hebrew are taken from the Greek alphabet. (The details are given in Appendix 2.)

The absence of 9 from the system has contributed to the awe and esteem which numerologists have for this number. The celebrated palm-reader and numerologist Cheiro says there is no 9 because 'the ancient masters of occultism knew that in the "Highest Sphere" the number 9 represents the 9-lettered name of God'.[5] This is mumbo-jumbo and the real explanation is much simpler. There is no 9 in the Hebrew system because the Hebrew letters which stood for 9, 90 and 900 have no equivalents in our alphabet.

Whichever system you prefer, the method of finding your number is the same. Write down your name and the number equivalents for each letter. Then add the numbers. If the total has two figures or more add these figures together and repeat the process until you reach a single figure, which is called the 'digital root'. For example:

FRANCIS T. BAKER

$$8 +2 +1 +5 +3 +1 +3 +4 +2 +1 +2 +5 +2$$

Total $39 = 12 = 3$

The numbers total 39. Add 3+9 to give 12. Add 1+2 to give 3. 3 is the digital root of 39 and the number of the name Francis T. Baker.

You should write down the name by which you usually think of yourself. If Baker does not normally use his middle initial, he should leave it out. If he thinks of himself as Frank instead of Francis, he should put down Frank Baker. Mr., Mrs. and Miss should not be included, as they are not part of your individual name. When a woman marries she changes her name. The number of her maiden name shows her personality and fortune before she married. The number of her married name shows how marriage has affected her.

The number found by this method is the most important number contained in your name. It shows your character and personality, the type of life you will lead, the path you follow through life's jungle. Your name contains other numbers as well. You can find the total of all the vowels and the total of all the consonants. Francis T. Baker's vowels add to 8, his consonants to 4. (Y is treated as a vowel only when there is no other vowel in the word. In Lynn Y is a vowel, in Billy it is a consonant.)

The total of the *vowels* is often called the Heart Number, and it reveals your inner character, the self which is hidden under the shell of your exterior, the person you are at heart. It indicates your deepest interests, ambitions, likes and dislikes. The total of the *consonants* is usually called the Personality Number, and it gives the clue to your outer personality, your manner and behaviour, the impression you make on those around you. This distinction goes back to Hebrew. When Hebrew is written down only the consonants are written, no vowels. (The letter *aleph*, A, is really a 'breathing' in Hebrew, not a vowel.) Because the vowels are not shown in written Hebrew the total of the vowels reveals your hidden self, the person you are under the surface. The total of the consonants, which are shown, indicates the personality which you show to the world.

Many numerologists stress the importance of still another number—the Birth Number—which is found by adding up your date of birth. If you were born on November 14, 1928, for instance, your Birth Number is 9.

November 14 1928

11   +14+1+9+2+8 = 45 = 9

This number is an indication of the stamp which the mysterious forces that move the universe impressed on your character and destiny at the moment when you were born. It will affect you all your life and it may not harmonise with the number of your name. If it does not, you can expect to be torn by inner conflict and you may seem to be always struggling against fate.

People whose names add to *one* have great fixity of purpose and an unswerving drive towards achievement in their own particular line. They are *single*-minded, or *one*-track-minded. They are powerful characters—positive, obstinate, self-reliant and self-assertive, ambitious and aggressive. They have excellent powers of concentration and good memories. They lead, create, originate and invent. They are pioneers, always drawn to the new and the unusual. Extremely independent people, they do not take orders well or co-operate easily with others. They resent advice and usually refuse to follow it. They are not always very pleasant people. They tend to have little real interest in friendship or love and usually have few close friends. If they are friendly and sympathetic, it may be because they think it is to their advantage to be so. They are likely to dominate everyone around them, sometimes to the point of tyranny. They are essentially people who 'look after Number One'.

People whose number is *two* have the qualities which are traditionally regarded as feminine. They have soft, sweet natures. They are quiet, tactful, conciliatory. They are *even*-tempered, lovers of peace and harmony. They tend to play *second* fiddle and make excellent subordinates, conscientious, tidy and modest. They are followers rather than leaders, and if they do not get their own way they do it by persuasion and diplomacy, not be asserting themselves. Often they are shy and self-conscious. They are likely to change their minds frequently and tend to put things off and generally shilly-shally. There is also a dark and sinister side to the 2-character which may show itself in cruelty, malice and deceit.

Like other magical thinkers, numerologists accept the theory that the association of two things in the human mind indicates a real connection between them. 'To play second fiddle' is not a mere figure of speech to the numerologist, but evidence of a link between the number 2 and subordination.

If your number is *three* you are brilliant, imaginative, versatile and energetic. You express yourself boldly, vividly and on all possible occasions. Threes sparkle and glitter. Witty, lively, charming, they are likely to be extremely successful in life. They are often highly talented, especially in the arts. They take things lightly and easily and they tend to be lucky—they seem to succeed without really trying. Proud and independent-minded people, they are ambitious, commanding, sometimes dictatorial. Their faults are a tendency to spread their efforts wastefully in too many directions and an inability to take anything seriously. They are also inclined to be overanxious for popularity and other people's approval.

Four is the number of solid, practical, uninspired and uninspiring people. They lack any creative spark, but they may be efficient organisers and administrators. Down-to-earth, calm, steady, industrious, respectable, they think of themselves as pillars of society. They like routine and detail and hard work. They have an unfortunate tendency to be stern, grim, repressive, plodding, suspicious and resentful of anyone whose ways are not like their own. There is an odd streak in the 4-nature, which comes out in fits of melancholy or sudden outbursts of rage and violence. Fours are not likely to be successful in life and any success they have will not be won easily. Four is traditionally the number of poverty, misery and defeat. Most modern numerologists try to gloss this over as far as they can, but their picture of 4 is not a happy one.

A *five* is a much brighter person altogether. He is restless and jumpy, clever, impatient. He lives on his nerves. The unusual and the bizarre fascinate him. He loves travel, new people, different surroundings. Five are jacks of all trades and masters of none, attracted by everything but held by nothing. They enjoy gambling, speculation and risks. They make excellent salesmen. They are adventurous, attractive people, quick-tempered, sometimes conceited and sarcastic. They detest responsibility and avoid it. They hate to be tied down or in a rut. Often inconsiderate and self-indulgent, they are resourceful, resilient, many-sided people, hard to analyse or pin down. For reasons explained later, the key to 5 is the fact that it is the number of sex. (The word 'sex' adds to 5, incidentally.) Fives have interesting but highly unstable love lives and the dark side of their nature may show itself in excess, debauchery or perversion.

Six is the number of harmony, domesticity and peaceful happiness. Sixes are equable, kindly, reliable, well balanced. They have a great talent for friendship and for home and family life. They are loyal, conscientious, idealistic and affectionate. Wholesome and conventional, unlike the fives, and without the brilliance of the threes, they may be more successful than either in the long run, especially in the arts or in teaching. Although they are capable and thorough workers, they usually lack any real flair for business. They are happiest in a quiet circle of friends and family. They are sometimes inclined to be smug and self-satisfied, fussy and gossipy, obstinate and conceited.

Seven is the number of the scholar, the philosopher, the mystic and the occultist. Sevens are natural recluses. They like to withdraw from the maddening bustle of the world and be alone to mediate and reflect. Dignified, reserved, self-controlled, serious, they have no patience with foolishness or frivolity. They care nothing for money and very little for physical comfort. They have powerful and penetrating intellects, but there is also a dreamy side to their character, highly imaginative, sometimes fey and strange. They are often extraordinarily bad at explaining themselves and their ideas and they tend to dislike being questioned or argued with. They are sometimes deeply unhappy people, pessimistic, disappointed, aloof, superior, witheringly sarcastic.

Eight stands for power, money and worldly involvement. It is the number of material success or failure. Eights are strong, tough, practical people, successful businessmen or politicians, but their course through life is never easy. They do not accumulate money with the careless ease of the threes. Their careers are built on struggle, strain, effort, care and drudgery. They conduct their operations cautiously and tenaciously, without inspiration. They can be hard, materialistic, selfish, sometimes tyrannical and unscrupulous. They are not very attractive characters and they may be keenly and sadly aware of the fact. Beneath their often grim and chill exterior there is likely to be a layer of wild eccentricity, waywardness and rebelliousness. They have the capacity for massive success, but they constantly face the possibility of resounding failure.

Nine is the number of high mental and spiritual achievement. Nines are large-minded, visionary, idealistic. Romantic, passionate, impulsive, they are people of wide sympathies and great charm. They have an intense urge to help other people and to serve the cause of humanity at large. They make brilliant scientists, teachers and artists. Strong-willed and determined people, inspired and inspiring, they are often condemned by their duller contemporaries as wild, unorthodox and impractical. They are easily imposed on, they constantly fall in and out of love, and they have a genuine horror of ugliness, poverty, old age and unhappiness, for themselves and everyone else. They can be uncharitable and intolerant when opposed. Their desire to do good may be expressed in a repellently conceited and egocentric way. Sometimes they seem to be too busy loving their fellow men in general to bother about the feelings of individuals. But on the whole the numerologist's picture of 9 is an attractive and inspiring one. The names of Presidents Lincoln and Kennedy both add to 9.

Any number above 9 is usually reduced to its digital root, but numerologists sometimes make an exception for the numbers 11 and 22. The name George Washington, for instance, adds to 65; 6 + 5 gives 11. The normal rule adds 1 + 1 to give 2, but some authorities halt the addition process at 11, especially as 2 does not fit noticeably well with Washington's character and achievements.

Eleven and 22 are particularly fortunate and excellent numbers, representing a higher plane of experience than the numbers from 1 to 9. *Eleven* is the number of revelation and martyrdom. Elevens are people who have a special message to give to the world. They may become great teachers and preachers, inspired visionaries in religion, science, politics or the arts. They are nine on a higher plane and they have similar virtues and failings. Intensely subjective, they live by the light of their own inner vision and they may not always understand the real characters and needs of the people around them. They can sometimes be accused of loving their ideals better than their fellow men. They are powerful personalities of great vigour and moral courage, convinced of the rightness and importance of their mission and prepared to make any sacrifice for it. The names Winston S. Churchill, Einstein, Pablo Picasso and Florence Nightingale add to 11.

Twenty-two is the number of the *master*. It is difficult to say anything about the person whose number is 22 without lapsing into a string of superlatives. This is the number of the truly great man, combining in an almost superhuman personality the best qualities of the other numbers—the driving energy of 1, the persuasiveness of 2, the brilliance of 3, 4's capacity for solid work, 5's versatility, the balance and harmony of 6, the reflective wisdom of 7, 8's worldly abilities, 9's devotion to humanity, 11's mission and inner vision. As creator, teacher, organiser, 22 is immensely successful, admired and respected by all who come in contact with him. There is only one flaw. The man who could be a Napoleon of politics, philosophy or business may choose instead to be a Napoleon of crime. Twenty-two is not only the number of the great tycoon (John D. Rockefeller adds to 22), it is also the number of the master black magician.

Numerologists say that 11 and 22 must be handled with caution. If your name adds to 22, it is natural to think of yourself as a 22-character instead of continuing the addition to arrive at the ominous and depressing number 4. But those who can really rise to the heights of 22 are very rare and it is probably more realistic to ignore 11 and 22 unless you find them popping up in pleasing profusion from your name and birthdate.

One obvious objection to numerology is that your name was given to you largely by chance—you happened to be born into a family names Jones, Smith or whatever it is, and you were named by parents who did not know anything about numerology and would not have accepted it if they did. But numerologists are magical thinkers and so they do not believe in chance. Like everything else, a person's name is the product of the inexorable forces of the universe. Numerologists say that before a child is born the forces of the universe which stamp the child's character and destiny are so impressed on the subconscious minds of the parents that they are bound to choose a name which expresses the character and destiny. Alternatively, the soul which will enter the child's body—a soul which is the survivor of many past lives—chooses a suitable name. 'The Soul', the American numerologist Florence Campbell says, 'has taken many journeys in the past and *knows* its present needs. The Soul wants progress upwards on the Great Spiral and *chooses* for the incarnating ego the vowels whose total shall accomplish this purpose.'[6]

Another problem is that you may have several different names—your full name, the name by which you think of yourself, the names by which various other people know you. Some people may know you by a nickname, others by your first name alone, others by your last name alone. An actor or writer may have one or more pseudonyms. You may have changed your surname, especially if you are a woman. You may have changed it more than once. Which name do you place under the numerologist's microscope?

The answer is that a thorough analysis examines all these names, because all of them reveal facets of your character. Your full name, given you at birth, is particularly likely to show the influence of fate or the forces of the universe. The names you have used since show how you have developed and expressed your character at different stages of your life. If you had a nickname at school the nickname shows what you were like at that time and what people thought of you then. If you are known at the office by your first name or last name alone, that name shows the impression you make at the office and how your underlying character expresses itself there.

As well as the numbers produced by the different versions of your name, the numbers given by the vowels alone, the consonants alone, and the birth date must also be considered. For really detailed analysis numerologists recommend examining the name letter by letter to see how many times each number appears and which numbers are missing. The pseudonym Marilyn Monroe, for instance, works out as follows:

$$\begin{array}{ccccccccccccc} \text{M} & \text{A} & \text{R} & \text{I} & \text{L} & \text{Y} & \text{N} & \text{M} & \text{O} & \text{N} & \text{R} & \text{O} & \text{E} \\ 4 & 1 & 2 & 1 & 3 & 1 & 5 & 4 & 7 & 5 & 2 & 7 & 5 \end{array}$$

The total of the whole name (showing overall character) is 2—the number of the eternal feminine. The vowel total (inner self) is 3—brilliance, artistic ability, sparkle, charm, luck. The consonant total (outer personality) is 8—power, wealth, worldly involvement. Taking the name letter by letter, the numbers which appear most frequently are 5—versatility, nervousness, restlessness, and the most suitable possible number for a sex goddess—and 1—drive, ambition, ruthlessness. Next come 7 (loneliness and introspection), 4 (hard work, unhappiness, defeat) and 2 (the eternal feminine again, but traditionally 2 is the most ominous and evil of numbers, though this is glossed over in modern numerology). It is significant that the name lacks a 6 (peace, adjustment, domesticity) and also lacks 8, which suggests that the worldly abilities of the consonant total were more apparent than real.

If a number is missing from your name, you will lack the qualities of that number and this is a challenge which you must overcome if you are to have a happy successful life. If your name shows the same number too many times your personality will be unbalanced by an excessive concentration of the qualities of that number. Hitler's title *Der Fuehrer*, for example, contains too many 5s (four of them in ten letters). Fives are usually nervous and jumpy, but such a concentration of 5 suggests mental instability, plus conceit, arrogance, excessive love of risks and total disregard of the interests of others. (The name Hitler adds to 2, which fits neatly into the old view of this number as evil and devilish, but it is not easy to see Hitler in the modern numerologist's terms as diplomatic, sympathetic and docile.)

Numerological personality-dissection is obviously complicated, and numerologists do not suppose that each of us can be neatly pigeonholed as one of nine distinct types. This is realistic and sensible of them, but it creates its own difficulty. It is extremely hard to weigh the various numbers and combinations of numbers which anyone's name contains and almost impossible to keep the element of wishful thinking out. Analysis of historical figures, on which numerologists rely heavily to prove the value of their art, is highly suspect. It is all too easy to fit anyone on to the Procrustean bed of numerology by stretching and emphasising all the characteristics which fit his numbers, while lopping off and failing to mention those which do not.

If you use numerology as a party trick, and it makes an amusing one, you may be surprised at the way in which your acquaintances seem to fit their numbers. The reason is the looseness and woolliness of numerologists' language, which is so broad and vague that almost any set of characteristics can be fitted into any number combination. (The same thing is true of astrology and other forms of fortune-telling.)

According to the numerologists, you can use numbers not only to assess your own character but also to improve your life and fortunes. If your name adds to 5 you should make sure that all matters of importance are postponed to days which add to 5—the 5th, 14th or 23rd of any month. If you back a horse it should carry number 5 and the race should be run on a day which adds to 5. If the jockey's name or birth date also adds to 5, you have a sure thing. Other people whose names total 5 will play significant roles in your life—you may harmonise well with them or there may be conflict because you are too much alike.

Health and diet can be considered numerologically. Nine-people must avoid the use of drugs as far as possible. They are peculiarly susceptible to addiction because the word 'drugs' adds to 9. Three-people should eat plenty of peaches, which add to 3 (but presumably they should never be content with one peach at a sitting, because a single peach adds to 4).

It is vital to live in a place which adds up to a suitable number. A city, like everything else, has its numbers and the one to concentrate on is the total of the vowels, which reveal the city's inner character. The vowels of Paris, city of wickedness and women, appropriately add to 2. London's vowels come to 5—many-sidedness and resilience—and New York's to 3—brilliance, glitter. Chicago's vowels total 9 and the American numerologist Montrose, founder of the Studio of Psychoanalysis by Numbers, says that because the vowels of both Chicago and Oakland (a suburb of San Francisco) total 9, Oakland will one day suffer a Great Fire as Chicago did.[7]

If nothing seems to go right for you even when you have done your best to act only on suitable days and live in a suitable place, the solution may be to change your own number by changing your name. (The idea was very prevalent among medieval Jews that a sick man's life could be saved by changing his name, which confused the angel responsible for bringing his life to an end.) The influence of the new number will slowly begin to make itself felt in your life and other people will begin to treat you differently. However, some numerologists condemn this as rank superstition and deny that you can change your destiny so easily.

One example of the effect of a change of name is the case of Napoleon. He originally called himself Napoleon Buonaparte, which adds to 1—the number of aggression and vaulting ambition, of leadership and domination. He later dropped the u from Buonaparte. This changed his number to 4, which foreshadowed the gigantic toil and burdens of his later years and his eventual defeat. If he had not changed his name in this way, the history of Europe might have taken a different course. There are several other significant numbers in Napoleon's career. He was born on August 1, 1769, which adds to 1. He became Emperor of the French on December 2, 1804—9, the number of high achievement. He died on May 5, 1821—4, the number of obscurity and defeat.

Numerologically, time moves in endlessly repeated cycles of the numbers from 1 to 9. We are living in the 1900s and $1 + 9 + 0 + 0$ gives 1. A 1-century is a period of beginnings, new developments, discoveries and inventions. The influence of 1 produces aggressive, driving forces in the world which relentlessly pursue their own ends and are reluctant to compromise or co-operate. It is a time of constant upheaval and revolution. It sees the rise of new countries and power blocs, new political, social and scientific theories. The two great wars of this century, the Cold War, revolutionary achievements in science, modern art, and the abandonment of Victorian conventions and standards are characteristic products of the influence of 1.

Within this uncomfortable 1-century we are passing through a 7-decade, the 1960s, which should modify the influence of 1 in the direction of withdrawal and introspection. We can expect a revival of interest in mysticism and the occult, a tendency for nations to concentrate their attention mainly on their internal politics and developments, increasing in psychoanalysis, especially in schools like the Freudian in which introspection is the principal method of therapy.

The last decade, the 1950s, was a time of harmony, balance and adjustment (influence of 6), at least as compared with the nerve-racked, unstable, war-torn

1940s (influence of 5), in which adventure, risks and travel came the way of many who would have preferred to avoid them. Before that the world struggled through the grim, poverty-stricken 4-decade of the 1930s, following the bright, glittering, expressive 3-decade of the 1920s.

Within the centuries and decades the influence of a new number comes into play with each year. Inside the years the same 1 to 9 cycle revolves as the months and days pass. These cycles affect everything in the universe, but besides them each of us has his own personal cycle. To find this, add your month and day of birth to the *current* year. The result is your Personal Year Number. If you were born on October 13 your Personal Year number for 1966 is 9—10 (October) + 4 (13th) + 22 (1966). In 1967 it will be 1 and your life will have begun a new cycle.

This number tells you what the year will be like for you and how to get the best out of it. For instance, in a 3-year you make new friends and enjoy social life and entertainment. You may make more money than usual with less effort than usual. Artistic activities should be rewarding. 'Pen that book,' says an American numerologist lightheartedly, 'compose a song . . . beautify yourself and your surroundings.'[8] In a 7-year on the other hand, you feel cut off, lonely, dissatisfied with your life and surroundings. Alternatively, since 7 is the number of secrets, you can have a clandestine love affair.

It is best if the numbers of your month and day of birth are as far apart as possible. Mozart was born on January 27, so that his numbers stepped up to the maximum possible extent, from 1 to 9. This is why he won fame in his lifetime and immortality in the history of music. A less edifying example is Al Capone, who was born on January 18 and so won fame in his lifetime and immortality in the history of crime.

One difficulty about numerological theories of time is that all the people born on any given date share the same Personal Year Number in every year which follows, regardless of their different backgrounds and circumstances. On the face of it, it does not seem likely that all the children born on August 1 of any year will experience similar conditions and behave in similar ways year by year for the rest of their lives. Another objection, which applies to all number theories involving dates, is that the modern Western calendar is not the only one in the world. Jews, Moslems and innumerable Asiatics use different calendars. If, as Western numerologists assume, our calendar is the one which indicates the number patterns of the universe, it seems odd that it should be of such comparatively recent date. Our present reckoning of years goes back to the sixth century A.D. and is now generally conceded to be inaccurate (because Jesus was probably born several years before A.D. 1). Our reckoning of months and days dates from 1582 at the earliest and was not accepted until much later in many Western countries (not until the eighteenth century in England). The reform of 1582, which chopped ten days out of the calendar, also moved New Year's Day from March to January and consequently affected the numbering of all subsequent years so far as the early months of each year are concerned.

Numerologists, who take no notice whatever of these objections believe that if you take your year of birth and add it to itself you will find an important year in your destiny. If you were born in 1930, 1943 was a significant year for you (and for everyone else born in 1930), because:

$$
\begin{array}{r}
1930 \\
\text{Plus } 1+9+3+0 = \quad 13 \\
\hline
1943
\end{array}
$$

Also, if an important year in the history of a person or a nation is added to itself, the result is likely to be another significant year. The stock example of this is taken from French history:

Fall of Robespierre	1794
Plus 1+7+9+4	21
Fall of Napoleon	1815
Plus 1+8+1+5	15
Fall of Charles X	1830

Another example is:

Accession of Louis XVI	1774
	19
Execution of Louis XVI	1793

Or, turning to English history:

Accession of George I	1714	Birth of Queen Victoria	1819
	13		19
Accession of George II	1727	Her coronation	1838

Louis the *Ninth* of France was born in 1215, which adds to *nine*. On the same principle, the following list can be constructed:

Louis the Ninth was born in 1215 (which adds to 9)
Charles the Seventh was born in 1402 (which adds to 7)
Louis the Twelfth was born in 1461 (which adds to 12)
Henry the Fourth died in 1610 (which adds to 8, which is 2×4)
Louis the Fourteenth came to the throne in 1643 (which adds to 14) and
    died in 1715 (which adds to 14) at the age of 77 (which adds to 14)
Louis the Eighteenth was born in 1755 (which adds to 18)

Eighteen, the number of the last king in this list, is twice the number of the first king listed and three times the number of kings mentioned.[9]

Pythagoras, the father of modern numerology, is supposed to have initiated at least one of his followers into the art of foretelling the future by numbers, but he and his modern disciples are mere tyros compared to the supermen who designed the Great Pyramid of Gizeh and built into it a detailed numerological prophecy of events up to and beyond our own time. A full account of Pyramid-mania would fill a book by itself, and the following is only a brief example, based on one authority.

Inside the pyramid there is an important ascending passage which is called the Grand Gallery. After a complex and baffling process of deduction, the point at which this gallery begins is taken to mark the birth of Christ on October 6, 4 B.C. Each inch of the gallery is assumed to equal one year of history. For the first 400 inches the stones of which the gallery is built are firm and in good condition, 'showing that the first 400 years of the Church . . . were progressive and vigorous growth.' Then the stones become scarred and broken. Pyramidologists say that the builders deliberately used broken stones to mark the inroads of the Visigoths under Alaric. The stones are in particularly poor condition at 622 inches and continue weak till 732 inches, when they improve. This shows the rise of Islam from the Hegira in A.D. 622 to Charles Martel's resounding defeat of the Mohammedans in 732. Another bad patch occurs from

1,000 to 1,300 inches, covering the periods when the Western and Eastern churches split and the Popes quarrelled with the Holy Roman Emperors.

At 1,844 inches the gallery ends in the Great Step, which rises abruptly three feet high from the floor of the passage. This obviously indicates 'a tremendous step upward on the path of humanity at that time'. Sad to say, searching the history books, no event in 1844 seems to fit this prophecy, but there is comfort in the thought that 'almost the whole lot of the discoveries and inventions in common usage have come into existence since the year 1844'. Humanity did not make any great *spiritual* advance, however, and the builders left the *higher* part of the Great Step in a crumbling condition because they foresaw this.

At this point the scale is altered to read one inch to one month. August 4, 1914, the day of England's entry into the First World War is marked by the beginning of the Low Passage, a dismal tunnel which can only be negotiated by crawling. The Low Passage ends at November 9, 1918, when the Kaiser abdicated, and so it forecast the length of the war. (The dates of British involvement in the war are shown because the Anglo-Saxons are the descendants of the Builders, the superior race who designed the pyramid. The miserable Egyptians merely supplied the labour.) A second Low Passage which runs from May 1928 to September 1936 clearly foretells the Depression. 1936, the year in which my authority was writing, was expected to be a vital year in the world's history. The dethronement of Satan was imminent, the Lamb was about to cast down the Dragon. Unfortunately, the builders' prophecy at this point was evidently either inaccurate or misunderstood.[10]

2. The Roots of Numerology

Number is the Word but is not utterance; it is wave and light, though no one sees it; it is rhythm and music, though no one hears it. Its variations are limitless and yet it is immutable. Each form of life is a particular reverberation of Number.

MAURICE DRUON *The Memoirs of Zeus*

It is not possible to read the numerologists for very long without discovering the importance which they attach to the term 'vibration'. 'Numerology is simply an extended study of vibration' and the numbers from 1 to 9 'make a complete cycle of vibration'. 'We live in a universe of vibrations and every person coming into this world has a vibration peculiar to the individual that is distinct from others.'[11]

The theory of the vibrating universe became popular in occultism in the nineteenth century, following discoveries about the nature of light, electricity and magnetism. In the early years of the century physicists demonstrated that light moves in waves and that electrical and magnetic impulses also travel in waves or undulations. At the same period it was accepted that the molecules of all substances are in a state of constant oscillating movement. Building on these ideas, occultists developed the theory that everything in the universe is undulating or vibrating. Different things vibrate at different rates of speed, and the essential nature or character of each thing is determined by its rate of vibration, in the same way that the different colours which we see are determined by differing wavelengths of light.

Although nineteenth-century physics seemed to give some support to this theory, it really depends on an analogy with sound, and particularly with musical sound. The numerologist's universe is like a gigantic musical instrument which has innumerable strings. The strings vibrate at various rates. There are nine basic rates of vibration—the nine notes which the instrument sounds—to which the numbers from 1 to 9 are assigned. Each string of the instrument represents a person or a place of a thing. Each vibrates at its own speed, making its own small sound which joins with the sounds of all the other strings to produce the overall note which the universe is sounding at any given moment. A man's name reveals his characteristic 'note', because his name contains the essence of his being, but he is also profoundly affected by his birth date because the universe's overall rate of vibration at the moment of his birth is indelibly stamped on his character and destiny.

This picture of the universe has been taken up enthusiastically by modern occultists, but it is not new to occultism. It goes back ultimately to Pythagoras and the discovery of the ratios of musical intervals.

Very little is known about Pythagoras. He was born on the island of Samos off Asia Minor and he is supposed to have travelled in Egypt, Babylonia and India, where he imbibed the ancient wisdom of the East. About 530 B.C. he founded a religious brotherhood and school of philosophy at Crotona, a Greek colony in southern Italy. The citizens of Crotona eventually grew irritated with Pythagoras and his disciples and expelled them.

Pythagoras and his early followers wrote nothing which has survived. Pythagoras apparently believed in reincarnation, in which most modern numerologists have followed him, and several curious maxims, some of which suggest fears of hostile magic, are attributed to him: spit on the cuttings of your nails and hair; when you get up roll the bedclothes together and smooth out the place where you were lying; do not wear a ring; never step over a crossbar; do not stir the fire with a sword; help a man who is loading, but not one who is unloading; when you put your shoes on begin with the right foot, but when you wash your feet begin with the left foot. My own favourite is 'be not possessed by irrepressible mirth'.

It may have been Pythagoras himself who discovered that the musical intervals known in his time—the octave, the fifth and the fourth—can be expressed in terms of ratios between the numbers 1, 2, 3 and 4. The pitch of a note depends on the length of the string producing it. Take a string, stop it and sound a note. Then double the length of string which you are sounding and the new note will be the octave of the original note. The octave can therefore be expressed as a ratio of 2 : 1. Similarly, the ratio of the fifth is 3 : 2 and the ratio of the fourth is 4 : 3.

The early Greek philosophers were concerned to find some principle of order in a universe which seemed chaotic. The discovery about the musical intervals may have suggested to the Pythagoreans that the principle of order was mathematical. If the relationship of notes in the musical scale can be simply expressed in terms of numbers, then perhaps all the bewildering and apparently disorderly phenomena of the universe can be reduced to numerical terms. This was the view of the universe which the Pythagoreans held, according to Aristotle, 'such and such a modification of numbers being justice, another being soul and reason, another being opportunity—and similarly almost all other things being numerically expressible'.[12]

Expanding on this, Nicomachus, a Pythagorean of the first century A.D., explained that the universe is constructed to a numerical pattern.

> All that has by nature with systematic method been arranged in the universe seems both in part and as a whole to have been determined and ordered in accordance with number, by the forethought and the mind of him that created all things; for the pattern was fixed like a preliminary sketch, by the domination of number pre-existent in the mind of the world-creating God, number conceptual only and immaterial in every way, but at the same time the true and eternal essence, so that with reference to it, as to an artistic plan, should be created all these things, time, motion, the heavens, the stars, all sorts of revolutions.[13]

The theory that all the phenomena of the universe are connected together in a great design or pattern is one of the fundamental assumptions of magic. The belief that this pattern is numerical is the foundation of numerology. When the magical theory that the name of a thing enshrines its essential nature is added, plus a method of translating names into numbers, the basic skeleton of numerology as a key to the mysteries of the universe is complete.

The numbers which determine the musical intervals are the first four whole numbers and together they produce 10 ($1+2+3=4 = 10$). In Pythagorean theory the numbers up to 10 are the essential numbers. Once you count beyond 10 you are using the same basic numbers over again. (This must have seemed obvious to primitive people who counted on their fingers.) The fact that 10 is produced by $1+2+3+4$ leads to the conclusion that these four numbers are the origin and basis of all numbers and are therefore the basis of everything in the universe.

This is confirmed when the basis of the construction of all solid objects is found in the same four numbers: 1 is assigned to the point, which theoretically has no dimensions; 2 to the line (connecting two points) which has length but not breadth; 3 to the triangle (connecting three points) which has length and breadth but not thickness. When a fourth point is added above the triangle and four points are connected, the simplest solid body—the tetrahedron—has been constructed.

Eliphas Levi's remark, in his *Doctrine and Ritual*, that the first four numbers are 'the source of all numerical combinations and the principle of all forms' is pure Pythagoreanism. One, 2, 3 and 4 are the basis of the numerical pattern which underlies the universe or, to put it more poetically, they are 'eternal Nature's fountain-spring', which was an epithet the Pythagoreans applied to a figure called the Tetractys which they held in great awe and veneration. It looked like this:

The Tetractys is a simple demonstration that $1+2+3+4 = 10$. It is an example of a primitive way of representing numbers—by pebbles or by dots, as they are still shown on dice. This way of showing numbers accounts for a great deal of ancient and modern numerological theory.

The Pythagoreans, like other Greek thinkers, were struck by the existence of pairs of opposites in the universe and believed that these opposites were an important factor in the universe's construction. This belief has been transmitted intact to modern numerologists and the major characteristics which they assign to the numbers fit neatly into a table of opposites:

1—active, purposeful, powerful, unsympathetic, leading, innovating.

2—passive, receptive, weak, sympathetic, subordinate.

3—brilliant, gay, artistic, lucky; easy success.

4—plodding, dull, uncreative, unlucky; hard work and failure.

5—versatile, adventurous, nervous, uncertain; sexuality.

6—simple, placid, domestic, settled; mother-love.

7—withdrawal from the world; mystery, secrets.

8—worldly involvement; material success or failure.

9—mental and spiritual achievement.

It is also clear that the *odd* numbers have much the more interesting and exciting characteristics. Against the driving force of 1, the brilliance and luck of 3, the adventurous versatility of 5, the wisdom of 7 and the achievement of 9, the even numbers are a poor-spirited crew.

This distribution of characteristics is another inheritance from the Greeks. The Pythagoreans listed ten fundamental pairs of opposites existing in the universe. Among these pairs were odd and even, one and many, right and left, male and female, good and evil. One, right, male and good were associated with odd numbers—many, left, female and evil with even numbers.

When numbers are represented by dots it is obvious that the odd numbers are male and the even numbers female. Three, 5, 7 and 9 appear as:

Two, 4, 6 and 8 are shown as:

It is immediately clear that, to use the polite language of Plutarch, the odd numbers have 'a generative middle part' while in each even number there is 'a certain receptive opening and, as it were, a space within itself'.

The masculinity of the phallic odd numbers is borne out by the fact that they are 'stronger' than the even numbers. If an even number is split in two, nothing but empty space is left. An odd number cannot be reduced to nothing so easily—a dot is left in the middle. And when odd and even numbers mingle together in addition, the odd *master* the even because the result or progeny is always an odd number. Obviously, odd numbers are male, thrusting and dominating, and even numbers are female, receptive and passive. The principles of numerology were worked out in ancient and medieval societies in which man was dominant, woman subordinate. The result is that the odd numbers have a near monopoly of vigorous, creative and admirable characteristics.

Another product of man-dominated societies is the identification of man with good and woman with evil. The Pythagoreans said that the female even numbers are evil because they can easily be reduced to nothingness, empty space, the primeval chaos in which the world was formed. The biblical commentator Hugh of St. Victor, writing in the twelfth century, took the general medieval view that even numbers stand for things which are inwardly empty and valueless, the corruptible and transitory, the things of this world. Two modern American occultists, H. A. and F. H. Curtiss, echo the same theory, for the same reason. 'Odd numbers are sacred because when we attempt to divide them into equal parts they leave the monad or 1 God standing unaffected between them . . . thus they reveal the Supreme Deity in the midst of his works.'[14] (F. Homer Curtiss was the founder of the Order of Christian Mystics, or Order of the 15, and also of the Fellowship of the Wisdom Religion.)

3. The Numbers Revealed

Some mathematicians believe that numbers were invented by human beings, others, equally competent, believe that numbers have an independent existence of their own and are merely observed by sufficientely intelligent mortals.

E. T. BELL The Magic of Numbers

Two is the first of the even numbers, which are female and evil, and so it is the number of woman and wickedness. The characteristics allotted to it are those traditionally associated with femininity—softness, sweetness, modesty, docility, subordination. Two-people achieve their ends by diplomacy and persuasion, because woman traditionally gets her way by artful persuasion and seduction. Woman plays the passive, receptive role in copulation and 2 is therefore the number of passive acceptance and receptivity (in the widest possible sense, so that for businessmen a 2-day is a good day for collecting accounts receivable).

The strain of cruelty, malice and deceit in the 2-nature comes from the number's connection with the Devil. Two is the most evil of numbers and two-pointed or forked objects are symbols of the Devil because 2 is the first number to break away from unity, the One or God. One is the number of God and 2, which is 1's opposite, is the number of God's arch-opponent. Early Christian writers noted that God did not see that 'it was good' after the second day's creations in Genesis. Medieval Jews were convinced of the dangers of repeating an action twice—for instance, twice taking fire from the hearth when there is an invalid in the house. The unclean beasts went two by two into Noah's Ark, but the clean beasts went in by sevens, and St. Augustine, who was an accomplished numerologist, commented 'that clean and unclean animals are in the ark; as good and bad take part in the sacraments of the church. That the clean are in sevens and the uncleans in twos. . . . The bad, again, are in twos as being easily divided, from their tendency to schism.'[15]

Four is inevitably a grim and ominous number because it is even, female and evil, and is made of 2 in two ways (2+2 and 2×2). Four is the number of solidity, because four points are needed to construct the simplest solid, the tetrahedron, and according to classical and medieval theory everything in the world is made of differing proportions of four elements—fire, air, earth and water—and characterised by differing mixtures of four qualities—hot, cold, wet and dry. The year is made of four seasons and the month of four weeks. The story of Christ is contained in four gospels. Raoul Glaber, writing in the eleventh century, connected the four gospels of which the divine message is composed with the four elements of which the world is made. He linked earth with Matthew because Matthew deals with Christ's incarnation in earthly form, water with Mark because he stresses the importance of baptism, fire with John because his gospel is the most spiritual, and air with Luke because his is the longest.[16]

Four is the number of solid matter and it is particularly the number of earth—a solid object bounded by the four cardinal points. People whose number is 4 are therefore solid and stolid, practical and 'down to earth', pillars of society in the same way that the earth supports the edifices of civilisation, stodgy and humdrum but subject to fits of melancholy (fog, mists, rain) and outbursts of violence (earthquakes and eruptions). They are toilers (farmers, gardeners, agricultural labourers) who work at hard, routine tasks for uncertain, often meagre, rewards. Four is an unlucky number because of this connection with dull, lifeless matter and with earthly existence, which many late classical and medieval writers condemned as a gloomy, toilsome, sin-ridden affair from which man could escape only by death and entry into the joyous life of the spirit. Sweat, misery and defeat are the lot of man on earth and the lot of 4-people in numerology.

Seven is the most mysterious and uncanny of the numbers and one of the most important in magic. Traditionally, the seventh son of a seventh son has magical powers. Seven is not produced by multiplication of any of the other numbers nor does it, multiplied, produce any other number in the first ten. It is unlike the other numbers in this way (for 9 = 3×3, 8 = 2×4, 6 = 2×3, 5×2 = 10, and so on) and so it is thought to be different from them, aloof, lonely and unable to communicate with them. It follows that if your number is 7 you are solitary, cut off from other people, unable to explain yourself and your ideas.

The mysterious importance of 7 is much older and more deeply rooted than this piece of numerological reasoning. The great Sumerian king Lugulannemundu, who possibly dates back to about 2500 B.C., built a temple in his city of Adab to the goddess Nintu. The temple had seven gates and seven doors and when it was finished it was dedicated with sacrifices of seven times seven fatted oxen and fatted sheep. Joshua and the Israelites marched around the walls of Jericho for seven days with seven priests bearing seven trumpets and on the seventh day they circled the city seven times and at the seventh time they shouted and the walls fell and they utterly destroyed the city. Revelation, one of the most popular books of the Bible for centuries, is packed with number symbolism and teems with 7s (the number occurs fifty-four times in all)—seven seals, seven trumpets, seven vials of wrath, seven thunders, seven spirits before the throne, seven golden candlesticks, seven heads of the Beast.

The significance of 7 comes from its connection with the moon. It is a widespread primitive belief that the cycle of life and death on earth—the birth, growth and decay of plants, animals and men—is connected with the waxing and waning of the moon as it goes through its endless cycle of births and deaths in the sky. The great classical astrologer Ptolemy said, 'The moon, too, as the heavenly body nearest the earth, bestows her effluence most abundantly upon mundane things, for most of them, animate or inanimate, are sympathetic to her and change in company with her; the rivers increase and diminish their streams with her light, the seas turn their own tides with her rising and setting, and plants and animals in whole or in some part wax and wane with her'.[17] A modern American astrologer applies the same principle to human life. 'When the New Moon comes into being, all Nature begins to renew itself; even you and I begin to gather new powers. It is Nature's way. From the New Moon up to the Full, she is giving out her strength, and we are waxing strong with it; from the Full Moon to the end, she is withdrawing her strength preparatory to giving it out again, and we are waning in our own powers because of this withdrawal.'[18]

The moon's cycle is made of four phases, each lasting about seven days. The Sumerians based their calendar on this cycle and this is the origin of the month of four weeks of seven days each, with extra days added to cover the period at the end of each cycle when the moon is not visible in the sky. In Babylonia every seventh day, marking the end of a stage in the moon's cycle, was sacred to Sin, the moon-god, and these days were felt to be unlucky and uncanny. This is probably the origin of the sabbath, the seventh day on which you rest, because it would be dangerous to do anything on a day which is uncanny.

If the moon rules life on earth, with a cycle running in periods of 7, by 'as above, so below' reasoning life on earth should also be run in periods of 7, and according to occultists it does. The human body renews itself every seven years. Occultists maintain that disease runs in 7s, with the crisis in most illnesses coming on the 7th, 14th or 21st day and lasting abut 3½ (half of 7) days. More importantly, menstruation in women, on which all human life depends, occurs in a cycle of 4+7 days and lasts about 3½ days.

The occultist's conclusion is that the number 7 governs the cycles and rhythms of life—birth, growth, disease, decay, death. For the same reasons, 7 is a number of completeness. Each stage of human growth is complete in seven years, each phase of the moon in seven days. Seven of anything makes a complete series. Seven planets are (or were until recently) all the planets. Seven days make a whole week. There are seven colours in the spectrum and seven notes in the musical scale, seven petitions in the Lord's Prayer, Seven Deadly Sins, seven features of the human head (two eyes, two ears, two nostrils, one mouth), seven orifices of the male body.

The characteristics of 7 in numerology—deep wisdom, interest in religion and philosophy, the search for inner truth, secrecy and mystery—follow from the occult significance of 7 as the number which holds the key to the underlying rhythms of life. This is powerfully reinforced by the most obvious example of 7 as a number of completeness—the creation of the world in seven days according to Genesis, which was essentially the creation of life. God finished the work in six days and rested on the seventh. The idea of the sabbath, of rest and reflection after toil and involvement, appears in the numerologist's 7-nature as withdrawal from the world, introspection and mediation.

People whose number is *one* are leaders and pioneers and a 1-year is a time of new beginnings, because 1 is the first of the numbers and 'leads' all the rest. One-people dominate others, because if 1 is added to any odd number it converts it to an even number and vice versa. They have great fixity of purpose and toughness of character, because whether it is multiplied or divided by itself 1 remains 1, which is not true of any other number. Several modern numerologists say that 1-people are proud and stiff-necked because the symbol 1 stands erect and unbending.

One is the number of God, the One. It stands for God the Father, the creator, the original of everything in the universe as 1 is the original number. The characteristics allotted to 1-people are very much those of Jehovah in the Old Testament—power and dominance, creativity and originality, determination, independence, self-assertion, refusal to co-operate with others or tolerate rivals.

Three is the number of creation because in numerological theory 1 alone, though potentially creative, is sterile. The word 'multiply' has a procreative meaning as well as a mathematical one, and however many times 1 is multiplied (fertilised) by itself it remains 1. Two does not solve the problem, because 2 merely produces a pair of opposites (• •) and 2 multiplied by 1 remains 2. To reconcile the opposites and create more numbers, 3 is needed ($3 \times 2 = 6$). 'Were God only one,' as Eliphas Levi explained, 'He would never be creator or father. Were He two there would be antagonism or division in the infinite, which would mean the division also or death of all possible things. He is therefore three for the creation by Himself and in His image of the infinite multitude of beings and numbers.'[19]

Lurking in the coverts behind this theory is the sexual symbolism of 3. Three is the first number to have a 'generative middle part' (• • •) and 3, or the triangle, is a natural symbol for the male genitals. Man's procreative equipment is threefold, and according to the principle of 'as below, so above' and the theory that God is man writ large it follows that God as procreator of the universe must also be threefold. 'Were God only one He would never be creator or father', because 1 (the erect phallus) alone is sterile. This is the basic numerological interpretation of the Trinity, the Threefold God.

Three is a potent number, because it represents the generative sexual force of the male and the highest spiritually creative force, through its connection with the Trinity. To the magician these forces are one and the same. The generative power of man and the creative power of God are manifestations of the same force on different planes. Three is used in magic in the hope of capturing this powerful creative force. Not surprisingly, 3 is particularly effective in love charms, and a method of finding the number of the girl a man should marry is to total his first name plus birth date and add 3.

The number 2 sets up a pair of opposites (• •) and stands for antagonism, opposition and the Devil, the arch-opponent of God. In magical theory all progress comes through the reconciliation of opposites. The middle dot of 3 (• • •) links the opposites of 2, reconciles them and transcends them in a higher harmony (as in $\therefore$, for instance). So 3 is the number of harmonious progress and if your number is 3 you progress easily and luckily through life, effortlessly gathering money and success on the way. Because 3 is the number of creation, 3-people have a strong urge to create and to express themselves and so they are talkative and witty and make fine creative artists. This is backed up by the fact that 3 is the number of the triangle, the first plane figure, and is therefore the number of 'surface'. Three-people are very much 'on the surface'—charming, sparkling, glittering. Their tendency to diffuse effort also comes from the triangle—they face three ways at once.

In Christian numerology 3 naturally stands for everything that is best, most perfect and most holy, because it is the number of the Trinity, but the association of 3 with the superlative is a much older doctrine. It comes out in the Greek word *trismegistos*—thrice-greatest, superlatively great—and the Latin *ter felix*—thrice-happy, happiest. Our notion of the superlative involves the third term in a series of three—good, better, best. The Pythagoreans called 3 the *perfect* number, because it has a beginning, a middle and an end (• • •), and anything which lacks a beginning or a middle or an end is plainly imperfect. Later, as Professor Bell sardonically comments in his *Magic of Numbers*, 'it was denied that 3 has either a beginning or an end, and people were burned at the stake for disagreeing'.

Three is also a number of completeness (beginning, middle and end, for example). Three of anything implies 'enough' and 'all'. The hero of a fairy story has three wishes, which somehow seems to be 'enough' wishes, and the heroine has three suitors. We say, 'I give you three guesses', with the feeling that three is enough. 'Three accounts for *all* time—past, present and future—and *all* space—length, breadth and thickness.

The association of 3 with both 'best' and 'all' may have originated in primitive methods of counting, or rather of not counting. Some primitive peoples had special words for 1 and 2, but for 3 or more used their word for 'many'. If 3 was connected with the idea of abundance in this way, it may naturally have become identified with 'best' and 'all'. The Babylonian term for a constellation, however many stars it might contain, was 'three stars'. In ancient Greece it was considered important to bury a dead body decently in the ground and not leave it lying about, but if circumstances made a proper burial impossible it was sufficient to drop three handfuls of earth on the corpse. In German folklore a werewolf must be stabbed three times in the brows to reveal the real person beneath the skin.

All numbers of completeness are important in magic, because they indicate how many times an action should be repeated. Because 3 implies 'enough' or 'all', to chant an incantation three times is magically to chant it enough times, or an infinite number of times. The instruction to repeat a process three times is constantly found in charms and spells. Three is sometimes combined with 7, another number of completeness. Pliny's *Natural History* recommends three times seven centipedes mixed in honey as a cure for asthma, and for scrofula three fingers of ashes of vipers taken in liquid for three times seven days. (Scrofula is a skin disease and vipers periodically cast their skins and appear in nice shiny new ones.)

Nine is another magically powerful number because it reduplicates the power of 3 ($9 = 3 \times 3$). A book on medicine, written about A.D. 400, gives the following cure for stomach upsets. Press the abdomen with the left thumb and say nine times, *Adam betam alam betur alem botum*. Touch the ground with the left thumb and spit. Say the words nine more times and again nine more times, giving a total of 3×9 repetitions. Pliny mentions a cure for spleen ailments. Take fresh sheep's milt (spleen) and apply it to the patient's body, saying 'This I do for the cure of the spleen.' Say this twenty-seven (3×9) times. Then plaster the milt into the bedroom wall and seal it with a ring.[20] In both these cures the effect of the words is to transfer the patient's ailment—to the earth in the first case, to the milt in the second (and the milt must be walled up because it has been magically linked with the patient and could be used against him)—but the words are only effective if the force of 3^3 is enlisted.

A sinister measuring charm is recommended by the Renaissance magician Cornelius Agrippa. Take the body of a dead man and a piece of rope. Measure the corpse with the rope—from the elbow to the end of the longest finger, from the shoulder to the end of the longest finger, and from head to toe. Do this three times, giving nine measurements altogether. Dispose of the dead body and keep the rope. Anyone afterwards measured in the same way with the same rope will fall into misery and misfortune.[21]

The real purpose of this charm is probably to kill anyone who is measured with the rope. The nine measurements have captured the deadness of the corpse and this can be transferred to a living body by imposing the same measurements on it. The measurements of a thing, like its name, *are* the thing. They state its dimensions and define its limits and so they contain its essential being. We say we have 'taken the measure' of a man when we have found out what he is like.

Nine is a number of completeness, because a human child is conceived, formed and born in nine months. Nine completes the series of the essential numbers. (From this point of view, 10 is merely a restatement of 1.) Also, 360 degrees make a complete circle and 360 reduces to 9. Ovid says in his *Fasti* that in Rome on certain days in May the ghosts of the dead were believed to return to their old homes. To expel them, the head of the house, after midnight, washed his hands in water and walked through the house, throwing black beans behind him and saying nine times, 'These I cast, with these beans I redeem me and mine.' He took care not to look over his shoulder as the ghosts gathered up the beans and followed behind him. Then he ordered the ghosts to leave his house, saying nine times, 'Ghosts of my fathers, go forth.' Not until then was it safe for him to look behind him. Beans were used to purge the house of the ghosts, because beans have laxative qualities. To repeat the two sets of words nine times was to repeat them enough times, or all possible times.

Nine stands for great spiritual and mental achievement in numerology, because it is the last and highest of the numbers from 1 to 9 and so it denotes the 'highest' qualities. Nine-people are really 3s writ large, with the higher characteristic of desire to serve humanity in place of the self-serving ambition of 3. Nine is the number of 'initiation', the end of one stage of spiritual development and the beginning of a new one, because it is the last of the units and is followed by the first of the tens. It is an amorous number, because it has the male sex-force of 3 reduplicated. The 9-nature may be egotistical, because 9 is an egotistical number. It always returns to itself. When 9 is multiplied by any other number the answer invariably adds to 9 ($2 \times 9 = 18$, which adds to 9, $3 \times 9 = 27$, which adds to 9, and so on), and if all the numbers up to and including 9 are added the total is 45, which again adds to 9.

Six is an even, female number, but it escapes the unluckiness of the other even numbers, because it is 'perfect'. A perfect number is one which equals the sum of its proper divisors other than itself. The proper divisors of 6 (apart from 6 itself) are 1, 2 and 3, and $1+2+3 = 6$. Nicomachus in the first century A.D. knew that 6, 28, 496, and 8,128 are perfect numbers. The next one—33,550,336—was apparently not discovered until the mid-fifteenth century. Because addition and multiplication of its component parts both give the same answer, 6 is regarded as a balanced, well-integrated, harmonious number, not torn by internal conflict, and so the 6-nature is balanced, well adjusted, contented, placid.

The tranquil and comfortable quality of 6 is strengthened by the fact that 6 is the number of female love and domesticity. This is because 6 is made of the first feminine number (2) multiplied by the first masculine number (3) and in love woman is multiplied (fertilised) by man. Six is the number of marriage, family and home, because traditionally female sexuality is legitimately expressed only in marriage. It stands for the perfect mother and housewife and 6-people are faithful, affectionate, reliable, wrapped up in home and children, efficient and hard-working (six days shalt thou labour), neat and tidy, conventional, gossipy and, it must be confessed, sometimes a little dull (even). They may be extremely successful in the arts, because they have the creative power of 3 twice (6 = 3+3).

Five is the number of male sexuality, because it is made of the first feminine number (2) added to the first masculine number (3) and in love woman is 'added' to man for his possession and pleasure. Where 3 is the number of sex for procreation, 5 stands for sexual enjoyment, sex for its own sake. It is the number of Don Juan—fickle, restless, loving risks and adventure, attracted by everything but held by nothing, avoiding responsibility, perhaps even debauched and perverted. Some of the 5 characteristics have a directly phallic reference—quickness, impulsiveness, jumpiness, elasticity and resilience. Five-people rebound quickly and they naturally hate being tied down.

In a wider sense, 5 stands for sensuality and the joys of the flesh in general, because it is the number of the five senses. In the twelfth century Hugh of St. Victor explained that 'because of the five senses, the number five naturally represents natural men who, though they are not shamefully dominated by carnal lusts, nevertheless pursue and love things that minister to the delight of their outward senses, since they do not know what spiritual delight means'. Five stands for the natural man, not only because it is the number of the senses but also because it is the number of Nature. It is made of 1 (the life-creating potential of God) plus 4 (matter) and when life is added to matter the result is the world of Nature, of animals, birds, plants and man. Five-people are many-sided, because the pentagon, symbol of 5, is a many-sided figure. For the same reason, and also because 5 is the halfway point between 1 and 9, they may be nervous and uncertain, looking backwards and forwards at the same time.

The significance of *eight* comes partly from the fact that it is made of 4+4. 4 is the number of earth and matter, so 8 stands for worldly involvement and material success or failure. 8 has double 4's capacity for defeat and so spectacular failure is an 8 possibility. But where 4 toils for little reward 8 may have great success in terms of money and power. Modern numerologists point out that the dual nature of the number is shown by the figure 8 itself—two circles, one on top of the other. The 8-nature may go up or down.

This idea is partly based on the fact that 8 in Christian number symbolism, far from being the number of worldly involvement, is the number of life after death. The possibility that after death the soul may go up, to heaven, is the numerologist's 'great success' and the possibility that it may go down, to hell, is his 'great failure'. Eight stands for life after death, because it follows 7. Seven is the number of life in this world (since it governs the basic rhythms of earthly life—birth, change, death) and 8, coming after 7, means the life of the world to come. As a result, 8 is the number of eternity and infinity, and the mathematical symbol for infinity is ∞—an 8 lying on its side.

Concealed behind all this is an anatomical interpretation of the number. Man's body has seven orifices, but woman's has eight and the eighth is the gateway through which new life enters the world. Eight is basically the number of 'new life'. In many churches the font is octagonal as a sign that baptism is the entry into a new life. In Jewish tradition a baby boy is named and begins his life as an individual on the eighth day after his birth. In the same way, life after death is 'new life'. Eight means worldly involvement, because at birth a new being becomes involved in the life of the world, and success or failure are the two great possibilities which confront him.

Among modern numerologists, Cheiro is particularly insistent on the ominous character of 8. He describes how Crippen was fatally dogged by the numbers 8 and 4. Crippen was born in 1862 (which adds to 8). His birthday was the 26th (8). The day on which his wife was last seen alive was the 31st (4) and her remains were discovered in his cellar on the 13th (4). Trying to escape, Crippen used the name Robinson (8 letters). He was recognised on board the *Montrose* (8 letters) on the 22nd (4) and brought back to England on the *Megantic* (8 letters). His formal arrest occurred on the 31st (4). His trial ended on the 22nd (4) of October (*octem* is the Latin for eight) and he was found guilty. When he was hanged he was 48 years old.

Eleven is the number of the faithful disciples of Jesus (the Twelve less Judas) and those whose number is 11 have a special message to give to the world as the Apostles brought the message of Christianity. This is backed up by the fact that 11 is the next number after 10. The numbers from 1 to 10 are the essential numbers in Pythagorean theory and stand for 'all things', the whole created world. Eleven is the beginning of a higher series of numbers and represents a higher, supernatural plane of knowledge and achievement. Eleven is inter-preted as God (1) added to the world (10), and so it is the number of revelation, the beginning of the knowledge of God. It is also the number of martyrdom, the entry into the higher life of heaven, and the Apostles were the first martyrs of the Christian church. Eleven-people are the saints and martyrs, the preach-ers and teachers, who are nearer to divinity than ordinary mortals and who announce the ways of God to man.

The importance of *twenty-two* comes from the twenty-two Hebrew letters, the creation account in Genesis and the twenty-two books of the Old Testa-ment. Occultists always cheerfully assert that the Old Testament has twenty-two books, although Christian versions of it have many more. The usual Jewish division of the scriptures gives a total of twenty-four books (five books of Mo-ses plus Joshua, Judges, Ruth, Samuel, Kings, Chronicles, Ezra and Nehemiah counted as one book, Esther, Job, Psalms, Proverbs, Ecclesiastes, Song of Solo-mon, Isaiah, Jeremiah, Lamentations, Ezekiel, Daniel, and the twelve minor prophets counted as one book). But Josephus, the Jewish historian of the first century A.D., and some other early authorities give the total as twenty-two, by combining Ruth with Judges and Lamentations with Jeremiah, and this is the number which interests occultists, because it coincides with the number of letters in the Hebrew alphabet.

For centuries Christians and Jews revered Hebrew as the divine language, the speech of the God of Israel. Hebrew was not only the language in which Jehovah revealed himself to the patriarchs and prophets and delivered the law and commandments to Moses, it was also the language which was used to create the universe. According to Genesis, God created the world by express-ing commands in words—'God said, Let there be light; and there was light.' What God did, in fact, was to *name* light and all the other creations, which immediately sprang into existence in response to God's utterance of their names, because the name of a thing contains the essence of its being.

The words which God used in creation were naturally assumed to be He-brew words. It was calculated by Jewish and Christian commentators that during the six days of creation God made twenty-two things in all—unformed matter, angels, light, the upper heavens, earth, water and air on the first day; the firmament on the second day; the seas, seeds, grass and trees on the third day; on the fourth, the sun, moon and stars; on the fifth, fish, aquatic reptiles and flying creatures; and on the six, wild beasts, domestic animals, land reptiles and man. (This is the list given by Isidor of Seville in the seventh century.[22])

God used the twenty-two Hebrew letters to create twenty-two things, which stand for 'everything that exists', because God created everything. So the twenty-two letters contain the secret of God's creation of the universe. Anyone who fully understands these letters understands the entire construction and mechanism of the universe. Twenty-two is the number of the *master*, the earthly equivalent of the Master on high who created all things by means of 22.

God made the world and revealed himself to man in a language which has twenty-two letters and in scriptures which have twenty-two books, and so 22 enshrines all the secrets of the universe, all knowledge of God, all wisdom, all truth. This is why books intended to illuminate the mysteries of God and the universe, and written by numerologically minded authors, are often arranged in terms of 22. The Revelation of St. John was written, probably deliberately, in twenty-two chapters. St. Augustine wrote his *City of God* in twenty-two books. Similarly, each volume of Levi's *Doctrine and Ritual* has twenty-two chapters and Aleister Crowley wrote *Magick in Theory and Practice* in twenty-two chapters. The members of the Wisdom, Knowledge, Faith, Love, Fountain of the World cult in California chant twenty-two times at their daily morning services, 'Love one. Love ye one another. Love all. Serve ye one another.' (The Fountain of the World is a sect of followers of the late Krishna Venta, who was believed to be Christ because he had no navel—meaning that he was not born of woman—and was killed with a bomb several years ago by dissident followers of his 'love one—love all' philosophy.)

The theory and structure of numerology is basically Greek in origin, but its underlying principles—the belief that the name of a thing reveals its essential nature, that names and all other things can be expressed in numbers, that the universe is constructed to a mathematical pattern and that this pattern involves opposites and their reconciliation—have received powerful support and their most important magical development in the Jewish system of magical theory called the Cabala.

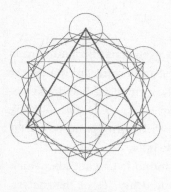

CHAPTER THREE

The Cabala and the Names of Power

THE Cabala is a body of occult doctrine, originally Jewish, which has been adopted with enthusiasm by non-Jewish occultists since the fifteenth century. Levi, Mathers and Crowley were all heavily influenced by it. Modern occultists are attracted to Cabala because of its age and its mystery, and because they can draw from it the great magical principles that the universe is a unity, that it has an underlying pattern connected with numbers and planets, that man is God and the universe in miniature, and that man can develop the divine spark within him until he masters the entire universe and himself becomes God.

The Cabala is often mystifyingly obscure and is so complicated that almost anything said about it is bound to be oversimplified. It is *hokmah nistarah*, 'the hidden wisdom', supposed to have been handed down in secret from generation to generation of the wise since the time of Abraham, to whom it was revealed by God. Modern cabalists say that those parts of the Cabala which have been written down and published do not contain its most profound secrets, which are revealed only to those who are worthy of them, passed on by word of mouth or in ancient documents which have never left the hands of initiates. Fortunately, comments by modern occultists throw some light on these inner secrets.

Apart from modern commentators, the Cabala itself consists of numerous writings by various anonymous authors. The most important are the *Sepher Yetzirah* (Book of Formation) in Hebrew, probably written in Babylonia between the third and sixth centuries A.D., and the *Zohar* (*Sepher ha-Zohar*—Book of Splendour) in Aramaic, the bulk of which was written in Spain soon after 1275, probably by the cabalist and scholar Moses de Leon.

Many of the basic ideas of the Cabala are also found in Gnosticism, which developed at the same time in the same area—the countries of the eastern Mediterranean about the time of Christ. Common to both is the importance attached to knowledge. Both claim to possess the *gnosis* or knowledge of God. This is not gained by rational enquiry or argument about the nature of God, which are rejected as useless. The knowledge of God comes through a direct divine inspiration or through sacred traditions which are themselves divinely inspired. This knowledge transforms the man who acquires it by making him a sharer in the divine being—to *know* God is to *be* God. The elect are not those who lead good lives, but those who are enlightened, who possess the knowledge of the divine. The sin which cuts man off from God is not any form of moral backsliding, but ignorance.

This theory of gnosis is one of the root-ideas of all occultism. It accounts for the contempt for conventional morality displayed by some of the Gnostics and cabalists, and it also, paradoxically, lies behind the Gnostic and cabalist mania for classification—the attempt to fit everything in God and the universe into a logical pattern. Knowledge is the key to the divine and the supreme knowledge must explain everything. This necessarily involves reason. The cabalists begin with the principle that it is absurd to think rationally about God, but this is itself a rational principle and the knowledge of God cannot be understood or conveyed to others except through the use of reason. Something totally irrational and disorderly is unfathomable and unexplainable, and despite his original rejection of reason the cabalist's thirst for knowledge ends in the imposition of a rigid rational pattern on God and the universe.

1. The Splendid Lights

In this book is written of the Sephiroth and the Paths, of Spirits and Conjurations; of Gods, Spheres, Planes, and many other things which may or may not exist.

It is immaterial whether they exist or not. By doing certain things certain results follow; students are most earnestly warned against attributing objective reality or philosophic validity to any of them.

ALEISTER CROWLEY *Magick in Theory and Practice*

The cabalists, like the Gnostics, set out to answer questions which confront any religious thinker. If God is good, how has evil entered the world which God created? If God is merciful, why is there pain and suffering in life? If God is limitless, infinite and eternal, what is the connection between God and a world which is finite, limited in space and time? By definition God is unknowable, for God is limitless and to be known is to be limited; but then how can man know God?

The Cabala gives two main answers to these questions. The first answer is that God is the total of all things. Every idea contains its own contradiction and God, who is the sum of all ideas, contains all contradictions. God is at one and the same time good and evil, merciful and cruel, limitless and limited, unknowable and knowable, and all these opposites are united in the greater whole which is God. The second answer is that the connection between God and the world is indirect. It is as if God were a mirror from which shines a great light. The light is reflected in a second mirror, which reflects it into a third, and this into a fourth, and so on. With each reflection the light and the mirrors lose something of their pure glow until at last the light shines dimly from the cracked and tarnished surface of our finite, evil world.

In the beginning all that existed was God and nothing. God sent out into the nothing an emanation from himself—often described as a light—and from this came a whole succession of emanations. There were ten of them altogether, each successive emanation containing less of the divine substance. The ten emanations are called the *sephiroth* ('numbers' or 'categories'). In typically paradoxical language, the *Zohar* explains that:

> The Aged of the Aged, the Unknown of the Unknown, has a form and yet has no form. He has a form whereby the universe is preserved and yet has no form because he cannot be comprehended. When he first assumed the form [of the first emanation] he caused nine splendid lights to emanate from it, which, shining through it, diffused a bright light in all directions . . . So is the Holy Aged an absolute light but in himself concealed and incomprehensible. We can only comprehend him through those luminous emanations which again are partly visible and partly concealed. These constitute the sacred name of God.[1]

The splendid lights of the sephiroth constitute the sacred name of God because they are God's identity. The universe *is* God and the sephiroth are parts of God, facets of God's or the universe's personality. They also provide a path by which man can reach God.

From classical times down to the sixteenth century it was generally accepted that the universe is made of nine spheres which are arranged like the skins of an onion, one outside the other. The outer skin is the sphere of God as Prime Mover. Inside it is the sphere of the stars and inside this again are the seven spheres of the seven planets. The innermost sphere belongs to the moon and the earth hangs inside it. In the early centuries after Christ the idea spread through the Mediterranean world that the soul comes originally from God and descends through the nine spheres to earth, where it is imprisoned in a human body. The soul longs for reunion with God and can achieve it by climbing back through the spheres to heaven. But each sphere is guarded by angels and the space between the earth and the moon is crowded with legions of devils. Even when the soul has successfully negotiated the devils, the guardians of the spheres will try to turn it back. Only those initiated into the secret traditions know the passwords which will make the guardians yield and open their gates for the soul to continue on its way to God. (Again, it is knowledge which clears the way for the soul, not the leading of a good life.)

When the soul leaves God and makes its way down through the spheres to earth, it gathers characteristics from each sphere in turn. Qualities of courage and ferocity come from the sphere of Mars, for instance, the ability to love from the sphere of Venus. These characteristics are added to the soul like skins or garments in layers, each layer outside the one before. The last garment or outer layer, which comes from earth, is the physical body. At the end of the process the soul is like an onion with several skins, a miniature image of the onion-shaped cosmos itself, though the layers are in the reverse order. When death comes, the soul sheds its skins, first the physical body and then the other layers one by one, as the soul rises through the spheres towards God.

The Cabala is based on this theory of the soul's descent and ascent through the spheres, though it has ten spheres instead of nine, because the cabalists were influenced by Pythagorean theory. Earth is given a separate sphere, the last sephira. Above this are seven sephiroth at the top which are the spheres of the stars and the Prime Mover. Man achieves union with God by climbing up through the sephiroth to reach their source. Each sephira is guarded by an order of angels and their guardians will try to turn the climber back. And in the lower spheres there are plenty of sinister intelligences that are very ready to trap an aspiring soul which is ignorant or careless.

Although many cabalists have led devout and blameless lives, thick veins of magic and sorcery are not far beneath the Cabala's surface. The essential doctrine of the cabalists is that death is not a necessary preliminary to the soul's ascent through the spheres. The soul can climb the ladder of the sephiroth while still in the body and man can make himself God on earth. The ten sephiroth are the great driving forces which move the universe and the impulses which move man. As he rises through the spheres the magician knows and becomes and controls the powerful force of each sephira. Paul Ricci, a Jew turned Christian who became Professor of Greek and Hebrew at the University of Pavia in 1521, said that the lore of the Cabala 'enumerates many sacred names to be invoked, and various bodily movements [breathing and posture exercises], by mean of which we attain more easily and beyond the use of nature to the glories of the Eternal Father *and our prerogatives in this world, which resemble them'.*[2] The process of the Cabala is a search for God, but it can also be an attempt to wield the magical power which belongs to man as the potential God.

Occult groups which teach the techniques of the ascent through the spheres frequently have ten ranks or grades, corresponding to the sephiroth. In Crowley's A ∴ A ∴ the student began as a Neophyte (sephira 10, the sphere of earth) and next became a Zelator (9, the moon), in which rank he had to achieve proficiency in certain practices which resemble yoga. As Practicus (8, Mercury) he completed his intellectual training and studied the Cabala, as Philosophus (7, Venus) he completed his moral training and was tested in 'Devotion to the Order'. The next grade, Adeptus Minor (6, the sun) involved the attainment of 'the Knowledge and Conversation of the Holy Guardian Angel', a rite of sex-magic to which Crowley attached great importance. As an Adeptus Major (5, Mars) the adept obtained a general mastery of practical magic, including such 'matters of detail' as securing wanted objects—'gold, books, women and the like'—opening locked doors, finding treasure or having armed men at command. ('Moral', Crowley says cheerfully, 'become an Adeptus Major!') It was also his duty to rule the members of the lower grades 'with balanced vigour and initiative in such a way as to allow no dispute or complaint; he must employ to this end the formula called "The Beast conjoined with the Woman" . . .'

The next grade, Adeptus Exemptus (4, Jupiter) 'completes in perfection all these matters'. The adept now either becomes a Brother of the Left-hand Path or crosses the abyss which lies between manhood and godhead to reach the three highest sephiroth and becomes a Magister Templi (3, Saturn) who tends his garden of disciples and obtains a perfect understanding of the universe. The magus (2, sphere of the stars) 'attains to wisdom, declares his law and is a Master of all Magick in its greatest and highest sense'. Finally, the Ipsissimus (1, sphere of God) 'is beyond all this and beyond all comprehension of those of lower degrees'. He 'is wholly free from all limitations soever, existing in the nature of all things without discriminations of quantity or quality between them'.[3]

'Ten is the number of the ineffable Sephiroth,' the *Sepher Yetzirah* says, 'ten and not nine, ten and not eleven. Understand this wisdom and be wise in the perception . . . The Ten ineffable Sephiroth have ten vast regions bound unto them; boundless in origin and having no ending; an abyss of good and of ill.' The sephiroth are 10, not 9 or 11, because they are the numbers from 1 to 10, the essential numbers of the Pythagoreans which are the basis of all things. The 'ten vast regions' are the departments of the universe which the driving forces of the sephiroth control.

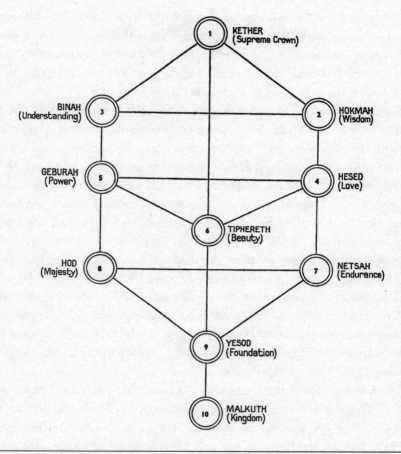

DIAGRAM 1 The Tree of Life

The sephiroth are usually shown in a diagram called the Tree of Life, which is an illustration of the underlying pattern of the universe and its fundamental unity. The Tree spreads its branches through the whole of creation and reconciles all diversity in unity, for though it has many branches it is one Tree and all the phenomena of the universe are leaves and twigs and branches of a connected whole. The Tree is a model of God, the universe and man. It is a classification of everything—nothing exists which cannot be placed in one or other of its ten pigeon-holes. The Tree consists of three triangles, with the tenth sephira, Malkuth, left over at the bottom. Each triangle contains two opposing forces and a third force which balances and reconciles them. The sephiroth run from right to left on the Tree, because Hebrew is written from right to left. Those on the right side of the Tree are male and positive, those on the left or evil side are female and negative, and the ones in the middle which reconcile the opposites are bisexual. The Tree does not always fit neatly with either astrology or numerology. The spheres of Saturn, Mars and Mercury are all classified as female, but the sphere of Venus is male. In some cases the significance of a sephira's number follows its standard meaning in numerology, but in others it does not.

The Tree is sometimes shown as a man's body—the upper triangle behind his head, the middle triangle his trunk and arms, the lower triangle his genitals and legs—and it is based on the analogy between man and God. The sephiroth are the steps of the processes by which God created the universe. If God is man writ large, this process must have paralleled the human creative process. In the Tree's first triangle male impregnates female and new life, the child or the universe, is born. In the second triangle father and mother nourish and guide the child through infancy and adolescence. In the third triangle the child grows up, the universe is a finished product.

The system of correspondences, greatly amplified by MacGregor Mathers and Crowley, identifies the 'ten vast regions' which the sephiroth control. Some of the correspondences are shown in Diagram 2. Mythical animals and classical gods are included, because they have their reality in the mind of man and therefore in the 'mind' of the universe.

The first triangle on the Tree shows the creative forces in God and the universe. *Kether*, the first emanation, is the force of God as Prime Mover, First Cause, the One. It is guarded by the four 'living creatures' of the first chapter of Ezekiel, which had 'the likeness of a man'. Its magical image—the mental picture on which the cabalist concentrates in meditation—is an old, bearded man, seen in profile. Zeus and Jupiter, the ruling gods of Greece and Rome, were the classical personifications of Kether. Its symbols are the crown, for kingship, and the point, which stands for 1. The soul which can reach this sphere achieves union with God.

God contains two great opposing forces or principles, active and passive, which are the next two sephiroth, the Father and Mother of the universe. *Hokmah* (2, male) is the active principle, the force behind everything which is positive, dynamic, thrusting, male. It is the force which originates and causes all activity and it rules all growth, evolution, change, movement. This is shown in its angels, the Wheels of Ezekiel which moved about, rolling to and fro, and which had 'the spirit of life' in them.[4] Hokmah corresponds to the life-giving Spirit of God, brooding on the waters in Genesis, and to the Logos of St. John's gospel, the creative Word with which God made the world. It is the Wisdom of God—God's active, creative thought. The analogy between mental creativity and sexual creativity is constantly drawn in occultism and also in language—the words 'genius' and 'genital' come from the same root. Hokmah's symbols are phallic, the phallus, the tower and the straight line, which is also a symbol of 2, connecting two points. In Greek mythology Uranus was the wise god who impregnated Earth and was the father of Nature and man.

The opposite sephira *Binah* (3, female) is the passive principle in God, called the Mother, the Throne, the Great Sea. Hokmah acts and Binah is acted upon, Hokmah thrusts and Binah responds. Hokmah is the active Wisdom of God, Binah the passive Understanding of God. Hokmah is the life-giving Spirit, Binah the waters of chaos which are lifeless, but from which, once fertilised, all things come forth. Binah stands for everything which is negative, malleable, potential rather than actual, female. Its symbols are female sex symbols, the cteis, the cup, the circle, oval and diamond. Its deities are mother-goddesses, including the sinister Hecate, the ruler of witchcraft and sorcery. Binah is the principle of inertia and stability, and anything which remains stable and unchanging is said to be under its influence.

Many of the Gnostics believed that the One became Two by thinking, so that there was a Mind and a Thought. The Thought was the first emanation from God and was the mother of all things. In the Cabala the Thought is split in two—the active Wisdom and the passive Understanding—and their union is the foundation of the universe. The rest of the sephiroth are the product of the union of Hokmah and Binah, which means that everything in the universe results from the interaction of active and passive, positive and negative. According to a modern English cabalist, Dion Fortune, 'everything rests upon the principle of the stimulation of the inert yet all-potential [Binah] by the dynamic principle [Hokmah], which derives its energy direct from the source of all energy [Kether, God]. In this concept lie tremendous keys of knowledge; it is one of the most important points in the mysteries.'[5]

The female sephiroth on the left of the Tree all combine good characteristics with distinctly evil and ominous ones. The perplexing contrariness of woman, who is maiden and hag, mother and harlot, tender and cruel, cold and passionate, illogical but discerning, passive but fecund, 'inert yet all-potential', is firmly built into the Cabala. Binah is the mother of all life, but is also the sphere of Saturn, the planet of death, fate, the cruel and inexorable scythe of Time, and in magic the force of Binah is used in attempts to kill. Crowley identifies Binah with 'the woman clothed with the sun, and the moon under her feet, and upon her head a crown of twelve stars' of Revelation, a personification of beauty and fertility, and also with 'Babalon', the Scarlet Woman, the Great Whore, 'Babylon the Great, the Mother of Harlots and Abominations of the Earth' who 'sitteth upon many waters . . . arrayed in purple and scarlet colour, and decked with gold and precious stones and pearls, having a golden cup in her hand full of abominations and filthiness of her fornication . . . drunken with the blood of the saints, and with the blood of the martyrs of Jesus'.[6] (*Every* idea contains its opposite, however, and Crowley says that Hokmah is the divine Word and the Lamb of Revelation, but also the Great Beast and the Dragon which attacks the woman clothed with the sun.)

Again, many of the Gnostics believed that the divine Thought fell into defilement, usually as a result of either curiosity or desire, and the eventual result was the creation of the visible world—the world which mingles life and death, love and hate, beauty and filth. The Gnostic Simon Magus maintained that the first divine Thought was the mother of various lower powers which created the world. These powers captured the Thought and kept her prisoner in the world, shutting her up in a woman's body. For untold ages she passed from one female incarnation to another, gradually sinking lower and lower into degradation until she became a common prostitute. Simon took about with him a woman called Helena and said that she was the fallen Thought, found by him in a brothel. He himself was God, come to redeem her. She had been the Helen for whose sake the Trojan War was fought, and this is the source of the story of Faust and Helen of Troy. Simon called himself Faustus, 'the favoured one'.

In human terms the sephiroth in the Tree's second triangle are father, mother and child. In the universe they are the forces which govern evolving life and the life-force itself. *Hesed* (4, male) stands for the kindly and merciful authority of the father, who protects the child and guides him along the right paths. Four is the number of solidity, the visible form of things, and Hesed is the force which organises things and builds them up. In the human body, for example, it governs the building up of food into tissue. It is the force behind all constructive energy, civilisation, law and order, justice, peace, love, benevolence. The unicorn stands for virility and power, as in Psalm 22—'But my horn shalt thou exalt like the horn of an unicorn.' Hesed's symbols are the sceptre, the wand and the crook— which are the king's, the magician's and the bishop's emblems of authority and are also phallic—and the pyramid and equal-armed cross, symbols of 4. The

Sephiroth	Planets	Guardian angels	Creatures, real or imaginary	Greek and Roman Gods	Magical image
1. Kether	—	Living creatures	God	Zeus, Jupiter	An old bearded king
2. Hokmah	—	Ophannim	Man	Uranus	A bearded man
3. Binah	Saturn	Arelim	Woman	Cybele, Rhea, Juno, Hecate	A mature woman
4. Hesed	Jupiter	Chashmalim	Unicorn	Poseidon, Jupiter	A powerful king on his throne
5. Geburah	Mars	Seraphim	Basilisk	Ares, Hades, Mars	A warrior in a chariot
6. Tiphereth	Sun	Shinanim	Lion, phoenix, child	Apollo, Adonis	A majestic king; a child sacrificed
7. Netsah	Venus	Tarsishim	Iynx	Aphrodite, Venus	A beautiful naked woman
8. Hod	Mercury	Benei Elohim	Twin serpents	Hermes, Mercury	A hermaphrodite
9. Yesod	Moon	Ishim	Elephant	Diana	A beautiful naked man
10. Malkuth	Earth	Cherubim	Sphinx	Demeter, Ceres, Persephone	A young woman, crowned and seated on a throne

DIAGRAM 2 **Correspondences of the Sephiroth**

angels are the flames of the fire from which the 'living creatures' appeared, and so stand for fatherhood.[7] The force of Jupiter is used in magical operations of friendship and in attempts to gain money and worldly success.

The opposite force is *Geburah* (5, female), which is the sphere of Mars and the force appealed to in operations of hatred and destruction. It is the strict and severe authority of the mother, who disciplines and punishes the child. Hesed builds things up, Geburah breaks them down. In the human body it rules the breaking down of tissue in the expenditure of energy. It lies behind all destructive energy, hate, rage, cruelty, war, havoc, retribution, Nature red in tooth and claw. The mythical basilisk is a ferocious creature whose breath and eyes deal death (though in modern biology the name is inappropriately applied to a harmless South American lizard). In plants the force of Geburah appears in the stinging nettle and in nux vomica, from which strychnine is obtained. Its symbols are those of violence and punishment—the sword, spear, scourge and chain—and also the pentagon and the Tudor rose, which are symbols of 5.

The interplay of Hesed and Geburah, of construction and destruction, governs all life in Nature. The balancing force between them is *Tiphereth* (6), the sphere of the sun. The sun unites them both in itself, shining warmly on men, beasts and crops with the nurturing benevolence of Hesed, blasting and withering them with the fierce heat of Geburah. Tiphereth is the vital energy of the life-force, the drive which impels life to continue. Its angels, the *shinanim*, ride in chariots like the chariot of the sun.[8] Christian cabalists associate it with Christ, who brought the promise of eternal life to men. Tiphereth is the 'son' of Kether (God) in the sense of being directly descended from it on the Tree and the symbolic association of Christ and the sun goes back almost to the earliest days of Christianity. In physical terms Tiphereth is the heart which pumps the life-blood through the body, in a circular motion like the sun's apparent circling of the earth. In psychological terms it is the enlightened consciousness, the human mind raised to the highest spiritual condition which it can achieve in any normal state. (The higher spheres can only be attained in supernormal states.)

Tiphereth's symbols are the Calvary cross and the cube, which stands for 6 because it has six sides. Six is the number of balance and harmony, and Tiphereth is the Tree's central sphere, to which the others are connected in a balanced arrangement. Its force is used in magical operations of harmony and friendship and also in attempts to discover buried treasure, because the sun is linked with gold. The spiritual experience of a soul which reaches this sphere is a realisation of the underlying harmony of all things and a vision of the Crucifixion, of death as the gateway to new life, as Christ died to rise again and as the sun sets in the evening to rise again at dawn. The golden lion, its mane like tongues of fire, is traditionally a beast of the sun. The child and the phoenix stand for mortality and immortality, the endless cycle of birth, death and new birth through which all life passes.

In the third triangle the child comes to manhood. The influences which play upon him are the opposing forces of animality and mentality, of impulse and thought. *Netsah* (7, male) is the Endurance of God and the Victory of God, the all-conquering and enduring forces of Nature. It stands for animal drives and proclivities, the senses and passions, instinct, unthinking reactions, the natural as opposed to the contrived. This is the sphere of Venus, ruler of Nature and desire, and its force is used in magical operations of love. The iynx or wryneck is a bird used in love charms. The wizards of classical antiquity spread-eagled the bird on a wheel and believed that in turning the wheel they turned the hearts of lovers. The spiritual experience of this sphere is a vision of triumphant beauty and its angels are the beautiful *tarsishim*, one of whom Daniel saw in a vision—'His body also was like the beryl (*tarsish*) and his face as the appearance of lightning.'[9]

Hod (8, female), the opposite sephira, is the sphere of mental faculties. It stands for the powers of imagination and fancy, inspiration, intuition, insight, which the cabalists regard as the higher capacities of the mind. Like the other sephiroth on the left of the Tree it has a decidedly evil side—reason and logic, which the Cabala distrusts, and all the constricting apparatus imposed on the mind through upbringing and training to regulate the impulses of the natural man, whose sphere is significantly placed on the good side of the Tree. Hod lies behind considered and unnatural reactions, schooled or conventional attitudes, artificiality, contrivance, ingenuity, and cunning. The *benei Elohim* are the 'sons of God', the fallen angels who looked on the daughters of men and saw that they were fair and taught them all arts and crafts, and they mark the contrast with the artlessness of Netsah. Mercury was the god of intelligence, communication, business and trickery, but also of magic, insight and true wisdom. The hermaphrodite was a common symbol for mercury, the metal, in alchemy. The twin serpents, emblems of wisdom and guile, come from

Mercury's staff, the caduceus. The force of Mercury is used in magical attempts to gain knowledge or see into the future and in operations of deceit.

Netsah and Hod are balanced and combined in *Yesod* (9), the sphere of the moon. The moon is the ruler of night, a light in the darkness, and Yesod is the dark depths of the personality in which the shining true self lies hidden. Nine is the number of initiation into the mysteries of occultism and promises high spiritual achievement. The moon is the mistress of magic and Yesod is the potential magical power of the self, which springs from the combination of man's highest mental faculties with the animal driving forces of his being. The angels are the 'messengers and ministers' (Hod—Mercury) of Psalm 104, which are also natural forces (Netsah)—'Who makest the winds thy messengers, fire and flame thy ministers'. The elephant shows the union of high intelligence and brute strength in the same creature and Yesod's plant is the aphrodisiac mandrake, the most powerful of all plants in magic.

The magical power of the self is linked with creativity. In Yesod the child becomes full grown, able to reproduce, to create both sexually and mentally. When the sephiroth are shown as a human body, Yesod is the genitals. It is a bisexual sphere and the moon is associated with the phallus of the male, because both increase and diminish, and with the sexual rhythm of the female. Yesod is the link between Tiphereth (the sun or the life-force) and Malkuth (the earth or the body) and Plutarch says of the moon, in *Isis and Osiris*, 'She is receptive and made pregnant by the sun, but she in turn emits and disseminates into the air generative principles.' In other words, moonlight is reflected sunlight and Yesod is 'the spout for the waters from on high', as the *Zohar* says, the channel between the creative power of God and the earth or earthly man. In magic, the force of the moon is used in operations of love and reconciliation and in necromancy, which is the bringing to life of dead bodies.

Finally, *Malkuth* (10) is the sphere of earth. Demeter and Ceres ruled fertility and agriculture, and Persephone represents crops and vegetation because she spent the winter underground with her husband Hades and returned to earth's surface in the spring. The *cherubim* are composite creatures, part human, part animal, part bird, which stand for the union of the elements from which all earthly things are made. But Malkuth is also the whole kingdom of God. It contains the forces of all the sephiroth within itself, and when the Tree is shown as a human body, Malkuth is the union of the whole body. Its number is 10, which means 'all things'. The sphinx of Thebes had a woman's head and breasts, a bull's body, a lion's paws, a dragon's tail and a bird's wings. It is a symbol of the four elements (bull, lion, dragon, bird) with the 'quintessence' (woman), the fifth element of classical theory, the pure material of which the heavens are made. It stands for the unity of all things, heaven and earth taken together. And the sphinx is also a symbol of the riddle, the universe as a great enigma which the mystic and the magician attempt to solve.

To explore the world of the sephiroth you must disentangle yourself from the world of everyday life. A man cannot wander through the landscape of the spheres until he is free from all the physical sensations, thoughts and worries which keep him tied to his usual surroundings. The physical and mental exercises of the cabalists are designed to achieve this.

The cabalist learns mastery of both his body and his mind. He trains himself to stay perfectly still for long periods of time and to do this in awkward positions—kneeling and resting on his heels, his back and head rigidly straight, his hands on his thighs; or standing on his right foot, holding his left ankle with his right hand, his left forefinger touching his lips. In these positions he must be able to breathe evenly and in a regular rhythm—for example, breathing in for ten seconds, holding the breath for thirty seconds, breathing out for twenty seconds, continuing in this way for an hour. He imposes all sorts of rules on himself. For a week or more he never allows himself to cross his legs or raise his left arm higher than his waist. He takes some common word, as common as 'and' or 'but', and does not let himself use it, or he avoids using any word which has a t or an s or some other letter of the alphabet in it. He picks a subject which particularly interests him and takes care not to think about it or anything connected with it for a week or longer. When he fails in any of these exercises, as he naturally will at first, he punishes himself. Crowley suggested cutting one's arm with a razor.

Concentration and imagination are vitally important in magic. The cabalist learns to concentrate his whole attention on one thing, at first a simple object, a black oval or a red triangle, later a moving object, a wheel turning or a pendulum swinging. He concentrates on imagined sensations—the smell of a rose, the feel of velvet, the ticking of a watch. He must imagine and concentrate with such intensity that the object or sensation is present in his mind to the exclusion of everything else, but he must also be able to banish it utterly from his consciousness at will. Eventually, he must be able to put himself into a trance in which he can totally disregard his body, focus his entire being on one thought, or prevent any thought whatever from entering his mind.[10]

Blind and deaf to anything which might tug him back to the normal world, the cabalist can adventure into the realm of the sephiroth. He imagines his own body as if it were standing in front of him. He must have a clear, vivid mental picture of it. Then he transfers his consciousness to the imaginary body, so that he sees through its eyes and hears through its ears. This body is his astral body, astral double or body of light, a replica of the physical body made of finer material. It is capable of moving freely through space and can pass through apparently solid objects. The world which this body perceives is the astral plane, which includes the ordinary physical plane, but extends beyond it. The threshold of this plane is in Yesod, the sphere of the moon, which in the old cosmology was the connecting point between the pure spheres of the heavens above it and the corruptible world of earth beneath it.

When he is comfortably settled in his astral body, the cabalist makes it rise high in the air. He will become aware of landscapes and figures, apparently human or animal. 'Such have a quality all their own', Crowley says. 'They are not like material things—they are not like mental pictures—they seem to be between the two.' The cabalist explores the strange country he has entered and speaks to any of the figures which approach him, but he must be cautious. The figures may try to deceive and ensnare him. 'Every spirit, up to God himself, is ready to deceive you if possible, to make himself out more important than he is; in short to lay in wait for your soul in 333 separate ways.'[11] These spirits are the equivalents in the universe of factors within the cabalist himself. The delusions into which they may entice him are self-delusions on a greater scale.

In this mysterious world the aspiring cabalist needs guide-posts to help him find his way about and avoid pitfalls. The guide-posts are provided by the system of correspondences, which lists the creatures, plants, colours, jewels, scents and symbols associated with the sephiroth and the Twenty-two Paths—twenty-two lines drawn on the diagram of the Tree of Life which connect the sephiroth together and are the paths the cabalist takes from one sephira to another. If the occult traveller believes he is in the region of Netsah, the sphere of Venus, and he sees a horse or a jackal he knows that something has gone wrong. The horse belongs to Mars, the jackal is a beast of the moon. He would expect to see doves or sparrows or a spotted beast, a leopard or a lynx perhaps, which are the creatures of Venus. If he is working up the twenty-second path, which leads from Malkuth to Yesod, and he meets a figure in a scarlet robe he knows he has strayed from the way. This path belongs to Saturn and the colour of Saturn is black.[12]

2. The Paths and the Tarot

> Here is the man with three staves, and here the Wheel,
> And here is the one-eyed merchant, and this card,
> Which is blank, is something he carries on his back,
> Which I am forbidden to see. I do not find
> The Hanged Man. Fear death by water.
>
> T. S. ELIOT *The Waste Land*

The *Sepher Yetzirah*, describing how the world was created, begins, 'In thirty-two wonderful Paths of Wisdom did Jah, Jehovah Sabaoth, the God of Israel, the Elohim of the living, the King of ages, the merciful and gracious God, the exalted One, the Dweller in eternity, most high and holy—engrave his name by the three Sepharim [means of expression]—Numbers, Letters and Sounds.' God used numbers, letters and sounds in creation because God is man writ large and three important human ways of expressing one's thoughts are by counting, writing and making meaningful noises. The 'thirty-two wonderful Paths of Wisdom' are the ten sephiroth or numbers and the twenty-two letters of the Hebrew alphabet.

The twenty-two Hebrew letters are associated with the twenty-two works of creation in Genesis and are believed to contain all wisdom, all truth, all knowledge of God and the universe. In the Cabala they are connected with the Twenty-two Paths, the roads which lead from one sephira to another. The letters and the paths account for everything in the universe and they are the soul's way to God and the magician's way to power, the steps in the process of spiritual expansion through which man can extend himself to cover the entire universe and control it. Their interpretation is enriched but also complicated by the fact that they are linked with the twenty-two major trumps of the Tarot pack.

The Tarot is a pack of curious cards which are the ancestors of our modern playing-cards. It is still used in fortune-telling and in a game called *tarocchini*, played in Italy and central Europe. Many occultists believe that the Tarot was invented by the ancient Egyptians, as a repository of their occult lore, and was brought into Europe by the gipsies. A different occult tradition says that the cards were designed by a committee of learned cabalists in Fez in A.D. 1200. Gnostic, Neoplatonic and Cathar influences have been seen in them, but the early history of playing-cards is lost in obscurity and no one really knows when or where the Tarot came into existence. The earliest undisputed references to cards in Europe do not come till the late fourteenth century. The mad king Charles VI of France was supplied with a Tarot pack in 1392 and some cards which are thought to have belonged to this pack are still preserved in Paris.

There is something extraordinarily fascinating about the Tarot. It opens strange windows into a world in which things are never quite what they seem, can never quite be grasped, a sunlit medieval landscape of tiny figures moving like marvellous toys—the Fool with cap and bells, the Emperor and Empress with a glittering cavalcade, Death at his reaping, the Hermit with staff and lamp, the Hanged Man swinging from his gibbet, the pale Tower falling. If they could be fully understood, occultists believe that these figures would reveal the secret of the inner mechanism of the universe, the hidden rhythms of the Dance of Life.

The early Tarot packs had varying numbers of cards and various names for the suits. What is now regarded as the standard pack has four suits of fourteen cards each—King, Queen, Knight, Page (our Knave), and the Ten down to the Ace. The suits are Swords (our Spades), Cups (Hearts), Coins or Pentacles (Diamonds) and Wands or Staffs (Clubs). It has been suggested that the suits are connected with the four sacred objects of the Grail legends—the sword, the cup, the dish and the lance. Besides these minor cards there are twenty-two others, the 'major trumps'. Their proper order is uncertain—the surviving trumps of the Charles VI pack are not numbered—but in the usual order they are:

0. The Fool
1. The Juggler
2. The Female Pope
3. The Empress
4. The Emperor
5. The Pope
6. The Lovers
7. The Chariot
8. Strength
9. The Hermit

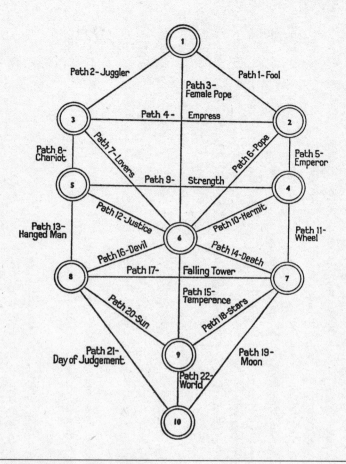

DIAGRAM 3 The Paths and the Tarot

10. The Wheel of Fortune
11. Justice
12. The Hanged Man
13. Death
14. Temperance
15. The Devil
16. The Falling Tower
17. The Stars
18. The Moon
19. The Sun
20. The Day of Judgement
21. The World

Although different packs have different designs, figures and symbols, there is a rough general similarity. A complete pack is illustrated in A. E. Waite's *Pictorial Key to the Tarot*. It was specially drawn for the book, with some of the cards 'rectified' to fit their true occult interpretation. Unfortunately, Waite's cards are

Path no.	Letters	Tarot trumps	Elements, planets and zodiac signs	Creatures	Plants	Colours
1	aleph	0. Fool	Air	Man, eagle	Aspen	Pale yellow
2	beth	1. Juggler	Mercury	Ape, ibis, swallow	Vervain, palm	Yellow
3	gimel	2. Female Pope	Moon	Dog	Hazel, almond	Blue
4	daleth	3. Empress	Venus	Dove, sparrow, swan	Rose, myrtle	Emerald green
5	he	4. Emperor	Aries (Mars)	Ram, owl	Geranium	Scarlet
6	vau	5. Pope	Taurus (Venus)	Bull	Mallow	Red-orange
7	zayin	6. Lovers	Gemini (Mercury)	Magpie, all hybrids	Orchid	Orange
8	heth	7. Chariot	Cancer (Moon)	Crab, turtle	Lotus	Amber
9	teth	8. Strength	Leo (Sun)	Lion	Sunflower	Greenish-yellow
10	yod	9. Hermit	Virgo (Mercury)	Virgin, anchorite	Snowdrop, lily, narcissus	Yellowish-green
11	kaph	10. Wheel	Jupiter	Eagle	Oak, poplar	Violet
12	lamed	11. Justice	Libra (Venus)	Elephant	Aloe	Emerald green
13	mem	12. Hanged Man	Water	Snake, scorpion	All water plants	Deep blue
14	nun	13. Death	Scorpio (Mars)	Scorpion, beetle, lobster, wolf	Cactus	Greenish blue
15	samekh	14. Temperance	Sagittarius (Jupiter)	Centaur, horse, dog	Rush	Blue
16	ayin	15. Devil	Capricorn (Saturn)	Goat, ass	Thistle	Indigo
17	pe	16. Falling Tower	Mars	Horse, bear, wolf	Absinthe, rue	Scarlet
18	sade	17. Stars	Aquarius (Saturn)	Man, eagle, peacock	Coconut	Violet
19	qoph	18. Moon	Pisces (Jupiter)	Fish, dolphin	Opium	Crimson
20	resh	19. Sun	Sun	Lion, sparrowhawk	Sunflower, heliotrope	Orange
21	shin	20. Day of Judgement	Fire	Lion	Red poppy, nettle	Orange-scarlet
22	tau	21. World	Saturn	Crocodile	Ash, yew, cypress	Indigo

DIAGRAM 4 Correspondences of the Twenty-two Paths

singularly ugly and many occultists have quarreled with his 'rectification'. Illustrations of older cards, including some from the magnificent Charles VI pack, can be found in Hargrave's *History of Playing Cards*.

There are almost as many interpretations of the Tarot—occult, Christian, gipsy, psychological—as there are interpreters. The cards contain such a richness of symbolism and suggestion that no two people are likely to react to them in quite the same way. Most occultists would probably agree with one modern commentator that 'it may be that the deepest occult wisdom of the Tarot cannot be put into words at all' and 'in the end, the seeker is told only what he cannot find for himself'.[13]

Modern cabalistic interpretations bristle with erotic symbolism. The meaning of each trump depends partly on its design and number, but mainly on its position on the Tree. The difficulty which plagues all Tarot interpretation is the question of the placing of the Fool, which has no number and corresponds to the Joker of a modern pack. It is often assigned to path 21, but in Crowley's system it is placed on path 1, and this seems to give the most satisfactory results, though it has the disadvantage of putting the numbers of the trumps and paths out of step. Waite follows the same system, although he tries to conceal the fact.

The system of correspondences, which throws additional light on the meaning of each trump and path, is an expanded version of the one in the *Sepher Yetzirah*, which divides the Hebrew letters into groups of 3, 7 and 12, corresponding to 3 elements (fire, air and water—there is no room for earth in the classification), 7 planets and 12 zodiac signs. Some of the correspondences are shown in Diagram 4.

The trumps and paths can be considered from two different points of view. If they are followed downwards from the top of the Tree, they show the evolution of the universe from God; they are the paths which led from God to man. In the opposite order, starting from the foot of the Tree, they are the way of the soul's ascent to God. The cabalist begins at the foot of the Tree and works upwards, following the course of the 'Serpent of Wisdom', which coils itself round and round the Tree. This means that he travels *all* the paths—path 22 to reach Yesod, paths 20 and 21 to Hod, paths 17, 18 and 19 to Netsah, and so on. It is easier to follow this progress if the trumps are taken in reverse order.

21. *The World* corresponds to the twenty-second path, leading from Malkuth (earth) to the threshold of the astral plane in Yesod. The card shows a naked woman, holding a wand in each hand and dancing in a garland of flowers. She is the symbol of joy, lightness and release, the leaving of earthly

existence and the entry into a higher world. This is 'death' in a sense and so is the subduing of the mind and body through the cabalist's exercises. Saturn is the planet of death, and the ash, yew and cypress are associated with death and graveyards. The crocodile stands for the plunge from the solid 'dry land' of ordinary life into the flowing 'water' of a more ethereal and deeper plane of experience.

20. *The Day of Judgement.* A great winged angel blows a trumpet and the dead rise up from their tombs. 'What is it that within us sounds a trumpet,' Waite asks, 'and all that is lower in our nature rises in response—almost in a moment, almost in the twinkling of an eye?' The answer is 'desire', sexual or spiritual, and the card is a symbol of aspiration, the yearning for better things. It is one of several cards of death and resurrection—life gained through the 'death' or release and transformation of man's earthly nature. The nettle is the sting of death, the red poppy is blood and the sleep of death. *Shin* is the letter of the Holy Spirit and the *Sepher Yetzirah* links it with Fire, the passionate flames of longing which carry the divine spark upward.

19. *The Sun* shines on two children who are playing happily by a high wall. Its path leads to Hod (higher mental faculties) and it shows the descent of light from on high, the dazzling light of true intelligence which frees the mind from the petty concerns and restrictions of the world around it. The light purges away conventional and accepted ideas, beginning a process which is continued in the next card. Although he still thinks of himself as a separate being, the cabalist begins to identify himself consciously with the One Life of the universe, represented by the sun. Like the merciless and keen-sighted sparrow-hawk he soars towards the sun; like the flowers of the heliotrope he follows the sun's course.

The transition from the Sun to 18. *The Moon* is one from light to darkness. The moon hangs in the night sky, shedding drops of blood on a path which leads away into the distance between two towers. A dog and a wolf are howling at the moon and a crab crawls up on to the land from a pool. Eighteen reduces to 9, the number of initiation, shown here as the breaking of the hymen. The letter *qoph* is supposed to represent the back of the head and the card is a symbol of the underworld of the mind and the cabalist's penetration of the unknown. The falling blood is a menstruum, a fluid in which a solid body is dissolved, and stands for a state of flux in the mind in which the reassuringly solid bodies of self-certainty, accepted ideas and accustomed ways of thinking have been dissolved and washed away. Through this inner night the creatures of imagination and nightmare move—illusions and deceptions, dreams and fantasies. The dog and the wolf are the animal impulses of man, unleashed to cry for the moon, and the crab, Waite says mysteriously, is 'the nameless and hideous tendency which is lower than the savage beast'. Conversely, the card also stands for the formation of the solid from the nebulous, the fashioning of the child in the womb, the clothing of the products of the imagination with flesh. To some extent at least the wanderer on the astral plane is in a world created by his own imagination, but his imaginings are real, though they may be deceptive and dangerous. It is on this path that the magician learns the art of making talismans, which are concrete embodiments of his desires and ideas. The moon rules night and the depths of the mind, and Pisces (ruled by Jupiter in astrology) is the sign of the Fishes, the creatures which swim in the depths.

17. *The Stars*. A beautiful naked girl pours water from two vases on to the earth and into a pool. Behind her trees and shrubs are blossoming and in the sky is a great star surrounded by seven lesser stars. There are eight stars altogether and 17 reduces to 8, the number of new life. The girl is Nature, pouring out the water of life to revive the world in the springtime. She is also the water of life in woman, the secretions which give promise of bliss, and the water of life in the mind, the gentle flow of intuition which brings hope to the troubled spirit. The card implies potentiality, expectation, the shining possibilities of the future and is often connected with astrology and other methods of predicting the future. The eagle is a symbol of hope because it soars into the heights. Aquarius, the Water-pourer, was originally the womanish Ganymede, who poured nectar for the gods on Olympus. He was carried off by Zeus in the form of an eagle and the constellation of the Eagle is near Aquarius in the sky.

16. *The Falling Tower*. A flesh-coloured tower, its upper part shaped like a crown, is struck by a bolt of lightning and is beginning to crumble. Two men are falling from it headlong. An obvious symbol of ejaculation, it stands for the collapse of a false philosophy, for the perception, as one authority puts it, 'that the structure of knowledge built on the foundation of the fallacy of personal separateness is a tower of false science'.[14] The emergence of this perception is symbolised by the bear, which emerges into the world in spring from the solitary sleep of hibernation. The card is also a symbol of discipline, the testing of the cabalist's 'Devotion to the Order' (the opposite of personal separateness). The nature of this testing is suggested by Crowley's references to the card as 'the Massacre of the Innocents' and 'the winepress'. Absinthe and rue are bitter and Mars is the planet of violence and destruction.

The paths of the next three cards lead to Tiphereth, the sphere of the life-force. 15. *The Devil* has wings, horns and claws, and holds a man and a woman on a leash of chains. In Babylonia the number 15 was sacred to Ishtar, goddess of sexual love, and in numerology 15 is closely connected with sex. 5, the number of sex and the senses, adds to 15 by occult addition (1+2+3+4+5 = 15) and 15 is made of 5 multiplied by 3, symbol of the genitals. The Devil frequently appears as a goat (Capricorn) and the goat and ass are both symbols of lust. The Devil is the angel who rebelled from pride and was cast down to earth. The card is an emblem of power and mastery in this world, standing for the dominating forces of pride, ambition and lust.

14. *Temperance* is oddly named if its cabalistic interpretation is the right one. Fourteen means change and transformation, because the moon changes from new to full, and from full to new, in fourteen days. The card is a higher continuation of the World, connecting Tiphereth and Yesod. It shows a figure pouring liquid from a silver cup into a golden one. The silver cup is Yesod (the moon), the golden cup is Tiphereth (the sun) and the pouring liquid is the flood of a spiritual orgasm in which the soul mounts from a lower plane to a higher. Sagittarius, the Huntsman, is a centaur—half beast (lower) and half man (higher). The horse and the dog are the huntsman's animals and also stand for the passage from lower to higher, because they have been trained to help man. The hunter's chase is for knowledge, the discovery of the central driving force deep in one's own nature. Tiphereth is the sphere of human consciousness, Yesod of the unconscious, and C. G. Jung has observed that, 'If attention is directed to the unconscious the unconscious will yield up its contents, and these in turn will fructify the conscious like a fountain of living water. For consciousness is just as arid as the unconscious if the two halves of our psychic life are separated.'15

13. *Death* is a skeleton with a scythe. He is mowing a field of human heads, but hands and feet are growing in their place. This is a symbol of death and resurrection in Nature. The lopped heads are the seeds which fall to the ground and from which new shoots, the hands and feet, will grow. The card shows the beginning of a process which is completed in the next card and it corresponds to the stage of 'putrefaction' in alchemy, a condition of spiritual exhaustion and decay from which new life comes. The heads, which stand for the 'higher' civilised and constricting part of a man's being, fall to rot in earth and give life to the hands and feet, the grasping, moulding, propelling forces of the 'lower' nature. Thirteen is an unlucky number, partly because it is one more than 12,

which is 'completion', and partly because there were 13 at the Last Supper, from which Judas went out to betray Christ. But Christ rose from death to life and 13 is the number of necromancy, the art of raising the dead to life. 'Raising the dead to life' has an obvious phallic connotation and in astrology Scorpio, the Scorpion, rules the genitals and is in turn ruled by Mars, the planet of violent energy. The fierce wolf and the scarlet lobster belong to Mars. The beetle stands for the unending renewal of life in Nature, from the Egyptian scarab or dung-beetle which rolls its eggs along in a ball of dung, an emblem of the life-giving ball of the sun, resurrected each morning. And the beetle is also a symbol of the life-giving power of the 'dung' or 'decaying filth' of the depths of human nature.

The paths of the Hanged Man and Justice lead to Geburah, the force which breaks things down, and stand for Death and Judgement, the killing and purging of the false self which precedes the creation of the true, inner self. 12. *The Hanged Man* suggests, Waite says, 'a great awakening that is possible' and that 'after the sacred *Mystery of Death* there is a glorious *Mystery of Resurrection*'. Death is the gateway to life—not only to life in the higher world of the spirit after the death of the body but also to life in this world, because new human life results from the 'death' of the phallus in ejaculation. The Hanged Man swings limply from a gibbet, head downwards, with two bags of gold dangling from his hands and on his face an expression of pleased serenity. He is passion spent, the completion of a process, and 12 is a number of completeness, because from very early times the year and the day have been made of twelve units, an idea which was powerfully reinforced in numerology by the fact that Christ chose twelve disciples.

The Hanged Man's Hebrew letter is *mem*, which the *Sepher Yetzirah* links with Water (appropriately, because both *mem* and our M probably come from the Egyptian hieroglyph for water). Water is the blood of the soil, the bearer of life and fertility. It is 'the fount and origin' from the old belief that all things originally derived from water and that the chaos from which the world was formed was water. Water also means the 'deeps' of the human personality, and so do the snake and scorpion which live in dark and secret places. In the process of the Hanged Man the magician is drowned in the floodtides of his inner being. The false self which is destroyed is the whole 'higher' structure of outlook, attitudes, tastes, acquired mental and emotional habits, which cages the inner man. In a reversal of values—the Hanged Man is upside down on his gibbet—this structure is overturned and fragmented to release the waters of the depths. These waters are fertile. They carry the seed of new life, of something within the magician which is potentially his true self.

11. *Justice*, the Judgement which follows the Death in the Hanged Man, is a woman holding a sword in her right hand, scales in her left. She is justice in the sense of exact balance. The adept achieves a condition of passive equilibrium in which the conflicting elements of his nature are equally balanced. He does not prefer any idea or course of action to any other and he matches each idea or action with its opposite. He is undergoing a 'purgatory', the cleansing of his being through the cancelling out of warring tendencies, and the purgative drug bitter aloes is made from Justice's plant. Because it is one more than 10, 11 means 'a new beginning' and the card marks the conception of the true self, shown in the impregnation of female (the woman) by male (the sword and scales). The adept is 'in the womb', passive and inert, waiting to be born in the next card, the Wheel.

The paths of Strength, the Hermit and the Wheel lead to Hesed, the force which builds thing up, and it is in them that the magician's true self is built up within him. 10. *The Wheel of Fortune* is a wheel of seven spokes, presided over by an angel who holds a sword in one hand and a crown in the other. It stands for destiny, fate, the unvarying cycle of Nature, the ebb and flow of the iron tides of life and death, growth and decay, to which all things are subject. Ten is the number of 'all things' and Jupiter, to whom the soaring eagle and the rooted oak belong, was ruler of all. The Wheel is the occult law of Karma, the principle of 'as a man sows, so shall he reap'. The true self has been 'sown' in Justice and is 'reaped' in the Wheel. It is born, to become part of the revolving wheel of existence. The card stands for the intervention of the human in the life of Nature and on this path the magician becomes 'Lord of the Forces of Life'.

9. *The Hermit* is an old man wrapped in a cloak, carrying a lantern and a staff. His path joins Hesed (the Father) with Tiphereth (Christ, the sun, the life-force) and Waite says that he 'blends the idea of the Ancient of Days with the Light of the World'. Isolated and withdrawn from the world, he is yet a light and a beacon to others. *Yod* is the letter of the phallus, creative power, and in terms of sexual symbolism the Hermit means masturbation—the true self has reached puberty, as it were, the magician has found the Master in himself. Complete in himself, solitary and virgin, the Hermit's plants all have white flowers, emblems of purity, uninvolvement. He is a symbol of the fertility of absolute self-reliance.

8. *Strength* is a woman forcibly closing the jaws of a lion. Parallel to the Falling Tower, at a higher level, it is another emblem of discipline, Crowley's formula of 'the Beast conjoined with the Woman'. This is an orgiastic and perverse formula, which joins the opposite spheres of love and mercy (Hesed, the lion), cruelty and hate (Geburah, the lion). The woman's unnatural dominance of the lion implies the discipline of submission to the abnormal and distasteful. 'Nature is outraged by Magick; man is bestialized and woman defiled.' The pulsing excitement and self-discovery of this discipline is the beginning of a rapturous ecstasy which reaches its height in the next card, the Chariot, and breaks down the barriers for the release of the true self.

The Lovers and the Chariot rule the paths to Binah, crossing the abyss which separates the three highest sephiroth from the rest, the abyss between man and God. Occultists now follow Eliphas Levi's 'rectification' of 7. *The Chariot*. A warrior rides in a chariot drawn by two sphinxes, one white and one black. In the old packs, including the Charles VI pack, the chariot is drawn by horses. The sphinxes have been substituted to show that the charioteer has solved the riddle of the sphinx. They are black and white for the opposites which the magician has yoked in his own nature and on the front of the chariot is the lingam, symbol of the union of the sexes. The crab and the turtle, at home both on land and on the water, again suggest the opposites and the magician's passage from the 'below' of manhood to the 'above' of godhead.

The Chariot parallels the Hanged Man on a higher plane. In this 'death' the adept is not submerged in his own inner depths but in the life of the universe. To reach the godhead, he must destroy himself as an individual man and identify himself with the universe, which is God. He annihilates his mortal, human personality and returns to the womb of Binah or Babalon, the Mother of All, who is also the Whore. This is the alchemical process of 'exaltation', the making of the Philosopher's Stone, the absorption of man into the divine. It is achieved through an emotional and spiritual frenzy, which rises to a peak of ecstasy when the magician is flung out beyond the bounds of his own being into communion with all things (the sphinx—the four elements plus the quintessence); a reversed communion in which he pours himself into Babalon's golden cup. 'Thou shalt pour out thy blood that is thy life into the golden cup of her fornication', Crowley says in *Liber Cheth* (or *heth*, the Hebrew letter of the Chariot). 'Thou shalt mingle thy life with the universal life. Thou shalt keep not back one drop.'[16]

6. *The Lovers* shows a man choosing between two women, or a young couple with a child or a cupid, in the old packs, but Waite's version shows Adam

and Eve naked in Eden, the gulf between God and man crossed through the creation of humanity in the image of God. The card has various implications—love and innocence, temptation, free will, choice—but it is also a symbol of the union of opposites. To cross the abyss to the One, man must balance the opposites in his nature and reconcile them. The balance and union of the opposites is shown in Adam and Eve, who were originally one being, and in the Twins (Gemini), the magpie and all pied and crossbred or hybrid creatures.

In the passage of the abyss the magician has a choice, which is implied in the Lovers, the choice of Adam and Eve between obedience and disobedience to a higher law. If he accepts self-annihilation, he is 'reborn' when he follows the path of the Empress. If he refuses, he becomes a Black Brother, isolated from the rest of the universe in the hard and evil shell of his own egotism. 'Such a being is gradually disintegrated from lack of nourishment and the slow but certain action of the attraction of the rest of the universe, despite his now desperate efforts to insulate and protect himself, and to aggrandise himself by predatory practices. He may indeed prosper for a while, but in the end he must perish. . . .'[17] Crowley believed that this fate overtook MacGregor Mathers. Others believe that it overtook Crowley himself.

The paths of the Empress, the Emperor and the Pope lead to Hokmah, the active creative principle in God. 5. *The Pope* is called the Hierophant—one who reveals sacred things—by occultists. He is the Magus who has attained spiritual power and authority. He corresponds to the process of 'projection' in alchemy, in which the perfect substance or Philosopher's Stone is mingled with a base metal to turn it to gold, and he stands for the intervention of the divine in earthly life (a higher parallel to the Wheel). He holds the keys of heaven and hell, which signify the knowledge of good and evil, and his right hand is raised in the blessing called 'the sign of esotericism', the thumb and the first two fingers pointing upwards, the last two fingers folded on to the palm. This indicates a distinction between 'above' and 'below', God and man, the gold and the base metal, and the Pope is the *pontifex* or 'bridge-builder' who links them. The symbol of Taurus ♉ unites the symbols of sun and moon, ☉ and ☽, the 'above' from which light shines and 'below' which reflects it. Taurus is ruled by Venus and the Pope whose hand is raised in blessing is a symbol of 'the impersonal idea of Love'.

4. *The Emperor* is the *alter ego* of the Pope, the ruler of things material. He stands for worldly authority, organisation, government, law and order, the outward form and arrangement of things. He sits on his throne or leans against it,

holding a sceptre. The arms of the throne end in rams' heads, which come from Aries, the Ram, the sign of virile energy and domination. The Emperor is God or man imposing order and form on things, the Magus who 'declares his law' and dominates all things beneath him. The owl is the bird of Athene, the warrior-goddess of wisdom, and Hokmah is the Wisdom of God.

3. *The Empress* is pregnant, fair-haired and smiling. Her path links Hokmah and Binah, the active and passive or male and female principles in God, and she corresponds to Venus, the goddess of Nature and love. The sparrow and the dove are amorous birds and subject to Venus. The swan is a symbol of satisfied desire, its phallic neck joined to its cteic body. The Empress is often identified with the woman clothed with the sun in Revelation, standing for beauty, pleasure and fertility, the teeming life of Nature. Her pregnancy represents the evolution of godhead from infinite to finite through the creation of the universe. The magician must go through the same evolution to reach Hokmah. He has become one with the godhead in Binah and therefore infinite. On this path he is born again as a being both infinite and finite.

Kether (God), the cabalist's final goal, is reached by the paths of the Fool, the Juggler and the Female Pope. 2. *The Female Pope*, called the High Priestess by occultists, is a dark girl crowned with the triple tiara and the horns of the moon, sitting on a throne between two pillars, one black and one white. The pillars mean duality, opposites and woman. Between them is a veil—the unbroken hymen, virginity. Her path leads from Kether (God) down to Tiphereth (Christ) and in Christian terms she is the Virgin Mary. In occult terms she is *gnosis*, the ultimate knowledge of God, and she is the gateway to heaven (and so corresponds to the moon, which is 'the gateway to heaven' because it is the heavenly body nearest to the earth). Man must penetrate the virgin, or reconcile the opposites in his nature and destroy his own duality, to become the One. The magician will destroy all duality of action in the Fool, all duality of purpose in the Juggler. In the Priestess he destroys all duality of thought. The ultimate knowledge of God, for the cabalist, is the complete knowledge of oneself and in modern psychological terms the Priestess is the virgin unconscious or subconscious. 'It is, so to say, covered by a veil. Only when this veil is rent or penetrated by concentrated impulses originating at the self-conscious level may the creative activities of subconsciousness be released and actualized.'[18] Which is another way of stating the magical doctrine that 'everything rests upon the principle of the stimulation of the inert yet all-potential [the unconscious] by the dynamic principle [the conscious ego] . . .' If unity is not achieved in the mind, the card has a sinister side. The dog is the beast of Hecate, the moon in her most baleful aspect, the pale mistress of death and ghosts, of the virgin and sterile against the impregnated and fruitful.

1. *The Juggler* is called the Magician by occultists. He is the celestial Juggler who keeps the golden balls of life in endless play, a symbol of the single-minded creative will of God and man. One is the number of beginning, the First Cause, the erect phallus, and the swallow stands for spring—the beginning of a cycle, the quickening of life. The ape and the ibis belong to Thoth, the Egyptian equivalent of Mercury, god of magic and intelligence. Vervain is a magically powerful plant and the palm is an emblem of fertility and triumph. In modern psychological interpretations the Juggler is the ego, the conscious directing force in the human personality.

Taken in descending order, the trumps from the Juggler to the Pope recall some of the Gnostic accounts of the creation of the universe and in gipsy tradition these five cards are believed to represent the powers which rule the world.[19] The Juggler may stand for the divine Mind, the true God of Gnosticism, and the Priestess and Empress for the Thought which arose in the Mind. The Priestess is the Thought in its original purity, the Empress is the Thought after it had been impregnated by the Mind to become the mother of all things. Among the lower powers which descended from the Thought was the Demiurge or Cosmocrator, the maker of the visible world. He was sometimes said to be the creator of things material (the Emperor) and also of things spiritual (the Pope), in the sense of conventional religion and morality. Many of the Gnostics believed that the Demiurge was evil and some of them identified him with the Devil. The Emperor's path is a continuation of the Devil's on the Tree and he is called 'Sun of the Morning', which suggests a punning reference to 'Lucifer, son of the morning'. The Pope is also not free of ominous undertones. Simon Magus said that the powers which made the world set up standards of morality as a way of keeping men in bondage to them and Eliphas Levi pointed out that when the hand is raised in the Pope's 'sign of esotericism', the shadow which it casts is the head and horns of the Devil.

Finally, at the head of the major trump comes 0. *The Fool.* He is a jester in motley with a stick and bundle over his shoulder, close to the edge of a great cliff. He is happily chasing a butterfly, not looking where he is going, and his next step will take him over the cliff. A curious animal which may or may not be a large cat is bounding beside him. In the old cards it seems to be biting his leg. He corresponds to the first path, leading from Kether towards the rest of the sephiroth, and to the first Hebrew letter, *aleph*. The *Sepher Yetzirah* links *aleph* with Air. The eagle is lord of the air and the Egyptian hieroglyph for A was an eagle. The Fool is a symbol of foolishness or madness, but his is a divine folly. Air stands for 'spirit' and the Fool is the Spirit of God about to descend into the nothing—falling from the cliff—at the beginning of creation. And the Fool is also the perfected spirit of man approaching the One. The One pervades all things and is free of all limitations. It contains all qualities and yet it has no qualities, for to ascribe any quality to it is to limit it. The Fool is the 0 which contains all things but is no-thing. He is as free, as all-pervading and as insubstantial as the air. 'The wind bloweth where it listeth, and thou hearest the sound thereof, but canst not tell whence it cometh or whither it goeth: so is every one that is born of the Spirit.'[20]

The minor cards of the Tarot are used mainly in fortune-telling. The suit of Swords (Spades) is generally ominous and unlucky. The Nine of Swords is the card of death. The Ten foreshadows pain, sadness, desolation. The Eight means ill health and bad news.

The suit of Coins (Diamonds) naturally stands for money, business, prestige and worldly matters. The Knave of Diamonds is traditionally a card of ill omen and so is the King. There is a story that Joachim Murat, Napoleon's brilliant cavalry leader and the King of Naples, consulted the famous card-reader Mlle Lenormand, cut the pack and turned up the King of Diamonds. He tried three times more and cut the same card each time. He pleaded for another chance, but Mlle Lenormand threw the cards at him and told him he was destined for the gallows or the firing-squad. He was executed by firing-squad in 1815.[21]

The suit of Cups (Hearts) is generally fortunate and stands for love, laughter, happiness, good health. The Ten of Cups means lasting success, the Three pleasure, the Ace beauty and fertility.

Wands (Clubs) are connected with energy, enterprise and activity, probably because the wand is a phallic symbol. The Three of Wands, T. S. Eliot's 'man with three staves', is associated with trade and merchandise involving ships and the sea. 'Fear death by water.'

3. Gematria

Magic has power to experience and fathom things which are inaccessible to human reason. For magic is a great secret wisdom, just as reason is a great public folly.

PARACELSUS *De Occulta Philosophia*

The early Jewish cabalists believed that the Old Testament was directly inspired by God, but with their love of secrecy, their interest in the hidden and contempt for the revealed, they looked for the truth of God's meaning beneath the surface words of the scriptures. Some of them seem to have thought that the Bible was largely written in various kinds of code. To unravel the codes they used mathematical and anagrammatic methods which were of considerable antiquity, but were first brought into prominence in the Cabala by the influential German-Jewish scholar Eleazer of Worms and his followers in the thirteenth century.

One of these methods is *gematria*, which means converting the letters of a word into their number equivalents, adding them up and then substituting another word which adds to the same total. When Abraham was on the plains of Mamre, Genesis says 'and lo three men stood by him'. The Hebrew words for 'and lo three men' add to 701. The words for 'these are Michael, Gabriel and Raphael' also add to 701, so it was deduced that the three men were really the three archangels. 'Shiloh shall come' means 'the Messiah shall come', because Shiloh and Messiah both add to 358. The number 13 means 'love of unity', because the words for 'love' and 'unity' both total 13. A normal pregnancy lasts for 271 days, which is shown by the fact that the letters of *herayon* (pregnancy) add to 271. The ladder which Jacob saw reaching from earth to heaven is Sinai, because both *sulam* (ladder) and Sinai total 130; the law revealed from Sinai is the ladder from heaven to earth. A striking example of a genuine use of this type of code in the Old Testament comes from the Book of Daniel, in which the identity of the Seleucid king Antiochus IV Epiphanes is cloaked under the name Nebuchadnezzar, probably because the Hebrew letters of both names add to 423.

Two other methods are *notarikon*—taking the first or last letters of the words of a phrase and joining them to make a new word or, conversely, expanding a word into a phrase—and *temurah*, which involves anagrams and letter substitutions, taking the last letter of the alphabet for the first, the last but one for the second, or reading L for A, M for B, and so on. A word of power which protects a man against the weapons of his enemies is YHMHYH, which means nothing in itself, but is made of the final letters of the first six Hebrew words of 'Who is like unto thee among the mighty, O Lord?' The first and last letters of the words for 'Who shall go up for us to heaven?' can be formed into the words for 'God' and 'circumcision', which means that God ordained circumcision as the passport to heaven. The first word of the Bible—*berashith*, 'in the beginning'—has been subjected to innumerable twistings and turnings. If each of its letters is taken as the initial letters of a word, one result is 'In the beginning the Elohim [God] saw that Israel would accept the law.' Another is 'Ye shall worship my first-born, my first, whose name is Jesus', one of six examples of notarikon which persuaded a seventeenth-century Jewish cabalist to turn Christian.[22]

Many medieval Christians were convinced that Jews cursed the name of Jesus every day in their prayers. Evidence of this horrid practice was found in a Jewish prayer which mentions 'those who bow down to vanity and emptiness and pray to a god who saveth not'. It was discovered that the words for 'and emptiness' had the same number value as 'Jesus'. The Inquisition frequently blacked this passage out of Jewish prayer books and it was finally left out of the Ashkenazic ritual altogether after Frederick I of Prussia prohibited its use in 1703.[23] During the Second World War, after the German occupation of Greece, Jewish communities in Syria were terrified of invasion. Learned cabalists were consulted and following a night of calculation announced that they had succeeded in rearranging the Hebrew letters of 'Syria' to form 'Russia'. Everyone was much relieved and the Germans invaded Russia soon afterwards.[24]

Christians adopted the Jewish methods early and with enthusiasm. Jesus as Alpha and Omega, the beginning and the end, was symbolised as a dove, because *alpha* and *omega* add to 801 and so does the Greek for 'dove', *peristera*. The fish is a symbol of Christ, partly because the Greek word *icthus*, 'fish', can be expanded by notarikon into *Iesous CHristos THeou Uios Soter*, 'Jesus Christ, the Son of God, the Saviour'. St. Matthew, giving a genealogy of Christ's descent from Abraham and David, says 'So all the generations from Abraham to David are fourteen generations; and from David until the carrying away into Babylon are fourteen generations; and from the carrying away into Babylon unto Christ are fourteen generations.'[25] The number 14 may have been used here because the Hebrew letters of David (DVD) add to 14.

The most famous example of gematria is the Number of the Beast. In the thirteenth chapter of Revelation a beast comes up out of the sea, having seven heads and ten horns and ten crowns and on its heads the name of blasphemy. One of the heads had been 'wounded to death', but the wound had healed. 'Let him that hath understanding count the number of the beast: for it is the number of a man; and his number is Six hundred threescore and six.'

Many attempts have been made to solve this riddle, some of them of a pleasing eccentricity. One answer is that Napoleon was the Beast because the letters of his name make three groups of six—Napole(6) on Buon (6) aparte (6). Macaulay refused to accept this solution and said the House of Commons was obviously the Beast, because it had 658 members plus three clerks, a serjeant and his deputy, a chaplain, a doorkeeper and a librarian, making 666 in all. Other candidates for the honour have been the Pope, Luther, the Kaiser and Hitler. In a recent book—*Babylon Has Fallen!*—Jehovah's Witnesses maintain that the Beast stands for the prevailing political organisation of the world at any given time. When Revelation was written the Beast was the Roman Empire. It is now the United Nations.

Aleister Crowley thought that he was the Beast himself, an opinion in which many of his contemporaries concurred. He said he discovered the fact while still a boy with 'a passionately ecstatic sense of identity'. He often signed himself 'The Beast 666' or TO MEGA THERION, which adds to 666, 'The Great Beast' in Greek.

It is generally accepted now that the Beast was meant to stand for the Roman Empire and its seven heads for seven Emperors. Some manuscripts of Revelation give the number as 616 instead of 666, but this is probably the result of despairing efforts to make the passage fit either Nero or Caligula. The head which was wounded to death but healed looks like a reference to Nero. He was murdered in A.D. 68, but there were persistent rumours that he had risen again, had escaped to the East and would return with an army to take his revenge. At least three men pretending to be Nero appeared in the Near East in the next twenty years. The Hebrew letters of Nero Caesar add to 666 only if it is spelled with an extra N on the end. Without it, the name adds to 616. (The letter *vau* can stand for V or W or, as in this case, long O.)

$$N \quad R \quad V \quad N \quad Q \quad S \quad R$$

$$50 + 200 + 6 + 50 + 100 + 60 + 200 = 666$$

Verse 15 seems to refer to Caligula. It mentions 'the image of the beast', which people were forced to worship. In A.D. 30 Caligula ordered a Statue of himself to be set up in the Holy of Holies, the abode of Jehovah in the Temple at Jerusalem. He died before the order could be carried out, but the intended sacrilege horrified the Jews. Unfortunately, Gaius Caligula Caesar in Hebrew (GS QLGS QSR) only adds to 616, and so does *Gaios Kaisar* in Greek.[26]

Robert Graves provides a most ingenious solution of the riddle in *The White Goddess*. He takes the Latin letters for 666—D.C.L.X.V.I.—and reads them by notarikon as the initial letters of *Domitius Caesar Legatos Xti Violenter Interfecit*, 'Domitius Caesar violently killed the envoys of Christ'. Domitius was the original name of Nero, before he was adopted by the Emperor Claudius.

Gematria is a natural outcome of the belief that the apparent disorderliness of the universe conceals a rational pattern. Numbers and letters are a good basis for such a pattern, because they can both be formed into innumerable different combinations—the innumerable phenomena of the universe—and yet they are orderly and subject to logical rules of behaviour. In Hebrew and Greek numbers and letters are interchangeable and the modern numerologist who analyses your character and destiny by turning your name into a number is following the old principle of gematria.

Modern cabalists value the old methods as ways of discovering the true significance of the 'names of power' which have been handed down to them by tradition, and they also use them to find new names of power. For instance, the name Adam, used as a synonym for 'man', shows that man is God. Its Hebrew letters (ADM) add to 45, which is the total of all the numbers from 1 to 9. These numbers are the basis of all things, because the other numbers merely repeat and develop them. The basis of all things is God and so Adam = 45 = God, or Adam is 'the name of man as a God-concealing form'.

Another example is the great name of power AUMGN, which is Crowley's expansion of the Buddhist *OM*. In Hebrew the letters of AUMGN add to 100. 100 is made of 20+80. The letters for 20 and 80 are *kaph* and *pe* which turned into Greek are the initial letters of *kteis* and *phallos* (corresponding to the Wheel and the Falling Tower in the Tarot). This shows that AUMGN is 'a synthetic glyph of the subtle energies employed in creating the Illusion, or Reflection of Reality, which we call manifested existence' and 'indicates the Magical formula of the Universe as a reverberatory engine for the extension of Nothingness through the device of equilibrated opposites'.

AUMGN can also be analysed letter by letter through its Tarot correspondences; A is the Fool, U or V the Pope, M the Hanged Man, G the Female Pope, N Death. Briefly, A is the One or God, U is the manifestation of the divine in matter, and M is death. So far the word shows a catastrophe, the slaying of the god. But the apparent death in M is followed by G, which is the Knowledge of God, and N—generation and resurrection. The whole word shows a circular formula—God becoming man and man eventually resurrected as God. Armed with this word, the magician has 'a mantra of terrific power by virtue whereof he may apprehend the Universe'.[27]

4. The Names of Power

With the name of *Jod He Vau He* one commands Nature; kingdoms are conquered in the name of Adonai, and the occult forces which compose the empire of Hermes are one and all obedient to him who knows how to pronounce duly the incommunicable name of Agla.

ELIPHAS LEVI *The Key of the Mysteries*

In magical theory the 'real' name of a god or an idea contains the essence of the god or idea, and therefore enshrines its power. Using the name turns on this power automatically, in the same way that pressing the light switch turns on the light. The magician's motives in using the name are neither here nor there. A man's reasons for wanting the light on may be good, bad or indifferent, but they do not affect the supply of electricity.

The New Testament makes it clear that people could use the name of Jesus, or thought they could, to cast out devils and perform other marvellous feats even if they did not follow Jesus or accept his teaching. 'Many will say to me in that day, Lord, Lord, have we not prophesied in thy name? And in thy name have cast out devils? And in thy name done many wonderful works? And then will I profess unto them, I never knew you: depart from me, ye that work iniquity.' In a later passage, when certain Jews are trying to expel a devil, adjuring it by 'Jesus whom Paul preacheth', the devil's reply—'Jesus I know and Paul I know but who are ye?'—is entirely wrong-headed and contrary to all magical principle because a name of power ought to work automatically; but then devils are well known to delight in deception.[28]

In the ancient world there was a widespread belief in the existence of a secret name of infinite power which automatically controlled everything in the universe. A Greek magical incantation invokes a god 'whose hidden name is unspeakable, which when the daimones hear they cower, which when the sun and earth hear they turn about, which when Hades hears he is troubled, rivers, the sea, lakes and springs when they hear it are frozen, rocks when they hear it are broken'.[29] The name controls even the gods themselves. An Assyrian inscription of the seventh century B.C., itself was a translation of a much older text, describes how the great god Ea was called on for help against the seven terrible demons called *maskim*—those who lie in ambush. Ea says he is the only being who knows the supreme magical name. 'When it is uttered everything bows down in heaven, on earth and in the infernal regions. And this name alone can subdue the *maskim* and stay their havoc. The gods themselves are bound by this name and obey it.'[30]

In Jewish tradition the secret name of infinite power is the 'real' name of the God of the Old Testament. The *Sepher Yetzirah* explains that what God did in creating the universe was to 'engrave his name' and the *Zohar* says that the ten sephiroth 'constitute the sacred name of God', because God constructed the universe by extending his own identity. The real name of God *is* God, it *is* the universe and it contains and controls all things. The search for this name is one of the major preoccupations of cabalistic magic.

The Bible supplies several names of God which have been used in magic by Jews and Christians, including El, Elohim, Eloa, Sabaoth, Shaddai, Adonai, Jehovah, Yah and Ehyeh. El was an ordinary word for god in Phoenician and Assyrian as well as in Hebrew. Elohim, which is plural, and its singular Eloa were also common words for god in Hebrew and the same root appears in Aramaic and Arabic terms for god. Sabaoth is usually translated as 'Lord of Hosts', Shaddai as 'the Almighty', Adonai as 'the Lord'. Basically, all these names merely mean 'a god'.

The *personal* name of the God of the Old Testament is the Tetragrammaton, or name of four letters—יהוה, YHVH (*yod he vau he*, written from right to left in Hebrew). This is the name which appears as Jehovah in many versions of the Bible. It is a form of the verb 'to be' (*he vau he*) and means 'he is', 'he exists'. The first person form is Ehyeh, 'I am', revealed to Moses at the burning bush—*Ehyeh Asher Ehyeh*, 'I Am That I Am'. Yah or Jah comes from the same root and may be an early form of YHVH.

The Tetragrammaton has been held in great awe from very early times. The Jews were reluctant to pronounce it, out of respect and possibly for fear of hostile magic. It came to be spoken rarely and so softly that it could not be heard. By the time of Christ the Tetragrammaton was spoken once a year by the High Priest when he entered the Holy of Holies on the Day of Atonement and also, inaudibly, during the Priestly Blessing (Numbers 6.24-27) after the daily services in the Temple. In the ordinary services it was not pronounced at all and wherever it appeared in the scriptures it was read as Adonai (Lord) or Elohim (God). The result is that for hundreds of years no one has been quite certain how it should be pronounced. Jehovah is a medieval rendering and almost certainly does not coincide with any pronunciation of the name ever used in Hebrew. Modern scholars generally plump for Yahweh.

From the magical point of view, it is fitting that the name of God should be made of four letters, because it was the name used to construct the universe and 4 is the number of the way in which all things are constructed and organised. As the personal name of God and because of the awe with which it is surrounded, the Tetragrammaton has always been a particularly important name of power in magic. Some occultists have claimed to know its true pronunciation, but this is a secret of secrets, a great arcanum of the mysteries, revealed to none but the *élite*.

The Tetragrammaton and other biblical names of God are used in every type of conjuration, spell and magical operation. The *Key of Solomon* recommends a talisman which must be engraved on copper, the metal of Venus, to attract love. In the centre of a circle are two triangles with the divine names YHVH and ADNY (Adonai), three names of angels—Monachiel, Achides, Delgaliel—and the name Ruach, 'Spirit'. (The *Ruach Elohim*, the Spirit of God, broods on the waters at the beginning of Genesis.) The words in the surrounding circle are a garbled Latin version of Genesis 1.28, referring to Adam and Eve—'And God blessed them and God said unto them, Be fruitful and multiply and replenish the earth.' The sexual force inherent in these words, backed up by the power of the divine and angelic names, will arouse passion in any woman to whom this talisman is shown. Six names of power are used and the hour-glass design in the centre of the talisman has six sides. Six is the number of female love.

A grimoire called the *Grimorium Verum* says that the magician's inkwell should have the names YOD HE VAU HE, METATRON, YOD, CADOS, ELOYM, SABAOTH inscribed on it, to infuse divine power in the ink and to ward off evil influences. Metatron is the name of the angel who guided the Israelites through the wilderness and is interchangeable with Shaddai (the Almighty) because both add to 314. Cados is Hebrew *Kadosh*, 'the Holy One', a

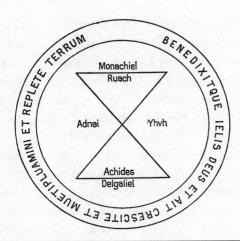

Monachiel
Ruach

Adnai   Yhvh

Achides
Delgaliel

(Circular text around talisman:) BENEDIXITQUE IELIS DEUS ET AIT CRESCITE ET MUETIPLUAMINI ET REPLETE TERRUM

DIAGRAM 5   Love Talisman from the *Key of Solomon*
(After Idries Shah, *The Secret Lore of Magic*)

title of God. Eloym is Elohim. (Brief details of the grimoires are given in Appendix 1.)

The biblical names of God, even the Tetragrammaton, did not satisfy magicians and constant search was made for the elusive 'real' name. The letters of the Tetragrammaton were rearranged in various permutations, by temurah—YVHH, YHHV, HVHY. Vowels were added to the consonants in various ways, to produce YAHAVAHA or YEHEVEH, for instance. Sometimes the letters of two divine names were mixed together, as in the name of power YAHD VNHY, an anagram of YHVH ADNY, Jehovah Adonai. In the early centuries after Christ names of God of 12, 42 and 72 letters or syllables were discovered and later still names of 8, 10, 14, 16, 18, 21, 22, 32 and 60 letters.

The name of 22 letters, a suitable number, since 22 means 'everything', first appears in the thirteenth-century *Sepher Raziel* (Book of the Angel Raziel), attributed to Eleazar of Worms. The name is ANQTM PSTM PSPSYM DYVN-SYM and is probably a permutation of letters from the words of the Priestly Blessing—'The Lord bless thee and keep thee: the Lord make his face to shine upon thee: the Lord lift up his countenance upon thee and give thee peace.' The name has no discernible meaning and contains no words known in Hebrew or Aramaic. The pronunciation is uncertain, but may have been *Anaktam Pastam Paspasim Dionsim*.[31]

The name of 42 letters is ABGYTS (possible pronounced *Abgitaz* or *Abigtaz*)

QDASTN NGDYBS BTDSTG HQDTNA YGLPZQ SQVSYT (possibly *Shakvazit* or *Shekuzit*). This is probably a rearrangement of the first 42 letters of the Bible and again has no known meaning. According to a fifteenth-century story, a cabalist called Joseph della Rayna tried to use the 42-letter name to gain power over the arch-devil Sammael (the angel who wrestled with Jacob) and his lieutenant Ammon of No. The two devils were forced to appear by means of a ring engraved with the names of power. They came in the form of fearsome snakes and Joseph's helpers ran away in terror. Joseph stood firm and placed on the head of Sammael a brass crown on which the name of 42 letters was written, saying 'Thy Master's Name is upon thee.' Sammael was vanquished, but cunningly persuaded the cabalist to seal the victory by burning incense to him. But this was an act of idolatry and it automatically freed the devils.[32]

The longest and some say the most powerful of the names of God is the name of 72 syllables, the Shemhamphorash or 'pre-eminent name', a title originally given to the Tetragrammaton. It comes from Exodus 14: 19-21, the passage about the Israelites crossing the Red Sea as the waters divided, with the chariots of Pharaoh in pursuit. Each of these three verses has 72 letters in Hebrew. They are written boustrophedon—verse 19 from right to left, underneath it verse 20 from left to right, and below this again verse 21 from right to left. Starting at the top right-hand corner and reading downwards, 72 syllables of three letters each are read off. The first syllable contains the first letter of verse 19, the last letter of verse 20 and the first letter of verse 21, and so on. According to tradition, Moses spoke this name at the Red Sea and its powerful force which parted the waters and allowed the Israelites to cross. The name's pronunciation is unknown and it is too unwieldy to be much used in magic.

One of the first great Christian cabalists, John Reuchlin, who lived in the fifteenth and early sixteenth centuries and whose books profoundly influenced Agrippa, pointed out that the name of 72 syllables is mathematically a derivative of the Tetragrammaton. The Tetragrammaton letters with their number equivalents are:

Y	H	V	H
10	5	6	5

$Y = 10$, $YH = 15$, $YHV = 21$, $YHVH = 26$, and if these totals are added, $10+15+21+26 = 72$. Reuchlin also said that the name of Jesus (the Pentagrammaton) is more powerful than the Tetragrammaton, because it adds the letter S to it—IHVH becomes IHSVH, Jesus (the letter *yod* can be read as Y, I or J). S is a letter of power because *Ruach Elohim*, 'the Spirit of God', adds to 300 and the letter *shin* (S) has the number value of 300, so that S stands for the Holy Spirit.

Magicians in search of names which contained power did not confine themselves to the Old Testament, and the rituals in the grimoires use names drawn from Jewish, Christian, Egyptian, Greek and Latin sources. A tremendous conjuration in the *Lemegeton* or *Lesser Key of Solomon* commands a demon to appear by an awe-inspiring battery of powerful names, including Y and V, which God revealed to Adam; Joth, which Jacob learned from the angel with whom he wrestled; Agla, which Lot heard and was saved from the destruction of Sodom; Schemes Amathia, which Joshua spoke and the sun stood still in the sky; Emmanuel, which Shadrach, Meshach and Abednego cried out in the burning fiery furnace and were preserved from the flames; Alpha and Omega, with which Daniel destroyed Bel and the dragon; Sabaoth, the name with which Moses brought down the plague of frogs upon the Egyptians; Escerchie Ariston, which turned the rivers of Egypt to blood; Elion, which brought the plague of hail; the names Hagios, Jetros and Paracletus; the three holy and secret names Agla, On and Tetragrammaton; and the name Primematum, which Moses uttered and the earth opened and swallowed up Corah, Dathan and Abiram.

Y and V are two of the Tetragrammaton letters and Joth is a variant of its first letter, *yod*. Agla, a great name of power which is frequently used in magic, is made by notarikon from the initial letters of the Hebrew phrase *Aieth Gadol Leolam Adonai*, 'Thou art mighty for ever, O Lord.' Medieval German Jews believed that if this name was written on a wooden plate and the plate thrown into a fire it would put the fire out. They explained this by expanding the name by reverse notarikon into *Allmächtiger Gott, Lösch' Aus*, 'Almighty God, extinguish it'.

Schemes Amathia is 'sun, be silent'. Shemesh was the name of the Canaanite sun-god and Shamash was the Babylonian sun-god. The reference is to Joshua's command, 'Sun, stand thou still upon Gibeon', which in Hebrew is 'Sun, be dumb upon Gibeon'. Emmanuel means 'God with us' and occurs only three times in the Old Testament, but it was later used as a title of Christ. Alpha and Omega are the first and last letters of the Greek alphabet and imply 'everything' and 'God' because they contain the whole alphabet between them—'I am Alpha and Omega, the first and the last', says the risen Christ in

Revelation. Escerchie Ariston comes from the Greek words *ischuros*, 'strong, mighty', and *aristos*, 'the best, the noblest'. Elion is a Hebrew title of God—*El Elyon*, 'God Most High'. Hagios is the Greek word for 'holy' and Jetros is Greek for 'the healer'. Paracletus is the Holy Ghost, the comforter of St. John's gospel—'And I will pray the Father, and he shall give you another Comforter, that he may abide with you for ever.' On was another name for the ancient Egyptian city of Heliopolis, at which the sun was worshipped. The priests of Heliopolis maintained that it was the centre of the earth and the place from which supreme power on earth ought to be exercised. Primematum is Latin for 'first made' or 'new made'. Referring to Corah, Dathan and Abiram, Moses told the Israelites, 'But if the Lord *make a new thing* and the earth open her mouth and swallow them up . . . then ye shall understand that these men have pro-voked the Lord.'[33]

Many of the names of power which roar and thunder through the rituals have no discernible meaning and their origin is unknown. A grimoire called the *Black Pullet* recommends various apparently meaningless names of power. To call up all the powers of heaven and hell the names are Siras Etar Besanar; to discover hidden treasures Onaim Perantes Rasonastos; to open any lock at a touch Saritap Pernisox Ottarim. The *Egyptian Secrets of Albertus Magnus*, which could scarcely have been written by the great thirteenth-century philosopher, reaches a high peak of unintelligibility with a charm to cure erysipelas in cattle. Write the following letters on an egg and give it to the afflicted animal to eat:

K a o r k S S O r E z o n r h

a r K O C tz tz a h u r o x K a o tz a

E a E S x i i x a r o t t o x

These letters may be an anagram of various names of power or they may be the initial letters of the names or they may be just a muddle. An anagram of Tarot can be seen in the last line.

The use of unintelligible and barbarous words in magic goes back to the Egyptian magicians who invented peculiar and scarcely pronounceable 'real' names for their gods, probably to prevent rival magicians from pronouncing them. The habit passed into western Europe through the Graeco-Egyptian magical texts of the early centuries after Christ, which are full of twisted and contorted names of no known meaning as well as Egyptian, Greek and Jewish names of gods and angels.

In some cases names of power have been altered deliberately, to conceal the real name or discover a better one, and in others the names have been muddled in translation or in being passed from one magician to another. A modern occult group were puzzled by the name of power Tegatoo, which they were trying to use, until they discovered that it was the battered remains of 'The Great Architect of the Universe'.[34] Another example is the name Pipi, which is a defence against evil and, if written on a shelled hard-boiled egg, opens the heart to wisdom and learning. One early alteration of the Tetragrammaton transformed to YHYH—יחיה. People accustomed to reading Greek, which, unlike Hebrew, is written from left to right, saw this as the Greek letters πιπι, pipi. Pipi eventually came back into Jewish magic from Greek as a name of power.

Another source of meaningless words in magic is the love of rhythm, rhyme and assonance. The following method of healing a fractured or dislocated bone comes from Cato the Censor's book *On Agriculture*, written in the second century B.C. Take a green reed about four or five feet long. Split it down the middle and have two assistants hold the pieces against your hips. Then chant *Motas vaeta daries dardares astateries dissunapiter*. Meanwhile, bring the ends of the split reed together in front of you, waving a knife above them. Hold the ends together and cut left and right. Then tie the pieces round the injured bone, repeating the same words or alternatively *Huat haut haut istasis tarsis ardannabou dannaustra*.

The chanted words have no meaning. Their virtue lies in the fact that they sound impressive. The *Egyptian Secrets* provide a very necessary charm 'To prevent a Person from Firing a Gun while you are looking into the Barrel'. Simply say *Pax Sax Sarax*. An early medieval cure for toothache is to say *Argidem Margidem Sturgidem* seven times on a Tuesday or a Thursday, providing the moon is waning (so that the toothache will wane, too).

Although nonsense-words like these are used only in magical operations of a low and simple order, the whole magical art of incantation depends heavily on impressive sound. The *Grimoire of Honorius* threatens a recalcitrant demon with:

If you do not obey promptly and without tarrying, I will shortly increase your torments for a thousand years in hell. I constrain you therefore to appear here in comely human shape, by the Most High Names of God, HAIN,

LON, HILAY, SABAOTH, HELIM, RADISHA, LEDIEHA, ADONAY, JE-
HOVAH, YAH, TETRAGRAMMATON, SADAI, MESSIAS, AGIOS, IS-
CHYROS, EMMANUEL, AGLA, Jesus who is ALPHA and OMEGA, the
beginning and the end, that you be justly established in the fire, having no
power to reside, habit or abide in this place henceforth; and I require your
doom by the virtue of the said Names, that St. Michael drive you to the
uttermost of the infernal abyss, in the Name of the Father, and of the Son,
and of the Holy Ghost. So be it.[35]

The magician works himself up into a state of ecstatic frenzy by intoning
words which roar and beat and swell and reverberate. The words must never
be said flatly, but rhythmically chanted. The sorcerers of classical times spoke
their incantations in a long ululation like the howl of a wolf. The strangeness
of the words used increases their self-hypnotising effect. 'The peculiar mental
excitement required', Aleister Crowley said, 'may even be aroused by the perception of the absurdity of the process and the persistence in it.' At the end of
his resources on one occasion, he recited 'From Greenland's Icy Mountains'
and obtained the desired results.[36]

There is no question that human beings are affected by the sound of certain
words and combinations of words. Effective oratory and verbal love-making
both rely partly on the pitch of the voice and the sound of the words used. Poetry
affects us through its sound and magicians generally prefer poetry which is
distinguished for its magnificence of sound. Crowley greatly admired Swinburne and his own verse was decidedly Swinburnian. In magical theory, if the
sound of certain words affects human beings, as it does, the same sounds will
affect the forces of the universe, for the universe is man on a greater scale.

Which combinations of sound will be effective can only be discovered by
trial and error. It is not enough to know the spelling of a name of power. It is
essential to discover the correct pronunciation, to produce the correct sound.
The correct sound can only be learned by trying out different pronunciations
until the magician finds the one which works.

To be able to pronounce effectively the very greatest of the names of power,
like Agla or the Tetragrammaton, is a mark of the master of the magic arts.
Crowley claimed that he knew how to pronounce 'the lost Tetragrammaton', at
the utterance of which the whole universe crashes into dissolution. He did not
explain the point, but his lost Tetragrammaton was probably the 'real' name of

God pronounced backwards. The real name of God was used to construct the universe. To speak it backwards is to reverse the process and destroy the universe. Similarly, the real name of the Devil is supposed to be the real name of God spelled backwards. One version of it is *Havayoth*.

In magic as in poetry, the effect a word creates is produced by the combination of its sound and its meaning, and the two things cannot really be disentangled from each other. Forceful words, impressively spoken and backed by authority—the commands of a drill-sergeant for instance—have a powerful effect on those who hear them. Magicians believe that in the same way forceful words, backed by the authority of the magician's will, have a powerful effect in magic. In some magical operations the words of an incantation are expected to be effective by themselves, with little or no other ceremonial.

An eighteenth-century French method of forcing a woman to submit to you is to touch any part of her body and chant *Bestarbeto corrumpit viscera ejus mulieris*, 'Bestarbeto weakens the innards of his woman'. *Corrumpo* means to weaken or to corrupt and is used here in the sense of turning the woman's insides to water. Bestarbeto is an obscure demonic or angelic power of some kind, but the real force of the charm is simply in the meaning of the words themselves. The fact that they are in Latin adds to their impressiveness.

A bathotic example of the supposed power of words to command demonic forces is a spell found by the Manchester police in 1865, when searching the house of an astrologer and magician called John Rhodes. It says, 'I adjure and command you, ye strong, mighty and most powerful spirits, who are rulers of this day and hour, that ye obey me in this my cause of placing my husband in his former situation under the Trent Brewery Company.'[37]

A conjuration in a British Museum manuscript for compelling an obstinate demon to appear relies mainly on the names of power which are used and the force of the words of the incantation. A fire is built of brimstone, dried manure and any other stinking stuff. The demon's name is written on virgin parchment and burned in the fire. The magician prays to God, by his just judgement against the serpent of Eden, to condemn and curse the disobedient demon. Then he appeals to the power of hell.

O thou most puissant prince Rhadamanthus, which dost punish in thy prison of perpetual perplexity the disobedient devils of hell, and also the grisly ghosts of men dying in dreadful despair, I conjure, bind and charge thee by Lucifer, Belsabub, Sathanas, Jauconill and by their power, and by the homage thou owest unto them, and also I charge thee by the triple crown of Cerberus his head, by Stix and Phlegiton, by your fellow and private devil Baranter, that you do torment and punish this disobedient N. until you make him come corporally to my sight and obey my will and command-ments in whatsoever I shall charge or command him to do. fiat. fiat. fiat. Amen.

Rhadamanthus was one of the judges of the underworld in Greek mythology. He was the younger brother of Minos, King of Crete, and the son of Zeus and Europa, who was carried off by Zeus in the form of a bull. Cerberus was the three-headed dog which guarded the gate of Hades. The Styx was the princi-pal river of the underworld, round which it flowed seven times. Phlegethon was another underworld river, made of flames instead of water. *Fiat* means 'let it be so', as does Amen, but Amen is a name of power in itself because its He-brew letters (AMN) add to 91 and Jehovah Adonai also adds to 91. In Greek, Amen adds to 99 and some early Christian manuscripts put 99 at the end of prayers, to signify Amen.

From the powers of hell, the magician turns to the reluctant demon him-self. (At the sign + the magician makes the sign of the cross.)

O thou most disobedient spirit N., I condemn thee by the virtue and power of the three most dreadful and mighty names of God Agla + On + Tetragrammaton + into the hands of these princes Lucifer, Satanas, Belsa-bub, Jauconill, to be tormented in the bottomless pit of hell for thy stubborn-ness, wilfulness, disobedience and rebellion: and furthermore as Christ Jesus cast out devils by the power of his divine godhead, by that power of Christ Jesus I cast thee into the tormenting pit of fire and brimstone until the latter day of judgement, except thou be obedient to fulfil my will and com-mandment in all things I have or shall ask or demand of thee, without any deceit, falsehood or delay. In nomine Patris + filii + et Spiriti Sancti + Amen. fiat. fi. fi.[38]

The author of this process has combined the names of power with language which is impressive in sound and clear in meaning into an incantation which expresses his will and which, he hopes, will effect it. Language is one of the supreme magical weapons. Through his use of language the magician taps the power of occult forces or intelligences, intoxicates himself into a frenzy in which his own powers are raised to their highest pitch, and expresses his commands in forceful words. At the back of his mind there is always the example of the great magical act in which the universe was created by the speaking of words. 'God said, Let there be light; and there was light.' Ideally, as Eliphas Levi said, 'In magic to have said is to have done.'

Some names of power shrink and expand. The best known of them is Abracadabra, which Defoe mentions in his *Journal of the Plague Year.* He said that many people behaved as if the plague was the result of possession by an evil spirit and believed they could ward it off by crossing themselves or with papers tied in knots, the signs of the zodiac or words and figures, especially the word Abracadabra written in a triangle. The word has been so widely used in magic that it has passed into the dictionary as a term for magical mumbo-jumbo in general, but it is still highly regarded by modern magicians.

The earliest mention of the word comes from Quintus Serenus Sammonicus, a doctor who was with the Emperor Severus on his expedition to Britain in 208. He was the author of a poem, which was well known in the Middle Ages, in which he says that Abracadabra is a cure for tertian fever. It should be written on a piece of paper, which must hang round the patient's neck for nine days and then thrown backwards over the shoulder into a stream running eastwards. The usual way of writing the word is:

ABRACADABRA
ABRACADABR
ABRACADAB
ABRACADA
ABRACAD
ABRACA
ABRAC
ABRA
ABR
AB
A

When the word is hung round the patient's neck his fever will gradually shrink away to nothing just as the word does. If the charm fails to work, Serenus recommends lion's fat or yellow coral with green emeralds attached to the skin of a cat and worn round the neck. These remedies seem to be connected with the sun. The lion and yellow both belong to the sun (and a stream flowing eastwards towards the rising sun). The sun supplies the world with heat and heat is the principal characteristic of fever.

Eliphas Levi makes great play with the 'magic triangle' of Abracadabra. Its eleven letters combine 1, the initiate, with 10, 'all things'. The first A is the One, AB shows the fertilisation of the Two by the One, from which all things were created. The next letter, R, shows 'the emission which results from the union of the two principles'. This is because, in Levi's system, R corresponds to the Moon in the Tarot. The drops of blood which fall from the moon are the 'emission' which follows the penetration of the virgin Two.[39]

The origin of Abracadabra is unknown and most of the attempts made to translate or explain it are not impressive. It may be connected with a Jewish charm to cure fevers, which goes:

> Ab Abr Abra Abrak Abraka
> Abrakal Abrakala Abrakal
> Abraka Abrak Abra Abr Ab
> 'And the people called unto Moses and Moses
> prayed to God and the fire abated.' [Numbers 11: 2]
> May healing come from heaven from all kinds of
> fever and consumption-heat to N. son of N.
> Amen Amen Amen. Selah Selah Selah.[40]

This charm must also be hung round the sufferer's neck. Its effect is to build up the heat of the fever to breaking-point and then gradually diminish it. Another Jewish charm involving a shrinking word, sometimes used against diseases of the eye, is Shabriri Briri Riri Iri Ri. Shabirir is a demon and the charm decreases his power by whittling away his name. In other cases a magician may build a name up, with the effect of steadily increasing power—ton rammaton grammaton ragrammaton tragrammaton Tetragrammaton. The *Key of Solomon* describes a crown which the magician must wear, in which is written Agla Aglai Aglata Aglatai.

Words or groups of words which read the same both forwards and backwards are powerful in magic. A palindrome has unusual force because it remains more determinedly itself than an ordinary word, which becomes gibberish if read backwards. For instance:

```
M  I  L  O  N
I  R  A  G  O
L  A  M  A  L
O  G  A  R  I
N  O  L  I  M
```

If you write this on parchment and place it on top of your head, the spirits will secretly reveal to you the truth of all things past, present and future. The square remains the same whether you read it downwards, upwards, from the left or from the right, and it is this which gives it its magic power. This is one of the magic squares from *The Sacred Magic of Abramelin the Mage*, which MacGregor Mathers translated and which influenced both Mathers and Crowley. The manuscript is in French and was written in the eighteenth century, but it is dated 1458 and claims to be a translation from an original in Hebrew.

The central doctrine of Abramelin is that the universe is populated by hordes of angels and demons. All the phenomena of the world are produced by the demons, working under the direction of the angels. The Nature of man is midway between the angelic and the demonic, and each man has attached to him a guardian angel and a malevolent demon. (This idea is much older than Abramelin.)

Abramelin says that initiates of 'the Magic of Light' can master and control the demons. This is achieved by a powerful will, purity and asceticism, and the use of words arranged in magic squares and written on parchment. With these squares the magician can acquire all knowledge and wisdom, the love of anyone he desires, and all hidden treasures, including statuary and ancient works of art. He can make himself invisible, cause spirits to appear and obey him, and create a zombie by reviving a corpse and making it behave as if it was alive for seven years. He can fly in the air—as a cloud, eagle, crow, crane or vulture. He can heal diseases, alter his sex, age and appearance, and cause hatred, discord, battles and general loss and damage.

Abramelin's squares are marred by the unfortunate fact that there are very few words in any language which fit the requirements of a magic square. Mathers explains that the words in the squares 'represent generally the effect to be produced or in other words are simply the Hebrew or other appellations of the result to which the square is to be applied', but he had little success in translating the words and many of them seemed to be meaningless collections of letters, arranged to read the same in all directions. Some of the squares do not even meet this requirement.

(a) R O L O R
    O B U F O
    L U A U L
    O F U B O
    R O L O R

(b) N A Q I D
    A Q O R I
    Q O R O Q
    I R O Q A
    D I Q A N

(c) S I N A H
    I R A T A
    N
    A X I R O
    H A R O Q

(d) C A S E D
    A Z O T E
    B O R O S
    E T O S A
    D E B A C

(e) S A L O M
    A R E P O
    L E M E L
    O P E R A
    M O L A S

Square (a) is for flying in the air in the form of a crow. Rolor may come from Hebrew *rol*, 'to move hurriedly'. (b) is used to gain the love of a girl who is promised to another and Naqid may mean 'remote offspring'. (c) is for causing a general war. Sinah means 'hatred'. The next square is the most sinister of all the Abramelin squares. The author says solemnly that 'this symbol should never be made use of' and goes on to explain that it should be buried in a place where the victim of the spell will walk over it. Mathers interpreted it as Cased—overflowing of unrestrained lust; Azote—enduring; Boros—devouring gluttonous; Etosa—idle, useless; Debac—to overtake and stick close. Square (e), which wins the love of a maiden if touched to her bare skin, is very like the most famous of all magic squares, the Sator formula:

S A T O R
A R E P O
T E N E T
O P E R A
R O T A S

This square was found scratched on fragments of wall plaster from a Roman villa in Cirencester. It has also been found inscribed on ancient drinking vessels and in bibles of the Carolingian period. The *Egyptian Secrets* recommend it for finding witches, because no witch can stay in the same room with it; for protecting cow's milk against witchcraft; for colic and against pestilence, poisonous air and sorcery. Like Agla, the Sator formula was believed to have the power of extinguishing a fire if written on a wooden plate and thrown into the flames. In 1742 in Saxony it was ordered that plates bearing this formula were to be kept handy for fire-fighting. A manuscript in the Bodleian says that the Sator square will magically obtain anything you want—'Write these words in parchment with the blood of a Culver [pigeon] and bear it in thy left hand and ask what thou wilt and thou shalt have it. fiat.'[41]

Many attempts have been made to translate the Sator square, without noticeably illuminating results. One version is 'Arepo, the sower (*sator*), delays (*tenet*) the wheels (*rotas*) by his works (*opera*)'. Another is 'the sower is at the plough (*arepo*), the work occupies the wheels'. Mathers interpreted it as 'the Creator (*sator*), slow moving (*arepo*), maintains (*tenet*) His creations (*opera*) as vortices (*rotas*)'. It is now generally accepted that the formula cannot be translated in this way at all. It is probably a Christian charm, an anagram of *Pater noster* and the letters A and O, twice repeated, so that it contains the first two words of the Lord's Prayer with Alpha and Omega, the first and the last, a symbol of Christ.

Magic squares containing numbers have played a less prominent part in magic than those which contain letters. The cabalists say that each planet has a magic square which can be used to attract the planet's influence. The squares of Saturn and Jupiter are:

Saturn				Jupiter			
4	9	2		4	14	15	1
3	5	7		9	7	6	12
8	1	6		5	11	10	8
				16	2	3	13

In a properly constructed square each number from 1 to the highest number used must appear once. Whether the numbers are added vertically or horizontally, each column must add to the same total. The Saturn square is the oldest magic square known and appears in the Chinese *I Ching*. It has three rows of three figures, because Saturn is the third sephira and similarly the square of Jupiter, which is the fourth sephira, has four rows of four figures.

The square of the sun has six rows of six figures, using the numbers from 1 to 36, and if all the figures in the square are added the total is 666. The deduction which magicians draw from this is that the Beast of Revelation is one aspect of the sun or the life-force. It is the savage, relentless pulsing power which drives all living things to procreate, to survive, to master their environment.

Modern magicians tend to be particularly fond of Graeco-Egyptian names of power, inherited from the Gnostic sects. The Christian cabalists of the Renaissance were fascinated by various Gnostic writings believed to have been written by Hermes Trismegistus, the supposed author of the Emerald Table. The bulk of these formed a collection called the *Corpus Hermeticum*, part of which was first translated into Latin and published in 1471. The Renaissance cabalists found in these 'Hermetic' books many of the occult theories which they also discovered in the Cabala, and the interest in Gnosticism has affected cabalistic magic ever since.

Among their numerous peculiarities, the Gnostics were addicted to tongue-twisting names of power involving batteries of consonants and strings of apparently senseless vowels. In a Gnostic book called *Pistis Sophia*, written in Coptic, a mixture of Egyptian and Greek, Jesus stands at the edge of the sea and prays to God.

> Hear me, my Father, the Father of every fatherhood, the boundless Light, Iao iuo iao uia psinother theropsin nopsither nephthomaoth nephiomaoth marakhakhtha marmarakhtha iaeu amen aman aman eitou ouraou ista amen amen soubaibi appaap amen amen deraaraiapaou amen amen sarsasartou amen amen koukiamiumiai amen amen iai iai touap amen amen amen main mari marie amen amen amen.

The high importance attached to the seven Greek vowels probably comes partly from the fact that there are seven of them and partly from the concealment of the vowels in written Hebrew. Vowels, which are hidden, are obviously of greater interest and importance than consonants, which are openly revealed. One Gnostic version of the 'real' name of God is, in English letters, Iaōŏūĕe.

Eliphas Levi and MacGregor Mathers were both enraptured by all things Graeco-Egyptian, but Aleister Crowley was the most thoroughgoing Gnostic of modern magicians. His important ritual called *Liber Samekh* is a genuine Graeco-Egyptian magical text with additions and alterations by Crowley himself.[42] In this ritual the magician recites a long string of names of power, including Iao and Iaeo, which are Gnostic equivalents of the Tetragrammaton,

Adonai and Sabaoth, which were both frequently used by the Gnostics, and Abraxas or Abrasax, a Gnostic deity whose name adds up to 365, the number of days in the year.

Some of the other names of power used, with Crowley's interpretations of their meaning, are SOTOU—'Thou, the Savior!' (from Greek *soter*, 'saviour'); AR—'O breathing, flowing Sun!' (Ra, the name of the Egyptian sun-god, backwards); ATHOREBALO—'Thou Goddess of Beauty and Love, whom Satan, beholding, desireth!' (Hathor was an Egyptian goddess, daughter of Ra); MRIODOM—'Thou the sea, the Abode!'; AROGOGORUABRAO—'Thou spiritual Sun! Satan, Thou Eye, Thou Lust!" A—'Thou Air! Breath! Spirit!' (from the Fool of the Tarot who corresponds to *aleph* and Air); AEOOU—'Our lady of the Western Gate of Heaven!'; OOO—'Satan, thou Eye, thou Lust!' (the Hebrew letter *ayin*, O, corresponds to the Devil in the Tarot and traditionally represents an eye); PHOTETH—'Abode of the Light!' (from Greek *phos*, 'light'); MA—'O Mother! O Truth!' (Ma was the Egyptian goddess of truth); GAIA—'Leap up, thou Earth!' (Gaea was a Greek goddess, a personification of the earth).

Crowley called this ritual *Liber Samekh* because the Hebrew letter *samekh* corresponds to Temperance in the Tarot, a symbol of orgasm and the soul's passage from a lower plane to a higher. He added the subtitles *Theurgia Goetia Summa*, 'High Supernatural Black Magic' (the second section of the grimoire called the *Lemegeton* is entitled *Theurgia Goetia*) and *Congressus cum Daemone*, 'Intercourse with the Demon', and described it as 'the Ritual employed by the Beast 666 for the Attainment of the Knowledge and Conversation of his Holy Guardian Angel'. This angel is an aspect of the magician's unconscious self and so is the demon of the subtitle. 'It is said among men that the word Hell deriveth from the word 'helan', to hele or conceal, in the tongue of the Anglo-Saxons. That is, it is the concealed place, which since all things are in thine own self, is the unconscious.' To know the angel and have intercourse with the demon, which are the attendant spirits of Abramelin the Mage, means to summon up and liberate the forces of the magician's unconscious. The performance of the ritual is accompanied by masturbation and the mounting frenzy with which the barbarous names of power are chanted is paralleled by rising sexual excitement, ending in a climax which is both physical and psychological and in which the magician's innermost powers are unleashed.

Crowley produced the final version of the *Liber Samekh* in 1921 for one of his pupils at the abbey of Thelema in Sicily—Brother Progradior, whose name among men was Frank Bennett, an ex-bricklayer in his fifties.[43] Progradior ('I will advance') was troubled by mysterious voices which he heard speaking to him and by painful headaches. Crowley believed with the Freudians that the principal cause of psychological troubles is the inhibition of unconscious sex-drives. The frenzy of the ritual was intended to overwhelm the conscious mind and sweep inhibitions away in the rising and swirling tides of the unconscious.

But the *Liber Samekh* is much more than a method of taking the libido out for a run. It is a ceremony in which the magician asserts his divine power and his mastery of the universe. The sexual force of the male is the human parallel to the creative power of God. In fact, raised to its highest pitch and directed by the will, the male generative force *is* divine creative power. The liberation of this force releases the power which controls all things in the universe. As the magician chants the barbarous names of power in the ritual, he creates 'vibrations'—sound waves in this case, charged with energy—which flow out from him and affect everything they touch. By vibrating the names in all directions, while turning inside his magic circle, he believes that he is radiating into the entire universe the power which he has called up from the recesses of his being. 'Come thou forth,' the magician commands the angel-demon which is his inner self, 'come thou forth and follow me: and make all Spirits subject unto Me so that every Spirit of the Firmament, and of the Ether, upon the Earth or under the Earth: on dry Land, or in the Water: of Whirling Air or of rushing Fire, and every Spell and Scourge of God, may be obedient unto me.'

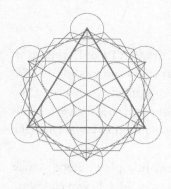

CHAPTER FOUR

The Stone and the Elixir

I N 1562 Agrippa wrote to a friend, 'Blessed be the Lord, I am a rich man, if there be truth in fable. A man of consideration, long my friend, has brought me seeds of gold and planted them over my furnace within long-necked flasks, putting underneath a little fire as of the sun's heat, and as hens brood over eggs we keep the warmth up night and day, expecting forthwith to produce enormous golden chicks. If all be hatched we shall exceed Midas in wealth, or at least in length of ears. . . .'[1]

This humorously deprecating attitude to alchemy was not shared by governments and kings, who pursued the search for gold with relentless enthusiasm. In the late sixteenth century the Senate of Venice hired a Cypriot alchemist to restore the republic's crumbling finances, but without success. Charles II of England built an alchemical laboratory underneath his bedchamber, heedless of the violent explosions which were often the only tangible results of alchemical operations. James IV of Scotland employed an intrepid alchemist who not only tried to make gold, unsuccessfully, but also attempted to fly in the air with a pair of feathered wings. He took off from the battlements of Stirling Castle, dropped like a stone and broke his leg. He explained that he failed because his wings included hen's feathers which naturally 'coveted the midden not the sky'. Coins were made from alchemical gold for Christian IV of Denmark in the 1640s and several other monarchs struck similar coins and medals. In 1675 an alchemist converted both copper and tin into gold in the presence of the Emperor Leopold I and two years later the same adept turned a silver medallion into gold. Examined in 1888, this medallion was found to have a specific gravity between that of gold and silver.

The alchemists' supreme goal was to make the Philosopher's Stone, which was believed to have the power of turning all things to gold. J. B. van Helmont, a seventeenth-century chemist and the inventor of the term 'gas', described the Stone in his *De Vita Eterna*. 'I have seen and handled more than once the Stone of the Philosophers: in colour it was like powder of saffron but heavy and shining, even as powdered glass. There was given to me on a certain occasion the fourth part of a grain, or the six-hundredth of an ounce. Having wrapped it in paper, I made projection therewith upon eight ounces of quicksilver, heated in a crucible, and immediately all the quicksilver—was congealed into a yellow mass. This being melted in a strong fire, I found eight ounces minus eleven grains of most pure gold.'[2]

Helvetius, a distinguished authority on medicine, was sceptical of alchemy, unlike van Helmont. In 1666 he was visited by a stranger who showed him three small lumps of Stone, 'each about the bigness of a small walnut, transparent, of a pale brimstone colour'. After much persuasion the stranger gave Helvetius a tiny piece of this material. When he complained that the piece was too small, the stranger cut it in two and gave him back only half of it. After the stranger had gone, Helvetius wrapped the Stone in wax and heated it in a crucible with half an ounce of lead. He doubted whether anything would happen, but within quarter of an hour the lead had turned into gold, which was tested and found to be of good quality.[3]

These accounts are clarity itself compared to the descriptions of the Stone given by most alchemists. They say it is something which exists everywhere in Nature, but is generally regarded as worthless. It is made of animal, vegetable and mineral; it has a body, a soul and a spirit; it grows from flesh and blood; it is made of fire and water. It is a stone, but it is not a stone, unknown yet known to everyone, despised and yet unimaginably precious, coming from God but not coming from God. Directions for making it are couched in various types of symbolic code. 'Bind the serf twice and imprison him thrice', says a book ascribed to the thirteenth-century alchemist and astrologer Arnald of Villanova. 'Put him once in whitest linen and if he is inobedient, incarcerate him again.

Make him receive himself. On the third night give him a white wife. And he will impregnate her. And thus she will give birth to thirty sons who will overcome their genitor.'[4] The Rosicrucian alchemist Michael Maier, who died in 1622, said 'From a man and a woman make a circle, then a square, then a triangle, finally a circle and you will obtain the Philosopher's Stone.'[5]

The alchemists wrapped their processes in veils of mystery which frequently confused other alchemists, and which make much of their art still impenetrable, because the processes were mystical as well as chemical. Alchemy is often treated as a largely imbecile prelude to modern chemistry, but this is its least interesting side. The Stone did not only turn metals to gold. It was also the spiritual transformation of man from a state of earthly impurity to one of heavenly perfection. Some alchemists never went near a laboratory and scorned the attempt to make gold as mere money-grubbing, but many of those who laboured hopefully over furnaces and stills believed that the Stone could be made only by one who had achieved a profound understanding of the inner mysteries of the universe. These mysteries could not be stated in plain language, even if the risk of revealing them to the unworthy was discounted. They could only be conveyed through symbolism and allegory, and the full richness of their significance could only be grasped through mystical experience.

1. The Foundations of Alchemy

> For behold, the kingdom of heaven is within you.
>
> LUKE 17.21

Alchemy, like all the magic arts, is based on the belief that the universe is a unity. The alchemists found a principle of unity and order in a substance called First Matter, which remains unchanged behind all diversity. First Matter is not matter in any normal sense of the term, but the possibility of matter. It can only be described in contradictory terms. It has no qualities or properties, but at the same time it has all qualities and properties, because it contains the possibility of all things latent within it. First Matter is what is left when all the characteristics of an object have been stripped from it.

Down to the eighteenth century, the later still in isolated cases, alchemists believed that the characteristics of an object could be stripped from it to reduce it to First Matter, to which other and better characteristics could then be added. They were supported by the prevailing theory of matter, developed by Plato and Aristotle and embellished by later philosophers, the theory of the four elements. According to this theory, which remained almost unchallenged until Robert Boyle attacked it in the seventeenth century, the universe was constructed by a god or lesser supernatural intelligence who created First Matter, or who found it in existence, moulded and animated it. The four elements of fire, air, water and earth were the first development from First Matter. Each of these elements combines two of the four primary qualities which exist in all things—hot, cold, wet and dry. Fire is hot and dry, air is hot and wet, water is cold and wet, earth is cold and dry. Everything is made of the four elements, and differences between objects or materials are caused by the differing proportions in which the elements are combined in them.

If one of the qualities of an element is altered, it turns into a different element. When fire, which is hot and dry, loses its heat it becomes cold and dry and changes into earth (in becoming ash). When water, which is cold and wet, is heated it becomes hot and wet and changes into air (in giving off vapour).

This theory was essential to alchemy, because it allows the possibility of transmutation. Gold is a mixture of the four elements in a certain proportion. The other metals are mixtures of the same elements in slightly different proportions. By changing the proportions in the mixture—through heating and cooling, drying and liquefying—the other metals could be turned into gold.

Modern occultists, many of whom believe that some of the alchemists did succeed in making gold, generally accept the theory of the four elements. 'Modern research confirms the old teaching that the Universe was created from the 4 Elements, Fire, Air, Water, Earth, in the order given, each growing as it were from its predecessor and all animated in turn by the Word breathed upon them at the Creation.'[6] But in modern occultism the four elements are four conditions in which energy can exist. Fire stand for electricity, air is the gaseous state, water the liquid state and earth the solid state. All things exist in one or other of these conditions, or in a mixture of them, and one condition can be changed into another.

The theoretical possibility of transmutation was confirmed in practice for the early alchemists by the metalworking technique of their day. Craftsmen in Egypt, where alchemy apparently originated in the centuries shortly before and after the birth of Christ, produced silver and copper alloys which had the appearance of gold, in such profusion that a complicated system of terms grew up for distinguishing between the different varieties of 'gold' on the market. A papyrus written in Greek about 300 A.D., found at Thebes in Egypt, contains several processes for manufacturing gold and silver from other metals and claims that the results will pass all the tests for natural gold and silver. In these and other early recipes the emphasis is on changing the colour of a metal, yellowing or whitening it until it looks like gold or silver.

The craftsmen of the ancient world were much concerned with the imitation of Nature, the use of alloys and dyes to make materials which resembled natural materials. The belief that Nature can be imitated became one of the fundamental theories of alchemy, summed up in the maxim that 'the most natural and most perfect work is to create that which is like itself'. Combined with this was the belief that the less valuable or 'base' metals are imperfections in Nature. Nature always aims at perfection and strives to make the most perfect metal, gold, the one least subject to tarnishing and corrosion. But Nature's process often goes astray and the result is the creation of the other, imperfect metals. When an alchemist tried to turn a base metal into gold, he believed he was freeing it from its impurities and transforming it into the higher state to which it naturally aspired. His gold would be genuine gold and his processes were usually intended to copy the processes by which gold is formed naturally in the earth.

In dealing with metals the alchemists thought they were dealing with life. They did not draw any clear distinction between animate and inanimate. In their world all things, including men and animals, are made of the same four elements and all things are alive (or as a modern occultist would interpret it, all things contain energy). Metals were thought to grow in the belly of the earth in the same way that a child grows in the womb. A German handbook on metals and mining printed in 1505 says, 'It is to be noted that for the growth or generation of a metal ore there must be a begetter and some subject capable of receiving the generative action,' and 'Furthermore, in the union of mercury and sulphur in the ore, the sulphur behaves like the male seed and the mercury like the female seed in the conception and birth of a child.'[7]

The parallel between metallic life and human life runs all through alchemy, a reflection of the magical principle that all things are made on the model of man. The first major step in the alchemical work was to reduce a base metal to First Matter, which 'killed' it by stripping away its outward form and released the spark of life hidden in it, in the same way that a man's soul is released from his body at death. The life-spark was then recombined with the First Matter to produce a metallic 'embryo' which would have a natural propensity to become gold, because Nature strives for perfection. Nourished in the proper way, the embryo would grow and eventually be born from the alchemist's furnace as the perfect gold, the Stone. Innumerable complications were added, but this was the main outline of the work.

The alchemists distinguished between the 'body' of a substance, its noncombustible part, and its 'spirit' or combustible and volatile part. When wood is 'killed' by being burned, smoke and ash are produced. The ash is the dead body of the wood and the smoke which rises to the sky is its spirit or spark of life.

The belief that a spark of divine life which has fallen from heaven is imprisoned in all matter came into alchemy from the complex of religious and philosophical ideas current in the eastern Mediterranean area about the time of Christ. Most of the Gnostics held this belief and the picture of the soul descending from God through the heavenly spheres to its captivity in matter, the body, is an example of it. The fact that Genesis contains two different accounts of the creation of man encouraged Jewish and Gnostic commentators to speculate on man's double nature, one celestial and spiritual, the other earthly and material. The Manicheans, who apparently took the idea of the divine spark from the Zoroastrians, said that in the beginning the evil powers of Darkness made envious war upon the divine realm of Light. Seizing some of the light and hoping to prevent its recapture, the dark powers embedded it in man, whom they created, so that mingled in man's darkness there is the divine light which the Manicheans called the 'living self' or 'luminous self', a predecessor of the astral body of modern occult theory. Some Christian Gnostics called it a spark or seed of light. In the New Testament it is called *pneuma*, the 'breath' or 'spirit'.

The Greek philosophers contributed to the theories about pneuma. Aristotle said that all things of earth change and decay because they are made of the four elements, which are changeable. He recognised the stability of species. A mother rat gives birth to a baby rat, not to an infant tortoise. Stability of species is now put down to the action of a chemical in living cells, DNA. Aristotle accounted for it by the action of an unchanging constituent in the male seed, pnuema.

The Stoic philosophers of the late centuries B.C. and early centuries A.D. continued along this track. They said that pneuma is something present in living creatures in addition to the solids and liquids of which their bodies are made. It moves in waves, like sound waves, and exists in different 'tones' or degrees of tension, on the analogy of the head of a drum which makes different sounds depending on its tension. This is an early form of the occult theory of the vibrating universe. The characteristics of any creature depend on the degree of tension of its pneuma waves.

A living body contains different types of pneuma. 'Cohesive pneuma' holds it together, 'vital pneuma' animates it and 'rational pneuma', existing only in creatures which think, gives it a mind. Rational pneuma is the Stoic equivalent of the spark fallen from heaven. It survives the death of the body, when it returns as a fiery vapour to its original source in the sky. This source is the universal pneuma, the substance which binds all things together in unity, the One.[8]

The alchemists, with their anthropomorphic view of the universe, believed that all matter contained a pneuma or spirit, which they identified as mercury, named for the god of intelligence and corresponding to the Stoic rational pneuma. The brightness and shininess of mercury may have suggested that it was the divine light imprisoned in matter and it was thought to be the life-principle of metals, probably because it is liquid. Liquids were believed to carry life—rainwater, blood, sperm and the contents of an egg being examples. If metals are alive, mercury is obviously the most alive of them all, because it moves about, hence its names *argentvive* and quicksilver, 'live silver'.

Mercury was the spirit of any individual piece of matter, the vapour given off during heating, and it was also sometimes regarded as the One, the unity underlying all diversity, in the same way that in Stoic theory the rational pneuma of individual creatures was part of the universal pneuma. Like the One, mercury combines opposites. It is a metal but also a liquid. It is liquid, but it does not wet a surface on which it rests. For this reason it was called 'the masculine-feminine' and was often pictured as a hermaphrodite. Mercury also appears as a unicorn tamed by a virgin, showing the reconciliation of opposites in it; as a lion and a unicorn fighting, a symbol of the antagonism of its opposites; as a dragon or winged serpent, showing its opposites of solidity (snake, earth) and mobility (wings, air, vapour).

The mercury of the alchemists was not ordinary mercury but *philosopher's mercury*, an ideal substance to which the mercury found in Nature is only an imperfect approximation. The alchemists believed in several other ideal substances and could find a warrant for them in Plato's theory of forms and also in Aristotle, who had explained that the four elements as we know them are not the true elements. The element air, for instance, is a refinement of the air that we breathe, which is a mixture of all four elements in which air preponderates.

The place of mercury in alchemy was affected not only by classical theory (which did not come to the medieval alchemists direct but through Arab writers, translated into Latin from the twelfth century onwards) but also by the Bible. Philosopher's mercury was identified with the Spirit of God which hovered over the water in Genesis. God made First Matter, an empty yawning darkness—'And the earth was without form and void; and darkness was upon the face of the deep.' The darkness condensed into the waters upon which the Holy Spirit moved. The Spirit animated the watery First Matter and moulded it into a pattern containing the possibility of all things. The action of the Spirit was seen as an impregnation and a hatching, recalling the old myths that the life of the universe is the result of the sexual activity of the gods. Orthelius, a late sixteenth-century alchemist, says that the Spirit 'brooded (*incubavit*) on the face of the waters' and 'lay upon the waters of old, impregnated them and hatched a seed within them, like a hen upon the egg'.[9] This was believed to have set the precedent for all subsequent creation. The first chapter of Genesis was said to contain all the secrets of the work of alchemy and some adepts devised processes which were intended to be a copy of the seven days of creation.

Orthelius also says that the Spirit was 'breathed into all things by the word of God, and embodied in them'. This idea was another early contribution to the theory of the vibrating universe. In Genesis, God creates by expressing commands in words and by expelling breath, as when God breathes into Adam's nostrils to bring him to life. Speaking or breathing sets up vibrations in the air and the modern authority quoted earlier on the animation of the four elements by 'the Word breathed upon them at the Creation' says that the breathing of the Word created the vibrations which permeate the entire universe. Occultists often link the spirit or divine spark in man with inspiration, which means literally something breathed into him. The first chapter of St. John enabled alchemists and occultists to identify the creative Word of God with the Holy Spirit of Genesis, with the life-principle, the divine breath breathed into Adam, and with the spark of divine light entrapped in matter. 'In the beginning was the Word, and the Word was with God, and the Word was God. The same was in the beginning with God. All things were made by him; and without him was not anything made that was made. In him was life; and the life was the light of men. And the light shineth in darkness; and the darkness comprehended it not.'

Mercury, or the 'spirit', slithers about bewilderingly behind a variety of disguises in alchemy. In the twelfth and thirteenth centuries it was generally accepted that metals were made of mercury and sulphur. Sulphur, which is highly inflammable, was seen as a fiery, active male principle in metals and mercury as a watery, passive female principle. Or sometimes they were regarded as the male and female principles within the double-natured mercury itself. The ideal philosopher's gold, the Stone, was thought to be the product of the combination of philosopher's sulphur and mercury in perfect balance, and joining these two ingredients, or reconciling the opposites, was an essential process in making the Stone.

In the ninth century an influential Arab alchemist, Rhazes, had suggested that metals contained a third, salty component. This idea became extremely important in later European alchemy and in the sixteenth century Paracelsus maintained that everything is made of philosophical mercury, sulphur and salt, though without abandoning the four elements. 'The world is as God created it. In the beginning He made it into a body, which consists of four elements. He founded this primordial body on the trinity of mercury, sulphur and salt, and these are the three substances of which the complete body consists. For they form everything that lies in the four elements, they bear in them all the forces and faculties of perishable things. In them there are day and night, warmth and coldness, stone and fruit, and everything else, still unformed.'[10] The attempt to reconcile 4 (the elements) with 3 (mercury, sulphur and salt) and 2 (opposites—day and night, and the rest) and turn them all into 1 (the Stone) was one of the principal preoccupations of later alchemy.

Alchemical theory now had a trinity in matter, corresponding to the divine Trinity and the threefold nature of man. In this classification, man's three parts are body, soul (emotions, desires, natural inclinations and propensities) and spirit (the higher mental faculties—inspiration, imagination, insight, moral discrimination and judgement). In metals, salt is the body—inert, passive and female. The fiery sulphur is the soul, corresponding to the burning passions of man, and is male. The opposites of sulphur and salt are linked by mercury, which is bisexual and corresponds to the spirit or mind of man, through which the soul's imperatives are translated into bodily action.

This was a return to the much earlier division of man into body—equivalent to the cohesive pneuma of the Stoics; soul—passions and appetites, the vital pneuma; and spirit—the rational pneuma, or on a universal scale the Logos of St. John, the Word of God which was also the Thought of God (Hokmah and Binah in the Cabala). According to the theory of the soul's descent through the spheres, the spirit is hidden inside the soul. When the soul rises again after death, it sheds its accumulated layers or skins one by one, until the whole soul is peeled away and the spirit is reunited with God.

Like the cabalists, the Gnostics and the devotees of the mystery cults did not believe that death was a necessary preliminary to the union of man with the divine. 'Saved by thy light,' a Gnostic prayer says, 'we rejoice that thou hast shown thyself to us whole, we rejoice that *thou hast made us gods while still in our bodies through the vision of thee.*'[11] In the mysteries of Mithras the initiate climbed up through seven gates on seven ascending steps, a mimicry of the soul's ascent through the spheres of the planets. In the mysteries of Isis the initiate put on or took off seven garments (or sometimes twelve). In both cases the result of the initiation was 'rebirth'. The initiate was reborn as the god. At the end of *The Golden Ass* of Apuleius, the hero is initiated into the mysteries of Isis. He does not reveal the details of the ceremony, though he says that he approached the very gates of death, but was permitted to return. Afterwards he emerged clothed in twelve stoles, a scarf with sacred animals worked on it called an Olympian stole, and a palm wreath symbolising the rays of the risen sun. '. . . . I was suddenly exposed to the gaze of the crowd, as when a statue is unveiled, dressed like the sun. That day was the happiest of my initiation, and I celebrated it as my birthday. . . .'

The attempt to become a god is the Great Work of magic and alchemy. The belief that man can attain the divine while still in the body, with the parallel between this process and the transmutation of base metals to gold, was grafted on to the metalworking techniques of the ancient world by Gnostic Graeco-Egyptian alchemists. One of them, Zosimos of Panopolis in Egypt, writing about A.D. 300, describes a dream in which he saw a priest sacrificing at a dome-shaped altar at the top of fifteen steps. He heard the voice of the priest saying, 'I have accomplished the action of descending the fifteen steps towards the darkness, and the action of ascending the steps towards the light. The sacrifice renews me, rejecting the dense nature of the body. Thus consecrated by necessity, I become a spirit.' The priest said he had suffered unbearable violence. He had been dismembered with a sword. His bones had been mixed with his flesh and 'burned in the fire of the treatment' and so, through the transformation of the body, he had become a spirit.

The word used for the domed altar, *phiale*, was also used for a dome-shaped glass receiver placed above distilling apparatus as a condenser of vapours. The dream probably describes the destruction of the 'body' of a metal by heating, with the rising of a vapour—the 'spirit'. But it also recalls the mystery-initiations. The descent of the steps into darkness and the return towards the light suggests the descent and ascent of the soul through the spheres. The dismemberment with a sword is the mock death that precedes rebirth. The burning in the fire of the treatment is the purging of the earthly nature and its transformation into spirit.

Later in the same dream Zosimos saw a crowd of people immersed in boiling water on the altar, burned and wailing. He saw a man of copper holding a tablet of lead. A spectator told him that 'the men who wish to obtain virtue enter here and become spirits after having escaped from the body'. Waking from the dream, Zosimos tells the reader to build a temple 'as of white lead, as of alabaster, having neither commencement nor end in its construction. Let it have in its interior a spring of pure water, sparkling like the sun. . . .' Then take a sword and find the narrow opening which is the entrance to the temple. A serpent lies at the entrance. Seize the serpent, kill him, flay him and use his body as a step to the entrance. You will find what you seek. The man of copper has become a man of silver and if you wish will become a man of gold.[12]

The temple has been interpreted as the alchemist's laboratory, the altar as his apparatus, the men as the ingredients of the work which become spirits or vapours, and the serpent as the difficulties of the work. But the dream obviously has a deeper significance. A modern occultist might interpret the temple which has no beginning or end as the true self which is eternal, symbolised as the body of a woman containing the sparkling water of life, the divine spark. The narrow entrance recalls Matthew 7.14, 'strait is the gate and narrow is the way which leadeth unto life', and the serpent which guards it is the animal nature of man which blocks the way to spiritual progress, but which, overcome and transformed, is the essential stepping-stone to the divine. The penetration of the narrow entrance is the mystical copulation, or union of opposites, which precedes the initiate's rebirth.

Alchemy grew up in the same area and at the same time as the Cabala. The writings of Zosimos have survived only in fragments, but an early commentary on them, the *Sacred Art* of Olympiodorus, says that he preached union with God, which is the supreme aim of the cabalists. He said that the process demands the stilling of the passions and the repose of the body, which the cabalists try to achieve through their exercises. He said that the alchemist should call upon the divine being within him and that those who know themselves know the god within, which is the cabalist doctrine of man as a God-concealing form. In later alchemy the making of the Stone was often shown as a tree, like the Tree of Life, its trunk and branches the successive steps in the work as the sephiroth are the rungs of the ladder to heaven.

The Philosopher's Stone is the ideal gold, the Platonic 'form' of gold, which permeates any substance and transforms it to its own golden nature. Because the early metalworkers concentrated on turning a base metal to gold by changing its colour, the Stone was frequently called the Tincture. Zosimos said that 'our gold which possesses the desired quality can make gold and tint into gold. Here is the great mystery—that the quality becomes gold and it then makes gold.'[13] 'Our gold' is what later generations would have called the Stone. It is the divine spark of Holy Spirit in tangible form. It is the One mystically solidified and it is man as God.

2. The Making of the Stone

Up from Earth's Centre through the Seventh Gate
I rose, and on the Throne of Saturn sate,
And many a knot unravel'd by the Road;
But not the Master-Knot of Human Fate.

There was the Door to which I found no key;
There was the Veil through which I might not see:
Some little talk awhile of ME and THEE
There was—and then and no more of THEE and ME.

The Rubaiyat of Omar Khayyam

A serious difficulty which confronted the apprentice to alchemy at the outset was that he did not know what raw material to work on. Many of the masters of the art would only say that the 'subject' of the work, the material to be worked on, was something which is found everywhere and universally regarded as valueless. Some adepts maintained that the subject of the work was the same as the apparatus in which it was carried on, the philosopher's egg or egg-shaped vessel from which the Stone would be hatched like a chick. Some helpfully suggested that the work should begin with spittle of the moon or semen of the stars or mucus of the stars. Others recommended vitriol, but by vitriol they evidently meant something else, as they expanded the word by notarikon into *Vista Interiora Terrae Rectificando Invenies Occultum Lapidem*, 'visit the interior of the earth and by purifying you will find the secret Stone'.

An alchemist who did not understand these instructions would have to proceed by trial and error. He might begin with a base metal or an alloy, but many other materials were tried. In his *Ordinal of Alchemy* the English fifteenth-century adept Thomas Norton of Briston sneered at those who experimented with grass, roots and herbs, various gums, vervain, mandrake, arsenic, antimony, honey, wax, wine, hair, eggs, dung, urine and vitriol, all without success.

The work might begin with gold itself, or gold would be added at some point in the operations, because it was said that whoever wishes to make gold must have gold to begin with.

From a spiritual point of view, it seems clear that the subject of the work was the alchemist himself. *Ars totum requirit hominem*, 'the art requires the whole man'. The alchemist was both the vessel of the work and the material in it. The valueless thing found everywhere is matter, which in man means the body and the animal nature that is closely linked with it. In matter there is concealed the spirit or divine spark, the moon-spittle or star-semen or star-mucus which is something fallen from heaven, or the vitriol found in the interior of one's own being. Whoever wants to make gold must begin with gold because a man cannot find truth unless he is true himself, or God unless he has God within him.

A common symbol of the work was a snake or dragon forming a circle by swallowing its own tail and bearing the Greek motto *en to pan*, 'all is one'. This motto has three words and seven letters, and 3+7 = 10, which stands for 'all things' and reduces to 1, unity. The Stone is the One which is also the All. In human terms it is the whole man, who in becoming the One becomes identical with the All, the universe and God. The work is circular, like the year and the cycle of Nature. It begins with the whole man—body, soul and spirit—and ends with the perfected whole man. Petrus Bonus, author of the *New Pearl of Great Price*, written about 1330, said that the old philosophers knew 'that God would become man on the Last Day of this art, when the work is accomplished. . . . Now, since no creature except man can unite with God, on account of their dissimilarity, God must needs become one with man. And this came to pass in Christ Jesus and His virgin mother.'[14] Many alchemists identified the Stone with Christ, who was both God and man, but their Christianity was decidedly unorthodox. The work is to be completed while still in the body. The Stone is the divine being that each man can crucify and resurrect in himself to attain a kingdom of heaven on earth.

The work seems to have proceeded along parallel chemical and mystical lines. The masters of the art said that the alchemist could not succeed except by the grace of God, and by prayer and austere devotion to the task. Concentration and imagination were also vital to success. The operations were slow and taxing, and the alchemist might have to repeat one process hundreds of times before it was completed. He was told to read all the authorities on the subject, however mutually contradictory they might be, and struggle to understand them. In the course of this long toil, it was evidently expected that the chemical development of the material in the vessel would be accompanied by a corresponding spiritual development in the alchemist. And when at last the final illumination came and the secret dawned in all its splendour on his mind, he would find that the work was not difficult at all and would scarcely be able to understand how he had been so blind before.

Some of the later alchemists abandoned laboratory work altogether and said it was unnecessary, but the neophyte had still to go through the same long labour of discovering what the work really meant, the same perplexities, false starts and misleading side-tracks, the same gradual growth of understanding. Knowledge, in fact, was the key to the Stone. When the alchemist understood what the Stone was, he had found it and had become it. In alchemy, as in all occultism, the truth is veiled behind symbols and paradoxes, because it has to be discovered for oneself. The occult arts are *arts*; their ultimate secrets can be learned, but cannot be taught.

Once the beginner had picked a raw material, he faced the difficulty of finding out what operations to perform on it. This was again a matter of lengthy trial and error. It was rare for the experts to agree on exactly what processes were needed to make the Stone or in what order they should be carried out. The early authorities generally said that there were four main stages in the work, distinguished by the appearance of four colours—black, white, yellow and red—in the material in the vessel. This sequence of colour changes appears in the oldest known book on alchemy, *Physika kai Mystika* (The Physical and the Mystical) written by Bolos of Mendes in Egypt about 200 B.C. It is probably connected with the four elements and the numerological significance of 4 as the number which governs the form and construction of things, including the making of gold. By the late Middle Ages the number of stages had been reduced to three—black, white and red—reflecting the trinity of mercury, sulphur and salt, and the significance of 3 as the number of creation, including the creation of gold. But these were only the main stages and the details of the work varied from one authority to another.

Some alchemists said there were seven processes in the work, others said there were twelve. The *seven* processes corresponded to the seven days of creation and also to the seven planets, because the influence of each planet was supposed to generate its own metal in the earth. The metals varied in degree of perfection from lead, the most impure, up to gold. The alchemist began with his raw material in its most impure 'leaden' state and gradually improved it till it had become the perfect gold, the steps in the work corresponding to the soul's ascent through the planetary spheres. (This is one reason why Saturn, the ruler of lead, corresponds to the World in the Tarot, the card which marks the beginning of the cabalist's upward progress.) The *twelve* processes were connected with the signs of the zodiac. The work was intended to copy the processes of Nature and the twelve months or zodiac signs make up the complete cycle of the year, in which Nature moves from birth to growth to decay, death and rebirth.

The English alchemist George Ripley gave a list of twelve processes in his *Compound of Alchemy*, written in 1470, and a very similar list was provided by another adept, Josephus Quercetanus, in 1576. The processes are calcination, solution, separation, conjunction, putrefaction, coagulation, cibation, sublimation, fermentation, exaltation, multiplication, and projection.[15]

Any interpretation of these processes, chemical or psychological, is necessarily conjectural, but the first steps, as far as putrefaction, were apparently supposed to purify the raw material and strip its characteristics from it, reducing it to First Matter and releasing its spirit or spark of life. Calcination meant heating the base metal or other raw material of the work in air until it was reduced to a fine powder or ash. Ripley said that this required a moderate heat, kept up for a year, which recalls an earlier Arab alchemist's enthusiastic comment, 'Calcination is the treasure of a thing; be not weary of calcination.' In destroying the outward form of the base metal, calcination was thought to remove all its surface qualities.

Spiritually, calcination probably stands for the purging fires of aspiration and self-discipline, symbolised in the Tarot by the Day of Judgement. The work begins with a burning discontent with oneself and one's life, a passionate longing for higher things. It is a process of self-watching and self-judgement, in which a man is constantly weighing himself and finding himself wanting. Combined with a fierce determination to do better, the result is the disintegration of the natural self. The outer, surface aspects of the personality are burned away and what is left is the 'powder' of the inner man.

The second step, solution, was to dissolve the calcined powder in 'a mineral water which shall not wet the hands'. This mineral water was mercury and some alchemists may have added ordinary mercury at this point, but more often, apparently, the vapours given off during calcination, which were identified as philosopher's mercury, were condensed into the mercurial liquid in which the powder was dissolved. Many alchemists complained of the difficulties of this process.

Reducing the raw material to a watery state was usually considered an essential early step in the work. 'Perform no operation till all be made water.' There was a widespread belief that all things originally derived from water and there was also, more specifically, the authority of Plato and Aristotle for thinking that metals are formed by the congealing of water in the earth. In the *Timaeus*, Plato classifies as water everything that can exist as a flowing liquid, including metals which flow when they are heated. Gold is water 'of a fusible kind' and copper is 'a shining and solid kind of water'. Aristotle said that there are two types of 'exhalation' or 'breath' which rise up from the earth when it is heated by the sun. One is more vaporous and moist, the other more smoky and dry. When these exhalations are trapped inside the earth they turn into metals and minerals. Metals 'are all produced by the enclosure of the vaporous [moist] exhalation, particularly within stones, whose drying compresses it together and solidifies it'. The metals 'are in a sense water and in another sense not: it was possible for their material to turn into water but it can no longer do so'. Each metal is 'the result of the solidification of the exhalation before it turns to water'.[16]

Since in alchemical theory metals are congealed water, to reduce a metal to water is to get back towards its First Matter and to purify the metal by freeing it from the defects of its 'growth' in earth. It is like the attempts made by some psychoanalysts to put a patient back into his early childhood, and some even pursue him into the womb (also an alchemical motif) to deal with the origins of his psychological defects.

Solution, which roughly corresponds to the Moon in the Tarot, is a process of deep self-examination and self-disgust. The calcined powder, which stands for the more enduring characteristics beneath a man's surface, is dissolved in mercurial water. The alchemist's underlying attitudes, prejudices, tastes, deep-rooted patterns of feeling and reaction, are dissolved away through the action of 'mercury', intelligent insight into himself. The difficulty of the process was to find the true philosophical mercury, the true insight, and it carries the danger of mental collapse, fear, despair, illusion and self-deception. The water of solution, the alchemists said, is a bitter water and C. G. Jung, drawing a parallel between alchemy and psychoanalysis, says, 'It is bitter indeed to discover behind one's lofty ideals narrow, fanatical convictions, all the more cherished for that, and behind one's heroic pretensions nothing but crude egotism, infantile greed, and complacency. This painful corrective is an unavoidable stage in every therapeutic process.'[17]

The ordeal of bitter water leads to the stage of separation. According to Ripley, this drew forth oil and water. It was not done by the operator but by God, which suggests that the alchemist left the watery material in the vessel alone to separate by itself. The intention was to separate the raw material's original components. These components might be the four elements or, in the earlier medieval theory, mercury and sulphur. Between them, mercury and sulphur combined the four primary qualities on which the elements themselves were based. Sulphur was hot and dry, corresponding to Aristotle's smoky and dry exhalation, and mercury was cold and wet, the vaporous and moist exhalation. The inflammable sulphur embodied the element fire (hot and dry), the liquid mercury the element water (cold and wet), hence the statement that the Stone is made of fire and water. In later alchemy, separation was meant to divide the raw material into mercury, sulphur and salt or spirit, soul and body.

Whether separation produced two, three or four components, its purpose was to purify the material still further and move one stage nearer to First Matter by getting back to the basic ingredients. The alchemist originally felt a sense of wholeness in himself and the work began with this as it will end in the perfected wholeness of the Stone. His examination of the sour wellsprings of his own behaviour destroys the sense of wholeness and he feels as if he were being cut in pieces or torn apart on a rack. T. E. Lawrence described the sensation in *Seven Pillars of Wisdom*. It was the result of self-loathing combined with physical exhaustion and in this particular case, interestingly enough, followed subjection to a sadistic, sexual 'discipline' (the Falling Tower in the Tarot). He found himself 'dividing into parts'. His body, which an alchemist would call salt, continued efficiently about its business, riding a camel. A second part of himself (mercury) 'hovering above and to the right bent down and curiously asked what the flesh was doing', while a third part (sulphur) 'talked and wondered, critical of the body's self-inflicted labour, and contemptuous of the reason for effort'. The two separated parts carried on a debate about the sense or stupidity of what the body was doing. Lawrence seems to have experienced a separation of opposites, the warring tendencies in himself. He called his condition a 'death-sleep', his Arab companion had to strike him to awaken him from it, and in some accounts of the alchemical work separation is immediately followed by the stage of 'death'.

Ripley and many other alchemists, however, follow separation with conjunction, the achievement of a balance between the warring opposites and their reconciliation. Sulphur and mercury are reunited. This was usually depicted as a marriage or copulation, and frequently as incest between mother and son or brother and sister because the sulphur and mercury came from the same original raw material. Sulphur, the soul or passionate nature was incestuously united with mercury, the spirit or dispassionate intellect. This attempt to end the intolerable separation, to find an inner balance, to come to peaceful terms with onself, was also symbolised as a re-entry into the womb. The son or the king or the dragon—the material of the work—creeps back into the body of his mother. It is an escape from pressures, not merely the pressures of the bustling world outside but also those of one's own spiritual condition. The alchemist has been purged of the characteristics and attitudes which are the 'defects of his growth'. The opposing tendencies which are the basic components of his nature have been separated, balanced and put together again. He is the child in the womb, his original self.

Conjunction could also be seen as the reunification of the four elements or the recombining of mercury, sulphur and salt. It required steady and moderate heating, a hard thing for the alchemist to achieve. He had no way of gauging the temperature in his furnace accurately and it was difficult for him to keep up a level heat.

The alchemist had now reached the first form of his material, before it had acquired imperfections through the accidents of Nature. It consisted of First Matter and an animating spark of life. The next step was to kill the material and release its life-spark, which was done by subjecting it to a moist heat, by warming the alchemical vessel in a water-bath, for instance, or in fermenting dung. The material lying at the bottom of the vessel should gradually turn black, a sign that it had become First Matter, a dead, featureless mass from which all characteristics had been removed including colour, black being regarded as the absence of colour. The material was believed to be rotting and the process was called putrefaction. Vapour—the life-spark or spirit or philosopher's mercury—was given off and the alchemists noted that putrefaction was accompanied by a foul smell, the 'grave stench'.

This was the first main stage of the work, the *nigredo* or black stage, called the Black Crow, Crow's Head, Raven's Head or Black Sun, and symbolised by a dead and rotting corpse or a black bird, a black man, a king slaughtered by warriors or a dead king eaten by a wolf. Different adepts led up to the nigredo in different ways. One simple method was to heat copper with sulphur, which would turn it into a black mass of copper sulphide—First Matter. Black and stinking as it was, the putrefying First Matter was potentially the marvellous

Stone, and the alchemists took the words of the Song of Solomon as a reference to it—'I am black but comely, O ye daughters of Jerusalem.'

It was essential for the material to rot, because putrefaction was thought to be a necessary precondition of life. Seed which fell to earth was believed to die and rot, releasing the life-principle which caused new growth (shown in Death in the Tarot). In classical times and in the Middle Ages it was accepted that frogs were generated from rotting mud, bees and other insects from the mouldering corpses of animals, wasps from dead asses, beetles from horses, locusts from mules. In a wider sense, the essential preliminary to rebirth was death, real or symbolic. The alchemists could quote St. Paul—'Thou fool, that which thou sowest is not quickened except it die', and 'So also is the resurrection of the dead. It is sown in corruption; it is raised in incorruption. . . . It is sown a natural body; it is raised a spiritual body.' They also had the authority of Jesus. 'Except a corn of wheat fall into the ground and die, it abideth alone: but if it die, it bringeth forth much fruit', which its spiritual corollary in the next verse, 'He that loveth his life shall lose it; and he that hateth his life in this world shall keep it unto life eternal.'[18]

The nigredo is the mock death of the mystery initiations. This is a primitive idea; among the Australian aborigines, for instance, a magician's initiation involved a sleep of death and rebirth. The alchemist is 'in the womb', fully turned in on himself, and he undergoes the mystical 'death' identified by the adepts with melancholy, a state of helpless dejection and spiritual rot in which the spirit or spark of life abandons the body and soul (the Hanged Man). The original self or First Matter dies in the black agony of nigredo.

A parallel was often drawn between the nigredo and the Crucifixion, from which the God-man rose to eternal life. The 'death' was a crucifixion in the sense of a suspension in suffering. It was symbolised by a snake nailed to a cross—'And as Moses lifted up the serpent in the wilderness, even so must the Son of man be lifted up.'[19]

The alchemist is now 'dead', putrefying in the slime of melancholy, but slowly a healing illumination comes with the gentle descent of philosophical mercury, true inspiration, the divine spark. The vapour given off during putrefaction hovers over the black material in the vessel like the Holy Spirit moving upon the dark waters of Genesis. It penetrates the First Matter, animates it and creates the embryo which will grow into the Stone. The process is described in an alchemical version of the Mass, written by Nicholas Melchior, who was astrologer to the King of Hungary in the early sixteenth century. (The parallel between the work of alchemy and the transformation of bread and wine into the body and blood of Christ in the Mass was drawn by many alchemists.) 'Then will appear in the bottom of the vessel the mighty Ethiopian, burned, calcined, bleached, altogether dead and lifeless.' The Ethiopian is the black First Matter. 'He asks to be buried, to be sprinkled with his own moisture and slowly calcined till he shall arise in glowing form from the fierce fire. . . . Behold a wondrous restoration or renewal of the Ethiopian!'[20]

Evidently, the vapour or spirit was condensed into a liquid which saturated the First Matter, while the vessel was heated. This was the alchemical 'bath of rebirth' and the alchemists saw the process as the rebirth through 'water and the spirit'. 'Except a man be born again, he cannot see the kingdom of God. . . . Except a man be born of water and of the Spirit, he cannot enter into the kingdom of God.'[21]

When the spirit and the First Matter had been rejoined, a white solid crystallised from the watery material in the vessel. This was the process of coagulation or congelation, corresponding to the appearance of dry land out of the waters on the third day of creation. The elements of the Stone flow together, Ripley says. The white solid is the White Stone or White Tincture which turns all things to silver. The appearance of the White Stone marked the second main stage of the work, the *albedo* or whitening, and the alchemists connected it with the white stone of Revelation 2.17. 'To him that overcometh will I give to eat of the hidden manna, and will give him a white stone, and in the stone a new name written, which no man knoweth saving him that receiveth it.'

In spite of the constantly repeated maxim *nihil extraneum*, 'nothing from outside', some alchemists were not above assisting the production of the white stone by adding new ingredients at this point. A little silver might be added with mercury, arsenic, antimony or tin, which would whiten the surface of the material in the vessel. Another method is given in the medieval *Allegoria Merlini*, which describes the work under the cover of a story about a king (the raw material) who drank so much water that his limbs were filled with it (solution) and he felt as if he was falling to pieces (separation). His doctors put him in a heated chamber and when they took him out he was dead (nigredo). The doctors took the body, ground it to powder, washed it and dried it. They added to it one part rock salt, two parts saltpetre and a little linseed oil, to make a paste. They put the paste into a crucible in which holes had been bored and placed another crucible underneath. Then they heated and melted the paste, so that the liquid ran down into the lower crucible, upon which the king rose up, resurrected.[22]

The White Stone is a new self, a new earth appearing out of the waters, peace, innocence, happiness, freedom from conflict. Silver is the metal of the moon and the White Stone shines in the alchemist's being like the moon in the night sky, turning the darkness to silver. From this point the third and final stage of the work leads to the *rubedo*, the red dawn which heralds the coming of the sun in splendour, the dazzling light of a new day.

The next step is cibation, in which the material in the vessel is 'fed with milk and meat moderately'. This nourishes the embryonic Stone, corresponding to the feeding of a baby, and may mean that fresh material was added to the vessel, though it is not clear what. Gerhard Dorn, a pupil of Paracelsus, recommended the addition of various ingredients in the later stages of the work, including human blood, celandine and honey. The blood would infuse life-energy into the Stone. Celandine would give joy and good spirits, because it was supposed to be a cure for night-blindness and, by extension, for melancholy, the 'night' of gloom. Honey stood for the sweetness of life and was also a preservative. It was the only sweetening substance in use until comparatively modern times and was used in antiquity to embalm dead bodies, because it prevents putrefaction. Dorn said that the honey or sweetness of life might change into a deadly poison and celandine, which gives clear sight, was perhaps an antidote to it.

In the remaining processes, from sublimation to projection, it is easier to take the chemical and psychological steps separately. The alchemist now adds to his 'growing' Stone the qualities which it must have when completed—perfect purity and stability, the ability to convert base metals to gold, and the ability to convert far more than its own weight in base metals.

Sublimation was a purification. The solid material in the vessel was heated until it vaporised and the vapour then rapidly cooled and condensed back into the solid state. This was repeated several times and was often symbolised by doves, swans or other birds flying up to heaven and descending again. The purpose was to rid the Stone's body of the original filth which accompanied its birth through putrefaction. The body was purged by converting it into vapour or spirit and discarding the residue, and the spirit was then reconverted into body. As a stage in the growth of the Stone, the solidification of the vapour recalls Aristotle's 'exhalations', solidified in the earth and becoming metals and minerals.

In the next step, fermentation, the material in the vessel turns yellow and becomes gold. Many alchemists said that gold should be added at this point to hasten the Stone's natural development into gold. Although it is not yet quite perfected, the Stone now acquires the ability to transmute base metals. It becomes a ferment or leaven, able to permeate, agitate and spur on the development of a base metal in the same way that yeast permeates dough and makes it rise. This quality comes from the Stone's soul or sulphur, the fiery driving component which excites and enlivens the base metal, and in fermentation the Stone's soul is united with its already purified body. Petrus Bonus explained that the Stone cannot change and colour other metals until it has been changed and coloured itself, 'and so our Stone is rendered capable of fermenting, converting and altering metals by means of a certain digestive heat, which brings out its potential and latent properties . . . when the artist sees the white soul arise, he should join it to its body in the same instant'.[23]

Exaltation brings the last colour change of the work, the rubedo or reddening. The alchemists evidently found that in the later stages of the work the material in the vessel was highly unstable. In exaltation, all the Stone's components were fused in unalterable harmony and unity. The body and soul, combined in fermentation, were now united with the spirit and the Stone became fixed and enduring. The heat of the furnace was raised to its highest intensity and the excited alchemist saw the marvellous spectacle for which he had laboured so long, the appearance of the true Stone of the Philosophers itself, the perfect red god, the Red Tincture or Red Elixir, the One.

On the fifth day of creation when God had made every living thing that moves except man, he commanded them 'be fruitful and multiply' and the same command was later given to Adam and Eve. The Stone needed one more quality, already latent within it, the ability to be fruitful and multiply itself by transmuting quantities of base metal far in excess of its own size and weight. This was produced through the process called multiplication or augmentation. The Stone was made fertile and fruitful in another conjunction or copulation or union of opposites, the royal marriage of soul and spirit, sulphur and mercury, king and queen, sun and moon, the red man and the white woman, standing for all the opposites which are reconciled in the One.

In the twelfth and last process, projection, the Stone was applied to a base metal to convert it to gold. This was usually done by wrapping a piece of it in wax or paper and heating it with the base metal in a crucible.

These final processes involve repeated balancing and combination of the Stone's components or opposites. The alchemists were necessarily concerned to achieve a proper balance of opposites so as to reconcile them. The *Book of Mercury*, by the famous Arab alchemist Geber or one of his followers, explains that in some cases the opposites are inextricably mixed together and cannot be balanced. 'No more will you find spirit which doess not contain a little body, nor body which does not contain a little spirit. Sometimes these two elements cannot be separated when one of them is too abundant, and the other too much lacking, so that there is a transformation and absorption of the part which is less in quantity by the part that predominates.'[24]

In human terms, this means that those who are overspiritual at the expense of the body and those who are overphysical at the expense of the soul are both far from perfection. The whole man is the balanced man. In psychoanalysis, Jung says, the problem of opposites is 'the dissociation of the personality brought about by the conflict of incompatible tendencies, resulting as a rule from an inharmonious disposition. The repression of one of the opposites leads only to a prolongation and extension of the conflict, in other words, to a neurosis. The therapist therefore confronts the opposites with one another and aims at uniting them permanently.'[25]

The same permanent union of opposites is the aim of magic and alchemy, but the alchemical processes involve more complicated considerations. The Stone has three components—body, soul and spirit—which are joined together in four steps.

> Sublimation unites body and spirit.
> Fermentation unites the spiritual body with the soul.
> Exaltation unites body, soul and spirit.
> Multiplication unites soul and spirit.

This repetitious pattern of unions is connected with the alchemists' attempts to reconcile the numbers 4, 3 and 2, and reduce them to 1. The riddle of the Sphinx was, 'What has four feet in the morning, two at midday and three in the evening?' Oedipus answered 'man', but another answer is 'alchemy', which began with the belief that all things are made of 4 (elements), then developed the theory that they are made of 2 (mercury and sulphur) and finally the theory that they are made of 3 (mercury, sulphur and salt). The adoption of a new theory did not cause the discarding of an old one; they continued to exist side by side. From the alchemist's point of view, the riddle was, 'How are 4 turned into 2 and then into 3, which is also 1?'

The 4 changes into the 2 because the four primary qualities of the four elements are all contained in the two opposites of sulphur (hot and dry) and mercury (cold and wet). But it is not enough to say that all things are made of 2, because 2 is the number of evil, hostility and reconciled opposites. All things must be made of 3, which joins the opposites in unity, but this 3 must contain the original 4.

The 3 contains the 4 in alchemy because mercury has a double nature. The trinity of mercury, sulphur and salt conceals a quaternity. Mercury can be seen as single or double, as required.

Sulphur	Soul	Male	Fire
Mercury	Spirit	Male-female	Air and Water
Salt	Body	Female	Earth

Michael Maier's solution to the Sphinx's riddle, quoted earlier, was 'From a man and a woman make a circle, then a square, then a triangle, finally a circle and you will obtain the Philosopher's Stone.' In sublimation, the alchemist takes 'a man and a woman', mercury (spirit) as male and salt (body) as female and joins them together or makes them into a circle. In fermentation, sulphur (soul) is added to make four or a square—salt (1)+mercury (2)+sulphur (1). In exaltation, these are regarded as three or a triangle, and they are joined or made into a circle which is the Stone, or 1.

Modern occultists juggle with the numbers from 1 to 4 in a similar way to produce a law which states that all activities or processes are triangular and at the same time quadrangular. One is the active element or power which initiates any process. Two is the passive element which serves as a fulcrum or basis for 1. Three is the combination of 1 and 2, the result of the action. But the three together make a new unit, which is 4, and 4 is also the active element of a new process, the 1 of the next triangle. This is the modern explanation of the 'saying of Mary the Prophetess', handed down through many generations of alchemists—'One becomes Two, Two becomes Three, and out of the Third comes the One as the Fourth.'

The Tetragrammaton, considered as the real name of God and therefore as the essence of all things, enshrines the same type of occult and alchemical formula. It has four letters, but it also has three, because one letter is repeated—YHVH, *yod he vau he*. The four letters are taken to represent the four elements, which contain two pairs of opposites, hot-cold and wet-dry.

Yod	Fire	Hot and dry	Male	Will
He	Water	Cold and wet	Female	Understanding
Vau	Air	Hot and wet	Male	Mind
He	Earth	Cold and dry	Female	Body

Yod (1) is the Father, the active principle in God and the universe. *He* (2) is the Mother, the passive principle. Their union produces a son, *Vau* (3), who corresponds to air, the product of the combination of fire and water, and to mind, the product of the combination of will and understanding. Finally, the daughter *He* (4) is produced, corresponding to earth and body, the solidification or materialisation of the first three.

The final *He* is the daughter and twin sister and bride of *Vau*, just as Eve was produced from Adam's body, was created by the same Father, and was Adam's wife (and Eve's emergence from Adam is the parallel to the emanation of God's Thought from God). *Vau* (mind) is the king's son who rescues the enchanted princess, *He* final (body), and marries her. The effect of this is to place her on the throne of her mother, the first *He* (understanding), and it is her youthful embrace which reawakens *Yod* (will), the All-Father, so that the process begins all over again. This family relationship symbolises the whole course of the universe.[26]

The course of the universe, in fact, is cyclical—the snake devouring its own tail—the Great Work is a circle. The Tetragammaton has 4 letters, which are 2 pairs of opposites, but the 4 are also 3 and the name runs in a circle to make 1, since it is the essence of God who is the One.

There is a sharp contrast between this system and the more conventional view that perfection is attained by shedding the body and animal nature altogether, as vicious and earth-bound. Here, body is joined with mind to become understanding, whose union with will completes the cycle and begins a new one. The occultist, as Dion Fortune said, 'does not try to escape from matter into spirit, leaving an unconquered country behind him to get on as best it may'.

In alchemy, the processes of sublimation, fermentation and exaltation correspond to the union of body and mind and their elevation to the throne of understanding. In sublimation, body is vaporised into spirit and spirit in turn condensed into body, so that the two are joined in a spiritual body. The 'original filth' purged from the body was sometimes said to be 'outward sulphur'. Some alchemists maintained that all things contain two sulphurs, inward and outward. The outward sulphur is stinking and impure dross, which must be removed, but the pure inwards sulphur is essential to the making of the Stone. For the more orthodox Christian alchemists outward sulphur probably meant the love of self and inward sulphur the love of God, but some alchemists, and the modern cabalists, do not take them in quite this sense. Sulphur stands for desires, feelings, motives. Inward sulphur means inner motives, the 'real will' beloved of Hegalian philosophers and modern occultists. Outward sulphur means superficial desires and interests. The removal of outward sulphur in sublimation spiritualises the body by freeing it from surface, worldly motives and concerns.

The alchemist is now left open to the free play of his inner driving forces. In fermentation the spiritual body is united with the soul. The fiery principle of inward sulphur, the soul or real will, works in the spiritual body as a ferment or leaven, changing and colouring the personality and transforming it to 'gold'. The process is one of intoxicated surrender to one's true inner self, a seething emotional disturbance and excitement which becomes an ecstasy (Strength in the Tarot). Modern occultists call the ferment 'the life in the juice of the grape' and 'the presence of Bacchus'.

Crowley hails Bacchus as man-woman, both divine and human—'drunk on delight of the godly grape, thou knowest no more the burden of the body and the vexation of the spirit'. The magician's ordinary self is 'a mob of wild women, hysterical from uncomprehended and unsated animal instinct; they will tear Pentheus, the merely human king who presumes to repress them, into mere shreds of flesh'. It is Bacchus, the true self, who will 'transform the disorderly rabble into a pageant of harmonious movements, tune their hyaena howls to the symphony of a paean, and their reasonless rage to self-controlled rapture'.[27]

Bacchus is 'doubly double', a god and an animal, a woman and a man. He is the true self, the human equivalent of God or Tetragrammaton, whose four letters are two pairs of opposites, and fermentation was thought to unite four components, mercury being double. Besides this, some of the alchemists said that mercury and sulphur are two pairs of opposites, not one. Mercury is outwardly mercury but inwardly sulphur and sulphur is outwardly sulphur but inwardly mercury. In other words, everything contains its own contradiction and whatever combines mercury and sulphur unites two pairs of opposites and is 'doubly double'.

The Bacchic frenzy of fermentation leads directly to exaltation, in which man becomes the Stone. The alchemists said that the material in the vessel was unstable, which suggests that the excitement of fermentation too often dwindled and broke down, with no lasting result. Exaltation was achieved only if the heat of the furnace could be raised to a sufficient pitch of intensity, only if the ecstasy could be carried to the highest peak of 'self-controlled rapture'. Then the Stone glowed brilliant red in all its glory in the vessel and the alchemist attained the ecstatic union with the divine. Body, soul and spirit were fused in the perfect and everlasting harmony of the whole man.

Exaltation corresponds to the Chariot in the Tarot and the charioteer has solved the riddle of the sphinx—the 4, the 3 and the 2 have become 1. When man becomes the Stone or the One, he becomes one with the universe. The process is a kind of death and the alchemist has achieved the full magical significance of the words quoted earlier—'Except a corn of wheat fall into the ground and die, it abideth alone; but if it die, it bringeth forth much fruit.'

The last two processes, multiplication and projection, are necessary because the work is cyclical. God is first 1, then 2 as a pair of opposites, and then through the union of the opposites 3, the Creator, from which follows 4, the creation of the physical universe. To halt the work with the Stone as 1, in exaltation, would be to cut the universe's lifeline. The human spirit which soars to union with the universe must become part of its unceasing process.

Love, in both multiplication and projection, is the completion of the work and its new beginning. 'Love', Eliphas Levi said, 'is one of the mythological images of the great secret and the great agent, because it at once expresses an action and a passion, a void and a plentitude, a shaft and a wound.'[28] In the royal marriage of multiplication, the One becomes Two and the Two are united—the union of *Yod* and *He* in Tetragrammaton, the Lovers in the Tarot. The wedding of sulphur and mercury stands for the fruitful union of all the opposites which are contained in the Stone.

From the union of the Two comes the fecundating power of the Third. In projection (the Pope in the Tarot) the Stone is mingled with a base metal, which is the alchemical parallel to the action of the Holy Spirit projected upon the waters in Genesis, animating First Matter and creating the phenomena of the universe with which the alchemist began. The work has come full circle.

For some adepts at least, the last stages of the work are connected with the astral body, for which they saw a warrant in St. Paul's distinction between the 'natural' and 'spiritual' bodies—'It is sown a natural body; it is raised a spiritual body.' 'Within the human body', Gerhard Dorn said, 'there is hidden a certain metaphysical substance, known only to the very few, whose essence it is to need no medicament, for it is itself uncorrupted medicament' and 'There is in natural things a certain truth which cannot be seen with the outward eye but is perceived by the mind alone. The philosophers have known it and they have found that its power is so great as to work miracles. . . . In this lies the whole art of freeing the spirit from its fetters' and it is 'the highest power and an impregnable fortress wherein the philosopher's stone lies guarded'.[29]

Several Renaissance occultists and alchemists mention what is now called the astral body or the astral light, the substance of which the astral body is composed—Dorn's uncorrupted 'metaphysical substance' or 'truth,' perceived by the mind alone. In his *Occult Philosophy*, Agrippa says that the human soul gains prophetic power when it transcends its normal bounds and escapes from the body to spread over space like a light escaped from a lantern. The experience comes through 'continued yearning heavenward from a pure body' (the Hermit in the Tarot) which carries the soul out of the body to pervade all space and all time. According to Paracelsus, man has three bodies—corresponding to body, soul and spirit—the 'elemental' or physical, the 'sidereal' or astral, and the 'illumined body' or 'spark of God', which recalls the 'luminous self' of the Manicheans. The astral body comes from the stars and consists of the accretions or layers added to the soul during its descent through the planetary spheres. It 'exceeds the measures of Nature'. It 'can neither be tied nor grasped' and can 'pass through walls and partitions without breaking anything'.[30]

The association of the astral with the soul, which stands between the body and the spirit or mind, accounts for the nature of the creatures of the astral plane, which are not like material things and not like mental pictures, but somewhere between the two. The astral plane, in modern theory, is the one in which desires, emotions and feelings move. It has the same relation to the physical plane as a man's emotions have to his body and beyond it is the 'mental plane', on which 'spiritual' beings move. Although the creatures of these planes are products of the mind and the imagination, to some extent at least, occultists believe either that they have an independent existence or that for practical purposes it is convenient to assume that they do.

Paracelsus said that the physical body is dead, but that the astral body is animated and volatile. The rising of vapour from a heated substance was believed to have its parallel in man, and the production of the 'spiritual body' in sublimation, the repeated transformation of a solid to a vapour and the vapour's reconversion to a solid, was the production of the ability to enter the astral plane and return to the physical body. The 'original filth' or 'outward sulphur' purged away in sublimation stands for the petty, surface motives and interests which tie a man to the physical plane. The increasing heat or frenzy of fermentation and exaltation leads to the point at which the alchemist is finally carried out beyond the bounds of his own being into a lasting union with the universe. He pervades all space and all time. He enters the impregnable fortress in which the Stone lies guarded.

3. The Elixir of Life

MAMMON   But when you see th' effects of the Great Medicine,
               Of which one part projected on a hundred
               Of Mercury, or Venus, or the moon,
               Shall turn it to as many of the sun;
               Nay, to a thousand, so ad infinitum:
               You will believe me.

SURLY   Yes, when I see't, I will.

MAMMON   Do you think I fable with you? I assure you,
               He that has once the flower of the sun,
               The perfect ruby, which we call elixir,
               Not only can do that, but, by its virtue,
               Can confer honour, love, respect, long life;
               Give safety, valour, yea and victory,
               To whom he will. In eight and twenty days
               I'll make an old man of fourscore, a child.

SURLY   No doubt; he's that already.

BEN JONSON *The Alchemist*

The adept who made the Philosopher's Stone had also made the Elixir of Life. Since it was divine and the perfect substance, the Stone was eternal and immortal. Its possession restored youth to the elderly, virility to the impotent, innocence and happiness to the world-weary. It healed the crippled, cured all diseases and resurrected the dead.

The American astrologer Marc Edmund Jones says that the occultist is expected to 'disentangle himself from the mere superficialities about him, and to strengthen his eternal matrix while doing so . . . he refines his personality until he has perfected the PHILOSOPHER'S STONE, i.e. the integrity of character through which he actually experiences a deathless significance among his fellows'.[31] But the immortality conferred by the Stone goes further than 'deathless significance'. The man who becomes the Stone has achieved true immortality. He has escaped the burden of successive mortal incarnations by becoming one with the eternal matrix, the One Life of the universe.

Some of the Masters, however, have chosen to remain on earth through a succession of bodily incarnations to help humanity. According to Cyril Scott, one of these is the High Initiate now known as the Hungarian Master, who lives in Europe and travels a great deal. He was once Proclus, a philosopher of the fifth century A.D., later 'a great English statesman and philosopher' (not named but probably Francis Bacon is meant) and later still the Count of St.-Germain. St. Paul is now a Cretan, principally occupied in watching over the Spiritualist movement. The High Initiate once known as Jesus occupies a Syrian body and lives in the Lebanon. He was earlier the Old Testament hero Joshua.[32] (This is because Joshua was the son of Nun and Jewish commentators believed that the true name of the Messiah would be Ji-Nun, 'son of Nun', or 'son of the Fish', which was one of the sources of early Christian fish symbolism.)

One of the most famous of all those who are supposed to have possessed the Elixir of Life is the Count of St.-Germain. 'The Comte de St.-Germain and Sir Francis Bacon', says Manly P. Hall, the leading light of the philosophical Research Society of Los Angeles, 'are the two greatest emissaries sent into the world by the Secret Brotherhood in the last thousand years.'[33] The Secret Brotherhood is a group of Masters, whose headquarters are said to be in the Himalayas and who are attempting to guide mankind along higher paths.

St.-Germain hobnobbed with the highest social circles in France, winning the favour of Madame de Pompadour in 1759 with his 'water of rejuvenation'. Immensely erudite and enormously rich, he was a skilful violinist, painter and chemist, had a photographic memory and was said to speak eleven languages fluently, including Chinese, Arabic and Sanskrit. He had found the Philosopher's Stone and used it to make gold and the magnificent jewels with which his person was literally besprinkled. He was believed to be over 2,000 years old and to be either the Wandering Jew or the offspring of an Arabian princess and a salamander. He delighted in reminiscing about the great ones of the past with whom he had been on familiar terms, including the Queen of Sheba and Cleopatra. He was a wedding guest at Cana when Christ turned the water into wine. There is a pleasant story of him describing a dear friend of long ago, Richard the Lionheart, and turning to his manservant for confirmation. 'You forget, sir,' the valet said solemnly, 'I have only been five hundred years in your service.'

St.-Germain attributed his astonishing longevity to his diet and his elixir. The elixir survives today as Saint-Germain Tea, a laxative made from senna. The diet consisted chiefly of oatmeal, groats and white meat of chicken, with a little wine occasionally. He also took elaborate precautions against catching cold. He is supposed to have died in Germany in 1784, but occultists believe that he was probably given a mock burial as, they say, Bacon was. It is said that he was frequently seen alive in the next century and was known to Bulwer Lytton.

Although to possess the Stone was also to possess the Elixir, there have always been plenty of rival elixirs and rejuvenators on the market, involving methods ranging from drinking human blood or eating vipers, strongly recommended by Madame de Sévigné in the seventeenth century, to inhaling the breath of young girls or sleeping with them, called 'sunamitism' from the story of David and the Shunamite damsel of 1 Kings 1. The search for magical renewal of youth and vigour still continues. At a conference of the California Medical Association in 1962 it was stated that health food stores 'tout nostrums with "magical properties" to pep up the blood, improve the complexion and instill vibrant youth' and that the American public spends $500 million a year on health foods and $350 million a year on unnecessary vitamins.

Alcohol has long been a popular elixir. Until recent times, in fact, alcohol was another term for the Elixir or 'water of life', as it is called in various languages—*aqua vitae, eau-de-vie, lebenswasser,* and the Irish *uisgebeatha,* now shortened to 'whisky'. In the early fourteenth century Arnald of Villanova identified it with alcohol in the modern sense, equating *aqua vini,* 'water of wine' with *aqua vitae,* but the word was not widely used in its modern meaning until the nineteenth century. Another name for alcohol was *aqua ardens,* because it is liquid and also burns; it was thought to be a combination of fire and water and so a form of the Stone. Some medieval alchemists thought that alcohol was a form of the quintessence, the pure fifth element of which the heavens are made. Placed in a still which was sunk in a dung-bed, the alcohol condensed in the still's projecting spout and was carried back into the still again, setting up a circulation. It then separated into two layers—a turbid lower layer, the earth or the four elements, which was rejected and a clear blue upper layer, the sky or quintessence. What this process actually produced was almost pure alcohol.[34]

A simple alcohol-elixir is Dr. Stevens' Water, a seventeenth-century cure-all and prolonger of life. Take one gallon of good Gascon wine and add one drachm each of ginger, galingale, cinnamon, nutmeg grains, cloves, fennel seeds, caraway seeds and origanum, and a handful each of sage, wild marjoram, pennyroyal, mint, red roses, thyme, pellitory, rosemary, wild thyme, chamomile and lavender. Bruise the herbs and grind the spices small. Add them to the wine and let the mixture stand for twelve hours, stirring frequently. Distil it, keeping the first distillate and the second and the third. This water 'comforts the spirits and vital parts and helps all inward diseases that come of cold and whoever uses this water moderately will make him seem young in his old age'.[35]

Gold was an obvious candidate for the Elixir, because the Stone was gold. The *Archidoxa Medicinae* or Elixir of Life of Paracelsus is believed to have been made from gold and he valued 'potable gold' as a medicine for purifying the blood and preventing miscarriages, as an antidote to poison, for keeping the Devil away if placed in a newborn baby's mouth, and especially for heart diseases, because gold and the heart are ruled by the sun. A sixteenth- or seventeenth-century recipe says that to make potable gold you begin with three pints of red wine vinegar and the ashes of a block of tin, burnt in an iron pan. Mix these together and distil them repeatedly. Then heat one ounce of gold in a crucible with white salt. Grind the mixture of gold and salt, heat it again, and wash it with water until there is no taste of salt left. Add it to the vinegar-tin mixture, one ounce to one pint, and evaporate it to the consistency of honey. Dissolve it in spirits of wine and you have potable gold.[36] It is significant that the recipe mentions alcohol and also honey and salt, both of which prevent decay.

Bacon, who is claimed by occultists as a great adept, said that the smell of earth is a tonic medicine. 'The following of the plough hath been approved for refreshing the spirits and procuring appetite.' Spring is the best time for this, before the earth has 'spent her sweet breath in vegetables put forth in summer', or fresh earth should be turned up with a spade. 'Gentlewomen may do themselves much good by kneeling upon a cushion and weeding.' Since the earth is the source of growing crops and vegetation, inhaling its vapours should preserve life, as Bacon hints. 'I knew a great man that lived long, who had a clean clod of earth brought to him every morning as he sate in his bed: and he would hold his head over it a good pretty while.'[37]

Another eminent English philosopher, Berkeley, hoped that he had found what might prove to be a 'universal medicine', a substance which carried the essence of life and cured all diseases, in 'tar-water', the dark resin exuded from pine-trees and firs mixed with cold water in the proportion of 1:4. He learned its uses on a mission to the American Indians. In *Siris*, published in 1744, he says that opium, mercury and soap 'bid fairest for Universal Medicines', but he has tried tar-water successfully on various ailments—including smallpox, asthma, coughs, pleurisy, indigestion, piles and scurvy—and believes there may be no limit to its capacities. It also preserved the gums and teeth, sweetened the breath and strengthened the voice. Berkeley suggested that the resin contained the 'vegetable soul' or 'the luminous spirit which is the form or life of a plant'. It was 'exalted and enriched' by the life-giving rays of the sun 'to become a most noble medicine: such is the last product of a tree, perfectly matured by time and sun'. Two months after *Siris* was published a Tar-Water Dispensary was opened in London and its use as a medicine became fashionable for a while.

Many occultists have speculated on the nature of life, what it consists of or in what substance it is contained, in the hope of using an 'essence of life' to stave off old age and cure disease. According to Paracelsus, the essence of life is contained in an invisible substance called 'mumia'. Blood, hair, sweat, urine and excrement all retain, for a time, the vital power of the body from which they come, and it is possible to make from them a 'microcosmic magnet' which contains mumia and attracts it, in the same way that magnetised iron attracts iron. If this applied to the afflicted part of a patient's body, it draws off diseased mumia from that part. The magnet is then mixed with earth and a plant is grown in the earth. The diseased mumia passes into the plant and the patient gets well. Paracelsus also used magnets to cure diseases caused by an imbalance or improper distribution of the basic components in the patient's body (and, much earlier, both Plato and Galen had said that disease is caused by imbalance of the body's elements or components). To cure hysteria in women, for example, Paracelsus placed one pole of a magnet above the uterus and the opposite pole of a second magnet below it, which regulated the movements of the 'nervous fluid' controlling the uterus and restored the fluid to its proper position. For epilepsy, the negative pole of a magnet was placed on the patient's head and the positive pole of another magnet of his stomach. This arrested the flow of nervous fluid to the brain, which had caused the epileptic fit.[38]

These ideas were carried further two hundred years later by Franz Mesmer and his followers. Mesmer published a thesis in 1766, in which he said that the movements of the planets affect the human body through an invisible fluid in which everything in the universe is immersed. He first thought this fluid was electricity, but he later called it the fluid of 'animal magnetism', because it acted principally on living creatures and had magnetic properties. He believed that

THE ELIXIR OF LIFE   171

just as a magnet has two poles, so man is magnetically divided in two, with poles in his left side opposite to those of his right side. Disease is caused by an imbalance of animal magnetism and can be cured by restoring a proper balance between the opposite poles. This can be done by stroking the body with magnets or by sheer will-power, because the fluid of animal magnetism responds to the trained will.

Mesmer went to Paris in 1778, set up a clinic and enjoyed a great fashionable success. His patients sat round a large oak tub which was filled with water, iron filings and powdered glass, and from which iron rods protruded. The patients applied these rods to the afflicted parts of their bodies while Mesmer marched about majestically in a pale lilac robe, passing his hands over the patients' bodies or touching them with a long iron wand. The results varied. Some patients felt nothing at all, some felt as if insects were crawling over them, others were seized with hysterical laughter, convulsions or fits of hiccups. Some went into raving delirium, which was called the 'crisis' and was considered extremely healthful.[39]

Mesmer's discovery that the magnetic fluid could apparently be controlled by the operator's will was the foundation of mesmerism and hypnotism. His theories have also influenced occultists and had a profound effect on Eliphas Levi. Levi identified the fluid of animal magnetism with the astral light, which exists in all the phenomena of the universe. It is both a substance and a force, a fluid and a type of light, and it was created by God's command 'Let there be light.' Like a magnet, it has opposite poles. It carries good and evil, it transmits light and propagates darkness. The astral body is formed of it and it can be controlled by the human will. It is the astral light, he explains in *Key of the Mysteries*, which is 'the fluidic and living gold' of alchemy and to control it is to achieve mastery of all things. 'To direct the magnetic forces is then to destroy or create forms; to produce to all appearance, or to destroy bodies; it is to exercise the almighty power of Nature.'

The belief in the existence of an Elixir of Life is a reflection of the magical theory that man is potentially divine. God is eternal and incorruptible, and it follows that somewhere, if man could only reach it, immortality waits for him, too.

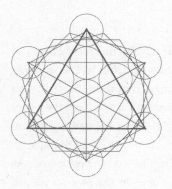

CHAPTER FIVE

Astrology

THE art of astrology is based on the theory of 'as above, so below', taken literally the belief that all events in the sky are paralleled by corresponding events on earth. Astrologers have connected virtually every important moment in history with movements of the planets, comets or eclipses, and the influence of the stars has been charted in the lives of innumerable people from Alexander the Great to Einstein. Both the birth and death of Julius Caesar were accompanied by comets, Wellington's defeat of Napoleon at Waterloo has been traced to the positions of Jupiter at Wellington's birth and Saturn at Napoleon's, the First World War was heralded by solar and lunar eclipses and has been linked with the positions of the sun and Mars in 1914, and American involvement in the Second World War was signalled by movements of Mars and Uranus. Modern astrologers believe that observation of the past conclusively proves that certain kinds of events occur on earth when the planets are in certain positions in the sky. 'Nobody', one of them says rather angrily, 'has been able to laugh that one off.'[1]

Astrology is concerned with the future, but its predictions are always based on analysis of the past. Past planetary positions will recur again and the time of their recurrence can be calculated. Astrologers know that Mars takes 687 days to go round the sun. They know what point in its orbit Mars has reached at any given moment and they can discover exactly what its position in the sky was or will be at any time in the past or future. If they find that there have always been dangers of war when Mars was in a certain position in the past, they predict that there will be danger of war again when Mars is in the same position in the future. In the same way, they forecast the effects of the other planets.

The astrologer's universe is like an immense simultaneous chess game. As the great driving forces of the universe move the pieces in the sky, so we are moved from square to square on the chess-boards of our lives. Some modern astrologers believe that the stars, or forces working through them, affect events on earth through vibrations or rays. Others do not attempt to explain the phenomenon at all, but the background to all astrology since classical times is the picture of the soul descending through the spheres to earth and gathering characteristics from each planet on the way. Man is made in the image of the universe. The planetary forces are inside us and each man carries the starry heaven and all its influences within himself.

There seems to be greater public acceptance of astrology at the present time than it has enjoyed since the seventeenth century, when it was thrown on to the rubbish heap with much of the rest of medieval science and philosophy. In a disturbing world, many people find modern science and philosophy either unintelligible or inadequate. Astrology offers a comprehensible explanation of human behaviour which, if its basic assumptions are granted, is attractively logical and orderly. At the same time it is sufficiently vague and complicated to escape the charge of being too simple an answer. And above all, it provides a convenient scapegoat—the sky—for all human folly, failure and inadequacy.

In the United States over 2,000 newspapers and magazines carry regular astrology columns. In Los Angeles astrologers advertise themselves in the papers, together with spiritual readers, card readers, psychics and the rest. (One recent ad says, 'Partner wanted, must have E.S.P., no investment.') Twenty American magazines deal entirely or mainly with astrology and it has been estimated that 5 per cent of the population fully believe that the future is written in the stars. In France the figure is said to be similar, possibly higher.[2] In Great Britain, where astrologers were lumped with 'charlatans, rogues and vagabonds' in the Witchcraft Act of 1735 and the Vagrancy Act of 1829, the astrologer is still widely regarded as a charlatan, but there is no longer any need for him to be a vagabond. Astrologers have set up their own professional organisations and there are schools which hold courses and set examinations in the subject.

Attempts have also been made to elevate the profession's status by the use of high-sounding titles—astro-scientist, astro-psychologist, solar biologist, astro-logue, astrologian.

In its earliest days in ancient Mesopotamia astrology was concerned with events affecting whole nations and peoples, not with the lives of individuals. The Greeks, who added most of its logical superstructure to astrology, also developed the interest in the fate of individual men and women which has dominated the art ever since. This branch of the subject, natal astrology, is still the most popular today.

1. Natal Astrology

We and the cosmos are one. The cosmos is a vast living body, of which we are still parts.
The sun is a great heart whose tremors run through our smallest veins. The moon is a
great gleaming nerve-centre from which we quiver forever. Who knows the power that
Saturn has over us or Venus? But it is a vital power, rippling exquisitely through us *all
the time.* . . .

Now all this is literally true, as men knew in the great past and as they will know
again.

D. H. LAWRENCE *Apocalypse*

In natal astrology your character and destiny are analysed in terms of the
position of the planets in the sky at the moment of your birth. These positions
are mapped in a 'birth chart' or 'horoscope'. It has often been argued that the
moment when you were conceived marked the beginning of your life and
should be taken as a basis, but this would obviously be difficult. The time of
conception is usually not known and cannot be calculated back from the time
of birth. Besides, as an American astrologer explains, when a baby draws his
first breath he inhales air, the 'causal substance' of the planet earth, and becomes an independent being. Until the moment of birth he is merely a part of
his mother.[3]

The astrologer needs to know the exact time of birth, which creates a difficulty because you may not know it and a difference of as little as an hour can
make a considerable difference to the positions of the planets in your birth
chart. One solution is to draw what is called a Hindu chart, which uses the
time of sunrise on your birthday, on the theory that the planetary positions at
the beginning of the day on which you began give a rough indication of your
personality and future. But most astrologers say that the indication is too
rough and they prefer the process of 'rectification'.

In rectification, charts are drawn for several likely birth moments. If you know you were born in the early morning, the astrologer can chart the positions of the planets at each hour from midnight to 6 a.m. He compares these charts with what he knows of your life and character, selects the one which seems to fit you best and uses it as the basis for his predictions. This process has considerable possibilities. If your astrologer's predictions never seem to come true, perhaps you have been misinformed about the time of your birth. By using a different time the astrologer may provide more accurate predictions and he will cheerfully go on to claim that he has discovered the correct time of your birth into the bargain. Rectification is not new. The eminent sixteenth-century mathematician Cardan so detested Luther that he altered Luther's birthday to give him an unfavourable horoscope.

When the moment of birth, real or rectified, has been determined, the astrologer charts the position of the sun, moon and planets in the sky at that moment. There is a good deal of disagreement among astrologers about the influences of the sun and moon. It is accepted that the *sun*, as the most important of the heavenly bodies, has a dominating influence on your character, but some authorities say that the sun rules the inner self and the moon the outer self, while others say it is the other way round. The sun is the world's power-house, the creator of light and heat, and so it is said to influence a man's creative power, vitality, will and ambition. Since the discovery that the sun stays still while the planets revolve around it many astrologers have concluded that the sun's position in the sky at your birth is the principle factor in creating your real self, the basic temperament which remains the same through all vicissitudes, the qualities and abilities which are central to your nature. Other astrologers, however, emphasise the sun's role in creating the 'lighted' or conscious part of the mind, the outer personality, appearance and physical characteristics.

Those who see the sun as the ruler of the real self take the *moon* as the mistress of the outer personality. The moon rules fluctuation, change, growth and decay, the ebb and flow of superficial relations and feelings above the hard rocks of your basic temperament. The moon receives light from the sun and reflects it, and so it governs receptivity and response, your reactions to other people and the world around you, acquired habits and mannerisms. But on the other hand the moon is also traditionally the ruler of night and the depths of the mind, the inner driving forces of a man's being.

The influences of the planets follow the characteristics of the gods for whom they are named. Astrologers are not so naïve as to say that Venus rules love because it is named for a love-goddess. Their argument is the other way round. After long study the ancients named Venus for the beautiful goddess of love, because they found that its influence was chiefly felt in matters of love and beauty. 'The planets were not named after the gods, the gods were named after the planets.'[4]

Mercury was the messenger of the gods and the god of intelligence, eloquence and merchandise. The planet rules your intelligence and especially your ability to communicate with other people, the messenger function. 'Mercurial' means active, sprightly, changeable, and if you are much influenced by this planet you will have these characteristics. Mercury was a celestial middleman—transferring messages, ideas, goods—and astrologers say that his planet influences you mainly through its connections with other planets. It tends to be a neutral force, which recalls the hermaphrodite as an alchemical symbol for mercury.

Venus rules love, affection, peace and harmony, beauty and appreciation of beautiful things. It governs your emotional make-up and your relationships with other people in love and friendship. The Babylonians named this planet for the goddess of love, and the Greeks and Romans followed suit, perhaps because it is most often seen in the early evening after sunset and in the early morning after sunrise, so that its appearances seem to set the bounds of night, the time for love-making.

Mars is the planet of belligerence, aggressiveness, activity, violent energy, determination. Its position in your birth chart indicates how active and energetic you are and in what ways. This is because the Sumerians and Babylonians connected the planet with blood, fire and the god of war, probably because of its reddish colour. Blood carries life and vitality, fire is active, energetic and destructive. Through the connection with red Mars was thought to be a particularly hot planet, and some modern astrologers say that it affects your tendency to become heated, in illness as well as in feelings, so that it influences your susceptibility to fever.

Jupiter, named for the father and ruler of gods and men, governs your ability to dominate, your tendency to fatherliness and 'joviality', to expansiveness and breadth of mind, and your ability to achieve prosperity and comfort. The Babylonians connected the planet with Marduk, a god who personified the sun in springtime, drying the land after the floods, bringing back order after chaos and presiding over the growth of crops. The result is that Jupiter is the planet of order and organisation, beneficence, success and money (growing crops).

Observation of its changing positions in the sky is the basis for astrological prediction of all fluctuations on the stock market. It also rules health and its symbol ♃ is still used to head prescriptions.

Saturn, like Mars, is traditionally an evil planet, occupied in frustrating the hopes of men and bringing upon them death, failure, catastrophe, misery and general gloom. This is because the Romans mistakenly identified Saturn, who was originally a harmless agricultural god, with the Greek god Cronos, possible because both of them had the sickle as an emblem. Cronos was the old and savage ruler of the Greek gods, who castrated his father Uranus with a sickle, ate his own children and was eventually tricked and overthrown by Zeus. Cronos in turn was wrongly identified with Chronos, 'Time', and so the planet rules the inexorable passing of time which eats its own children in turning all things to dust. In addition, Saturn is 'cold', because it is the furthest from the sun of the old planets and 'black' because its light is dim.

Modern astrologers, who tend to be all sweetness and light, prefer not to attribute evil influences to the heavens, and they see Saturn as 'the celestial taskmaster', governing your powers of self-discipline and self-control, your capacity for endurance and the bearing of responsibility. Their picture of Saturn is still not a very cheerful one and they seem in awe of a planet which they personify more often than any of the others. The Hollywood astrologer Carroll Righter, self-styled World's Greatest Astrologian, says of Saturn in his *Astrology and You*, 'Under his influence you get exactly what you have earned, not one whit more or less. . . . He is the planet of JUSTICE and only gives you that to which you are entitled.'

The discovery of planets which were not known to the ancient world has caused astrologers much hard work and considerable irritation over the last two hundred years. The new planets do not fit neatly into the astrological scheme of things. Astrologers have tried to discover the nature of their influences by calculating their positions in people's birth charts and gauging their effects on these people's lives. Important political and social events occurring after each new planet's discovery are also taken as clues to its astrological nature, but the main emphasis is still on the god for whom the planet is named.

Uranus was christened for the Greek sky-god who was deposed by Cronos and was the father of the Titans, the Cyclopes and the Hundred-handed Ones, who were probably personifications of the violent upheavals and convulsions of Nature—eruptions, tidal waves, earthquakes. It is the planet of sudden change, upheaval and revolution. Its influence may make you wilful, independent, impatient of restraints, wild and unconventional, likely to do or say peculiar and unexpected things. It is the planet of originality and invention, because Uranus was the father and originator of all living things. It is also the planet of electricity, because he was the god of lightning.

Neptune, named for the Roman god of the sea, is the planet of impressionability, because water is fluid and shifting and takes the shape of any container. It governs spiritual and psychic matters, the mysterious depths of things. As the ruler of dreams, Neptune is connected with the motion-picture industry. Under its influence you may be preacher, medium, mystic or occultist. Or you may be 'watery' in the sense of being vague, dreamy and impractical.

Astrologers are not certain about *Pluto*, but usually treat it as a planet of change and transformation, because Pluto was lord of death and the underworld, though they agree that its influence on human life has not yet been sufficiently studied.

To draw your birth chart the astrologer needs a method of describing exactly where each planet was in the sky at the time of your birth. To locate any position on the earth's surface we use a grid of imaginary lines, the lines of longitude and latitude, and we can state the position of any place on the earth in terms of these lines. In the same way astrologers use an imaginary measuring-rod, the *zodiac*, to describe the positions of the planets in the sky. The zodiac is an imaginary backcloth in the heavens. We see the sun, moon and planets moving across this backcloth and we can describe the position of a planet at a given moment by stating the point which it has reached on the backcloth. For accuracy in doing this, the zodiac is divided into twelve equal sections, called the *signs of the zodiac*, and the signs are divided into degrees. There are 30 degrees in each sign.

In Diagram 6 the sun, seen from the earth on April 4, appears to be half-way across the zodiac sign Aries, and Venus is half-way across the sign Gemini. These positions are stated as—sun at 15° Aries, Venus at 15° Gemini. By July 6 the earth has moved some way along its orbit round the sun, so that the sun now appears to be at 15° Cancer, with Venus at 15° Libra. The positions of the moon and the other planets could be shown and stated in the same way. (Venus is shown here only for purposes of illustration. Its positions would not be the same on April 4 and July 6 every year.)

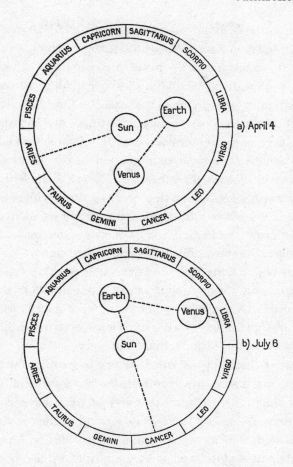

DIAGRAM 6 **The Sun in the Zodiac**

Viewed from the earth, the sun appears to move across the backcloth of the zodiac. The fact that it only 'appears' to do this and that it is really the earth which is moving does not upset the calculations of astrologers. To say that the sun is now passing through the sign of Libra, or that the earth is moving in such a way that the sun appears to be passing through Libra, is to state the same fact about the relative positions of sun and earth, and it is the relative positions with which astrologers are concerned.

In astrology the signs of the zodiac are *not* the constellations which have the same names. On March 21 each year astrologers say that the sun is in Aries.

In reality, the sun is not in the constellation Aries (though it was 2,000 years ago) but in the constellation Pisces. When an astrologer today says that the sun is in one sign of the zodiac it is really in the preceding sign, which seems to cast some doubt on all astrological findings for several hundred years past. But astrologers distinguish between the constellations and the signs. The constellations are groups of stars in the sky. The signs are artificial divisions of the sky and are not affected by precession of the equinoxes (the phenomenon which has caused the difference in the sun's apparent position in the constellations). This distinction was drawn by Ptolemy, the father of medieval and modern astrology, in his *Tetrabiblos*, but astrologers are on treacherous ground with it, because much of their doctrine comes from astrologers of the ancient world, to whom the signs and constellations were identical, and the names of the constellations have considerable influence on the astrological nature of the signs.

The apparent motion of the sun carries it through the full circle of the zodiac every year and it spends approximately one month in each zodiac sign. The day of your birth, regardless of the year, gives you one major factor in your birth chart, the sign occupied by the sun. Horoscopes in newspapers and magazines are based on this factor, the *sun-sign.*

Each sign of the zodiac is 'ruled' by one or more of the planets and the planet which rules a sign strongly affects the sign's characteristics. The origin of these rulerships is lost in the mists of antiquity, but they seem to be based on a logical system. According to Ptolemy, writing in the early second century A.D., the two signs which cover the period of maximum warmth are Cancer and Leo (July and August), and so they are ruled by the moon and sun, the bearers of light and heat. The two opposite signs, Aquarius and Capricorn, belong to Saturn because it is the coldest planet, the furthest from the sun. Jupiter, next to Saturn, rules the next two signs and Mars the next two. Mercury is never further from the sun than one sign in either direction, so it rules the signs next to Leo and Cancer, and Venus, which is never further than two signs from the sun, rules the next two signs.[5] Diagram 7 shows the signs, the planet which rules each sign (in the inner circle) and the dates during which the sun is in each sign. The new planets have upset the neat traditional arrangement and have to share the rulership of three of the signs.

The signs are divided into groups, called *quadruplicities* and *triplicities.* These groupings, again tradition, have an important effect on the astrological nature of each sign.

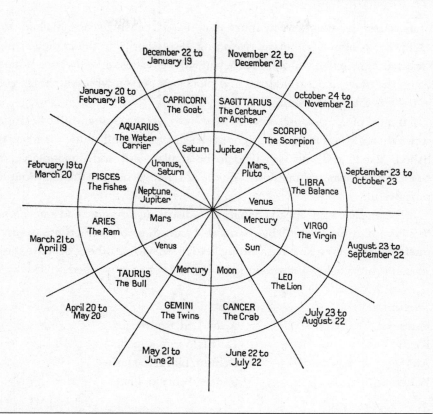

DIAGRAM 7 **The Signs of the Zodiac**

Quadruplicities	*Signs*
Cardinal	Aries, Cancer, Libra, Capricorn
Fixed	Taurus, Leo, Scorpio, Aquarius
Mutable (or Common)	Gemini, Virgo, Sagittarius, Pisces

When the position of each planet in the zodiac at your birth has been discovered, the number of planets in each quadruplicity is counted. If the sun, moon and all eight planets were in cardinal signs when you were born, for instance, you will have strongly 'cardinal' characteristics. The *cardinal* signs mark the beginning of each of the four seasons—spring, (Aries, March 21), summer (Cancer, June 22), autumn (Libra, September 23) and winter (Capricorn, December 22). When the sun enters each of these signs it is moving into a new section of its course, leading the way into a new season, causing seasonal changes on earth. By 'as above, so below' reasoning, if a majority of the planets were in cardinal signs when you were born, you will be restless and always anxious to be on the move, a natural leader and pioneer, a person who sets things going and starts things happening.

If most of your planets were in *fixed* signs, you are rather dull by comparison. When the sun is in these signs each season is in full swing, firmly established, 'fixed', and you will tend to be stable, solid and unadaptable. You suspect new ideas and methods, you dislike change, but you are tenacious and purposeful.

The *mutable* signs mean change, an old season giving way to a new one. If this is your group you will be changeable and adaptable, sometimes positively unstable. You may also have a strong bent for service to others, because the old season is unselfishly withdrawing so that the year can proceed on its way.

Triplicities	Signs
Fire	Aries, Leo, Sagittarius
Earth	Taurus, Virgo, Capricorn
Air	Gemini, Libra, Aquarius
Water	Cancer, Scorpio, Pisces

The number of planets in each triplicity in your chart is also counted. If your planets are predominantly in the *fire* signs, you have fiery characteristics—you are aspiring, warm, bright and cheerful, jumpy and excitable, able to burn with passion and feeling or better still with a hard gem-like flame. People not of your own kind may find you extremely alarming. An *earth* person is earthy—dependable and solid as the ground beneath our feet, cautious, practical, taciturn and quiet (except for occasional violent eruptions), possibly limited and narrow in outlook, perhaps even a 'clod'. *Air* people are light and lively, gay, intellectual, idealistic, free and easy, but sometimes rather 'airy-fairy' and too much inclined to 'talk hot air' with their heads in the clouds. The *water* group are naturally watery—sensitive, emotional, deep, intuitive, secretive, unstable, treacherous, perhaps 'wet', 'sloppy', or 'drips'. Astrologers do not regard this kind of thing as mere word-play and all the words in inverted commas in this paragraph come from Margaret Horne's *Modern Textbook of Astrology*, written as a textbook for courses at the Faculty of Astrological Studies in London. Astrologers share the magician's belief that an association between two things in the human mind is evidence of a real connection between the two things in the universe.

The astrological nature of each sign is a blend of the characteristics of the planet which rules it, the quadruplicity and triplicity to which it belongs, and the animal or object which it represents. (The animals and objects come from the Greeks. The Babylonian names of the signs were different in most cases.) *Aries*, for instance, is cardinal—implying movement, leadership, creativity—and fiery—implying drive, energy excitement. Its ruler is Mars, the planet of vigour and activity. Consequently, Aries is the most active and energetic of the signs, and if you were born when the sun was in Aries you will be driving, impatient, aggressive, possibly violent and destructive, a born leader and fighter. You will be creative and optimistic, probably egotistical and belligerent. Aries is the sign of the Ram and you will be very much like a ram, even a 'battering ram'. You should have the strong sexuality which rams are supposed to enjoy and you may look like one, with a long neck and well-marked eyebrows which with your nose make you resemble the astrologer's symbol for Aries—♈. That Ariens look like rams is not a modern discovery. Bartholomew of England, writing in the mid-thirteenth century, said that Ariens have 'a hairy body, a crooked frame, an oblique face, heavy eyes, short ears, a long neck'.[6]

The sign *Leo* is fiery but fixed and if it is your sun-sign you will have greater stability than the Ariens. Leos are lion-like, powerful, dignified, dominating, courageous, generous, honest, loyal and inflexible. They have fine heads of hair, short noses and large handwriting (paw marks). Extremely creative, they can be imperious, self-righteous, patronising and unable to co-operate with others. They are particularly successful as leaders of men in action—Caesar and Napoleon were both Leos (so was Mussolini). Much of this follows from the fact that the sun is Leo's ruler and Leos always go forward in life, because the sun never retrogrades. The planets sometimes appear to be moving backwards or 'retrograde' in the zodiac, but the sun never does this.

Sagittarius, the third fiery sign, is also a mutable sign and its natives are correspondingly fiery but changeable. Ambitious, clever and imaginative, they may show inconsistency and inability to concentrate. The ruling planet, Jupiter, brings them breadth of mind and a bold, generous character, but they can be domineering and Sagittarian women are inclined to air their opinions too loudly and too often. This is the sign of the Centaur and Sagittarians love travel, movement, hunting, the outdoors, sports and animals, especially horses (the Centaur being half horse).

In the Earth triplicity, *Taurus* is a fixed sign and the sign of the Bull. Taurus people are accordingly reliable, solid, patient, slow and careful, clumsy but tenacious. They are thickset and heavy-necked, usually placid, but with violent tempers. It is not a good idea to wave red flags in front of them. They love comfort and possessions, and are possessive in love. Venus gives them a liking for peace, harmony and beautiful things. Bulls are renowned procreators and Taureans may have great creative abilities. Shakespeare, Gibbon, Robert Browning, Kant, Brahms, Wagner, Sibelius and Salvador Dali were all born under this sign.

Virgo, earthy and mutable, is not a very promising sign. Its earthy character causes stolidity, quietness and dependability, its mutable character a bent for service to others. Virgos, of course, are virginal—cool, modest and prudent—and they tend to be old-maidish, fussy, critical, nervous and tense, overconcerned with their health. Mercury gives them intelligence, an attractive voice and a knack for languages.

Capricorn, the sign of the Goat, is earthy and cardinal. Its natives are solid, practical people, but also determined leaders, capable of leaping over all dangers and butting away all obstacles. Saturn brings them gravity, caution, a cool utilitarian cast of mind. They make excellent politicians. To look at, naturally, they are saturnine and have long faces like goats.

Gemini is the first of the Air signs and is also mutable. Its ruler is Mercury, planet of intelligence, communicativeness and restlessness. Geminians are intelligent, inventive and inquisitive, but also extremely changeable and jumpy, going up and down like mercury in a thermometer. They can be heartless and 'two-faced', because this is the sign of the Twins, but they are usually very loyal and devoted to their families (because the original Twins, Castor and Pollux, were noted for their brotherly affection).

Libra is airy and cardinal, implying movement and restlessness, lightness and intuitiveness. This is the sign of the Balance or Scales under the rule of Venus, which may make Librans attractive in looks or personality, fond of beauty and good at creating harmony around them. They have a 'balanced' quality about them and a pleasing tact. They weigh everything carefully in their scales and they often find it hard to make up their minds or make definite decisions. They are restless and easily become discontented. They are neat and precise, dislike ugliness and dirt, and have a great need for sympathy and friendship.

Aquarius is airy but fixed, the sign of the Water Carrier, ruled by Uranus and Saturn. Aquarians are brilliant and inventive (airy) and also persistent and determined (fixed). They are much concerned to help others (water carrying), pouring themselves out on the world, as it were, but they can be fanatical, tactless, and independent to the point of perversity (influence of Uranus). They are sociable people who tend to wear odd clothes and have noticeable ankles. They are prone to accidents involving electricity and are unusually likely to be struck by lightning. Washington, Franklin, Lincoln, General MacArthur and Adlai Stevenson are included among Aquarians.

Cancer, the Crab, is the cardinal Water sign. If you were born with the sun in Cancer you may be relieved to hear that you are not expected to look exactly like a crab. Your round, pale face comes from the moon, Cancer's ruler. Your characteristics are crab-like, though. You are much given to movement, travel and exploration (cardinal qualities). Under the surface, you are shy, timid, introspective (watery qualities). Your caution and your excellent memory, combined with your understanding of current trends (the moon), may make you a successful businessman, like John D. Rockefeller, Sr., and Marshall Field, who were Cancers. Sensitive, protective and home-loving, you like to collect things. When trouble comes, you naturally tend to scuttle for cover.

A *Scorpio* person unites the deep qualities of the watery signs, the stability of the fixed signs, and the characteristics of the scorpion. Scorpios are darkly secretive, intense, passionate. They have invincible will-power, sharp and resilient minds and characters. They have a knack for acquiring great wealth. They are terrible and relentless enemies. They should keep their feet firmly on the ground and be careful about their diet (because scorpions are scavengers).

Lastly, *Pisces* is watery and mutable. The wretched Pisceans, ruled by the vague and impressionable Neptune, are excessively changeable, emotional, dependent on others, nervous, muddled, easily upset and almost incapable of making definite decisions. They are the Fishes and first they swim upstream, then they swim down. But they are friendly, sympathetic people and they often have considerable artistic talent and an intuitive understanding of the mysterious and the intangible. Sometimes they are evasive and slippery, like fish. They are fond of the water and swimming, naturally. They should have protuberant eyes and slightly vacant expressions.

Your sun-sign is of great astrological importance, because it has a dominating effect on your basic character, but your personality is also affected by the positions of the moon and the planets in the zodiac when you were born. The zodiacal position of a planet indicates the particular way in which that planet will affect your character and life. For instance, one of the characteristics of

Taurus is a liking for food, drink and comfort. If Mars, the planet of vigour and activity, was in Taurus at your birth it may be that your Martian energy is particularly directed to food, drink and comfort, so that you tend to overeat, drink too heavily and generally overindulge yourself. Venus is the planet of love. If Venus was in the balanced, harmonious sign of Libra when you were born your love-life should be pleasant, gentle and peaceful, but if Venus was in the dark and passionate sign of Scorpio you are likely to have fierce and tempestuous love affairs.

Not only does the influence of a planet show itself in a different way in each zodiac sign but the strength of the influence may vary. Traditionally, each planet has a sign in which its influence is 'strong', a sign in which it is 'exalted' or powerful and a sign in which it is 'debilitated' or weak. For example, Saturn is strong when it is in Capricorn, exalted when in Libra, weak when in Aries. Venus is strong in Taurus, exalted in Pisces but weak in Virgo, which seems logical.

Astrologers use special tables, called Ephemerides, to find the positions of the sun, moon and planets at your birth. These tables also show which sign was on the eastern horizon at the time and place of your birth. The point where your eastern horizon appeared to intersect the zodiac is called the *ascendant* and the sign on the horizon is said to be 'on the ascendant'.

In diagram 8 point A is your birthplace and the ascendant is marked ASC. On this particular day the sun was at 15° Aquarius. If you were born at sunrise, the eastern horizon from point A intersected Aquarius and so Aquarius is both your sun-sign and the sign of the ascendant. At midday the sun is still at 15° Aquarius, but the earth has revolved on its axis in such a way that the eastern horizon now intersects Taurus and Taurus is the sign on the ascendant. By sunset the earth has revolved still further, the eastern horizon from point A intersects Leo and Leo is the sign on the ascendant, though the sun-sign is still Aquarius.

The sign on the ascendant, the sign which was rising over your eastern horizon at the time of your birth, is an extremely important factor in your birth chart. This sign is supposed to have great influence on your personality and destiny, and the planet which rules the ascendant sign is the ruling planet of your life. Born at midday, as in diagram 8, with the sun in Aquarius and Taurus on the ascendant, your characteristics will be a blend of Aquarius-Taurus qualities, subject to the influence of Venus, which rules Taurus and is therefore

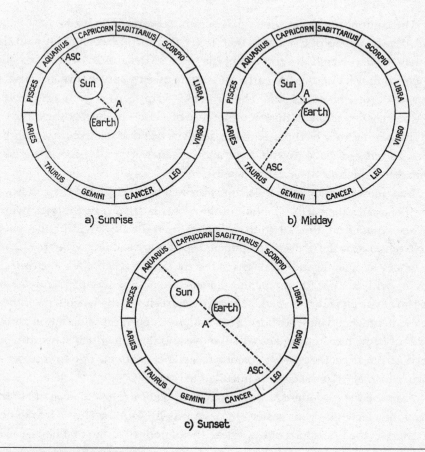

a) Sunrise

b) Midday

c) Sunset

DIAGRAM 8 **The Ascendant**

your ruling planet. Born a few hours later at sunset, you will be a mixture of Aquarius-Leo qualities and your ruler is the sun, which rules Leo.

All children born between January 20 and February 18 have the same sun-sign, Aquarius, but they will not have identical personalities, because their ascendant signs will differ with the time and place of each child's birth. Their sun-sign characteristics may be modified by those of any of the eleven other signs. This greatly increases the number of personality-types available to astrologers. As the positions of the moon and the planets also have to be taken into account, it is clear that astrological character-analysis is not simple or uncomplicated. (However, two children born at the same time and within a few miles of each other will have identical birth charts, which has been one of the principal arguments against astrology for centuries.)

The complications have only just begun, however. The birth chart is intended to be a map of the sky as seen from your birthplace. Not only do the planets move through the zodiac but the signs of the zodiac themselves also appear to move, circling the earth once every twenty-four hours, because of the earth's rotation on its axis. The sun at 15° Capricorn at your birth could have been at any point on the circumference of a circle in the sky, the centre of the circle being your birthplace. To pin down its position relative to your birthplace, astrologers have invented yet another imaginary division of the sky, again into twelve sections, called *houses*.

Imagine a gigantic wheel. Its rim is formed by the signs of the zodiac, so that it encircles the earth. The hub of the wheel is at your birthplace. Twelve spokes radiate from the hub to the wheel's rim in the sky, dividing the wheel into twelve parts, the houses. The hub and spokes are stationary, but the rim of the wheel is revolving and the signs of the zodiac, stretched along the rim, are moving with it. The sun, moon and planets are moving independently along the rim at various rates of speed. The birth chart shows the wheel's position at the moment when you were born. This is a pre-Copernican illustration and in reality it is the hub and spokes which move and the rim which stays still, but this does not affect the relative position of a planet or zodiac sign to your birthplace, which is what the chart is intended to show.

Suppose the ascendant at your birth, the point on the zodiac or rim of the wheel intersected by your eastern horizon was 10° Cancer. This is marked on the chart as the first spoke of the wheel, the boundary of the first house, as in diagram 9 (in which the numbers of the houses are shown at the centre). The other zodiac signs follow round the wheel in order. The first house begins at 10° Cancer, the second at 10° of the next sign, Leo, the third at 10° of the next sign, Virgo, and so on. The planetary positions can now be marked in. The sun was at 20° Scorpio and appears in the fifth house of the chart, which covers the stretch of the sky from 10° Scorpio to 10° Sagittarius. The moon at 11° Taurus is just inside the eleventh house, which begins at 10° Taurus. Mercury at 9° Aquarius falls in the seventh house, which ends at 10° Aquarius. If you imagine yourself standing at your birthplace at the centre of the chart, your eastern horizon intersects 10° Cancer, the ascendant, your western horizon intersects 10° Capricorn and the point in the sky immediately above your head is 10° Aries. You can see the moon and Mercury above you in the sky, but it is night-time and you cannot see the sun, which is at the other side of the earth.

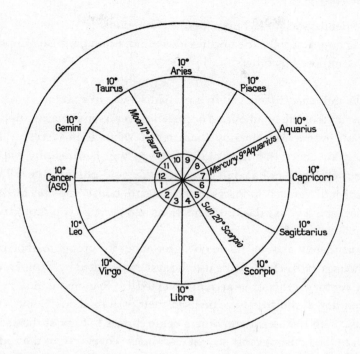

DIAGRAM 9 The Houses

The house position of a planet is supposed to reveal the department of life in which its influence will show itself. The departments of life are, briefly:

House	Department of Life
1	Personality and appearance.
2	Money and possessions.
3	Mental capacities, knowledge, self-expression, short journeys.
4	Childhood environment.
5	Children, pleasures, love affairs, risks and speculation.
6	Health, work, services rendered (by you to others or by others to you).
7	Close relationships in marriage, love, business.
8	Death; legacies and other sources of gain.
9	Religious and philosophical views, travels, dreams.
10	Career, status, reputation, responsibilities.

11   Friends, social life, hopes, desires, ambitions.
12   Enemies, secrets, the unconscious mind, limitations (self-imposed
       or imposed by others).

A planet's influence affects you in a particular way in a zodiac sign and in a particular area of life in a house. For instance, Venus in Pisces is supposed to produce an impractical, dreamy character. If Venus is in Pisces in the fifth house of your chart, this may mean that you will be dreamily impractical about your children and also that you should avoid plunging heavily on the stock market. If Venus is in Pisces in the eleventh house, you may be dreamily impractical about your hopes and ambitions and perhaps you should wake up to reality.

Unfortunately, astrologers do not agree about the proper method of drawing the houses in the chart. Some use the system invented by Campanus in the eleventh century, others the system invented by Regiomontanus in the fifteenth century, and others have devised their own methods. Some begin the first house with the ascendant, others begin it near but not at the ascendant. Some space the houses evenly so that each house covers 30° of the zodiac, but others space the houses unevenly. The inevitable result is that different astrologers give different interpretations of the same planetary positions, because they place the planets in different houses.

Diagram 10 is a sample birth chart. Since it is intended only as an illustration, I have shown the names of the planets and signs where an astrologer would use symbols. In this chart the houses are not equal in extent—the sixth house covers 33°, while the seventh covers 30°. The ascendant is at 10° Leo, but in this case the first house starts near but not at the ascendant. If you want to draw your own chart, *Astrology for Everyone* by the well-known British astrologer Edward Lyndoe has helpful tables and instructions, which I have used in drawing this diagram, but many astrologers do not accept Lyndoe's house-division system.

The first point to consider is the sign on the ascendant. The ruling planet of this sign is the ruler of the person's life and the affairs of the house occupied by the ruling planet will be of special importance in his life. In diagram 10, Leo is on the ascendant, so the ruling planet is the sun, which should produce a powerful, vital, creative life. The sun is in the first house, which suggests that this man's personality and appearance will be particularly important factors in his life. His sun-sign is Leo, implying a commanding, powerful and power-

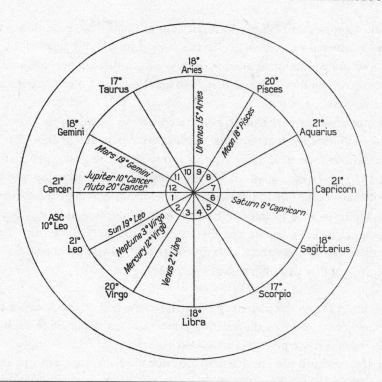

18°
Aries

17°
Taurus

20°
Pisces

18°
Gemini

21°
Aquarius

Uranus 15° Aries

Moon 18° Pisces

Mars 19° Gemini

21°
Cancer

Jupiter 10° Cancer
Pluto 20° Cancer

21°
Capricorn

ASC
10° Leo

Saturn 6° Capricorn

21°
Leo

Sun 19° Leo

Neptune 3° Virgo

Mercury 12° Virgo

Venus 2° Libra

18°
Sagittarius

20°
Virgo

17°
Scorpio

18°
Libra

DIAGRAM 10   **Sample Birth Chart**

loving character, but this is modified by the fact that the moon is in Pisces, which suggests that his inward reactions to things may tend to be emotional and confused. The moon in the eighth house means an interest in psychic re-search or some other form of speculation about life after death. (If Neptune is in the eighth house, you should die in your sleep or under anaesthetic. Ve-nus in the eighth house means an easy death.)

Counting by quadruplicities, the majority of the planets (six out of ten) are in cardinal signs, suggesting movement, leadership, creativity. The rest are all in mutable signs, implying changeableness, instability. The impression of in-stability is heightened by the fact that there are no planets at all in the fixed signs. The triplicities give a more balanced effect—two planets in Fire signs, three in Earth signs, two in Air signs, and three in the Water group.

Neptune and Mercury are together in the second house—money and pos-sessions. Neptune is an impressionable planet, and in this house suggests a ten-dency to be easily swindled in money matters, but this may be mitigated by the fact that Neptune is in Virgo, which ought to produce a more cautious, critical attitude to other people. Mercury in the second house and 'exalted' in Virgo means a strong possibility of making money as a middleman or agent or in some field connected with communication. Perhaps this person might write popular books on psychic research.

Uranus in Aries in the ninth house suggests an aggressively (Aries) free-thinking and independent (Uranus) attitude to religion and philosophy (ninth house). Saturn 'strong' in Capricorn in the sixth house is not promising for health and may cause a cold, calculating attitude to work and employers. One authority says that Mars in the twelfth house means 'dangers of violence', but luckily Jupiter is also in the twelfth house and the same authority says this means 'Success. Enemies are not able to cause trouble'. On the other hand, a different authority interprets Mars in the twelfth house as 'considerable administrative ability usually produces success'.

Besides interpreting the planetary positions in the zodiac and the houses, the astrologer also considers the relative position of each planet to each other planet. These relative positions are called *aspects*.

In diagram 10, Jupiter and Saturn are opposite each other, with an angle of close to 180° between them. Jupiter is directing its rays or vibrations at the earth from one side and Saturn is directing its rays or vibrations from the other side. The two planets are said to be 'in opposition', hostile and in disagreement. This celestial disagreement will have disagreeable effects on the subject of the birth chart. Jupiter is the planet of prosperity and success. Saturn's opposition will tend to limit success and thwart ambition. Any two planets in opposition have unpleasant effects on earth. For example, in cases where the sun in Leo is in opposition to the moon at the time of birth, the baby is likely to be afflicted with a squint (presumably caused by trying to look at the sun and moon in opposite directions at the same time).

When two or more planets occupy the same position in the chart or are within a few degrees of the same position, they are 'in conjunction' and their influences, playing on the earth from the same direction, are mingled together. In diagram 10, Jupiter and Pluto are almost in conjunction: so are Mercury and Neptune. Whether a conjunction is favourable or unfavourable depends on the planets involved. Venus in conjunction with the sun at a man's birth can inject his character (sun) with the soft influences of Venus to cause effeminacy. A conjunction of the two evil planets, Mars and Saturn, has been dreaded for hundreds of years as a terrible omen. Lyndoe expects this conjunction in a birth chart to produce 'a malicious temperament with even a possibility of sadism'. Traditionally, a conjunction of sun and moon at birth produces a lunatic—a personality (sun) overaffected by *luna*, the moon. Modifying this, Lyndoe says that a conjunction of sun and moon will cause periodic bouts of depression.

There are numerous other aspects which can be taken into account. In the old days they were plainly labelled good or bad, but modern astrologers prefer to call them positive or negative, easy or difficult. The bad or difficult aspects are connected with the evil and ominous numbers 2, 4 and 8. Planets are in opposition, the worst possible aspect, when there is an angle of 180° between them, which is the zodiac circle divided by 2. A square (90° angle between two planets) divides the zodiac circle by 4 and a semisquare (45° angle) divides it by 8. Sesquiquadrate (135° angle) is square plus semisquare. The last bad aspect is quincunx (150° angle). A quincunx is a group of five objects formed into a *square*, which is probably the reason for this aspect's ominousness.

The good or easy aspects are connected with the comparatively favourable numbers 3, 5, 6 and 12, especially with 3, the luckiest of numbers. Trine (120° angle between two planets) is the zodiac circle divided by 3. A grand trine— three or more planets in an equilaterial triangle on the chart—is an excellent omen. Other good aspects are sextile (60° angle) which divides the zodiac by 6, semisextile (30° angle) which divides it by 12, quintile (72° angle) which divides it by 5, and biquintile (144° angle) which is two quintiles.

The effects of these aspects again vary with the planets involved. A bad aspect of Mars to Jupiter will give you a streak of wildness and extravagance, but a good aspect of Mars to Uranus produces a compelling personality with well-developed muscles. Adolf Hitler's birth chart shows Mars square to Saturn, which produces manic-depressive personalities. The zodiac signs also affect the picture. People born with the sun in Capricorn but with Saturn (Capricorn's ruler) badly aspected to Mars will show revolutionary tendencies and will take a gleeful delight in watching other people suffer. *Predicting Events* by Zain, a textbook for courses in astrology at the Church of Light in Los Angeles, says that Edison was bound to lose money in companies promoting his inventions because at his birth Mars in the second house (money) was square (unfavourable) to Uranus (inventions) in the fifth house (speculation).

There are many other complications. To mention only one, the influences of non-zodiacal constellations can be taken into account. Vivian Robson, a leading authority on this subject, noted that the constellations in the sky usually bear little or no resemblance to the objects they are supposed to represent, but that the objects turn out to be accurate symbols of the constellations' influence on earthly life. 'The constellation of the Dog, for example, actually influences dogs, ridiculous as it may appear.'[7] The influence of the constellation Argo, named for a ship, is connected with the sea and particularly with drowning. Argo was in the eighth house (death) of Shelley's horoscope and the poet duly died by drowning. The constellation Hair of Berenice affects baldness. When Mars is in the constellation Andromeda in bad aspect with the sun and moon, it causes death by hanging, decapitation, crucifixion or impalement.

Reduced to its simplest form, as recommended in many astrological textbooks for beginners, the process of analysing a birth chart amounts to connecting together a set of key words and then translating them into meaningful language. The nature of a planet, a zodiac sign or a house is summed up in one or more key words which can be linked into a sentence.

Suppose you had Jupiter in Scorpio in the third house of your chart. This could be interpreted as: the *expansive* influence of Jupiter will show itself *passionately* (Scorpio) in *mental capacities* (third house). If your astrologer repeated this statement to you as it stands you would probably not be greatly impressed. He has to translate it into words which mean something. The trouble is that the number of ways in which he can do this is almost limitless. He might say that you will have a strong desire to broaden your interests and mental outlook, or he might tell you your mind is obsessed by sex, or he might say any one of a hundred other things. And he could equally well have stated the same planetary position in entirely different key words as: the influence of Jupiter to *prosperity* will show itself *secretively* (Scorpio) in *short journeys* (third house), which perhaps might mean that you should be able to make money as a bookmaker.

The woolliness of astrological language is one of the reasons for the constant failure of astrologers to agree on the interpretation of a given set of planetary positions. A chart can be interpreted in so many equally legitimate ways that two different astrologers are almost certain to produce two different interpretations. The fact that many astrological predictions are so all-embracing that they can scarcely fail to come true is also due to the vagueness of the astrologer's language as well as to his natural caution.

2. Mundane Astrology

Nearly all professional astrologers are ignorant of their own subject, as of all others.

ALEISTER CROWLEY Magick in Theory and Practice

Mundane astrology is the branch of the subject which deals with nations and peoples. Just as a chart can be drawn for an individual, so it can be drawn for a nation. The chart shows the planetary positions in the zodiac and the houses at the time and place required. The significance of the houses is adapted to national affairs. The second house, for instance, governs the national wealth and the national debt, and the seventh house, which rules love, marriage and business relationships in an individual's chart, rules foreign affairs in a nation's chart.

An interesting example is the horoscope of the United States, as interpreted by the celebrated American astrologer Evangeline Adams. It is not always easy to decide on a moment of birth for a nation, but in this case it is taken to be 3:03 a.m. on the fourth of July 1776. At that moment Gemini was on the ascendant, which accounts for the versatility and restlessness of Americans ever since. Gemini's ruler, Mercury, is America's ruling planet. Mercury is the middleman planet of business and communication and American brilliance in business, especially in salesmanship and advertising, is the natural consequence of Mercury's dominant position. The behaviour of Uranus has also been an important factor in American history. This planet stands for sudden change, violent upheaval and revolution. It was in the ascendant sign Gemini in 1776 when the thirteen colonies rebelled against the British. It next returned to Gemini in a grim conjunction with Mars and Saturn in 1860, the year of the outbreak of the Civil War. Writing in 1931, Evangeline Adams saw that Uranus and Mars would again be together in Gemini in 1942, and predicted that U.S.A. would probably be at war in that year.[8]

Clues to the influences of Uranus, Neptune and Pluto have been found in events occurring after each of these planets was discovered. Although the new planets are 'new' only in the sense of being recently discovered, astrologers believe that they have made themselves felt in the world only since their discovery. The identification of Uranus in 1781 has been followed by revolutions and violent upheavals in the world, notably the French Revolution of 1789. The planet also cast its shadow before it by sparking the American revolution of 1776. Neptune has shown its spiritual and psychic influence in the rise of Spiritualism, the growth of interest in psychic and occult matters and the development of psychology and psychoanalysis since it was discovered in 1846. Pluto was identified in 1930. The Depression, the Second World War and the manufacture of the atomic bomb suggest that its influence has been appropriately hellish.

An important event for mundane astrologers is a conjunction of Saturn and Jupiter, which occurs once every twenty years. Kepler and other eminent astrologers of the past believed that the Star of Bethlehem was a conjunction of Saturn and Jupiter in Pisces. Later authorities generally agree, but place the conjunction in Aries. Since 1842 the conjunctions of Saturn and Jupiter have invariably occurred in Earth signs, which accounts for the Industrial Revolution and for modern materialism and concentration on practical matters (relieved only by the spiritualist influence of Neptune since 1846).

The modern astrologer's Great Year is a period of approximately 26,000 years, divided into twelve sections which correspond to the signs of the zodiac. Astrologers do not agree about the precise dating of these periods, but they say that in the ninth and tenth centuries B.C. the world was passing through the Age of Leo. At that period the sun at the vernal equinox, the beginning of spring about March 21 each year, was in the constellation Leo. As Leo's ruler is the sun, this age was naturally marked by sun worship. About 8000 B.C. the world entered the Age of Cancer, as a result of precession of the equinoxes. The sun was then in Cancer at the vernal equinox. Cancer is a Water sign and if the Great Flood ever occurred it can confidently be dated to this age, which was also marked by moon cults and the worship of female divinities because Cancer is ruled by the moon. The Age of Gemini, 6000 to 4000 B.C., saw the invention of writing, because Gemini's ruler Mercury is the planet of communication. From 4000 to 2000 B.C. the Age of Taurus brought in bull worship, the worship of the Golden Calf and also the construction of pyramids, ziggurats and other large and solid edifices on the earth because Taurus is the fixed Earth sign. After the Age of Aries, which astrologers believe was conspicuous for ram worship, the Age of Pisces began about 1 A.D.

Pisces is a mutable sign and the immediate consequence of its appearance at the vernal equinox was the growth of Christianity, which stresses unselfishness and service to others. Pisces is the sign of the Fishes, and so Jesus chose fishermen to be his disciples and the early Christians used the fish as a symbol. In astrology opposites are supposed to attract each other, which accounts for the importance of the Virgin in Christianity, as Virgo is the sign opposite Pisces. (The use of 'Lamb of God' and 'Good Shepherd' for Christ does not seem to fit Pisces, but can perhaps be explained as a hangover from the Age of Aries.) Pisces is a watery sign and the Piscean Age has been one of watery confusion and emotionalism. The approaching Age of Aquarius, beginning about the year 2000, will be a more orderly, constructive and intelligent period because Aquarius is a fixed Air sign. It is hoped that the nations will follow the celestial Water Carrier's example of service to others and that the new age will be a time of international harmony and the brotherhood of man.[9]

Of course, the future can be foretold in much more detailed terms than these. For centuries mundane astrologers have diligently turned out almanacs of predictions for each coming year. Predictions addressed to Louis XI of France in 1476 forecast that women would quarrel with their husbands and that many men would leave their wives. Saturn at mid-sky in the spring was expected to cause a rise in the prices of things governed by Saturn, including lead, iron, magnets, black stones, elephants, camels, bears, ostriches, crows and all black birds, and bread. War was forecast for early March with deceptive peace offers about March 20.[10] Modern astrologers tell us what to expect of the future in more cautious and less specific terms. At the time of writing, the sun in Libra is sextile (favourable) to the moon in Leo and this is a favourable sign for world peace moves and may herald a summit conference. The energetic force of Mars moving into Leo will cause some long-established governments to totter. In the United States conflict between liberals and conservatives, rising living costs and a late Christmas shopping rush can be expected.

Swift's *Predictions for the Year 1708 by Isaac Bickerstaff, Esq.* could almost be reprinted today as a satire on this kind of thing. Bickerstaff makes various pleasantly absurd forecasts for 1708, including the statement that near the end of August 'much mischief will be done at Bartholomew Fair by the fall of a booth', which is the eighteenth-century equivalent of a forecast of rising prices or dispute between liberals and conservatives now. He goes on to say that Partridge, a celebrated astrologer and almanac-maker of the day, will die at 11 p.m. on March 29 of a raging fever. Swift followed this up on March 30, 1708, by publishing an anonymous newsletter describing the death of Partridge the night before. Many readers accepted this at its face value and presumed that Partridge really was dead. Three other wits produced a pamphlet, ostensibly written by Partridge, hotly maintaining that he was still alive and complaining that he was greatly inconvenienced by the report of his death and could not go out of doors because he was being dunned for his funeral expenses. Partridge himself was finally drawn in. He included in his almanac for 1709 a statement that he was alive and in perfectly good health, to which Swift replied with a pamphlet containing cogent reasons to prove that Partridge was certainly dead, whatever he might say to the contrary.

Modern mundane astrologers have one great advantage over their predecessors—the fact that most people do not believe them. A disastrous example of inaccurate astrological prediction is the forecast of a Great Flood for the year 1524. Astrologers all over Europe realised that there would be conjunctions of all the planets in Pisces in February 1524. Obviously this must portend some fearsome and extraordinary event and since Pisces is a watery sign, the astrologers expected a Flood which would rival Noah's. The result was widespread panic. By mid-January it was said that 20,000 people had fled from London alone, seeking higher ground. The Prior of St. Bartholomew's prudently stocked a fortress at Harrow-on-the-Hill with two months' supplies and took all necessary precautions to keep other people out. A man at Toulouse built himself a Noah's Ark after the biblical pattern, though whether he collected two animals of every species to join him in it is in doubt. The Elector of Brandenburg took refuge on the highest available mountain on the day foretold by his court astrologer and awaited the dread event. When no drop of rain had fallen by four o'clock, the Elector sent his coach back to his castle. The court astrologer had at least the satisfaction of seeing the coachman and four horses struck dead by lightning at the gate. The Great Flood never materialised, though 1524 did turn out to be an unusually wet year.[11]

Many astrologers in medieval times were also doctors and diseases were thought to be caused by planetary influences. Fourteenth-century astrologers believed that a conjunction of Saturn, Jupiter and Mars in Aquarius corrupted the air and caused the Black Death. In the early sixteenth century astrologers were much concerned with the origins of syphilis. Agostino Nifo attributed it to a conjunction of Saturn and Mars in Pisces. In his poem *Syphilis*, Girolano Fracastoro said the disease was caused by a conjunction of Saturn, Jupiter and Mars in Cancer, which corrupted the air. Petrus Maynardus, who taught medicine at Padua, said that only men born under Scorpio, the sign which rules the genitals, were subject to it and predicted that it would disappear altogether after a conjunction in 1584.

Modern astrologers still connect disease with the stars. Heart trouble, spinal meningitis and muscular rheumatism of the back are aggravated when Mars is passing through Leo. When Mars is in Cancer we are all in danger of stomach upsets and digestive troubles. Uranus in Cancer 'pretty much precludes the permanence of one's health'. Mars and Saturn in certain relationships with the moon in a birth chart presage chronic ill health.

Traditionally, each sign of the zodiac is associated with part of the human body.

Aries	head	*Libra*	kidneys, buttocks
Taurus	neck	*Scorpio*	genitals
Gemini	shoulders, arms, lungs	*Sagittarius*	hips, thighs
Cancer	stomach	*Capricorn*	knees
Leo	heart, back	*Aquarius*	ankles
Virgo	intestines	*Pisces*	feet

You are likely to suffer from ailments in the part of the body ruled by your sun-sign. Born under Aries, you will probably be afflicted with head injuries and headaches and also with kidney complaints from the opposite sign, Libra. Born under Pisces, you can expect trouble with your feet and intestinal disorders, from Virgo. The reader will now see why Aquarians are supposed to have noticeable ankles and Scorpio's rule of the genitals accounts for many of its characteristics. 'Penetrating' is a word often used to describe the Scorpio nature.

3. Astrology and Daily Life

In what manner does the countenance of the sky at the moment of a man's birth determine his character? It acts on the person during his life in the manner of the loops which a peasant ties at random around the pumpkins in his field: they do not cause the pumpkin to grow, but they determine its shape. The same applies to the sky: it does not endow a man with his habits, history, happiness, children, riches or a wife but it moulds his condition. . . .

KEPLER, *quoted in* ARTHUR KOESTLER *The Sleepwalkers*

One of the attractions of astrology for many people is that by showing them their star-given virtues and failings it helps them to make the best of their lives. Like all magical thinkers, astrologers put a high value on balance and equilibrium. They disapprove of excess, extremes, extravagance and eccentricity. You may lack balance because of the planetary positions at your birth. A person of great drive and enthusiasm may fail in life without favourable aspects from Saturn which will give him realism and orderliness of mind. A practical, down-to-earth person needs favourable influences from Jupiter to broaden his interests and give him ways of expansion. But the planets do not doom you to failure or unhappiness and once you know your deficiencies you can try to correct them.

'The stars impel, they do not compel', is a favourite astrological maxim and most modern astrologers, in theory at least, do not believe that a man is inevitably destined to follow the track mapped out for him at birth in the heavens. Human beings have free will and we can assert ourselves against the stars. In practice, astrologers are curiously split-minded about this subject. They claim a very high degree of accuracy for their predictions—Lyndoe, for instance, claims to be right 80 per cent to 90 per cent of the time—and if they are right, most of us must follow docilely along our star-impelled courses. But the astrologers are not deterred by the thought that the more accurate their forecasts, the less chance they can have of helping us to alter our destinies, and they think of themselves not as mere fortune-tellers but as counsellors who show us the way to happiness and success.

Naturally, they are much concerned with love and marriage. Before you marry you should have your own and your prospective partner's birth charts checked to make sure that the two of you are compatible. If you were really sensible you would take the stars into account before even beginning to involve yourself with a possible husband or wife, which might save you the embarrassment of having to break off an engagement on the advice of your astrologer. As a rough guide, one theory is that you will be happiest with someone born under the zodiac sign opposite your own. In astrology 'opposites attract' and two people born under opposite signs should make a balanced, harmonious couple. This is a reflection of the magical doctrine that all progress comes through the reconciliation of opposites.

Another traditional theory says you should marry someone who is in your own triplicity but not someone who is in your quadruplicity. The 'fiery' Aries man should marry a 'fiery' Leo or Sagittarius woman, but he ought to avoid a 'cardinal' Cancer, Libra or Capricorn woman at all costs. This is because your triplicity is a group of 3. Three is the number of the reconciliation of opposites and also the number of procreation and fertility, so it is a favourable number for marriage. Your quadruplicity is a group of 4, which is the ominous number of misery and defeat.

Astrologers recognise that many people entangle themselves in love affairs and marriages without taking the precaution of consulting the stars and most astrological magazines give advice to the dissatisfied and the lovelorn. At least one expert can tell a wife whether her husband has been unfaithful to her or not if the husband's place, date and time of birth are supplied.

Once married, you can consult the stars to find the correct time for having children who will be a credit to you. An American astrologer says, 'It is now possible for astrologically guided unions to produce congenial children, with desired characteristics and a reasonable certainty of sex.'[12]

Besides acting as marriage counsellors, astrologers can determine which days in the future will be favourable for any conceivable activity. The Ephemerides of the fifteenth-century astrologer Regiomontanus included notes of favourable times for new enterprises, sowing, planting and cultivation of vines, taking a bath or having one's hair cut. Modern astrologers are equally thorough. Astrological magazines list good days for baking, sewing, dancing, giving a party, buying a car, taking photographs, pouring concrete, buying new clothes, having your hair cut to stimulate growth (when the moon is waxing) or having it cut to retard growth (when the moon is waning). Some magazines give 'lucky moon days', which are usually based on the Mansions of the Moon.

The moon travels through the entire zodiac in a little over twenty-seven days. The Mansions of the Moon mark the sections of the zodiac traversed by the moon each day. Agrippa called the first Mansion, which starts at 0° Aries, the Ram's Horns, and said that the moon in this stage of its course causes discord and journeys on earth. The second Mansion, beginning between 12° and 13° Aries, is favourable for finding buried treasure and for preventing prisoners from escaping. According to Pliny's *Natural History*, the twentieth day of the moon is good for curing warts. The sufferer should go out into the country at night, lie down flat in a path, gaze steadily at the moon, reach above his head and rub the warts with whatever he first touches.

The moon is important for day-to-day matters, because it changes its position in the zodiac more rapidly than the sun or the planets, but astrologers can chart all the planetary positions and aspects for any day in the future for any project you have in mind. For example, an astrologer might warn you against buying a house when Mercury is in a difficult aspect with Mars and might tell you to wait till Mercury (the planet of trade) is in conjunction or easy aspect with Jupiter (prosperity).

If you are buying or selling an animal, the sixth house in the chart is important, because it governs four-footed animals. A moment when the moon is in Capricorn and the sixth house should certainly be a good time to buy a goat. Astrologers also consider the sixth house in forecasting the results of horse races. One method is to draw a chart for the time and place of the race and check the planetary positions against the colours which will be carried by the horses. The old planets have colours which are traditionally associated with them,* and for racing purposes the new planets represent stripes (Uranus), hoops or checks (Neptune) and spots (Pluto). If a horse will be carrying scarlet colours its planet for the race is Mars and if Mars is well aspected, especially if it is in the sixth house, the horse's prospects are good.

*See above, page 24.

By calculating planetary positions and aspects for any day in the future, astrologers discover the planetary trends of the moment and show you how to take advantage of them. In all the multitudinous activities and problems of your life you can get yourself right with the stars and help them to help you. The branch of astrology which selects a favourable moment for the future is *electional* astrology. An allied branch, *horary* astrology tells you how a project will turn out by charting the planetary positions at the time when the idea of the project first came into your mind.

Current planetary trends are the second factor on which horoscopes in newspapers and magazines are based, the first being your sun-sign. At the time of writing Neptune is in Scorpio. Neptune is an impressionable planet and so Scorpios are being warned against trickery and deception. 'You can avoid difficulties best by keeping to yourself.' 'Make your personal needs your own private business.' 'Keep emotions and money both where they belong.' Uranus, the planet of sudden change and upheaval, is in Virgo and so Virgos are being told to 'guard against the unexpected'. 'Don't be rushed into decisions.' 'A trouble-free week if you steer clear of arguments.' 'Avoid making a major change or decision.'

A more complicated method of predicting the influences of the stars on your life in the near future is provided by astrological *progression* systems. Karl Krafft, one of Hitler's astrologers, said that 'the birth chart remains impregnated, once and for all, with everything concerning the individual, since his constellations still play a part at the moment of his decease'.[13] But the planets did not suddenly vanish from the sky when you were born. They have continued to influence you since. A progression system is a method of measuring the planetary influences on you since your birth. Unfortunately, the astrologers have not been able to agree on any one system.

When an astrologer draws a progressed chart, he makes a curious and important assumption. He says, 'Let X days in the sky equal Y years on earth.' The difference between the various progression systems is largely a difference in the figures which are inserted for X and Y. Astrologers do not explain the equation itself. They compare it to the scale used in drawing a map—one inch to one mile, for example—but they defend it simply by saying that it works.

In the system most frequently used, one day in the sky is taken to equal one year on earth. Suppose you were born at 10 a.m. on June 1. The movements of the planets between that time and 10 a.m. the next day governed the first year of your life, their movements in the next twenty-four hours governed the second year of your life, and so on. If you are now beginning your forty-first year, your life to date has been influenced by the planetary movements during the first forty days of your existence.

The progressed chart for the coming year shows the sky at 10 a.m. on July 11 in the year of your birth, the beginning of your forty-first day of life. The ascendant and the house boundaries are calculated for that day and time at your birthplace. The zodiac sign on the ascendant and the sign occupied by the sun in this chart will affect your personality in the year ahead and so will any planet in the first house. If the progressed ascendant is in Gemini, for instance, this will give a lighter, airier cast to your personality in the coming year, though without destroying your basic natal characteristics. Your ruling planet for this year will be Mercury, Gemini's ruler, and the affairs of the house occupied by Mercury will be important. There will be minor changes in the affairs of the house occupied by the moon, because the moon rules fluctuation. There will be activity in the affairs of the house occupied by Mars and probably disagreements and disputes about them. If Jupiter (expansion) is in the first house (appearance) you may put on weight in the year ahead and if Saturn (restriction) is in the eighth house (sources of gain) people who owe you money will be reluctant to pay up. Aspects to the moon, ruler of women, will affect your relations with women. Adverse aspects to Mercury may cause you to be absent-minded, make clerical errors, give people the wrong change or say the wrong things.

The idea that a day in the sky equals a year on earth might be defended on the ground that the zodiac makes a complete revolution in the sky in one day while the earth takes one year to complete its orbit round the sun. It may also be connected with the old belief that 36,000 years make one Great Year. When a Great Year ends the universe will go back to the beginning like a restarted gramophone record and everything that has happened will happen all over again. Some classical authorities, including Plato, thought that the natural span of man's life should be 100 years (of 360 days each year). If a man lives 100 years and the universe 36,000 years, it can be said that the life of the universe moves at 360 times the speed of human life, so that the development of the universe in one day is the equivalent of man's development in 360 days, or one year.

4. Astrology and Magic

If we would call any evil Spirit to the Circle, it first behoveth us to consider and to know his nature, to which of the planets it agreeth, and what offices are distributed to him from the planet.

Fourth Book of Agrippa's *Occult Philosophy*

Astrology is essentially a magical art. Astrologers believe that the course of our lives is laid down for us in the stars, but they also hold the contradictory belief that we can use the influences of the stars to our own advantage. If you wait to buy a house until Mercury and Jupiter are in certain positions in the sky, you are following a procedure which is just as magical as the medieval cure for lunacy which prescribes tying a herb round the patient's neck with a red cloth when the moon is waxing in the sign of Taurus. In one case the moon's influence is used to cure a lunatic, in the other the influences of Mercury and Jupiter are used to secure a satisfactory house.

Most people who believe in astrology would probably reject the medieval lunacy cure, but if they are consistent they should not doubt it because it smacks of magic. In practice, modern astrologers keep decidedly quiet about this subject. An American magazine lists favourable days for making an appointment with your doctor, having dental treatment or having your eyes tested, but it does not list favourable days for undergoing surgery or taking medicine. Astrologers who say that the stars influence health usually do not provide astrological remedies. This is not a sign that astrologers want to avoid magic, but a confession that their system has failed to work when applied to medicine.

Medieval astrologers were less cautious. Alexander of Tralles, a medieval authority of great influence, advised wearing a verse of Homer, engraved on a plate of copper (the metal of Venus) at a time when the moon was in Leo or Libra, as a cure for gout. Arnald of Villanova made a seal of lead, the metal of Saturn, in the form of a lion (the sign Leo, standing for strength and courage) for Pope Boniface VIII to limit (influence of Saturn) the pain of an operation for stone. Apparently it worked, as Boniface is said to have valued it highly. Both these remedies involve the use of a *talisman*—the copper plate or the seal.

A talisman is an object—a precious stone, a ring, a plant, a piece of paper—usually carried in the hand, hung from the neck or tied to the body. An astrological talisman is used to attract the influence of the planet. It must be made of a material associated with the planet and it should be constructed at a time when the planet is radiating its influence with maximum power, when it is in the ascendant or at mid-sky or well aspected or in an appropriate zodiac sign. Julianus Ristorus, professor at Pisa University in the early sixteenth century, owned a ring which had been engraved with certain characters when the moon was at mid-sky and 'strong' in Cancer. He used it to cure ailments of the shins and feet. He had another ring, engraved when Saturn was badly aspected, which he used to ward off mosquitoes.

Rings intended to attract the influences of the planets should be made of the following materials:

Sun	Diamond or topaz set in gold.
Moon	Pearl, crystal or quartz set in silver.
Mercury	Opal or agate set in quicksilver.
Venus	Emerald or turquoise set in copper.
Mars	Ruby or any red stone set in iron.
Jupiter	Sapphire, amethyst or cornelian set in tin.
Saturn	Onyx or sapphire set in lead.

The uses of talismans ran far beyond the cure of disease. In 1318 the Archbishop of Aix resigned his see after he had been accused of practising the 'forbidden, damnable and mathematical art' of divination. It was said that a Jewish astrologer had carved seals on the Archbishop's pastoral rings to avert disease and bring him good fortune. In England in the late fourteenth century formal rules were drawn up for the conduct of duels in the marshal's court, including a provision that the adversaries must fight with conventional weapons only. Each was to swear on oath that he carried no stone of power or herb or 'characters' (magical letters or symbols) or any other charm. At the same period, in 1386, Robert Tresillian, condemned to death for treason, announced at the scaffold that he could not die as long as he kept his clothes on. The executioners stripped him and found talismans, painted 'like unto the signs of heaven' (the zodiac signs) and the head of a devil painted and the names of many devils on parchment. They took these away and hanged him up naked and he died.

The medieval magician and astrologer Cecco D'Ascoli described the manufacture of a talisman to attract love. The talisman is made of tin, the metal of Jupiter, planet of success. The molten tin must be poured into the mould when Venus is in Taurus or Pisces. Venus is 'strong' in Taurus and 'exalted' in Pisces and as the metal is poured out the powerful influence of Venus alters the proportions in which the elements are mingled in the tin, so that it becomes an effective love charm. (Cecco D'Ascoli was eventually condemned by the Inquisition as a heretic. He and his astrological writings were burnt together at the stake in Florence in 1327.)

Francis Barret's *The Magus or Celestial Intelligencer*, published in 1801, says that if you carry a talisman engraved on silver when the moon was well aspected you will be pleasant, cheerful and honoured by others, you will be able to make journeys in safety, your wealth will increase and your health will be good. If you make a talisman of lead when the moon is adversely aspected and bury it under or near a house, it will bring evil to those who live in the house.

A magical textbook called the *Great Albert* describes a talisman which will bring good luck in gambling. To make this talisman, take a large piece of virgin, unused parchment. On the first Thursday (day of Jupiter, the planet of prosperity) of the new moon at the hour of Jupiter and before sunrise, write on the parchment *non licet ponare in egoborna quia pretium sanguinis*. Then wrap the severed head of a viper in the parchment and tie it up with a red silk ribbon. Hang it on your left arm when you are going to gamble and all will be well. The Latin words are a corruption of Matthew 27.6. When Judas Iscariot remorsefully returned the thirty pieces of silver to the chief priests they decided that it was not lawful to send the money to the treasury, because it was the price of blood, *non licet eos mittere in corbonam quia pretium sanguinis est*.[14] Because the thirty pieces of silver could not be returned to the treasury, your stake cannot be lost to the bank when these words are written on your talisman.

Modern astrologers are generally silent on the subject of talismans. Edouard Chatelherault gives directions for making planetary talismans in his *You and Your Stars*, though he does not specifically say that he expects them to work. W. T. and K. Pavitt, in their book on talismans and zodiacal gems, doubt many of the old claims made for talismans, but believe that they may have power in some cases and give a modern magical explanation of their action. 'Many people are prepared to admit that there may be some active power in a thought made concrete in the form of a Talisman or Amulet.' The talisman provides a focus for the magician's concentration on the object of his spell, in the same way that a wax image provides a focus for his hatred or his lust.

Astrological considerations have always been extremely important in magic. Magicians link the planets with the great forces which move the universe, as in the Cabala, because the ancients identified the planets with the gods. To control the planetary influences is to control the driving impulses beneath the surface of things. This is made possible by the fact that the stars behave in a regular and predictable way, which was one of the reasons for astrology's firm grip on the classical world. The old nature-gods behaved arbitrarily and un-predictably, like the forces which they personified—lightning, thunder, wind, earthquake. In the planets the Greeks discovered gods who followed strict and changeless laws and in his old age Plato found the true gods in the sky. All forces which obey immutable laws, like the planets and the numbers, are vital to magic, because the magician can rely on them to work in the way which he requires at the time when he needs them.

The influence of a planet can be magically captured through the use of things which are linked with it—using red, iron and the number 5 to tap the force of Mars, for example. Or the starry influences can be drawn down to earth through a magical link created by words, as in an interesting love charm from the *Grimorium Verum*, which uses the force of the moon and a star and is described as 'an experiment of the wonderful power of the Superior Intelligences'. The magician begins by drawing on virgin parchment two concentric circles surmounted by a cross. On the western arm of the cross is the symbol of the sun ☉, on the eastern arm the symbol of the moon ☽, and on the northern arm a star. He writes the name of the woman he desires in the inner circle and on the other side of the parchment the names of power Melchiael Bareschas.

At eleven o'clock at night, armed with this talisman, the magician goes outside and puts the parchment on the ground, with the woman's name downwards. He puts his right foot on the parchment, his left knee on the ground, and holds in his right hand a lighted candle of white wax, large enough to burn for an hour. Then he concentrates on the highest star in the sky and begins his incantation. 'I salute and conjure you, O beautiful Moon, O beautiful Star, O brilliant light which I hold in my hand.' These words link the moon and the star with the candle. 'By the air that I breathe, by the breath within me, by the earth which I touch, I conjure you.' This channels the celestial forces through the air, through the magician's breath, into his body, through the parchment bearing the woman's name and into the earth. They are 'earthed' as a precaution. Otherwise the magician might be destroyed by them, as by lightning. The incantation continues:

By all the names of the spirit princes living in you; by the ineffable name ON which created all things; by you, O resplendent Angel Gabriel, with the Planet Mercury, Michael and Melchidael. I conjure you by all the Holy Names of God, that you send down power to obsess, torment and harass the body, the soul and the five senses of N., she whose name is written here below, so that she shall come to me and submit to my desires, liking no one in the world, and especially thus N., for as long as she shall be indifferent to me. So shall she endure not, so shall she be obsessed, so suffer, so be tormented. Go then, quickly. Go Melchidael, Bareschas, Zazel, Firiel, Malcha, and all those who are with you. I conjure you by the Great Living God to obey my will and I, N., promise to satisfy you.

This incantation is repeated three times. Then the magician burns the parchment with the candle. He is burning the woman's name with the celestial force which has been linked with the candle, which should cause her to writhe in fiery torment until she submits to the spell. The next day he puts the ashes of the parchment in his left shoe and keeps them there till the woman comes to him.[15]

Another way of enlisting planetary influences in a magical operation is to perform the ceremony on the day and in the hour of the appropriate planet. Each day and each hour has its planetary ruler. Sunday is ruled by the sun, Monday by the moon, Tuesday by Mars (Tiw, the Teutonic war-god), Wednesday by Mercury (Woden), Thursday by Jupiter (Thor), Friday by Venus (Freya),

Saturday by Saturn. The planet which rules the day rules the first hour after sunrise and the succeeding hours of daylight are ruled by the other planets in the following order:

1. Sun   5. Saturn
2. Venus   6. Jupiter
3. Mercury   7. Mars
4. Moon

At sunset a new progression begins. The first hour after sunset is ruled by the planet which is fifth in order from the planet which rules the day. For example:

	Thursday (day of Jupiter)	*Friday* (day of Venus)
1st hour after sunrise	Jupiter	Venus
2nd hour after sunrise	Mars	Mercury
3rd hour after sunrise	Sun	Moon

and so on for the remaining hours of daylight.

1st hour after sunset	Moon	Mars
2nd hour after sunset	Saturn	Sun
3rd hour after sunset	Jupiter	Venus

and so on for the remaining hours of night.

The next sunrise marks the start of a new day and the effect is that each planet rules the first and eighth hours of daylight and the third and tenth hours of night on its own day.

Rules for deciding which planetary influences are needed for different types of operation are provided by the *Key of Solomon* and another grimoire, *True Black Magic*. Briefly, the days and hours of the planets are suitable for:

Sun   Gaining money or the support of powerful people; gaining or causing friendship and harmony; finding buried treasure.

Moon   Raising the spirits of the dead; operations of love and reconciliation; seeing visions; becoming invisible; theft; operations connected with water, the sea, shipping and travel.

Mercury   Obtaining knowledge; discovering the future; operations connected with commerce, merchandise, deceit and theft.

Venus   Works of love, lust, pleasure and friendship.

Mars   Killing, destroying or causing hatred, discord and unhappiness; raising the spirits of the dead, especially those murdered or killed in battle; operations connected with military matters.

Jupiter   Gaining wealth, position or friendship; gaining good health; becoming invisible.

Saturn   Works of death, destruction or injury; raising souls from hell; obtaining knowledge; all operations connected with buildings (because in the Cabala Saturn is the force of stability and inertia).

A waning moon is favourable to works of hatred and discord. The moon when almost obscured favours operations of death and destruction, and also becoming invisible. Nothing should be attempted when the moon is in conjunction with the sun, as this causes all projects to fail.

Some magical textbooks classify the 'spirits' or supernatural intelligences which the magician hopes to master in terms of their planetary affiliations. The *Arbatel of Magic* lists seven 'Olympic Spirits' who rule the planets—Aratron (Saturn), Bethor (Jupiter), Phaleg (Mars), Och (Sun), Hagith (Venus), Ophiel (Mercury) and Phul (Moon). Each of them has troops of subordinate spirits at his command and each governs his planet's department of life and has the corresponding magical powers. Bethor rules wealth and status, as Jupiter does in astrology, and he can confer riches and high rank on the magician. Similarly, Hagith rules love and beauty, confers these benefits on the magician and converts copper, the metal of Venus, to gold instantaneously.

Each Olympic Spirit has his own magical symbol, which is his 'mark' or signature and is equivalent to his 'real' name. But the *Arbatel* says that knowing a spirit's symbol does not automatically give power over it, which is a contradiction of the usual magical doctrine. The spirit can only be summoned by praying to God to send him. Profound meditation and a sincere love of God are necessary before such a request will be granted.[16]

Other authorities say that planetary spirits can be summoned or planetary influences attracted by the use of 'images', which are real or mental pictures intended to express the planet's nature. In 1489 Marsilio Ficino, a Florentine philosopher and doctor, published a medical textbook *Libri de Vita*, in which he recommended the use of 'images' for attracting favourable influences. Students,

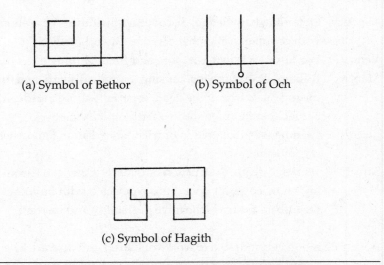

(a) Symbol of Bethor   (b) Symbol of Och

(c) Symbol of Hagith

DIAGRAM 11 **Symbols of Planetary Spirits from the *Arbatel of Magic***

he said, sometimes become ill or depressed after working too hard, and this is because thought and study belong to Saturn, which rules the melancholy temperament and is antagonistic to the vital forces of life and youth. Overworked students and elderly people whose vital forces are on the wane should try to lure influences from the favourable planets Jupiter, Venus and the sun. To gain health and happiness, for instance, make an image of Venus—a picture of a beautiful young girl dressed in white or yellow and holding flowers and apples. It has been suggested that Botticelli's *Primavera* may have been intended as a talisman of Venus of this kind.

Ficino put his planetary images forward hesitantly, afraid that he might be accused of practising magic, but a hundred years later Giordano Bruno adopted the same idea with hearty enthusiasm. He supplies various images of the sun, for example—Apollo with a bow but no quiver, laughing; an archer killing a wolf, a crow flying above him; a man with a beard and helmet riding a lion, a golden crown above his head and on his helmet a cock with a conspicuous crest of many colours. These pictures are symbols of the sun's nature in the same way that the Tarot cards are believed to be symbols of universal forces or paths to the ultimate truth. By meditating on them, according to Bruno, the planet's influence can be brought down into the human personality. You can master the planetary forces, in fact, by concentrating on their characteristic symbols. Bruno was condemned as a heretic and magician by the Inquisition. He was burned alive at Rome in 1600.[17]

Some of Ficino's planetary images seem to have been taken from a book on magic and astrology called *Picatrix*, which was originally written in Arabic, probably in the twelfth century. Another magical textbook, the *Fourth Book* added to Agrippa's *Occult Philosophy* but probably not written by Agrippa himself, describes the spirits of the planets in very much the same way. A spirit of the sun may appear as a king holding a sceptre and riding a lion, as a king seated on a throne with a globe beneath his feet, as a queen, a lion, a cock or a sceptre. The spirits of Venus show themselves as girls playing and luring the magician to join them, as a naked girl, a king riding a camel, a she-goat, a camel or a dove. A spirit of the moon may take the form of an archer riding a doe, a huntress with bow and arrows, a little boy, a cow, a goose or an arrow. A spirit of Mars appears as a man in armour, a king astride a wolf or a lion with a naked sword in his right hand and the severed head of a man in his left, as a horse, as a stag or as wool. The shapes of the spirits of Jupiter are a king with drawn sword riding a lion, eagle or dragon; a mitred priest; a girl crowned with laurel; a bull, stag or peacock; a sword. A spirit of Mercury comes as a king riding on a bear, a beautiful youth, a woman holding a distaff, a dog, a she-bear, a magpie, a rod. Finally, the spirits of Saturn appear as a bearded king riding a dragon, an old bearded man, an old woman, a boy, a dragon, an owl, a black garment, a sickle, a juniper tree.[18]

These descriptions probably have the same basic purpose as the planetary images of Ficino and Bruno. They help the magician to summon and master the planetary spirits by concentrating on their characteristic forms. They have a parallel in the wealth of symbolic descriptions and pictures which alchemists included in their works as objects of meditation, in an attempt to convey ideas which they could not express exactly in ordinary language. In alchemy, to understand the Stone was to find it. Similarly, in magic to know the nature of a spirit is to master and control it.

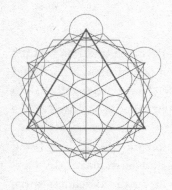

CHAPTER SIX

Ritual Magic

THE magician's central preoccupation is with the exercise of power, but his use of his powers is as various as his methods. From a tremendous ceremony in which he displays his mastery of all the forces of the universe, he may turn to something as trivial as afflicting an enemy with boils. At one moment weltering in the graveyard procedures of necromancy, at the next he is slyly turning people into animals. (Aleister Crowley could do this and once he turned the poet Victor Neuburg into a camel.)

The grimoire called the *Lemegeton* lists the names and powers of seventy-two devils and an analysis of their functions—most of them have more than one—gives an interesting picture of the magician's uses of power. The *Lemegeton's* major interest is in the gaining of knowledge. More than half the devils listed include teaching as one of their functions. They teach the magician sciences, arts, philosophy, mathematics, logic, languages, astronomy and astrology, the occult powers of herbs and jewels. One of them teaches handicrafts, one grammar, one the languages of animals and birds, and one, rather surprisingly, ethics. In addition, many of the demons reveal secrets or show the events of the past, present and future, and some find things which have been lost or stolen. This emphasis on knowledge and secrets reflects the tradition that the rebel angels who lusted after the daughters of men taught them all arts and crafts. It is also a reflection of the occult importance of knowledge rather than virtue as the key to spiritual progress and the belief that knowledge of the universe is synonymous with its control.

A second group of devils cause death, destruction and hatred. They bring murder, war and bloodshed or they stir up storms and earthquakes. Two torment people with putrefying sores and one brings an agonised death in three days from festering wounds. Two destroy the victim's sight, hearing or intelligence and two rob important people of high position and status. Several change people into other shapes, animal and human.

The next group are concerned with the magician's own wealth and status. They provide him with riches and treasure, give him the friendship and favour of other people, bring him high worldly position, a good reputation, cunning, courage, wit and eloquence. Three of them turn base metals into gold or money.

Twelve demons provide good familiar spirits as servants. Eleven procure the love and complaisance of women and one makes women show themselves naked. Three control the souls and bodies of the dead. Others make the magician invisible or provide pleasing illusions—one can show any person in a vision, one gives the illusion of running waters, one of musical instruments playing, one of birds in flight. Four devils transport people safely from place to place. One warms water for baths. One turns water into wine and one reprehensibly turns wine into water.

The mixture of the trivial and the important is typical of magic and so is the mixture of good and evil. The demon named Glasyalabolas teaches all arts and sciences, which seems admirable, but he also incites murder and bloodshed. Raum reconciles enemies, but is equally ready to destroy cities. Flauros will destroy and burn the magician's foes, if desired, and if not desired will gladly discourse on matters of divinity. Seere is 'indifferently good or bad and will do the will of the operator'.

Magical operations, like those of the *Lemegeton*, which involve conjuring up a 'spirit'—an occult force personified as an angel or demon—have a long history and tradition. The basic pattern of the ceremonies is already found in the Graeco-Egyptian magical texts, which date from about A.D. 100 to 400, and is repeated in medieval and modern textbooks, though with many variations in detail. First the magician prepares all the necessary accessories—his sword, his wand, perfumes, talismans, the magic circle, pentagrams and hexagrams. When everything is ready, he summons the spirit to appear in a succession of powerful incantations. Finally, he gives the spirit its orders and dismisses it.

1. Preparations and the Magic Circle

These metaphysics of magicians
And necromantic books are heavenly:
Lines, circles, scenes, letters and characters:
Ay, these are those that Faustus most desires.
O, what a world of profit and delight,
Of power, of honour, of omnipotence
Is promised to the studious artisan!
All things that move between the quiet poles
Shall be at my command: emperors and kings
Are but obeyed in their several provinces
Nor can they raise the wind nor rend the clouds;
But his dominion that exceeds in this
Stretcheth as far as doth the mind of man.
A sound magician is a mighty god:
Here, Faustus, try thy brains to gain a deity.

MARLOWE's *Faust*

The first essential is that the magician must be magically 'consecrated', which means that he must set himself apart from the everyday world and his ordinary life. A magical operation of any difficulty cannot be performed in a normal condition of mind or body. One of the Graeco-Egyptian texts tells the magician to remain pure for seven days. Then on the third day of the new moon he must go to the bank of a river, the Nile in this particular case, where he builds a fire of olive wood on an altar made of two upright bricks. Before sunrise he ceremoniously circles this altar. As soon as the rising sun clears the horizon, the magician cuts off the head of a virgin white cock. Throwing the head into the river, he drains the cock's blood into his right hand and laps it up. He burns the carcass on the fire and himself dives into the river. He then climbs back on to the bank, being careful to step backwards, takes off his wet clothes and puts on new ones. Finally, he must go away without looking over his shoulder.[1]

In this process the magician is purified and set apart from his ordinary self by the week of chastity, the virginity of the cock which he has imbibed with its blood, the plunge into the river and the new clothes which symbolise his 'new' self. He must climb out of the river backwards and go away without looking behind him to avoid making any link between his new and old selves.

All the grimoires insist on the virtues of continence, fasting and cleanliness. The *Grand Grimoire*, for instance, says that the magician must abstain from the company of women for an entire quarter of the moon and may eat not more than two meals a day during that period. Each meal is preceded by a prayer in which the magician devotes to God his soul, his heart, his inward parts, his hands, his feet, his desires, his entire being.

Eliphas Levi recommended a thorough wash before beginning a magical operation and that the atmosphere of the place where the ceremony is to be held be purified by burning a mixture of the juice of laurel leaves, camphor, salt, white resin and sulphur. Laurel juice is an intoxicant. Camphor is traditionally supposed to have the power of preserving chastity. Salt is white for purity and is a protection against evil forces. When the spirit is evoked and has breathed in the fumes from this mixture, it has eaten the magician's salt, in effect, and is restrained from harming him. Levi also said that the operator should have the minimum of sleep before the ceremony and should abstain altogether from intoxicating drink and the eating of meat.

There is a mixture of motives behind this insistence on purity and fasting. Although he may intend to kill, torture or indulge his lust, the magician purifies himself because he will call on God for assistance and he will use divine names of power to control the spirit he evokes. This spirit is a powerful occult force and a dangerous one, and abstinence is a method of avoiding contamination through the entry into the body of impurities which the spirit might be able to seize on. Many primitive peoples fast and swallow emetics or purges before taking part in sacred ceremonies, and in classical times people who went to gather particularly powerful herbs were warned to fast and be chaste, to wear white clothes or go naked, and sometimes to chew garlic, the smell of which would dismay the demonic forces they were likely to disturb.

Much the most important reason for abstinence, however, is that it heightens the magician's powers. The refusal to concern himself with food or drink or women allows him to devote himself utterly to the ceremony which he is to perform. Chastity banks up his sexual energy, fasting and going without sleep weaken the body and give strange powers to the mind. Some modern magicians recommend the opposite of the traditional procedure. Drink, drugs and sex can be used to produce a state of mingled exhaustion and exaltation in which the magician's powers are raised to their highest pitch, but it is essential that the magician does not indulge himself for pleasure, which would distract him from the necessary iron concentration on the business in hand, but with the clear and sole purpose of building up his magical energies. The force to be evoked may show itself by taking temporary possession of the magician or one of his assistants and one of those present should be weakened to the point of exhaustion by drink, drugs, wounds and the ceremony itself, so that he can put up the least possible resistance to the invading force.

The ceremony should be held in a secluded place where no one is likely to interrupt. If the place has an atmosphere of mystery, romance or evil, so much the better. The ceremony can be performed in the ruins of a castle, a church or a monastery, in a graveyard, in a wood or a desert, or at a place where three roads meet, sacred to Hecate, the goddess of sorcery. The operations can also be performed perfectly well in a private house, in which case the room should be hung and carpeted in black and all doors and windows should be locked.

The grimoires say that the operator needs numerous instruments and accessories. The details of their manufacture are usually so absurdly complicated as to be almost impossible of performance. The vital requirement is that everything used must be 'virgin'. The magician must either make his instruments or 'magical weapons' himself from previously unused materials, and this is preferable, or he must buy them brand new and especially for his operations. The virtue of a thing which is virgin is that its innate force has not been dissipated by use, but, beyond this, to use any object which is second-hand or has been employed for non-magical purposes is to risk terrible dangers. The previous owner or the previous use may have linked the object with influences which are not in harmony with the ceremony the magician intends to conduct. Powerful forces are brought into play in magical operations, and if something goes wrong the power 'shorts' and the magician or his assistants may, at the very least, be knocked down or struck unconscious by it. This is an unpleasant and dangerous experience, though the person usually recovers. On the other hand, the experience does have a certain back-handed advantage, as Crowley pointed out. 'But it does encourage one—it is useless to deny it—to be knocked down by a demon of whose existence one was not really quite sure.'[2]

Another reason for demanding that the magician make his own paraphernalia is that in doing so he fully involves himself and all his capabilities in the work. Magic is not for the incompetent, the fainthearted or those who lack application and determination.

The magician will need a sword and a sharp knife or dagger. These should be forged or bought on the day and in the hour of Jupiter, planet of success and prosperity, at a time when the moon is waxing. An incantation must be said over them to infuse them with power. For example, from the *Grimorium Verum*:

> I conjure thee, form of the instrument, by God the Father Almighty, by the virtue of Heaven and by all the stars which rule, by the virtue of the four elements, by that of all stones, all plants and all animals whatsoever, by the virtue of hailstorms and winds, to receive such virtue herein that we may obtain by thee the perfect issue of all our desires, which also we seek to perform without evil, without deception, by God, the Creator of the Sun and the Angels. Amen.[3]

A magic wand or rod is another important weapon and one of the supreme emblems of magical power, partly because it is a phallic symbol. The use of ceremonial staffs or wands is very ancient and they have been found near prehistoric hearths. Moses and Aaron used their magic rods to smite the land of Egypt with plagues. The wand also belonged to Hermes, who led the souls of the dead down to the underworld, and it became an emblem of all who rule over the dead. In the *Odyssey* Circe changes the comrades of Odysseus into swine with her *rhabdos* or wand. The rhabdos was eventually personified as a demon. Rabdos, the strangler, is one of the devils listed in the *Testament of Solomon*, which says that he was formerly a wise man of great learning—Hermes.

The wand must be made of hazel. (A hazel rod is also used in water-divining.) According to the *Grand Grimoire*, the rod should be 19½ inches long, cut at sunrise so that it captures the vigorous energy of the newly reborn sun. It must be cut with the magic knife, which should be stained with blood, again to capture the energy. The magician must pray to Adonai, Elohim, Ariel and Jehovah to endow the wand with the power of the rods of Jacob, Moses and Joshua, the strength of Samson, the righteous wrath of Emmanuel, and the thunders of mighty Zariatnatmik, who will avenge the crimes of men at the Day of Judgement. The name Ariel means 'hearth of God' and in the Old Testament is applied to Jerusalem—'Woe to Ariel, to Ariel, the city where David dwelt.'[4] It later became the name of a spirit whose best known appearance is in *The Tempest*.

Pointed steel caps are fixed on to the two ends of the hazel rod and mag-netised with a lodestone. The magician then commands the rod by the names of Adonai, Elohim, Ariel and Jehovah to obey his will, to attract all substances he wishes to attract and to sunder and reduce to chaos all things he wishes to destroy.

Until they are needed, the sword, knife and wand should be wrapped in an expensive silken cloth, of any colour except black or brown. Before they are used they should be purified and consecrated by sprinkling them with water, preferably holy water, and 'fumigating' them—exposing them to perfumes. The sprinkling should be done with a bunch of mint, marjory and rosemary tied with a thread, or alternatively with a bunch of vervain, periwinkle, sage, mint, valerian, ash, basil and rosemary. The perfume used is either ecclesiasti-cal incense or is made by burning aloes wood, mace, storax and benzoin. (Ben-zoin is a resin which is one of the principal ingredients of both church incense and Friar's Balsam.)

The magician's robes are another important factor. The *Magical Elements*, attributed to Peter of Abano, but probably not written by him, recommends robes which have been used by a priest in his services, because of the sacred force inherent in them. This is a rare example of an exception to the 'virgin' rule. The *Fourth Book* added to Agrippa's *Occult Philosophy* suggests a robe of white linen, fitting closely and covering the whole body down to the feet, tied with a girdle. All undergarments should be made of linen or silk and should be white for purity. Shoes must also be white and the magician ought to wear a white hat or crown with names of power written on it—for example, YHVH in front, Adonai at the back, El on the right side, Elohim on the left, according to the *Key of Solomon*. Names of power and powerful designs or symbols can also be drawn or embroidered on the robe.

Although the grimoires recommend white robes, in operations of an un-questionably evil nature or which clearly involve the powers of darkness trap-pings of black and red would be closer to the nature of the work and more effective. Buttons, buckles, hooks and knots should be avoided as far as possi-ble because fastenings may impede the flow of power from the magician. Ger-ald Gardner, a member of a modern witch coven, says that witches work naked, so as not to impede the release of magical force which their ceremonies gener-ate in their bodies.[5]

When the magician washes himself his actions represent the cleansing of his mind from all irrelevant thoughts. Conversely, donning the robe is a symbol of his assumption of a suitable frame of mind. He first repeats a short banishing formula from Psalm 51. 'Purge me with hyssop and I shall be clean; wash me and I shall be whiter than snow.' Then comes the consecrating formula which dedicates him to his task. In the *Lemegeton* it is, 'By the mysterious power of this garment I put on the armour of salvation in the strength of the Most High, Ancor, Amicar, Amides, Theodonias, Anitor, that my purpose be achieved, O Adonai, through thy power, to whom be honour and glory for evermore.'

Once the magician is robed he can proceed to an extremely important preliminary, the drawing of the magic circle. The circle must be drawn properly and when the spirit has been summoned the magician leaves the circle at his peril. MacGregor Mathers says that without a correctly constructed circle 'the invocation to visible appearance of such fearful potencies as Amaymon, Egyn and Beelzebub would probably result in the death of the Exorcist on the spot; such death presenting the symptoms of one arising from Epilepsy, Apoplexy or Strangulation'. Mathers was present at an operation in which the magician accidentally leaned forward slightly over the edge of the circle and received a shock which struck the magic sword from his hand and hurled him staggering back into the circle.[6]

The circle has been considered powerful in magic from time immemorial, though it is not known why. Perhaps it is a perfect figure because every point on the circumference is equidistant from the centre, but whatever the reason, the use of a circle to mark the boundary of a sacred or protected area is very old, as at Avebury and Stonehenge. The Babylonians drew a circle of flour round the bed of a sick person to protect him from demons, and similarly it was customary among German Jews in the Middle Ages to draw a circle round the bed of a woman who had just given birth to a child. An envoy of Rome delivering a message to a foreign and hostile ruler would draw a circle round himself with his staff, apparently as a sign of his inviolability.

According to the ninth book of the *Enquiry into Plants* by the pioneer botanist Theophrastus, a pupil of Aristotle, it is best to draw a circle round certain dangerously powerful plants before digging them up. In gathering black hellebore, whose root has strong purgative properties, you should draw a circle round it and cut it facing east and saying prayers to the gods. Three circles should be drawn round that most deadly of plants, the mandrake. To dig up the noisome gladwyn, *iris foetidissima*, draw a circle round it three times, cut it with a two-edged sword and leave wheat-cakes in its place in payment for it. In all these cases it seems that the circle is drawn to keep at bay the earth-spirits which may hurry to the spot when a plant belonging to them is gathered.

Magic circles do not appear frequently in the Graeco-Egyptian texts, but in medieval and modern magic the circle is of paramount importance. It should be nine feet in diameter, drawn with the point of the magic sword or knife, or with chalk or charcoal. It can also be drawn with vermilion paint, which has power partly because of its colour and partly because it is usually made of mercury and sulphur, the components of the Stone. A second circle, eight feet in diameter, is drawn inside the first, so that the completed circle looks like a round plate with a narrow rim. Names of power are written in this rim as a barrier against the forces to be evoked. Crosses, bowls of water and such plants as vervain, anise and St. John's wort, which devils are said to dislike, should be placed in the rim. Water, holy water if possible, should be sprinkled round the outside of the circle. (The magic circle used by modern witches is slightly different. It is nine feet in diameter with two outer circles, each six inches further out.)

There must be no gap or break in the circle through which evil forces might get into it. Care must be taken not to scuff or blur its lines. A gap is left for the magician and his assistants to enter the circle and once they are in their places the gap is closed. Sometimes the assistants are placed outside the main circle in smaller circles of their own.

Diagram 12 shows a simple circle from a French manuscript, using the names of power Alpha, Omega and Agla, signs of the cross and the words *Dominus adjutor meus*, 'the Lord my helper'.[7] The *Grimoire of Honorius* uses the same type of circle with, written in the rim, ✝ *Et Verbum caro factum est* ✝ *Jesus autem* ✝ *transiens per medium illorum ibat*—'And the Word was made flesh. . . . But Jesus, passing through the midst of them, went his way', the force of which will keep the magician unscathed in the midst of the powers he has summoned up.

An eighteenth-century version of the *Key of Solomon* recommends a more complicated arrangement—three concentric circles within a square, with the names of power Adonai, El, Yah, Eloa, Ehyeh and Tetragrammaton. The *Lemegeton* says that the Triangle of Solomon should be drawn outside the circle and two feet away from it. The spirit is conjured into this triangle, from which it

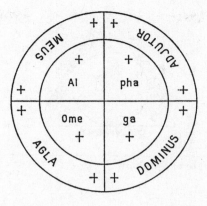

DIAGRAM 12 A Magic Circle

will not easily escape. The name inside the triangle is Michael. The origin of Anexhexeton, or Anaphexeton, said to be 'the name which Aaron spoke and became wise', is obscure but it may be connected with the Greek words *anaphero* and *ekphero*, to 'bring forth' or 'put forth'. Numbers 17.8 describes how 'the rod of Aaron . . . brought forth (*exenenke*) buds and bloomed (*exenthesen*) blossoms. . . .' In this way God designated Aaron and the tribe of Levi as the priesthood of Israel.

In some of the later textbooks a much more ominous note enters into the instructions for making the circle. According to the *Grand Grimoire*, it should be made of the skin of a young goat, cut into strips and fastened down with four nails taken from the coffin of a dead child. Inside the circle a triangle is drawn, in which the magician and his assistants stand. Two wax candles are placed in the circle, one to the left of the triangle and the other to the right, each set in a circlet of vervain. Along the base of the triangle is written IHS, standing for Jesus and *In hoc signo vinces*, 'In this sign conquer.' A brazier of burning charcoal is placed in front of the magician and the fire is fed with camphor and brandy.

A German grimoire called *Doctor Faust's Grosser und Gewaltiger Meergeist* (Doctor Faust's Great and Powerful Sea-Spirit), supposedly published in 1692 and claiming to be a translation of a Latin original by the famous Faustus himself, says the circle should be made of lead, the metal of death, with the names of power hammered into it. Inside it is a triangle made with three chains from a gibbet and nails which have been driven through the head of a man broken

DIAGRAM 13 **The Triangle of Solomon**

on the wheel. The chains and nails must be hammered and welded together with copper on Good Friday night between eleven and midnight, and at each stroke of the hammer the magician must say, 'Peter, bind it.' Each of the magician's assistants carries a dagger in his left hand and in his right a wax candle which has burned by the bier of a corpse and has afterwards been blessed by a priest. The magician himself wears a blue robe and for his girdle a cloth which has been used by an executioner to wipe his sword after beheading a criminal.[8]

Eliphas Levi, who sometimes let his imagination run away with him altogether, said that when the circle was to be used for evoking evil forces it should be drawn with the point of the magic sword, with the inner circle made of strips of lamb's or kid's skin, nailed down with four nails from the coffin of an executed criminal. Inside this is a triangle, with candles made of human fat to left and right, set in black wooden candlesticks and encircled with vervain. Along the outer edge of the circle four objects are placed—the head of a black cat which has fed on human flesh for five days, a bat which has been drowned in blood, the horns of a goat which has had intercourse with a girl, and the skull of a parricide. The magician wears a seamless black robe, without sleeves, and a cap of lead, engraved with the symbols of Venus, Saturn and the moon.[9]

These grisly properties, which might not always be very easy to obtain, are recommended by the authors of the textbooks mainly to send a delightful chill down the reader's spine, but they also illustrate the fact that the circle is not intended only to keep at bay the evil forces outside it but also to concentrate the forces inside it. The grim accessories create the right atmosphere for the ceremonies which follow and they contribute a force of their own, the force inherent in things connected with death, agony, violence and perversion. The four nails are a protection against demons because they are made of iron, but their link with a man who has been executed gives them the powerful energy of the resentment and hatred which he felt at the moment of death. If the man was tortured to death, the force of his agony and rage is believed to be even stronger. The candles of human fat contain life-energy and so does the cloth stained with blood. The head of the cat fed on human meat, the drowned bat, the goat's horns and parricide's skull are conductors of the fierce, intoxicating currents of energy aroused in the performance or contemplation of acts which are perverted, cruel and abominable.

The circle is a focus for these forces and also for the energy which the magician brings to the work from the depths of his own being. The *Grimoire of Honorius* provides an interesting incantation for the magician to chant while drawing the circle. The words are muddled and confusing, but a modern cabalist would probably interpret the incantation as a method of summoning up the divine power from within the magician, to concentrate it in the circle.

> O Lord, we fly to thy power! O Lord, confirm this work! That which is working in us becomes like dust driven before the wind, and the Angel of the Lord coming, let the darkness disappear, and the Angel of the Lord ever pursuing; Alpha, Omega, Ely, Elohe, Elohim, Zabahot, Elion, Sady!

> Behold the Lion who is the Victor of the Tribe of Judah, the Root of David. I will open the Book and the seven Seals thereof. I beheld Satan as a bolt falling from Heaven. It is Thou who has given us power to crush dragons, scorpions and all Thine enemies beneath Thy feet. Nothing shall harm us, by Eloy, Elohim, Elohe, Zabahot, Elion, Esarchie, Adonay, Jah, Tetragrammaton, Sady!

The confusion of 'I' and 'Thy' here suggests that the 'Angel of the Lord' may be the divine energy which bursts forth from the magician, dissipating the darkness and driving the dust of his normal self before it like the wind. He identifies the angel and himself with the Lion of Judah, the Lamb of Revelation, which opened the book with seven seals, and with Christ who beheld Satan falling from heaven. Then he delivers a triumphant paean in praise of his own divine power. He is the innocent of hands and clean of heart and he is also the King of Glory.

The earth is the Lord's and all those who dwell therein, because He fixed it upon the seas and made it in the midst of the waves. Who shall go up into the mountains of the Lord? Who shall be received in His Holy Place? The innocent of hands and clean of heart, who hath not received his soul in vain and hath not sworn false witness. The same shall be blessed of God and shall obtain salvation. He is of those who seek Him. Open your gates, ye princes, open the Eternal Gates and the King of Glory shall come in. Who is the King of Glory? The Lord Almighty, the Lord mighty in battle. Open your gates, ye princes. Lift up the Eternal Gates. Who is the King of Glory? The Lord Almighty. He is the King of Glory. Glory be to the Father, and to the Son, and to the Holy Ghost. Amen.[10]

A modern formula for drawing the magic circle is given by the English cabalist who wrote under the name of Dion Fortune. The magician faces east and makes the sign of a cross on his forehead and chest. This is not the Christian cross but the equal-armed cross which stands for the four elements and the four cardinal points. Touching his brow, the magician says, 'To Thee, O God [touching his solar plexus], be the Kingdom [touching his right shoulder], and the Power [touching his left shoulder], and the Glory [clasping his hands], unto the ages of the ages. Amen.' The magician is proclaiming his mastery of the universe—the elements or cardinal points—and 'God' is himself. He next imagines that he has a great cross-handled sword in his right hand. Holding it point upwards, he says, 'In the Name of God I take in hand the Sword of Power for defence against evil and aggression.' He imagines himself towering up to twice his normal height, 'a tremendous armed and mailed figure, vibrating with the force of the Power of God'. He draws the circle on the floor with the sword, imagining a line of golden flame following the sword's point. Then, facing east, he clasps his hands and raises them above his head, saying, 'May the mighty archangel Raphael protect me from all evil approaching from the east.' He repeats this formula facing south, west and north in turn, but substituting the names Michael, Gabriel and Uriel respectively.[11]

In this case the circle has been drawn *deosil*, clockwise, from east to south to west to north, following the direction of the sun. In operations which are consciously evil or dedicated to the Devil, the magician should move the opposite way, *widdershins* (from Anglo-Saxon *wither sith*, 'to walk against'), which is moving against the sun and is therefore an unnatural and perverse motion, attractive to evil forces. The seven terrible *maskim* of Babylonian theory, the devilish

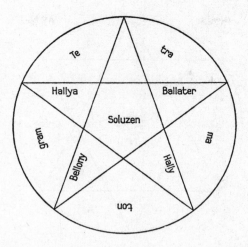

DIAGRAM 14 The Pentagram of Solomon

counterparts of the planetary gods, moved against the sun; they rose in the west and went down in the east. Witches danced widdershins at the sabbath.

Before the ceremony itself begins all irrelevant or disturbing forces must be banished from the circle. Pentagrams and hexagrams are used for this and also act as additional defences during the ceremony. The origin of the belief that the pentagram is a barrier against evil is unknown. The stock medieval explanation of its power is that the five points of the star stand for the five wounds inflicted on the body of Christ and for this reason devils are terrified of it. In modern theory, the pentagram represents God or man (1) added to the physical universe (4—solidity, the elements) and is a symbol of the divine power which man has over the universe. It is also an emblem of man, because a man with his arms and legs stretched out is a living pentagram, the points of the star being his head, hands and feet.

Pentagrams should be drawn in the rim of the circle and outside it. The Pentagram of Solomon (from the *Lemegeton*) should be embroidered on the magician's robe or drawn on parchment or other material and carried in his hand. The pentagram with one point upwards repels evil, but a reversed pentagram, with two points upwards, is a symbol of the Devil and attracts sinister forces because it is upside down and because it stands for the number 2. It represents the great Goat of the witches' sabbath and the two upward points are the Goat's horns.

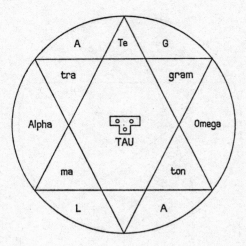

DIAGRAM 15 **The Double Seal of Solomon**

The hexagram or Seal of Solomon is another powerful symbol which may be drawn inside or outside the circle. Solomon is said to have owned a seal-ring on which the real name of God was engraved and which enabled him to master all spirits and demons. Arab writers said that this seal was in the shape of a six-pointed star and so this symbol is used in magic to control spirits. In modern theory the hexagram stands for the combination of both 'above' and 'below', represented by its two triangles, one pointing up and the other down. It is an emblem of man as God. It is also a symbol of the Philosopher's Stone, because it unites the symbols of fire △ and water ▽. The Double Seal of Solomon, as shown in the *Lemegeton*, combines a circle, a hexagram and names of power. It should be drawn or embroidered on the magician's robe.

A small brazier should be placed inside the circle. A charcoal fire is lighted in it and various substances are burned. The fumes attract spirits and the spirits can make visible forms for themselves out of the smoke. This notion may be connected with the fact that when charcoal is burned part of the smoke condenses as soot, which was regarded as the manifestation of a 'spirit'. For instance, Petrus Bonus says of soot in his *New Pearl of Great Price*, '. . . here a spirit, as it were, has evaporated from the fire and has assumed a corporeal form'.[12] It is significant that many of the substances recommended for burning in operations of sorcery give off fumes likely to cause stupor, hallucinations or delirium—hemlock, henbane, black hellebore, indian hemp, opium, all of which are powerful narcotics. One formula for summoning devils requires the burning of coriander, hemlock, parsley, liquor of black poppy, fennel, sandalwood and henbane. Fumes from burning henbane can cause convulsions and temporary insanity.

If the spirit to be summoned or the operation to be performed is connected with one of the planets, as many as possible of the substances belonging to the planet should be used to produce the correct fumes and scents. The odours of Saturn are mostly sinister and evil-smelling—asafoetida, civet, henbane, galbanum, musk, myrrh, mandrake, opium, scammony, sulphur, the powdered brains of a black cat. Civet and musk belong to Saturn as the planet of Time because they are both used in perfumery to make long-lasting scents. Galbanum is a resin and was included in the sacred incense of Jehovah, the recipe for which is given in Exodus 30.34. Scammony is another resin and a purgative.

For operations of Jupiter, the magician burns aloes wood, ash branches, cedar, ambergris, powdered lapis lazuli, saffron, storax, peacock's feathers, stork's blood and the brain of a young stag. Aloes wood has a powerful and pleasing fragrance when burned. Napoleon was passionately fond of it. Ambergris, which is secreted in the intestines of sperm-whales, also has a powerful and pleasant smell.

The scents of Mars come from benzoin, dragon's blood, human blood, euphorbium, hellebore root, powdered lodestone, pepper, sulphur and tobacco. Most of these belong to Mars because they are hot, acrid or red. Dragon's blood is a red exudation from certain varieties of palm-tree and is now used for staining violins. Euphorbium is a sharp, acrid resin.

The sun rules aloes wood, ambergris, cinnamon, cloves, frankincense, myrrh, musk, eagle's brain and white cock's blood. Cinnamon and cloves belong to the sun as the preserver of life on earth because they are preservatives—it is now known that their oils have powerful bacteria-killing properties. Myrrh and frankincense are also preservatives. Myrrh was used by the ancient Egyptians in embalming corpses and was offered to Ra, the sun-god, when in his zenith at midday.

Venus rules ambergris, galbanum, coral, aloes wood, musk, benzoin, myrtle, rose, red sandalwood, storax, sparrow's brain and pigeon's blood. Ambergris is probably included because of its connection with the sperm-whale. The rose and the myrtle belong to Venus for their beauty and sweet scent, musk because it is aphrodisiac. A perfume made of ambergris, musk and sandalwood was very popular with the beauties of Charles II's court. Coral is traditionally supposed to promote fertility.

The scents of Mercury come from mace, mastic, cinquefoil, cloves, narcissus, white sandalwood, storax, wormwood and the brain of a fox. Mastic is a resin. Wormwood belongs to Mercury because the alchemists connected wormwood with the 'bitter water' of the process of solution which was also 'mercurial water'. In the eighth chapter of Revelation a great star falls from heaven, 'and it fell upon the third part of the rivers and upon the fountains of waters'. The name of the star was Wormwood and it made the waters bitter and many men died of the bitter waters.

The moon rules camphor, frankincense, menstrual blood, jasmine, ginseng, mandrake, onycha, the dried heads of frogs and the eyes of bulls. Ginseng is a stimulant plant whose root is used in China as a cure for mental or physical exhaustion. Onycha was one of the ingredients of Jehovah's incense and was probably obtained from a species of Red Sea snail with a white, transparent shell. The sea and the white colour connect it with the moon.

It is sometimes necessary to use fumes to keep evil spirits back. Sulphur, myrrh, red sandalwood, rotten apples, vinegar, wine galls and arsenic mixed in the dregs of wine can be burned for this purpose.

Fumes may go some way to explain the curious and unpleasant experience of three men named Weber, Gessner and Zenner in a lonely hut in a vineyard near Jena in Germany on Christmas Eve, 1715. According to Weber, the only survivor, they went to the hut to summon up a spirit which would lead them to buried treasure. For protection they had a rosary and various magic symbols, and they wrote Tetragrammaton in pencil on the outside of the door before going into the hut. Inside, each said the Lord's Prayer three times. They drew a magic circle on the ceiling—an odd place for it—and lit a fire in a flower pot. The fumes were extremely thick. They opened the door to clear the atmosphere, then closed it again. Gessner began the conjuration to summon the spirit. He repeated an incantation three times, but no spirit appeared. Weber then chanted an incantation to Och, the ruling spirit of the sun in the *Arbatel of Magic*. This incantation included the names of power Tetragrammaton, Adonai, Agla and Jehovah. He began to repeat it a second time, but suddenly everything seemed to go dark before his eyes and he fell unconscious. He last saw Gessner and Zenner sitting at the table, apparently unaffected.

The three were found next day. Gessner and Zenner were dead and Weber seemed near death. When he revived, Weber could not speak, but could only make strange, frightening noises. Watchmen were left to guard the hut overnight. It was bitterly cold and the fire was lit again. The following morning one watchman was dead and the other two were unconscious. When they came round both insisted they had been attacked by evil spirits during the night. The ghost of a small boy kept scratching at the door of the hut, finally opened it and glided about inside.

Weber eventually recovered, though he was physically and mentally shattered, suffering from nervous tears, pains in the back and stomach, vomiting, and an aversion to food. The obvious explanation, that fumes from the fire caused all the trouble, does not account for all the facts. Both Gessner and Zenner had fouled themselves, which suggests a sudden, severe shock rather than poisoning by fumes. In addition, Zenner's body was covered with terrible weals and scratches, his tongue protruded from his mouth, and his neck and face were covered with burnt powder-marks.

The local officials investigated the incident soberly and meticulously, without recourse to torture. What may have happened nobody can tell, but according to Professor Butler, a sane authority as well as a distinguished one, the published account rings convincingly true.[13]

2. The Sacrifice and the Summoning

GLENDOWER I can call spirits from the vasty deep.
HOTSPUR   Why, so can I, or so can any man;
           But will they come when you do call for them?
                              SHAKESPEARE *Henry IV, Part 2*

Most of the processes in the textbooks involve the killing of an animal, usually a young goat, at some stage in the operations. In the older grimoires this is done long before the ceremony itself begins and the animal's skin is used to make parchment. Pentagrams and hexagrams are drawn on the parchment and used for protection and to control the spirit when it appears. However, it is clear that in some cases the slaughter of the animal is also a sacrifice, an offering to God to obtain divine favour or sometimes an offering to the spirit itself. In the *Grimorium Verum*, for instance, the magician cuts the throat of a virgin kid with a single stroke of the magic knife, naming the spirit he intends to evoke and saying, 'I slay thee in the name and to the honour of N.' In the *Key of Solomon* he cuts off the kid's head with one blow, naming the spirit and saying, 'O high and powerful being, may this sacrifice be pleasing and acceptable to thee. Serve us faithfully and better sacrifices shall be given thee.' White animals, the *Key* says, should be offered to good spirits and black animals to demons.

In the later grimoires the sacrifice tends to be more closely associated with the ceremony itself and in modern rituals the victim is sometimes slaughtered at the height of the ceremony. This is done to increase the supply of force in the circle. In occult theory a living creature is a storehouse of energy, and when it is killed most of this energy is suddenly liberated. The killing is done inside the circle to keep the animal's energy in and concentrate it. The animal should be young, healthy and virgin, so that its supply of force has been dissipated as little as possible. The amount of energy let loose when the victim is killed is very great, out of all proportion to the animal's size or strength, and the magician must not allow it to get out of hand. If he is unsure of himself or lets his concentration slacken, he may be overwhelmed by the force he has unleashed.

It is an ancient magical principle that blood is the vehicle in which an animal's life-energy is carried. The spirit or force which is summoned in the ceremony is normally invisible. It can appear visibly to the magician by fastening on a source of energy on the physical plane of existence. It may do this by taking possession of one of the human beings involved in the ritual. Alternatively, it can seize on the fumes of fresh blood, or on the smoke from the brazier, but blood is more effective.

The most important reason for the sacrifice, however, is the psychological charge which the magician obtains from it. The frenzy which he induces in himself by ceremonious preparations, by concentration, by incantations, by burning fumes, is heightened by the savage act of slaughter and the pumping gush of red blood. This idea seems to lie behind the simple recipe for summoning the Devil given in a version of the *Red Dragon*. Take a black hen which has never been crossed by a cock, it says, preferably seizing it by the throat so that it makes no noise, to prevent dissipation of energy. Take it to a crossroads and on the stroke of midnight draw a circle on the ground with a rod of cypress (a graveyard tree and an emblem of death). Standing in the circle and concentrating your magical powers to their highest pitch, tear the live bird in two with your hands and say *Euphas Metahim, frugativi et apellavi*. Then turn to the east and command the Devil to come to you. He will come.

It would obviously be more effective to sacrifice a human being because of the far greater psychological 'kick' involved. Eliphas Levi said that when the grimoires talk about killing a kid they really mean a human child. Although this is highly unlikely, there is a tradition that the most effective sacrifice to demons is the murder of a human being. In 1465 a jury in Norfolk found that John Caus and Robert Hikkes had summoned up a spirit and promised to sacrifice a Christian to it if it led them to buried treasure. The spirit did and they found more than one hundred shillings, but they cheated the spirit by baptising a cock with a Christian name and burning it. In 1841 treasure-hunters in

Italy murdered a boy as a sacrifice to a demon which they believed would find buried treasure for them.[14]

Aleister Crowley could not pass over such an opportunity to scandalise his readers. 'For the highest spiritual working one must accordingly choose that victim which contains the greatest and purest force. A male child of perfect innocence and high intelligence is the most satisfactory and suitable victim.' Montague Summers took this seriously, as he took everything else, and quotes it with gratified horror, in spite of Crowley's footnote in which he says that he performed this sacrifice an average of 150 times a year between 1912 and 1928!

In practice, human victims normally being in short supply, the magician's bloody sacrifice is the killing of an animal or the wounding of the magician himself or one of his assistants, whose skin is gashed till the blood runs. If this is combined with the release of sexual energy in orgasm, the effect is to heighten the magician's frenzy and the supply of force in the circle still further. This is the other 'sacrifice' which Crowley and other modern magicians skirt mysteriously around—'with regard to which the Adepts have always maintained the most profound secrecy' and which is 'the supreme mystery of practical Magick'. It is extremely difficult to perform it effectively, 'because it is a great effort for the mind to remain concentrated upon the ceremony. The overcoming of this difficulty lends most powerful aid to the magician.'[15]

When at last everything is ready, the circle drawn, the brazier lit, the magician and his assistants in their places, the summoning of the spirit begins. It is likely to be a long and exhausting business. First, the magician concentrates on the spirit to be evoked, shutting out all extraneous thoughts and sensations. Then he begins an incantation in which he gently commands the spirit to appear outside the circle.

There is no agreed form of words for the incantations. Hitting on a formula which will work is a matter of trial and error. The essential points are that the names of power must be correctly pronounced—also a matter of trial and error—and that the magician should use words which are clear and commanding and through which he can work himself up into an intoxicated ecstasy of power.

The following incantations all come from the *Lemegeton*, which has perhaps the most impressive array of incantations of any of the grimoires.[16] The opening formula is:

> I conjure thee, O Spirit N., strengthened by the power of Almighty God, and
> I command thee by Baralamensis, Baldachiensis, Paumachie, Apolorosedes

and the most powerful Princes Genio and Liachide, Ministers of the Seat of Tartarus and Chief Princes of the Throne of Apologia in the ninth region.

I conjure and command thee, O Spirit N., by Him who spake and it was done by the Most Holy and Glorious Names Adonai, Elohim, Elohe, Zebaoth, Elion, Escherce, Jah, Tetragrammaton, Sadai. Appear forthwith and show thyself to me, here outside this circle in fair and human shape, without horror or deformity and without delay.

Come at once from whatever part of the world and answer my questions. Come at one, visibly and pleasantly, and do whatever I desire for thou art conjured by the Name of the Everlasting Living and True God, Heliorem. I also conjure thee by the real name of thy God, to whom thou owest obedience, and by the name of the Prince who rules over thee.

Come, fulfil my desires and persist unto the end in accordance with my will. I conjure thee by Him to whom all creatures are obedient, by the Ineffable Name Tetragrammaton Jehovah, by which Name the elements are overthrown, the air is shaken, the sea is turned back, fire is quenched, the earth shudders, and all the hosts of things in heaven, of things in earth, of things in hell, do tremble and are confounded.

Speak to me visibly, pleasantly, clearly and without deceit. Come in the name Adonai Zebaoth, come and do not linger. Adonai Saday, the King of Kings, commands thee!

If the spirit does not appear, this incantation is repeated again and if necessary a third time. The gentle and kindly tone which the magician takes at first is gradually replaced by a fiercer, prouder, more commanding note. If the spirit has not appeared after the third repetition, a second and much stronger incantation is chanted. The spirit is ordered to show himself, in a pleasing form and without deception, by a battery of names of power, listed earlier.* This incantation ends with:

By the dreadful Day of Judgement, by the Sea of Glass which is before the face of the Divine Majesty, by the four Beasts before the Throne, having eyes before and behind, by the Fire which is about the Throne, by the Holy Angels of heaven and the Mighty Wisdom of God.

*See above, p. 120.

By the Seal of Basdathea, by the name Primematum which Moses uttered and the earth opened and swallowed up Corah, Dathan and Abiram, answer all my demands and perform all that I desire. Come peaceably, visibly and without delay.

This conjuration should also be repeated three times if necessary. According to modern occultists, the magician must work himself up to a higher and higher pitch as the words roar and thunder from his lips, as the fumes well up around him, as the sweat stands out on his body. At the moment when his excitement becomes almost uncontrollable he should stop short on the brink of surrender to it, again and again, until it is not longer possible or conceivable to hold back and the full force of his inner being bursts forth.

If the spirit has not appeared in response to the second incantation, the magician delivers a third conjuration in which he threatens the spirit, commanding it to appear by the seven secret names with which Solomon controlled all demons—Adonai, Perai, Tetragrammaton, Anexhexeton, Inessensatoal, Pathumaton and Itemon (apparently from Greek *pathumeo* 'to be idle', and *itamos* 'hasty', 'reckless'). The magician threatens by Eve, by Saray, to curse the spirit and hurl him into the bottomless pit, the lake of eternal fire, the lake of fire and brimstone, to remain there till the sounding of the last trump. 'Come therefore in the holy names Adonai, Zebaoth, Amioram. Come, Adonai commands thee.'

This should certainly force the spirit to appear and if so, he must be greeted politely but firmly. The magician should face the spirit all the time and should be on his guard. The spirit may be surly and obstinate, refusing to obey the magician's orders, or he may tell lies or try to lure the magician out of the circle. The magician must keep control by concentrating the full power of his will and the assistants should not speak to the spirit, as they might interrupt the flow of power from the magician.

It is possible, however, that a peculiarly obstinate spirit may still refuse to appear even after the first three incantations have been three times repeated. In this case the magician girds himself to the task once more and delivers the 'Curse of the Chains'.

O spirit N., who art wicked and disobedient, because thou has not obeyed my commands and the glorious and incomprehensible Names of the true God, the Creator of all things, now by the irresistible power of these Names I curse thee into the depths of the Bottomless Pit, there to remain in unquenchable fire and brimstone until the Day of Wrath unless thou shalt forthwith appear in this triangle before this circle to do my will. Come quickly and in peace by the Names Adonai, Zebaoth, Adonai, Amioram. Come, come, Adonai King of Kings commands thee.

The magician writes the spirit's name and 'seal' or magic symbol on a piece of parchment which he puts into a black wooden box with sulphur, asafoetida (an evil-smelling gum made by drying the juice from the root of the plant *Ferula asafoetida*) and any other stinking stuff which is to hand. The box is tied with iron wire. Because the spirit's name and symbol are in the box, symbolically the spirit himself is in it and the iron wire prevents him from escaping, since demons are powerless against iron. The magician hangs the box on the point of his sword and holds it over the fire, saying

I conjure thee, Fire, by Him who made thee and all other creatures of this world to burn, torture and consume this spirit N. now and for evermore.

The spirit is now told that unless he appears immediately his name and symbol will be burned in the box and afterwards buried. If he does not come, the magician says

O spirit N., because thou art still disobedient and unwilling to appear, now in the name and by the power of the Almighty and Everlasting Lord God of Hosts Jehovah Tetragrammaton, sole Creator of heaven, earth and hell and all things contained therein, supreme Lord of all things visible and invisible, I curse thee and deprive thee of all thine office, place and power. I bind thee in the depths of the bottomless pit, there to remain until the Day of Judgement in the lake of fire and brimstone prepared for rebellious spirits. May all the company of heaven curse thee. May the Sun, the Moon, the Stars, the Light of the hosts of heaven curse thee into unquenchable fire, into unspeakable torment.

As thy name and seal are bound in this box, choked with sulphurous and stinking substance and about to burn in this material fire, so in the Name of Jehovah and by the power and dignity of the three Names Tetragrammaton, Anexhexeton, Primematum, may all these drive thee into the lake of fire prepared for the damned and accursed spirits, to remain there until the Day of Wrath, no more remembered before the face of God who shall come to judge the quick and the dead with the whole world by fire.

The magician drops the box into the flames and the spirit, unable to resist this last terrible threat, will immediately appear. The fire should be quenched at once and the spirit greeted pleasantly with sweet perfumes, but he must be shown the Pentagram and Seal of Solomon to keep him in order.

When the spirit has been given his orders or has answered the magician's questions, the ceremony ends with the formal licence to depart. This is an extremely important part of the ritual. The magician cannot leave the circle until the spirit has gone and he cannot be sure that the spirit has gone until he has formally ordered him away. The *Lemegeton* formula is:

> O spirit N., because thou hast answered my demands I hereby licence thee to depart, without doing injury to man or beast. Go, I say, but be ready and willing to come whenever duly conjured by the sacred rites of magic. I conjure thee to withdraw in peace, and may the peace of God ever continue between me and thee. Amen

If the spirit refuses to depart, the situation is extremely dangerous. The magician must summon the full resources of his will, repeat the licence to depart and burn vile-smelling substances. Even if no spirit has appeared at all and the operation seems to have been a failure, the licence to depart must be spoken, because the spirit may be lurking outside the circle unknown to the magician.

Modern magicians find the incantations of the grimoires crude and tedious, though they can be effective because they are simple and direct. Crowley said that he himself and others known to him had evoked spirits by these processes, but success seemed to be obtained more in spite of the ceremony than because of it.

The most striking of Crowley's own rituals is the *Liber Samekh*, in which the magician summons up a 'spirit' which is really the divine power within himself. It is based on a Graeco-Egyptian magical text which the Order of the Golden Dawn recognised as particularly valuable and important. Crowley used it in a series of evocations in 1911 and in 1921 revised it for the use of a pupil, Frank Bennett.*

---

*See above, pages 131–3.

The usual preparations must be made, the circle drawn, and the 'incense of Abramelin' kindled—a mixture of myrrh, cinnamon, olive oil and galingal (an aromatic root), which gives a pleasant smell. The magician chants the first part of the conjuration, which describes the essential nature of the spirit.

> Thee I invoke, the Bornless One.
> Thee that didst create the Earth and the Heavens.
> Thee that didst create the Night and the Day.
> Thee that didst create the darkness and the Light.
> Thou art Asar Un-Nefer (Myself made Perfect): Whom no man hath seen at
>   any time.
> Thou art Ia-Besz (the Truth in Matter).
> Thou art Ia-Apophrasz (the Truth in Motion).
> Thou hast distinguished between the Just and the Unjust.
> Thou didst make the Female and the Male.
> Thou didst produce the Seeds and the Fruit.
> Thou didst form Men to love one another and to hate one another. . . .

In the first line of the original the spirit was 'the headless one'. Crowley substituted 'bornless' as a reference to the eternity of the godhead. Most of the lines refer to pairs of opposites which are united in the One.

> Hear thou Me, for I am the Angel of Ptah-
>   Apophrasz-Ra: this is Thy True Name, handed
>   down to the Prophets of Khem.

The magician summons the spirit by pronouncing its 'real' name. Ptah was an Egyptian god of intelligence and thought, sometimes held to be the maker of the world. Ra was the sun-god. Khem is an old name for Egypt. The real names of the spirit and the magician are the same, because the spirit is the magician's true self.

The magician moves about the circle to each of the cardinal points and invokes the spirit by reciting long strings of barbarous names of power, which enshrine its nature and attributes. He feels a swift, fierce current of creative energy pulsing through him and he builds up a clear mental picture of the spirit, as if it was standing in front of him.

This is the Lord of the Gods:

This is the Lord of the Universe:

This is He whom the Winds fear.

This is He, Who having made Voice by His commandment is Lord of all
      Things; King, Ruler and Helper.

The last line refers to God's creation of the universe by word of mouth, by 'voice'. The magician orders the spirit to make all spirits subject to him—every spirit of the firmament and the ether, of the earth and under the earth, of dry land and of water, of whirling air and rushing fire, and every spell and scourge of God. He has now 'summoned up' a spirit from his inner self. He next chants another string of barbarous names in which, with a passion rising to ecstasy, he identifies himself with the spirit. At the climax the full force of his magical power gushes from him, he loses all consciousness of his normal self and becomes the mental picture which he only saw before.

I am He! the Bornless Spirit! having sight in the feet [meaning, 'that they
      may choose their own path']; Strong, and the Immortal Fire!

I am He! the Truth!

I am He! Who hate that evil should be wrought in the World!

I am He, that lighteneth and thundereth!

I am He, from Whom is the Shower of the Life of Earth!

I am He, whose mouth ever flameth!

I am He, the Begetter and Manifestor unto the Light!

I am He, the Grace of the Worlds!

'The Heart girt with a Serpent' is my name.[17]

Ra, the sun, is 'the heart' and Ptah, god of wisdom, is 'the serpent'. The command to make all spirits obedient to the magician is repeated again, but this time it is spoken as if by the spirit itself, as if it was the spirit's will to show itself by taking possession of the magician's body. The magician seems to be filled with a great inner light and he hears his own voice chanting far off, distant and strange, as if it came from outside him.

Crowley used this ritual in 1911 to summon a spirit called Abuldiz, but the results were not very satisfactory. He is supposed to have obtained a far more striking success two years before, using the stock methods of the grimoires.

In 1909 Crowley and his friend and pupil Victor Neuburg visited Algiers and went on southwards into the desert. They decided to conjure up a 'mighty devil' called Choronzon. The magic circle was drawn in the sand and the Triangle of Solomon, from the *Lemegeton*, outside it. The name Choronzon was written in the triangle and they cut the throats of three pigeons, one at each angle of the triangle, and poured the blood on to the sand.

Crowley wore a black robe with a hood which enveloped his head but had eye-slits. He crouched in the triangle, to allow the demon to take possession of him. Some occultists have claimed that as a result of this rash act he was obsessed by the demon for the rest of his life. Neuburg remained in the circle. He called upon the archangels and their legions to protect him and chanted an incantation from the *Grimoire of Honorius*.

Crowley held a topaz and, looking into it, he saw the demon appear in the depths of the stone, crying the words which are supposed to open the Gates of Hell, *Zazas, Zazas, Nasatanada, Zazas*. The demon blustered, boasted and raged, speaking in Crowley's voice and also in his style—'I have made every living thing my concubine, and none shall touch them, save only I. . . . From me come leprosy and pox and plague and cancer and cholera and the falling sickness.'

Neuburg thought he saw not Crowley but a beautiful woman in the triangle. She spoke softly to him and looked at him longingly, but he realised that she was really the demon, trying to entice him out of the circle. Suddenly there was a loud, wild laugh and Choronzon appeared visibly in the triangle. He heaped flattery on Neuburg and asked permission to come and put his head under Neuburg's feet to adore and serve him. Neuburg recognised this as another ruse, an attempt to get into the circle, and refused. Choronzon, who was now in the shape of Crowley but naked, begged for water to quench his thirst. Neuburg again refused, commanding the demon to obey him by the Names of God and by the Pentagram. Choronzon was not in the least subdued by this and Neuburg, who was becoming increasingly frightened, threatened him with anger and pain and the torments of hell. But Choronzon answered magnificently, in the manner of Marlowe's Mephistopheles. 'Thinkest thou, O fool, that there is any anger and any pain that I am not, or any hell but this is my spirit?'

The demon broke into a torrent of furious and obscene blasphemies. Neuburg was frantically trying to write down all Choronzon's words and while his attention was distracted Choronzon craftily threw sand from the triangle on to the line of the circle, broke it and sprang into the circle. The unfortunate

Neuburg was flung to the ground as the raging demon tried to tear out Neuburg's throat with his fangs. Neuburg desperately invoked the Names of God and stabbed at Choronzon with the magic knife. The demon was overcome and writhed back into the triangle. Neuburg repaired the circle while the demon turned back into a beautiful woman and again attempted a seduction, but in vain. In the end Choronzon admitted defeat, but as the energy of the pigeons' blood was now exhausted he disappeared and the operation came to a close.

Crowley, who said that during all this he 'dwelt apart' in his robe and hood, noted that Choronzon appeared as a woman, as a wise man, as a wriggling snake and as Crowley himself. He had no fixed form, because he was the maker of form. He was 'the terror of darkness, and the blindness of night, and the deafness of the adder, and the tastelessness of stale and stagnant water, and the black fire of hatred, and the udders of the Cat of slime; not one thing but many things'.[18]

There is not much doubt that the procedures of ritual magic are likely to cause hallucinations. The magician prepares himself by abstinence and lack of sleep, or by drink, drugs and sex. He breathes in fumes which may affect his brain and senses. He performes mysterious rites which tug at the deepest, most emotional and unreasoning levels of his mind, and he is further intoxicated by the killing of an animal, the wounding of a human being and in some cases the approach to and achievement of orgasm. Through all this he concentrates on a mental picture of the being he hopes to see. It does not seem at all unlikely that at the high point of the ceremony he may actually see it.

Although such manifestations may often be the results of hallucination, or sometimes of deliberate deception, occultists believe that this is not always the case. They say that self-intoxicating procedures are necessary because the spirit is not a part of the normal, everyday world and so it cannot be experienced in normal states of mind. The spirit may show itself in a form created for it by the magician's imagination, but it is a real force. It may be a force or intelligence which exists independently of the magician, and if so it is no more imaginary than the forces of electricity of gravity, or it may come from within the magician himself, in which case it is no less real than the forces of ambition or pride or desire which we recognise in ourselves. Behind all this, of course, is the perplexing question of what reality consists of, and whether it is sensible to regard those things which we seem to perceive in 'normal' conditions as real, but those which we seem to perceive in 'abnormal' states of mind as unreal.

3. The Lords of Darkness

The Black Rider flung back his hood, and behold! he had a kingly crown; and yet upon no head visible was it set. The red fires shone between it and the mantled shoulders vast and dark. From a mouth unseen there came a deadly laughter.

J. R. R. TOLKIEN *The Lord of the Rings*

The grimoires and the demonologists classify the spirits which the magician may attempt to summon up in various different ways. There are spirits of the seven planets and the days of the week, of the hours of night and day, of the zodiac signs and of the cardinal points, some of them good and some evil.

There are also the 'elementals'. In the fifth century Proclus divided spirits into five groups, four of them connected with the elements of fire, air, water and earth, and a fifth group which live underground. Psellus, in the eleventh century, added a sixth category—*lucifugum*, 'fly-the-light'. In sixteenth- and seventeenth-century authors the fire-spirits are usually described as living in the upper heavens and having no contact with men. The spirits of air are ferocious and violent. They hate human beings, cause storms, and can make themselves visible bodies out of air. Water-spirits, which are cruel, passionate and deceitful, generally appear in female shape. They wreck ships and drown swimmers. Spirits of earth live in the woods. Some are friendly to men, but some set traps for them and lead travellers astray. The spirits who live underground are exceptionally malicious. They attack miners and treasure-hunters, cause earthquakes and eruptions, and lure people below ground to their deaths. The fly-the-lights, which naturally never appear in the day-time, are entirely beyond human understanding or control—mysterious, restless, icily malignant. They pursue and kill those incautious enough to travel by night.

These spirits are the medieval and modern survivals of the wide-spread primitive belief that all Nature is alive as man is, that spirits live in every stream and mountain, in clouds and breezes, in trees and fields and hedgerows, in boulders, crags and caves. They are unpredictable and mischievous as Nature is, sometimes kindly but more often cruel.

The grimoires are mainly concerned with much bigger game—the ruling princes of evil, the fallen angels, the great lords of darkness themselves. An early catalogue of demons appears in the *Testament of Solomon*, which dates from about A.D. 100 to 400. It describes how an angel from God brought Solomon the magic ring which gave him power over all devils by forcing them to tell him their real names. Beelzeboul, prince of devils, and Asmodeus, the devil of lust who is part spirit and part man, are among the evil spirits mentioned. The names of the devils come from Jewish, Greek, Egyptian, Assyrian, Babylonian and possibly Persian sources. Their functions are listed, as in the later grimoires. One sets fire to crops, one strangles babies, one wrecks ships. Many of them cause diseases. One brings eye ailments, another migraine, another fevers, another inflammation of the tonsils. This is an inheritance from the primitive tradition that any disease is caused by or itself is a demon, which survives in Crowley's Choronzon, who was leprosy, pox, plague and the rest.

A later version of the *Testament* gives a different list of devils, including Asmodeus, Astaroth and Mahomet. Most of their names are contorted and of unknown origin. This version set a pattern for the grimoires by giving the 'character' of each demon, the magic symbol which controls it because it is the demon's 'mark', equivalent to its real name.

In the *Grimorium Verum* and the *Grand Grimoire* the three supreme powers of evil are Lucifer, Beelzebuth and Astaroth. When summoned by the magician, Lucifer appears as a handsome boy, Beelzebuth as a gigantic fly, Astaroth as a human figure, pied black and white. Their immediate subordinates are named, with their special functions and 'characters'.

Other lists are given in the *Lemegeton* and in *Pseudomonarchia Daemonum*, by the sixteenth-century demonologist John Wier or Weyer, a pupil and friend of Agrippa. Wier provides a complete hierarchy of hell, which includes Beelzebuth, supreme chieftain of the infernal regions, Satan in second place, Euronymous who is Prince of Death, Moloch the Prince of the Land of Tears, Pluto the Prince of Fire, Baalberith, the arch-demoness Proserpine, Astaroth, Adrammelech, Nergal, Baal who commands the infernal armies, Lucifer who dispenses the justice of hell, Chamos, Melchom, Behemoth, Dagon, Asmodeus who rules gambling-houses, and Antichrist who is sadly fallen in state since he is now the mere mime and juggler of hell. Some demons are ambassadors to certain countries, including Mammon (England), Belial (Turkey), Rimmon (Russia), and Thamuz (Spain).

As has often been observed, devils are usually other people's gods, and this is true of many of those listed by Wier and the *Lemegeton*. Some of them were originally gods of the Hebrews' neighbours or of the Canaanites whose territory the Hebrews invaded and occupied. Mentioned with rage and contempt in the Old Testament as rivals of Jehovah, they came to be regarded as diabolical powers.

Beelzebub, Lord of the Flies, was the chief of demons in Jewish popular belief at the time of Christ, who was accused of casting out devils by Beelzebub, 'the prince of devils'.[19] He was originally Baalzebub, god of the Philistine city of Ekron, to whom King Ahaziah sent for an oracle, much to the annoyance of the prophet Elijah. The name may mean 'lord of flies' or 'lord who drives flies away' or that divination by the flight of flies was practised by the god's priests. (The history of Satan or Lucifer, usually regarded as chief of devils, is considered in Chapter 7.)

Baal means 'lord' and was a title given to many local deities in Syria and Palestine. The supreme Baal was the great fertility god of the Canaanites, whose worship involved the sacrifice of children by burning. 'They have built also the high places of Baal, to burn their sons with fire for burnt offerings unto Baal.'[20] Attempts have been made to connect him with the Celtic sun-gods Belenus and Belinus and with Beltane, the Celtic fire-festival on the first of May, but the connection seems to rest on a false etymology. The *Lemegeton* says that Baal appears with a toad's or cat's head and has a hoarse voice. He imparts wisdom and invisibility.

Children were similarly sacrificed to Moloch, a Phoenician and Canaanite god, and to Adrammelech, whose cult was probably brought into Samaria by colonists from Syria. Chemosh was worshipped by the Moabites and Milcom by the Ammonites. Dagon was the great god of the Philistines, who placed the Ark of Jehovah in Dagon's temple when they had captured it from the Israelites. The force of the Ark destroyed Dagon and hewed his statue in pieces. Rimmon was a Syrian god. Naaman the leper bowed himself down in the temple of Rimmon at Damascus.

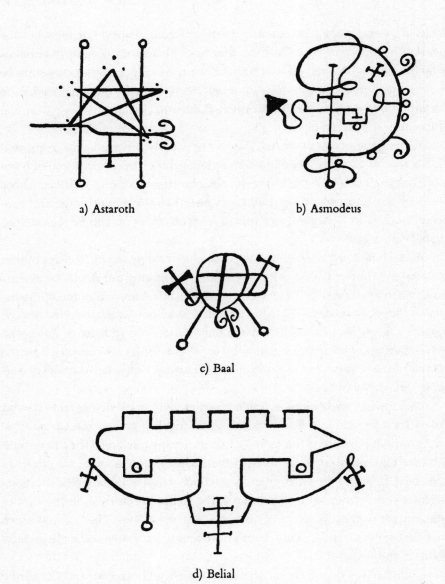

a) Astaroth

b) Asmodeus

c) Baal

d) Belial

DIAGRAM 16   **Magic Symbols of Devils from the *Lemegeton***

Another devil who was originally a Canaanite god, Baalberith, 'lord of the covenant'—a god who presided over agreements, in fact—was among the many devils, including Beelzebub, Astaroth and Asmodeus, who took possession of Sister Madeleine de Demandolx of the Ursuline convent at Aix-en-Provence in the early seventeenth century. Under their influence, she saw visions, danced and sang love-songs, writhed in indecent postures and told blood-chilling tales of sodomy and the cannibal eating of children at witch revels she had attended. It was determined that her confessor, Father Gaufridi, had seduced and be-witched her. After torture, he was strangled and burned at Aix in 1611.

Ashtaroth was the great goddess of Canaan and Phoenicia, the equivalent of the Babylonian Ishtar. She was worshipped with lascivious rites which were constantly condemned by the Old Testament prophets. The goddess became a male demon who appears like a beautiful angel, but has very bad breath. He teaches the sciences and reveals the events of the past, present and future.

Nergal, the ruthless, the crouching one, comes from further afield. He was the Babylonian lord of the underworld and the equivalent of Mars, ruler of war, plague, flood and destruction. Tammuz was originally a Sumerian shepherd-god, whose cult became popular in Syria and Phoenicia.

Asmodeus, the devil of lechery, sensuality and luxury, frequently appears in Jewish literature and seems to have always been a devil. Traditionally, he has the feet of a cock, a bird noted for sexual vigour. It was Asmodeus who killed the seven husbands of Sarah in the *Book of Tobit*. He may be derived from the Persian *Aeshma Daeva*, the fiend of the wounding spear who is the demon of passion, jealousy and rage, of his name may come from Hebrew *shamad*, 'to destroy'. The *Lemegeton* says he must always be invoked bareheaded.

Belial (or Beliar), the worthless one and the demon of lies, also seems to have been an evil spirit from the start. His name may be a contraction of He-brew *beli ya'al*, 'without worth'. The Jews sometimes regarded him as the chief of devils and he is the leader of the forces of evil in *The War of the Sons of Light and the Sons of Darkness*, one of the Dead Sea scrolls. 'But for corruption thou hast made Belial, an angel of hostility. All his dominion is in darkness, and his purpose is to bring about wickedness and guilt. All the spirits that are associated with him are but angels of destruction.'[21] When summoned, he appears as a beautiful angel and speaks in a deceptively soft, pleasant voice.

Mammon, the devil of avarice, was not a god but a word. His name comes from Aramaic and means wealth or profit. He was regarded as a demon be-cause Jesus said, 'Ye cannot serve God and mammon'.[22]

Pluto and Proserpine come from Rome, Eurynomus from Greece. Pluto was the Roman lord of the underworld and Proserpine (Persephone) was his queen. Eurynomus appeared in a famous painting of the descent of Odysseus into the underworld, in the Hall of the Cnidians at Delphi. He was shown sitting on a vulture's skin, half black and half blue like a meat-fly, showing his teeth in a carrion grin and chewing the flesh of corpses.

Among numerous other devils in the *Lemegeton* are Phoenix, said to be an excellent poet, and Amon, originally an Egyptian god whose name means 'the hidden one' and who was united with Ra as a sun-god, Amon-Ra. He appears like a wolf with a snake's head, vomiting flames. He procures the love of women and also reveals the future. Cimeries, who rides a black horse and rules all the spirits of Africa, probably takes his name from the Cimmerians, a people mentioned by Homer who lived in mists and darkness in the farthest West. Balam is a three-headed devil who rides a bear and carries a hawk on his wrist. He predicts the future and is probably Balaam, a greedy sorcerer in the Old Testament and in the New a symbol of avarice or of idol-worship and immortality.[23]

That demons appear in grotesque and horrifying shapes is an old tradition. The Babylonians thought that evil spirits were so hideous that they might run away if shown themselves in a mirror. They had the bodies of dogs, eagles' legs, lions' paws, scorpions' tails, human skulls for heads, goats' horns and the wings of birds. The demon locusts which appear in the ninth chapter of Revelation have the bodies of war-horses, human faces, long hair and golden crowns, lions' teeth, clashing wings and the stinging tails of scorpions. (Their leader, the Angel of the Bottomless Pit, whose name in Hebrew is Abaddon, the destroyer, is in Greek Apollyon, who appears in *Pilgrim's Progress*.) The early Christian Fathers described devils as appearing in human form and also as lions, leopards, bulls, bears, horses, wolves, snakes and scorpions, or as composite creatures.

The grimoires describe a devil's appearance so that the magician can be sure that the right one has appeared, but the descriptions also recall the planetary talismans of Ficino and Bruno and the planetary spirits of the *Fourth Book of Occult Philosophy*. They may have been intended to help the magician to summon the spirit by concentrating on its characteristic form.

According to the Cabala, the evil powers sprang from the left-hand pillar of the Tree of Life, especially from the sephira Geburah, the severity and wrath of God. Evil came from this sphere as if God's wrath had somehow spilled over from it. In the *Zohar* and later cabalistic books, evil spirits are often called *kelipoth*, 'husks' or 'shells'. They are the waste or litter or filth which the organism of the universe gives off.

By the thirteenth century the idea of ten evil sephiroth, the counterparts of the ten divine sephiroth, had developed. They are ruled by arch-demons under the supreme command of Sammael, the fell angel of poison. MacGregor Mathers listed them as:[24]

1. Satan and Moloch	6. Belphegor
2. Beelzebub	7. Baal
3. Lucifuge	8. Adrammelech
4. Ashtaroth	9. Lilith
5. Asmodeus	10. Naamah

Lilith and Naamah, in Jewish tradition, are demonesses who throttle newborn babies and seduce men in their sleep, sucking their blood. Naamah's origins are not known. Lilith was probably the *lilitu* originally, an Assyrian demoness who had wings and long, dishevelled hair. Her name was confused with the Hebrew word for 'night', *layil*, and so she was described as a hairy night-fiend. There is a story that King Solomon at first suspected the Queen of Sheba of being Lilith, because she had hairy legs. She is probably the 'terror by night' of Psalm 91—'Thou shalt not fear for any terror by night . . .'—and legend says that she was Adam's first wife, created by God out of filth and mud. From Adam's union with her sprang Asmodeus and hosts of other demons. Eve was not created until later. This story does not appear in the Bible, but justification for it was found in Genesis 5.3, which says that Adam lived 130 years and then 'begat a son in his own likeness, after his image' on Eve. This was thought to imply that he had previously begotten sons, the demons, who were not in his own likeness and image.

4. Necromancy and Psychic Attack

The Church does not deny that, with a special permission of God, the souls of the departed may appear to the living, and even manifest things unknown to the latter. But, understood as the art or science of evoking the dead, necromancy is held by theologians to be due to the agency of evil spirits. . . .

The Catholic Encyclopaedia

Necromancy means literally 'divination by the dead' and one of its principal aims is to discover the future. The dead, no longer bound by the limitations of the mortal, physical plane, can see the events of the future and can be compelled to reveal them. Moving on a shadowy plane surrounding the physical one, they can also see the location of buried treasure and they know the nature of spirits and demons, and how best to communicate with them.

Opponents of Spiritualism sometimes describe it as modern necromancy, but the Spiritualists have different aims and their methods are milk-and-watery in the extreme compared to the methods of necromancy, which is one of the ugliest and most dangerous of magical operations. It is considered peculiarly dangerous because the nastiness of its procedures stirs up evil currents or attracts evil forces which may fasten on the magician.

For nine days before the ceremony the necromancer and his assistants prepare for it by surrounding themselves with the aura of death. They dress in musty grave-clothes, filched from corpses, and these must not be taken off until the operation is finished. When they first put these on they recite the funeral service over themselves. They abstain from even the mere sight of a woman. They eat dog's flesh and black bread, baked without salt or leaven, and they drink unfermented grape-juice. The dog is the creature of Hecate, the goddess of ghosts and death and sterility, the terrible and inexorable one, the dweller in the void, who is invoked with averted head because no man can see her and remain sane. The absence of salt is a symbol of putrefaction after death, because salt is a preservative. The bread has no leaven and the grape-juice is unfermented to stand for matter without spirit, the physical clay without the spark of life. The bread and the grape-juice are also the necromantic equivalents of the bread and wine of communion, unleavened and unfermented as a sacrament of emptiness and despair.

Through these preparations the magician puts himself in touch with death, into a corpse-like state in which he is in rapport with the real corpse he intends to disturb. When everything is ready he goes to the grave, either between midnight and one in the morning—the first hour of the new day, a suitable time for raising the corpse to life—or at sunset, the first hour of the new day in the older tradition. A magic circle is drawn round the grave. The assistants carry torches and burn a mixture of henbane, hemlock, aloes wood, saffron, opium and mandrake.

They open the grave and the coffin, exposing the corpse. The magician touches it three times with the magic wand, commanding it to arise. One formula is:

By the virtue of the Holy Resurrection and the agonies of the damned, I conjure and command thee, spirit of N. deceased, to answer my demands and obey these sacred ceremonies, on pain of everlasting torment. Berald, Beroald, Balbin, Gab, Gabor, Agaba, arise, arise, I charge and command thee.

In a longer process, involving the body of a suicide, the magician commands the spirit by the mysteries of the deep, the flames of Banal, the power of the east, the silence of the night and the rites of Hecate, to show itself and reveal why it took its own life, where it is now and where it will be hereafter. The magician taps the carcass nine times with the wand and says, 'I conjure thee, spirit of N. deceased, to answer my questions as thou hast hope for the rest of the blessed and ease of all thy sorrow. By the Blood of Jesus which He shed for thee, I conjure and command thee to tell me what I ask.'[25]

They take the body and arrange it with its head to the east, the direction of the rising sun, and with its arms and legs in the position of the crucified Christ, so that it will rise from the dead. At its right hand they place a dish containing a little wine, mastic and sweet oil, which they set alight. The magician conjures the spirit to enter its old body again and to speak, 'by the virtue of the Holy Resurrection and the bodily posture of the Saviour of the world' and 'on pain of torment and wandering thrice seven years, which by the force of sacred magic rites I have power to inflict on thee'.

When this incantation has been repeated three times, the spirit returns to its old body, which slowly rises until it stands upright. It answers the magician's questions in a faint, hollow voice. Then the magician rewards the spirit by giving it rest. He destroys its body—burning it or burying it in quicklime—so that it can never again be troubled and called back by sorcery.

Written in the time of Nero, the description of a necromantic operation in Lucan's *Pharsalia* is well in tune with modern magical theory. Sextus Pompey, son of Pompey the Great, is anxious to discover what fate holds in store and decides to consult the dead, to be sure of a clear and accurate answer. 'Though it may be well enough for the oracles and prophets who serve the Olympians to give riddling responses, a man who dares consult the dead deserves to be told the truth.' The ceremony is performed by the witch Erichtho, who had 'kept on good terms with the infernal powers by squatting in tombs'. She had behaved as if she was a corpse, in fact. She also surrounded herself with things redolent of death—gobbets of flesh and bones from children's funeral-pyres, grave-clothes and pieces of human skin, the nails, tongues and eyeballs of buried corpses.

For the ceremony itself Erichtho demanded a recent carcass with sound lungs which would speak audibly and clearly. Older corpses 'only speak incoherently'. According to occult theory, some of a body's energy remains in it after death, but this energy is gradually dissipated. A recent corpse was found and taken to a dark place, screened by yews. Erichtho cut into the corpse's chest and poured into its veins a mixture of warm menstrual blood, the froth of rabid dogs, a lynx's guts, the hump of a corpse-fed hyena, the sloughed skin of a snake, and the leaves of plants on which she had spat. All these were intended to instil a kind of poisonous life into the corpse. Next she chanted an outlandish incantation which seemed to mingle the barking of dogs and howling of wolves, the screech of an owl, the roaring of wild beasts and hissing of snakes, the crash of waves on rocks, the murmur of forest trees and the bellow of thunder. She invoked Styx and the Elysian Fields, the euphemistically-named Kindly Ones, who torture damned souls, Proserpine and Hecate, Hermes the Thrice-Great who leads men down to get the three Fates, Charon who is hell's ferryman, Chaos, and 'the true ruler of the Earth, who suffers endless agony below, since the gods are so long a-dying'.

At the end of the incantation a ghost appeared, but at first it obstinately refused to enter the corpse. Erichtho threatened it in the name of all the powers of hell and gradually the dead body's blood grew warm and began to circulate, the lungs began to work, the muscles to move, and the corpse jumped up and stood erect, pale and tense. It answered the questions which Pompey put to it and was given its reward, to be burned to ashes.

In Aleister Crowley's novel *Moonchild* an operation of necromancy is begun at sunset. The sorcerers work barefooted, to draw up the powers of earth from the volcanic strata below. They cover the ground with nauseous slime and sprinkle it with sulphur. The magic circle is drawn in the sulphur with a forked stick, a sign of the Devil, and the grooves filled in with powdered charcoal. The corpse is placed at the centre of the circle, its head to the north—the side of shadow. One assistant holds a lighted candle of black wax, the other leads a goat on a leash and carries a sickle. The master-sorcerer lights nine small candles and sets them about the circle. (The constant appearance of the number 9 in necromancy may be connected with the old nine spheres, through which the soul rises after death.) He impales four black cats alive on iron arrows, so that their agony will frighten away undesirable spirits, and places them at the four cardinal points.

The sorcerers intend to evoke a demon from the goat. They will then identify the goat with the corpse, so that the demonic power will be transferred into the corpse and will bring its spirit back to life. As the ritual proceeds, the necromancer chanting incantations, the goat bleating, the tortured cats squalling, 'it seemed to all of them as though the air grew thick and greasy; that of that slime were bred innumerable creeping things, monsters misshapen, abortions of dead paths of evolution, creatures which had not been found fit to live upon the earth and so had been cast off by her as excrement'. As the incantations work to their climax the goat stirs and bounds under the manipulations of the master-sorcerer (it can be assumed that these are sexual manipulations). They recognise that the demon is present and stab the goat to the heart. The reeking blood spurts over them, its smell mingling with the stench of sweat and the odour of the decomposing corpse.

The arch-sorcerer begins his final conjuration. They hack off the goat's head, slash a gaping cavity in the belly of the corpse and thrust the head of the goat into it. Other parts of the goat are pushed into the corpse's mouth. This is the identification of corpse and goat. Suddenly, one of the assistants flings himself on to the two carcasses, tearing them with his teeth and lapping the blood. He is the weakest of the group and it is through his mouth that the dead man's spirit, now demon-inspired, will speak. He sits up, his face beaming with delight, and answers their questions rapidly and commandingly.

In some cases the dead are summoned to attack a person the magician wishes to harm or master. A Graeco-Egyptian text gives the following method of compelling a woman to submit to the magician. He makes a wax doll to represent the woman and pierces it with thirteen needles, through the brain, eyes, ears, mouth, hands, feet, belly, anus and genitals. At sunset, he places the doll on the grave of someone who died young or by violence. Then he conjures the corpse in the grave by Persephone, Ereshkigal (the Sumerian queen of the underworld), Adonis, Hermes, Thoth and Anubis (the jackal-headed Egyptian god of the dead), by the gods of the underworld and all the legions of the dead untimely snatched from life, and commands it to rise up and stalk through the streets, to go to the woman's house and bring her to him and obsess her. 'And awaken at my behest, whoever you may be, whether male or female. Betake yourself to that place and that street and that house and bring her hither and bind her. Bring N.N. hither, daughter of N.N. . . . Let her sleep with none other, let her have no pleasurable intercourse with any other man, save with me alone. Let N.N. neither drink nor eat, nor love, nor be strong nor well, let her have no sleep except with me. . . .'[26]

This process amounts to a rape by means of a zombie, one of the 'living dead', a corpse which the magician has animated and which is subject to his will. Alternatively, another person can be attacked by enlisting a demonic power. Dion Fortune described the methods and symptoms of 'psychic attack' in her book *Psychic Self-Defense*. She herself was first drawn to occultism by experiencing an attack of this kind, which shattered her health for a long period.

To evoke a demonic force against an enemy, the magician performs a ceremony of Mars, the planet of violence and destruction. He drapes the room in scarlet, wears a scarlet robe, and uses instruments of iron with a naked sword as his magic wand. He lights five torches, because Geburah, the sphere of Mars, is the fifth sephira. He wears a red ruby and the astrological symbol of Mars engraved on a pentagon of steel. He invokes 'the arch-devil of the fifth Infernal Habitation'—Asmodeus, the demonic force corresponding to Geburah. The magician offers himself as the channel through which this force can manifest itself. To direct it at the victim a link is needed—a lock of the victim's hair, a nail-paring, or something he has often worn or handled. Failing this, the magician can create an artificial link by identifying something in his possession with the victim. For instance, he might formally baptise an animal with the victim's name and then torture and kill it. Or he may concentrate his hatred on some object which is then left in the victim's house or buried where he will step over it.

Concentration is essential. Occultists believe that the magician's will can be turned on other people like a ray or a beam. If he is projecting hatred or cruelty, evil spirits will be attracted by the current of force and will join in the operation. One way of killing an enemy by concentration is called the Black Fast. Mabel Brigge, executed at York in 1538, was said to have confessed to killing a man by abstaining from meat, milk and all dairy foods, meanwhile concentrating on the victim's death. A modern example of magical concentration occurred in Germany in 1938, when General von Fritsch was tried on false charges, faked by the Gestapo. Himmler, the Gestapo chief, was anxious about the outcome of the trial and assembled twelve S.S. officers (the number of a coven) in a room near the court. He made them sit in a circle and concentrate their minds so as to control the proceedings. But von Fritsch was cleared despite their efforts. The same method was turned against the Germans two years later when, it is said, the English witches prevented the invasion of England by directing at Hitler's brain the thought that he could not cross the Channel.[27]

Another way of launching a psychic attack is through an artificial elemental. Occultists say that elementals—the minor and brutish spirits of fire, air, earth and water—exist in Nature, but that it is also possible to make an artificial one, with a temporary lease on life. The magician forms in his mind a clear picture of the creature he intends to create. By concentrated imagination and will-power, and by feeding into the mental picture his own violent emotional forces—his hatred, cruelty or lust—he can endow the creature with life and send it out to attack an enemy. It may appear in animal form—as a toad or a snake or a wolf perhaps—or as something which is part human and part animal. It will not be visible to ordinary sight, but the person attacked by it will see it and so will anyone who is clairvoyant.

The symptoms of a successful psychic attack are said to include extreme fear, anxiety and mental distress, bruises on the body—sometimes in the form of a goat's hoof or an ace of clubs—broad smears of slime, sometimes with footprints in them, the smell of decomposing flesh, poltergeist phenomena and inexplicable outbreaks of fire, and a curious and sinister sound called 'the astral bell', which may vary from a clear bell-like note to a faint click. The seventeenth-century demonologist Francesco-Maria Guazzo, a friar who frequently acted as adviser to the judges in witch trials, included among symptoms of bewitchment slow wasting and emaciation of the body with intense lassitude of mind, convulsions, tearing pains near the heart, heavy pulse, spasms of the neck or stomach, sexual impotence, feelings of intense heat or cold in the stomach, sweating in cold weather, and gummy eyelids.

In 1746, John Wesley, preaching in Cornwall, was told by a woman that his sermon had given her relief from a spell cast on her seven years before, which had caused her fear and horror of mind and also bodily agony. She felt as if her flesh was being torn by red-hot pincers. In 1878 at Salem, Massachusetts, a legal action was brought by Lucretia Brown, a follower of Mrs. Eddy in the early days of the Christian Science movement, against Daniel Spofford, another of Mrs. Eddy's followers. The allegation was that by projecting 'malicious animal magnetism' against her Spofford had caused her mental pain and suffering, severe spinal pains and neuralgia. Mrs. Eddy, who was herself inclined to claim that her enemies directed malicious psychic currents against her, gave evidence for the plaintiff, but the court dismissed the action.

Occultists say that symptoms associated with psychic attack can also be caused by malevolent spirits in cases where something has gone wrong in a magical operation. Evil beings may show themselves in appalling nightmares or in noises, pools of slime or blood, moving balls of light and disgusting stenches. Eliphas Levi said that on some occasions, after performing occult experiments, he was woken in the night by the sensation of a hand trying to strangle him. His books and papers were disturbed and thrown about, the timbers of the building creaked ominously and he heard heavy blows on the ceiling. Dion Fortune mentions the case of a man who used a magic square from the *Sacred Magic of Abramelin*, but was unable to control the force he had unleashed. He began to suffer from terror at night, especially at the sight of the new moon. When at last he saw the creature which was obsessing him, it had a beard, long flowing hair and closed eyes. One night a red snake uncoiled itself from under his bed and to get away from it he jumped out of the bedroom window, ten feet from the ground. Next time he saw the being its hair had changed into snakes. Later, a great red obelisk crashed through the bedroom wall, smashing mirrors and windows. All these experiences were 'hallucinations', but he lived in real terror for months until he was rescued by the help of another occultist.

Similarly, the occultist who explores the astral plane runs the risk of failing to bring his astral self back into his physical body. The astral body may then wander away out of his control and may be attacked or obsessed, causing nightmares, hysteria, fainting fits, headaches, in extreme cases even paralysis or insanity. These symptoms will wear off in time, but may still cause permanent damage, in the form of inability to concentrate, follow an argument, keep a promise or persist in any given course of action, all of which recalls Guazzo's 'lassitude of mind'.

5. Low Magic

. . . facilis descensus Averno;
noctes atque dies patet atri ianua Ditis.

The gates of hell are open, night and day;
Smooth the descent, and easy is the way.

VIRGIL *Aeneid*

Besides the great operations of ritual magic, necromancy and psychic attack, there are numerous processes of a comparatively minor and vulgar order, often classed as 'low magic'. These processes do not demand the knowledge, persistence and dedication required for the operations of ritual magic, but they follow sound magical principles. Many of them are ways of gaining another person's compliance in love.

A simple medieval method is to buy a small hand-mirror, without haggling. Take the mirror out of its frame and write the name of the girl you desire three times on the back of the glass. Then find two dogs which are copulating and hold the mirror in such a way that they are reflected in it. Hide the mirror for nine days in a place which the girl passes frequently and afterwards carry it with you and she will submit to you. What you have done is to create a magical link between the girl, the sex act which you captured in the mirror, and yourself, the mirror's owner.

An unpleasant charm intended for a woman who wants to ensnare a man allows her to get literally 'under his skin' by feeding him the products of her body. She takes a very hot bath and afterwards, while perspiring profusely, covers herself all over with flour. When the flour is thoroughly saturated, she wipes it off with a white linen cloth, which she wrings out into a baking-dish. She cuts her finger- and toe-nails, adds hairs from all parts of her body, burns them to a powder and mixes it with the floury liquid in the dish. Then she stirs in an egg, bakes the mixture in the oven and serves it to the man of her choice.

In using hair or other parts of the body it is essential to make sure that they come from the right person, as is suggested by the cautionary tale of John Fian, schoolmaster of Saltpans in Lothian, which is told in a pamphlet of 1591, *News from Scotland*. Fian conceived a passion for the older sister of one of his pupils and persuaded the little boy to bring him three of her pubic hairs. When the boy tried to take these hairs from the sleeping girl, she woke and cried out. Their mother came in and, discovering what had happened, took three hairs from the udders of a young heifer and gave them to the boy, who passed them on to Fian. Fian 'wrought his art upon them' and in a little while the heifer came to him, 'leaping and dancing upon him', and pursued him everywhere, 'to the great admiration of all the townsmen of Saltpans'.

Many love-charms involve the use of supposedly aphrodisiac plants and herbs, which are powdered and put into the food or drink of the woman desired, or hidden in her room or left in any place which she often passes. Recommended plants include lettuce, endive, purslain, valerian, jasmine, crocus, coriander, fern and pansy. Cyclamen appears in love-charms, perhaps because in classical times its roots were used as pessaries. The *Enquiry into Plants* says the roots should be burned and the ashes marinated in wine and formed into little balls. Periwinkle should be beaten into a powder, wrapped round with earthworms and mixed with leeks. Laurel is used in love-charms because chewing its leaves induces delirium. The Greeks thought the carrot attracted love, probably because of its shape. Poppy and deadly nightshade work not by inducing desire but by drugging the victim to leave her helpless.

The most powerful plant in love-magic, and also the most dangerous to the operator, is the poisonous mandrake, *atropa mandragora*. Atropa refers to Atropos, the oldest of the three Fates, whose shears sever the thread of each man's life when his time comes. The meaning of *mandragora* is not known. It is a pre-Greek word, possibly coming from Asia Minor or Persia originally.

The mandrake has magical power because its root often resembles a human body. Writing in the twelfth century, Hildegard of Bingen said that 'because of this likeness which it has to man, it is more amenable to the influence of the Devil and his wiles than other plants'. Mandrakes were classified as male or female. The male is white mandragora, which has a thick root, black outside and white inside. Its leaves spread out close to the ground and it has heavily scented blossoms and yellow berries, which have a soporific effect if eaten and were used as a narcotic and anaesthetic. The female black mandragora is similar, but its root is often forked. There is also a third type, called morion or fool's herb.[28]

The root of the mandrake contains a narcotic juice which, distilled in wine, can cause death, insanity or delirium. The Greeks regarded it as a highly dangerous plant and the *Enquiry into Plants* says that anyone who wants to dig one up should draw three circles round it with a sword and face west. His assistant should dance round the plant, whispering erotica to it. The root was used to cure gout and insomnia, but principally in love-potions. One of Aphrodite's titles was Mandragoritis.

Later the belief grew up that it was too dangerous for a human being to drag the mandrake out of the ground. In the dark of night the earth must be carefully loosened around the root and a string tied from the root to the neck of a black dog. The operator then moves well away and throws pieces of meat to the dog, just out of reach. Straining to get the meat, the dog pulls the mandrake out of the ground. The operator must cover his ears, or better still stuff them with wax or cotton, because as it is torn from the earth the mandrake utters a terrible cry, which no one can hear and live. The dog is killed by the mandrake's screech and is buried in its place.

Later still it was believed that the mandrake grows from the moisture which drops from a hanged man on the gallows. The basis of this belief may be the fact that a man who is hanged frequently ejaculates. His semen, falling to the ground, would provide suitable nourishment for a plant effective in love-magic.

Once out of the ground, the mandrake should be washed in wine every Friday evening and wrapped in a red or white silk cloth, renewed each new moon. It answers all questions put to it, keeps its owner's enemies at bay, and induces pregnancies in barren women. Any gold coin left beside it overnight will be doubled by the morning.

The *Grimorium Verum* provides a method of making yourself invisible which is often quoted. Begin on a Wednesday before sunrise with seven black beans and the head of a dead man. Put one bean in the head's mouth, two in its eyes, two in its ears. The grimoire does not account for the other two beans, but presumably they go in the nostrils. Trace a pattern of your own design on the head with your fingers and bury it in the ground, facing upwards. Water it with good brandy every morning before sunrise. On the eighth day, as you are doing this, a spirit will appear and say, 'What are you doing?' You reply, 'I am watering my plant.' The spirit will ask you for the brandy bottle, telling you that he wants to do the watering himself, but you must refuse. If you persist in refusing, he will show you the pattern which you traced on the head. You can now be certain that this is the spirit of the head and not a deceiving spirit. Give him the bottle and let him water the head. Next morning, the ninth day, the beans will be sprouting. Take them, put them in your mouth and look in a mirror. You should see no reflection of yourself, because the beans carry the invisibility of the dead and buried head. Do not swallow the beans, as you can only become visible again by taking them out of your mouth.

The same grimoire gives a method of harming an enemy. Dig up an old coffin in a graveyard and remove the nails from it, saying, 'Nails, I take you that so you may serve to turn aside and cause evil to all persons whom I will. In the Name of the Father, and the Son, and of the Holy Spirit. Amen.' Then find a footprint, which has been made by your enemy. Drive one of the nails into the footprint, saying *Pater noster upto in terra*. This seems to be an appeal to the Devil, meaning 'Our father who art on earth', in parody of the Lord's Prayer. Hammer the nail well in with a stone and say, 'Cause harm to N. until I remove thee.' The only way to call off this spell is to pull the nail out again and say, 'I remove thee so that the evil which thou hast caused to N. shall cease. In the Name of the Father, and of the Son, and of the Holy Spirit. Amen.'[29]

Finally, a useful magical implement is a Hand of Glory, which enables the magician to rob people's houses with impunity. It is the hand of a man who died by hanging and it holds a candle made of his fat, the light of which prevents anyone who sees it from moving. The *Little Albert* ('Marvellous Secrets of the Natural and Cabalistic Magic of Little Albert'), published in 1722, says that the hand must be cut from the corpse and wrapped in a piece of winding-sheet. It is squeezed thoroughly to make sure that all the blood has drained from it. Then it is pickled for fifteen days in an earthenware jar with pounded salt, peppercorns, saltpetre, and 'zimort' or 'zimat', but it is not known what this is. The hand is afterwards dried in the heat of the sun during the dog-days, from July 3 to August 11, when the Dog Star, Sirius, rises and sets with the sun. The influence of the sun is probably intended to contribute to the dazzlingness of the Hand's light and the influence of the Dog Star to its dangerous and frightening quality. It was believed that dogs were dangerous and liable to rabies during the dog-days. If the sun's heat is not sufficient, the hand is heated in a furnace fed by bracken and verain. The fat which runs from the hand is collected and mixed with wax to make a candle, which is stuck between the dead hand's fingers. The lifelessness and bloodlessness of the hand reach any observer through the light of the candle and strike him as motionless as the dead.[30]

The Hand of Glory is not a mere figment of Little Albert's imagination. Writing in the mid-fifteenth century, Petrus Mamoris said that some people 'carry with them the hand of a corpse to which the sacraments have been applied and with which they make the sign of the cross in reversed fashion over some sleeper, causing him to sleep for a whole day without waking, so that they may rob his house at leisure'.[31] In 1831 burglars broke into a house at Loughcrew, County Meath, in Ireland, armed with a dead man's hand which clutched a lighted candle. But the hand failed to work. The alarm was given and the burglars ran away, leaving the hand behind them. A gang of poisoners, out to collect life insurance, who committed several murders in Philadelphia in 1939, used the Hand of Glory to terrify witnesses and victims. In this case it was believed that the Hand could be used to kill or injure. It was sometimes an actual human hand, severed at the wrist and mummified, or was made of bone or ivory, with the thumb and the two middle fingers folded on to the palm, the index and little fingers pointing up like a pair of horns, which is traditionally a sign of the Devil.

The hand with three fingers closed and two open is devilish because it denies the Three and affirms the Two.

In most of the processes in the grimoires demons are subordinate to the magician, or can be subordinated. But there is another group of rituals in which the force of evil is master and is worshipped—those connected with the pact with the Devil, the witches' sabbath and the Black Mass.

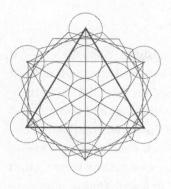

CHAPTER SEVEN
The Worship of the Devil

THE Devil is a legacy of the widespread human tendency to attribute the origin of evil to non-human influences. In primitive societies evil and misfortune are usually thought to come from the gods. The powers which created the universe and rule it are the ultimate authors of all things and they are given the responsibility for the presence of evil as well as the credit for the existence of good. In matters which are too trivial to be the concern of the gods primitive people put harm and suffering down to the malice of evil spirits, which are less powerful than the gods but more numerous.

The Jews in early times believed in various supernatural beings to whom evil could be ascribed. Jehovah was originally regarded by his followers as only one among many gods. The other gods belonged to the neighbours of the Jews and were regarded by Jehovah's prophets as evil powers, hostile to Jehovah and his people. In the same way the early Christians did not dismiss the pagan gods as fictions, but believed that they were real and were evil beings—demons.

The early picture of Jehovah as one god among many was replaced by the belief that he was the only God, the sole creator of the universe and all things in it, as described in Genesis. It logically followed that Jehovah himself must be the source of evil as well as good, as the prophet Amos said. 'Shall there be evil in a city and the Lord hath not done it?' The same belief is stated in Isaiah—'I form the light, and create darkness: I make peace, and create evil; I the Lord do all these things'—and again in Ecclesiasticus—'Good things and bad, life and death, poverty and wealth come from the Lord.'[1] This conviction that the origin of evil is in God survived in the Cabala, in which the evil powers are an offshoot or overflow from the sephiroth, which are emanations from God. It accounts for the relative insignificance of the Devil in Jewish tradition, as compared with Christian, because a supernatural evil power is unnecessary unless God is believed to be entirely good.

In the Old Testament, Jehovah frequently brings evil upon men by direct action. Angry with the Jews on one occasion, Jehovah put the idea of taking a census into David's mind so that he could then punish this crime by sending a pestilence that killed seventy thousand men. But on some occasions Jehovah worked through subordinate spirits. When he was angry with Ahab and intended to bring him to his death, Jehovah consulted the host of heaven who were gathered about his throne and said, 'Who shall persuade Ahab, that he may go up and fall at Ramoth-gilead?' The host of heaven argued the point inconclusively until a spirit came to stand before Jehovah and said, 'I will persuade him . . . I will go forth and be a lying spirit in the mouth of all his prophets.' Jehovah agreed and Ahab was duly killed.[2]

Besides the spirits which attended on Jehovah and made up his court, the angels of later Jewish and Christian belief, the Jews also believed in malignant demons and hairy spirits which infested lonely and barren places. But in these early traditions there is no sign of any belief in the Devil, the great prince of evil who is the arch-enemy of God. The figure of the Devil loomed up later and passages in the Old Testament which originally had nothing to do with him were taken as scriptural authority for his existence.

1. The Origins of Satan

Better to reign in Hell than serve in Heaven.

MILTON *Paradise Lost*

The name Satan comes from a Hebrew word meaning 'adversary'. In the older books of the Old Testament, written before the Jews were carried away into exile in Babylon in the sixth century B.C., a satan is merely an opponent. The angel of God 'stood in the way for an adversary (*satan*)' against Balaam. A satan was not necessarily supernatural. The Philistines refused to accept David, because they were afraid he would turn his coat in battle and become their satan or adversary.[3]

In two later passages, written after the exile, 'the satan' appears. He is an angel and a member of God's court who acts as an accuser of men before God. In the book of Zechariah, possibly dating from the late sixth century B.C., the prophet sees Joshua the high priest standing before God to be judged. The satan stands at Joshua's right hand 'to resist him' or argue the case against him. There is already a suggestion that the satan is excessively zealous as a prosecutor, because God rebukes him for accusing a righteous man.[4]

In the first two chapters of Job, perhaps written about a hundred years after Zechariah, the satan is still the accuser of men and he now seems definitely malignant. The sons of God present themselves before Jehovah and the satan is with them. In words which were probably intended to have an ominous ring, the satan says he has come 'from going to and fro in the earth and from walking up and down in it'. Jehovah praises Job as a righteous man, but the satan argues that it is easy for Job to be faithful to God, because he is happy and prosperous. As a test, Jehovah allows the satan to kill Job's children and his servants and his cattle, but Job refuses to curse God for these catastrophes, saying philosophically, 'The Lord gave and the Lord hath taken away; blessed be the name of the Lord.' The satan is not at all content with this. 'Skin for skin, yea, all that a man hath will he give for his life. But put forth thine hand now, and touch his bone and his flesh, and he will curse thee to thy face.' Jehovah lets the satan afflict the unfortunate Job with a plague of sore boils all over his body, but Job still remains faithful.

In this story the satan is determined to destroy Job's credit with God and he is the direct instrument of Job's punishment. But he acts only under God's instructions and he is felt to be performing a useful function. He tries to bring to the surface the wickedness inherent in men. Later, it was thought that the satan's malicious zeal must make him as repulsive to God as he was to man. In 1 *Enoch*, a Jewish book which is not included in the Old Testament but influenced the early Christians, there is a group of satans who by this time are not welcome in heaven at all. Enoch hears the voice of the archangel Phanuel 'fending off the satans and forbidding them to come before the Lord of Spirits to accuse them who dwell on the earth'. There are also 'angels of punishment' who seem to be identical with the satans. They are seen preparing instruments of punishment for 'the kings and the mighty of this earth, that they may thereby be destroyed'.[5] These passages were probably written in the first century B.C.

It was from this notion of an implacable angel who accuses men and punishes them that the Devil of medieval and modern Christendom eventually grew. When the Old Testament was first turned into Greek, 'the satan' was translated as *diabolos*, meaning 'an accuser', with the implication of a false accuser, a slanderer, and this is the word from which our 'Devil' comes.

Later Jewish writers tended to separate good and evil, and to see Jehovah as entirely good. They found the actions of Jehovah in some biblical stories distinctly unedifying and so they put them down to an evil angel. When the story of David numbering Israel and God's vengeance for this crime was first told—in 2 Samuel, which may date from the early eighth century B.C.—Jehovah puts the idea of taking the census into David's mind. But when the same story is retold in 1 Chronicles, possibly written in the fourth century B.C., it is Satan who is responsible. 'And Satan stood up against Israel, and provoked David to number Israel.' This is the only use of Satan as a proper name in the Old Testament.[6]

In later Jewish writings and in Christian theory the figure of Satan becomes clearer and his powers are magnified until he is the great opponent of God and man, almost—but never quite—beyond God's control. It was natural for people to wonder how the satan, originally a valued if unpleasant official of God's court, had fallen from grace to become God's enemy. One explanation was found in the story of the Watchers, the germ of which appears in Genesis. When the race of men began to increase in numbers, 'the sons of God saw the daughters of men that they were fair; and they took them wives of all which they chose'. In those days 'there were giants in the earth' and the daughters of men bore children by the angels which 'became mighty men which were of old, men of renown'. The story may have been meant to account for the supposed existence of giants and heroes in early times, but, intentionally or unintentionally, the next verse connected it with the coming of evil to the earth. 'And God saw that the wickedness of man was great in the earth, and that every imagination of the thoughts of his heart was only evil continually.' It was because of this that God decided to destroy mankind in the Flood.[7]

There are several possible references to this story in other Old Testament books, but the first full version of it in its later form is given in 1 *Enoch*, in passages probably written in the second century B.C. 'And it came to pass when the children of men had multiplied that in those days were born unto them beautiful and comely daughters. And the angels, the children of the heaven, saw and lusted after them, and said to one another: Come, let us choose wives from among the children of men and beget us children.' These angels were of the order of Watchers, the sleepless ones. Their leader was Semjaza—or in other passages, Azazel. Two hundred of them descended to earth on Mount Hermon. They took wives 'and they began to go in unto them and to defile themselves with them'. They taught their wives charms and enchantments, botany and the cutting of roots. Azazel taught men to make weapons of war, swords and knives and shields. He also introduced the evil art of cosmetics.[8]

Their human wives had children by the Watchers—great giants who ate up all the possessions of men. 'And when men could no longer sustain them, the giants turned against them and devoured mankind, and they began to sin against birds and beasts and reptiles and fish, and to devour one another's flesh and to drink the blood.' God sent the archangel Raphael to imprison Azazel in the desert till the last judgement, when he was to be hurled into eternal fire. The other Watchers were made to look on while their children, the giants were killed. Then God told the archangel Michael to bind the angels in the valleys of the earth until the day when they would be cast into everlasting torment in an abyss of fire. But the earth was not purged of evil. Demons issued from the bodies of the dead giants and have remained in the world ever since, causing wickedness, destruction and oppression.[9]

One passage sympathetically suggests that the sin of the angels was not so much lust as a longing to enjoy the comforts of family life, as men do, and this is the first hint of a theme which was developed later—the idea that some of the angels were jealous of man. God explains to the angels that because they are immortal and need no descendants they have not been given wives and children.[10] But to later ages the point of the story was that evil and bloodshed and forbidden arts came to earth through an appalling crime against Nature, the physical union of the angelic and divine with the mortal, which produced monstrosities—the giants. It seems likely that the medieval insistence on, and horrified fascination with, the sexual relations of witches with the Devil owes something to the legend of the Watchers. The story is the diabolical counterpart of a revered mystery of the Christian faith—the descent of the Divine to a mortal woman and the birth of the Saviour.

Some of the early Christian Fathers, including St. Augustine, rejected the legend of the Watchers and found the origin of evil in a revolt against God by a great archangel who rebelled through pride. Their scriptural authority was the famous passage in Isaiah which foretells the approaching doom of the King of Babylon.

> How art thou fallen from heaven, O Lucifer, son of the morning! How art thou cut down to the ground which didst weaken the nations! For thou hast said in thine heart, I will ascend into heaven, I will exalt my throne above the stars of God: I will sit also in the mount of the congregation upon the sides of the north: I will ascend above the heights of the clouds; I will be like the most High. Yet thou shalt be brought down to hell, to the sides of the pit.[11]

This was the foundation of the Christian doctrine of the Devil's attempt to make himself the equal of God and his expulsion from heaven in punishment. As an explanation of the satan's fall from grace it had the advantage of fitting the tendency of later Jewish and Christian writers to exalt Satan's status to almost the position of an independent god. Lucifer, it was said, had been the archangel's name in heaven and Satan was his name after his fall.

This passage in Isaiah may refer to a legend of the beautiful morning star who walked in Eden, blazing in jewels and light, and in his insane pride attempted to rival God. 'Lucifer, son of the morning' is in Hebrew Helel ben Shahar, 'day-star, son of the dawn'. The Jews, Arabs, Greeks and Romans identified the morning star (the planet Venus) as male. In Greek it was called *phosphoros* and in Latin *lucifer*, both words meaning 'light-bearer'. It has been suggested that the story of Lucifer may have been based on the observation that the morning star is the last proud star to defy the sunrise, and the belief that it must have been punished for its defiance.[12]

The legends of Lucifer and the Watchers both find the origin of evil in the fall of divine beings, driven to sin by pride or by lust and condemned to hell in punishment. It was natural for them to be combined, with the Watchers becoming Lucifer's followers. There are already hints of this possibility in 1 *Enoch*. In one passage the Watchers are said to have been corrupted by the satans, who led them astray and caused their sin, and in another Azazel, the leader of the Watchers, is described as 'a star fallen from heaven'.[13]

By the first century A.D. Lucifer and Satan and the Watchers had all been connected together and the serpent of Eden had been added to the story. A book called 2 *Enoch* says that the archangel Satanail tried to make himself the equal of God and seduced the Watchers to rebel with him. They were all banished from heaven and to revenge himself for his fall Satanail tempted Eve in Eden. According to the *Vita Adae et Evae*, Satan was expelled from his glory among the angels because he refused to worship Adam, which the angels were ordered to do by God. Michael told him that God would be angry, but Satan said, 'if he be wroth with me, I will set my seat above the stars of heaven and will be like the Highest.'[14] Then God hurled Satan and his followers down to earth and Satan tempted Eve in revenge. Here the Devil's rebellion from pride is combined with the idea of angelic jealousy of man.

There is no suggestion in Genesis that the serpent who tempted Eve was the Devil, but Christian writers generally accepted that the serpent was either the Devil's agent or the Devil himself in disguise. On this basis St. Paul constructed the central doctrine of Christianity, that Adam's crime plunged all subsequent generations into the power of the Devil and the toils of sin and death, from which God sent his Son to release them. As Adam's disobedience brought death to men, so Christ's willing submission to death brought men eternal life. 'For as in Adam all die, even so in Christ shall all be made alive.'[15]

Jesus and his followers evidently believed that the Devil has authority over this world, at least in the sense that he rules worldliness, luxury and pride. During the temptation in the wilderness, according to St. Matthew, the Devil showed Jesus 'all the kingdoms of this world and the glory of them, and said, in words which go to the heart of Satanism, 'All these things will I give thee, if thou wilt fall down and worship me'. In St. Luke the Devil specifically says that power over all the kingdoms of this world has been granted to him, 'for that is delivered unto me; and to whomsoever I will I give it'. Jesus called the Devil 'the prince of this world' and St. Paul called him 'the god of this world'. Embarrassing use was later made of these passages by Gnostics who maintained that the Devil rules this world because he created it, and that God is far away.[16]

Another strand in the later picture of the Devil was his identification with Leviathan, a monstrous primeval dragon or serpent which had challenged Jehovah. Isaiah says that God will punish 'Leviathan, the piercing serpent, even Leviathan that crooked serpent.'[17] The legend of Jehovah's victory over Leviathan may be connected with Babylonian and Canaanite myths. In Babylon the god Marduk's defeat of the great dragon Tiamat, who tried to overthrow the gods, was celebrated each year. In the Canaanite myth of Baal, the god kills the sea-dragon Lothan (*ltn*) or Leviathan.

> When thou smotest Leviathan the slippery serpent,
> (And) madest an end of the wriggling serpent,
> The tyrant with seven heads. . . .[18]

Leviathan and the Devil, who were both opponents of God, both prideful and both to be punished, are linked together in Revelation. A great red dragon appears, with seven heads. The dragon's tail drew down a third of the stars and cast them to the earth. 'And there was war in heaven: Michael and his angels fought against the dragon; and the dragon fought and his angels, and prevailed not; neither was their place found any more in heaven. And the great dragon was cast out, that old serpent, called the Devil, and Satan, which deceiveth the whole world: he was cast out into the earth, and his angels were cast out with him.' A voice from heaven is heard rejoicing because 'the accuser of our brethren is cast down, which accused them before our God day and night'.

And the voice cries woe to the inhabitants of the earth, 'for the devil is come down unto you, having great wrath, because he knoweth that he hath but a short time'.[19]

In this tremendous vision most of the main threads of the later Christian conception of the Devil are drawn together—'the satan' who accused men before God; the war in heaven, with the forces of God led by Michael; the expulsion of Lucifer from heaven; the fallen angels or stars who were his followers; the seven-headed dragon Leviathan; and the belief that the Devil's vengeful fury has been let loose on earth. It is not clear whether the description of the Devil as a deceiver was meant to refer to the serpent of Eden, but the generations of Christians who knew this passage probably identified 'that old serpent' as the subtle tempter of Paradise.

It was the Christians who gave the Devil almost the position of a god. Convinced of the stainless goodness of God, they sensed and feared the presence of a great supernatural Enemy, the quintessence of all evil. That the Devil sinned through pride became and remains the orthodox Catholic belief.

In the Middle Ages and the early modern world the Devil was a familiar reality. He figured in popular tales, stage plays, mumming dances; he was preached from pulpits; he leered or frowned from the walls and windows of churches. He and his legions were everywhere, subtle, knowing, malicious and formidable.

Evil has its own perverse allure and the greater the powers with which the Devil is credited the more his attraction is increased. The Devil, like God, has been constantly pictured in the image of man, and Christians have believed in the great archangel's revolt against God, in part at least, because it strikes a responsive chord in the human heart. Lucifer is man in rebellion and his pride seems a more worthy explanation of the origin of evil and is, paradoxically, less discreditable to the Prince of Darkness than the lust of the Watchers. The result has been the tendency to see the Devil as a titanic romantic figure, as he is in *Paradise Lost*—the arch-rebel against authority, fearless, determined, defiant in the face of superior force, unhumbled in defeat—and to accord him a willing or unwilling admiration. With all the magnificence of the Devil's pride and power, it is not surprising that some have attempted to enter his service.

People who worship the Devil do not regard him as evil. To the Satanist the supernatural being who is the Enemy of Christendom is a good and benevolent god. But the word 'good', applied to the Devil by his followers, does not carry its Christian or conventional meanings. Satanists believe that what Christians call good is really evil, and vice versa, though there is an ambivalence of attitude in Satanism, as in black magic, a perverse pleasure in doing things which are felt to be evil combined with a conviction that doing these things is really virtuous.

Worship of the Devil as a good god naturally involves the belief that the Christian God the Father, the God of the Old Testament, was and remains an evil god, hostile to man and the enemy of morality and truth. In full-blown Satanism, Jesus Christ is also condemned as an evil being, though sects accused of devil-worship in the past have frequently not believed this.

If God the Father and God the Son, the creators of Jewish and Christian law and ethics, are thought to be evil, the necessary result is a denial of the whole Judaeo-Christian moral code and the conventional rules which are based on it. The followers of the Devil are intensely excited by and preoccupied with sensual pleasure and worldly achievement. They admire pride, strength and force. They revel in self-assertion and dominance, lust, dirt, violence, cruelty and all passionate sensations. Christian piety, with its virtues of otherworldliness, self-denial, humility, cleanliness of heart and mind, they condemn as spineless, colourless, dead. They wholeheartedly echo Swinburne's accusing line—'Thou has conquered, O pale Galilean, and the world has grown gray from thy breath.'

As in black magic generally, actions which are conventionally condemned as evil are valued for their psychological and mystical effects. Devil-worshippers usually believe that the attainment of perfection and the experience of the divine come through an ecstasy achieved in a sensual orgy which is likely to involve perverse sexual practices, homosexuality and flagellation, sometimes cannibalism. Because the Christian churches, especially the Roman Catholic, are regarded as abominable institutions devoted to the worship of an evil god, their ceremonies are parodied and degraded. Doing this is not merely to make a gesture in the Devil's cause; it captures and twists to Satanic uses the power which is believed to be inherent in the Christian rituals.

Preoccupied with this world and this life, his worshippers believe that the Devil rules the world and that the immediate rewards of his service are pleasure and power. After death, they expect to be reborn on earth, or, in some cases, they hope to go rejoicing to a hell which is not an infernal torture-chamber but a place where all pleasures are intensified and the capacity to experience them greatly increased. They believe that the Devil will eventually vanquish and overthrow the God of the Christians and return in triumph to the heaven from which the Christian God wrongfully ejected him. In that day Satan's faithful flock will reap their reward of eternal power and eternal bliss.

Holding one or more of the beliefs which make up this pattern of Satanist theory has frequently been enough to bring down an accusation of devil-worship. Many sects and groups have been accused of it, but genuine Satanists have probably always been rare, as they are today. The accused sects cloaked themselves in secrecy, to avoid persecution, and it is often impossible to tell whether they were consciously devoted to adoration of the Christian Devil or not. Even the true character of witchcraft in Europe is still violently disputed, in spite of great quantities of evidence. But there is a common factor in the accusations made, justly or unjustly, against suspected devil-worshippers—the reversal of Christian values.

The early development of Satanist theory was influenced by widespread acceptance of dualism, the belief that opposing gods of good and evil exist independently of each other. By itself dualism does not imply devil-worship, but it creates a favourable background for it. There is more incentive to enlist in the Devil's ranks if he is on more or less equal terms with God than if he is subordinate to God and acts only on God's sufference, as in orthodox Christian belief.

The central belief of the Gnostic sects, accused of Satanism by orthodox Christians, was dualist. 'For any Gnostic', it has been observed, 'the world is really hell.'[20] Convinced that the world is thoroughly evil, the Gnostics could not believe that it had been created by a good god. They thought that the supreme God, the principle of good, is far away in the distant heaven. The world was made and is governed by lesser deities, called Archons, 'rulers', who are either actively hostile to God or do not know that God exists. For some Gnostics the Archons were the gods of the planets, the guardians who barred the way to the human soul when it tried to ascend through the spheres after death.

The chief of the Archons was frequently identified with the God of the Old Testament, who was in Gnostic eyes an evil, savage, vindictive and treacherous deity. According to their Christian opponents, Simon Magus and another Gnostic teacher, Menander, both believed that the world was made by archangels who were in rebellion against the supreme God. Saturninus, who taught at Antioch in the early second century, said that the world was made by seven rebellious angels, led by the God of the Jews, who inspired Moses and the Old Testament prophets to lead mankind astray.

Christian eyebrows were inevitably raised at this insistence on the wickedness of God the Father and the belief that the world is ruled by rebel angels, but the Gnostics did not stop there. They believed that man was created by the Archons and is fundamentally evil, though he does contain the divine spark. Some said that the man the Archons fashioned could not stand up and wriggled about on the ground like a large helpless worm. The supreme God took pity on him and sent down the divine spark which gave the poor creature human life and an erect posture. Theories of this kind struck at the roots of Christianity, for if man was evil from the beginning and did not fall from grace in Eden, Christ could not have come to atone by death for man's fall.

Pursuing this train of thought enthusiastically, some Gnostics identified Jehovah as the Devil, others said that the Devil was a good angel, an opponent of Jehovah and the Archons. They reversed all the Old Testament values, condemning the patriarchs and prophets, and praising Jehovah's opponents. In Gnostic theory the serpent of Eden was a saviour, sent by the supreme God to teach Adam and Eve the knowledge of good and evil, so that they could see the evil nature of the world Jehovah had created. Some Gnostics admired Cain and pointed out that his peaceable offering of crops was rejected while Abel's blood-sacrifice was accepted, because the evil lord of this world delights in blood. Other Gnostics reverenced the Sodomites, Corah, Dathan and Abiram, Pharaoh and the Egyptians, and all those condemned in the Bible for worshipping other gods and failing to walk in the ways of Jehovah.

Some went so far as to condemn Jesus as the son of the evil Jehovah and glorified Judas Iscariot for ridding the world of this incubus. The majority believed that Jesus was a divine saviour who came to free men from the God of the Jews, but even so, their views were so unorthodox as to smell strongly of sulphur and brimstone. According to St. Irenaeus in his book *Against Heresies*, written in the late second century, Saturninus taught that Jesus was not really crucified. Simon of Cyrene was executed in his place while Jesus stood by invisibly and watched, laughing. It followed that anyone who professed the Crucified had been fooled by the Archons and remained a slave to them, while whoever denied him knew the true disposition of things and was free of the Archons.[21]

To these drastic reversals of Christian beliefs some Gnostics added a corresponding reversal of Jewish and Christian moral standards. The general Gnostic emphasis on knowledge, received through an inspiration from God, as the only key to the divine naturally led to a contempt for conventional morality,

because a man did not reach heaven by leading a good life but through possession of the gnosis. Some Gnostics led lives of severe austerity, to free themselves
from the tangles of the wicked world. They particularly detested the procreation of children, for it added to the stock of human lives enslaved to the Archons. But others took the opposite course. The followers of Valentinus, Irenaeus
says, believed that a man who had received the gnosis had become 'spiritual
substance', a god in effect, and could not be corrupted by anything he might do.
Secure in godhead, they seduced their female disciples and indulged all the
lusts of the flesh 'with the utmost greediness'. Similarly, the followers of Simon
Magus led profligate lives and practised magic.[22]

The Gnostics could argue that there was a positive virtue in evil living. For
them the world was thoroughly evil and its accepted moral codes had been
invented by the Archons to keep men in subjection. The evil Jehovah had delivered the law and commandments to Moses and inspired the harangues of
the prophets. The way to escape from slavery, to frustrate the scheme of the
Archons and attain salvation, was to break all the conventional rules.

Some Gnostics apparently carried this idea to a point which does not fit
with their dualistic tendencies but which is close to the heart of magical theory.
They said that good and evil are meaningless labels and that the way to perfection is to experience everything. 'For they maintain', Irenaeus says of Gnostics who held that the world had been created by the Devil, 'that things are evil
or good simply in virtue of human opinion. They deem it necessary, therefore,
that by means of transmigration from body to body, souls should have experience of every kind of life as well as every kind of action', so that 'their souls,
having made trial of every kind of life, may at their departure not be wanting
in any particular'. Transmigration from body to body was necessary unless in
one life the adept could do 'all those things which we dare not either speak or
hear of, nay which we must not even conceive in our thoughts'.[23]

All these Gnostic ideas fit into the general pattern of Satanism; indeed,
they largely established it. There is no evidence that any of the Gnostics consciously worshipped the Devil, but it is not surprising that orthodox Christians thought they did.

After the triumph of Christianity and its adoption as the state religion of the
Roman Empire, Gnostic theories were kept alive by obscure heretical sects in
the East and were eventually transmitted into western Europe. The principal
sects involved in this process seem to have been the Messalians of Armenia,

who moved slowly westwards after the fourth century and reached the Balkans by the eleventh century; the Paulicians, who flourished in Armenia and Asia Minor from the fifth century and were deported to the Balkans in 872; and the Bogomils, who were well entrenched in Bulgaria by about 950, seem to have drawn many of their doctrines from the Paulicians and Messalians, and spread westwards in their turn.[24]

In the twelfth century the principal Bogomil centres were in Bosnia, northern Italy and southern France. They seem to have acquired a dominating influence over the Cathars (from Greek *catharoi*, 'the pure'), whose first communities had appeared in the north of Italy in the early eleventh century. A hundred years later the south of France was riddled with Catharism, which was supported by many of the local nobility. The first Cathar bishop in northern France established himself there about 1150 and the movement penetrated into Flanders and western Germany. In 1167 a Bogomil bishop travelled through northern Italy and southern France, visiting the Cathar faithful and setting up new bishoprics.

The Cathars said that the God of the Old Testament was Satan, the lord of this world, which he created. He governed the human body, death, and all material and temporal things. Some thought he was originally a fallen angel, but others took the dualist view that he had existed as an independent rival of the true God since the beginning of time and would continue to exist for all eternity.

The moral views of the Cathars were also highly obnoxious to orthodox Christians. Like many Gnostics earlier, they thought it sinful to procreate children, which replenishes the stock of the Devil's world, and they observed that the command to be fruitful and multiply was given to Adam and Eve by Satan—Jehovah. Their high adepts, the Perfect, who were reverenced as embodiments of Christ by the faithful (another danger signal in orthodox eyes), lived in strict austerity, refraining from sex, violence, all food of animal origin, lying, owning property and taking oaths. But the lower ranks of Cathars, who were far more numerous, did not observe these rules. On the contrary, they were enslaved to the Devil in any case and nothing they did could very well harm them. It was better for them to indulge their lusts casually than to marry, for marriage was an abomination designed to produce children.

Besides encouraging debauchery, the Cathars were accused of believing that any form of sexual intercourse which would not lead to the conception of a child was preferable to one which would, and they were suspected of unnatural vice. This is how the word *bougre*, originally applied to Cathars to mean

'Bulgarian' (i.e. Bogomil), acquired its modern meaning. The fact that the male Perfect lived together in pairs, and the female Perfect likewise, stimulated accusations of homosexuality.

The Cathars believed themselves to be the true Church of Christ. They denounced the Church of Rome as an institution of the Devil, not only because it worshipped a god they identified as Satan but because they thought it infected through and through with the worldliness and fleshly indulgence which the Devil ruled and delighted in. The Roman Catholics returned the compliment with interest. It seemed clear that a sect which encouraged vice and reversed so many accepted Christian values must be in league with the Evil One. Additional evidence of Satanism was found in the fact that when a Cathar was initiated as one of the Perfect he formally renounced the Roman Church and his Catholic baptism. If this was not already a stock requirement for enlisting in the Devil's service, it became one.

Whether any of the Cathars did worship the Devil is not known. It is possible that some of them concluded that if the Catholic God was really the Devil, then the Catholic Devil might be the true God. In any event, Rome was convinced that they did, and in the early thirteenth century Pope Innocent III organised an armed crusade against the Cathars in the south of France. They were accused of adoring the Devil in the form of a goat or a cat at meetings which Catholics called 'synagogues of Satan' (from Revelation 2.9). Under torture some of them confessed to this, and to singing songs to the Devil, slaughtering stolen children and drinking potions made from their bodies. They flew through the air to their meetings on broomsticks or poles smeared with oil, while devils took their places at home. The same accusations were later made against witches.

Several other sects preserved dualist and Gnostic beliefs, probably influenced directly or indirectly by the Bogomils and Cathars. About 1125 a French peasant called Clementius of Bucy taught that the altar of a Catholic church was the mouth of hell and that it was sinful to marry and beget children. His followers were said to avoid this sin by devoting themselves to homosexuality and lesbianism, but they did hold occasional promiscuous orgies. Babies born as a result of these were burned and a communion-bread was made from their remains.

In 1184 the Waldensians or Vaudois, who still survive in Europe as a Protestant sect, came under the anathema of Rome. They were accused of worshipping the Devil and holding orgiastic meetings at night, at which a dog appeared and sprinkled the worshippers with its tail. Also accused of cannibalism, they acquired such a reputation that sorcery became popularly known in France as *vauderie* and witches as *vaudoises* (and this is the origin of the word Voodoo).

Early in the next century rumours circulated of the hideous Satanic rites practised by a sect in Germany called Luciferans, and in 1227 the Pope sent Conrad of Marburg to root out heresy and reform the Church in Germany. Conrad was a sadistic fanatic who had been spiritual director of St. Elizabeth of Thuringia and had delighted in beating and humiliating her. He descended on the Luciferans in the fierce conviction that he was called to do battle with Satan himself. The confessions he extracted were apparently made without torture, but under the threat of death if the victim did not confess. If these confessions were accurate, the Luciferans were full-blown Satanists. They worshipped the Devil as creator and ruler of the world, complained that he had been unjustly and treacherously banished from heaven, and believed that he would overthrow the God of the Christians and return to heaven, when they would enjoy eternal happiness with him. They revelled in whatever displeased the Christian God and hated whatever pleased him. At Easter they would go to Mass, keep the consecrated hosts in their mouths and spit them out into a cesspool to show their contempt for Christ.

When a man was initiated as a Luciferan he was taken to one of their meetings and made to kiss a toad on its backside or mouth. Or sometimes the thing he kissed looked like a duck or a goose and was the size of an oven. Then there came to him a man with black eyes who was pale, emaciated and icy cold. Possibly, he represented the Devil as lord of death. The initiate kissed him and lost his Catholic faith in that instant. Then everyone sat down to a feast and a large black cat appeared, emerging from a statue which was always present. The initiate, the leader of the group and any other members who were worthy of the honour kissed the cat's backside. The leader said, 'What does this teach?' A member answered, 'the highest peace', and another added, 'And that we must obey.' The candles were put out and there was an indiscriminate heterosexual and homosexual orgy. Afterwards the candles were relit and the figure of a man appeared from a dark corner. The upper part of his body shone like the sun, but from the hips down he was black like the cat. The leader cut off a piece of the initiate's clothing and gave it to the shining man, saying, 'Master, I give this to you which has been given to me.' The shining man answered, 'You have served me well, you will serve me more and better. I leave to your care what you have given to me.' Then he disappeared.[25]

This account of an initiation carries a certain conviction and it could have been stage-managed without too much difficulty. There are traces, in modern times, of a tradition among witches that Lucifer, 'the light-bearer', was the sun, an identification which could easily be made when the Devil was regarded as the ruler of life on earth. The shining man may perhaps have been intended to represent the Devil as both the sun of day-time—the shining upper half of the figure—and the sun of night, the black lower parts standing for the black sun, passing under the earth through the regions of darkness before the next sun-rise. The black sun can be imagined as the leader of the stars, which follow his course towards the western horizon and disappear beyond it—the stars fallen from heaven.

The obscene kiss on the backside of an animal or person representing Satan became a stock charge in allegations of devil-worship, but where it originally came from is not known. It was evidently a symbol of utter submission and perhaps also of the reversal of conventional values.

Conrad of Marburg was assassinated in 1233, but the hunt for Satanists continued. About 1286 Pope Honorius IV ordered the persecution of a group of German heretics who preached that men and women ought to refrain from wearing clothes and working with their hands. This would restore them to the state of innocent perfection enjoyed by Adam and Eve in Eden. The belief was considered dangerous, because its adherents frequently condemned marriage and it encouraged vice. It has bobbed up now and again in Europe and the United States and is perhaps the origin of the notion that nudism is physically and psychologically healthy. In 1925 Adamites were discovered near Oroville, California. Anna Rhodes, the priestess of the cult, believed that she and her husband were Eve and Adam and their home the Garden of Eden, re-created. The sect held naked orgies in the Rhodes farmyard, dancing round a bonfire and sacrificing animals. On at least one occasion a lamb was burned alive, though whether this was a deliberate blasphemy—the lamb being a symbol of Christ—is not clear.[26]

In 1307 French and English members of the Order of Knights Templar were tried on charges of worshipping the Devil in the form of a cat; worshipping an idol and wearing girdles which had touched the idol's head; renouncing Christ, the Virgin and the saints; stamping, spitting or urinating on crucifixes; homosexual vice; and ritual homosexuality on admission to the Order—the candidate kissed his leader and kisses were exchanged on the navel, the anus, the base of the spine or the phallus. It was also said that they did not believe in the Eucharist and that the Order's priests omitted the *Hoc est corpus meum*, 'This is my body', from the canon of Mass.[27]

Large numbers of Templars confessed to some of the charges, especially to those of renouncing Christ, insulting the Cross, obscene kissing and homosexual vice. Some confessed under torture, some without torture but probably in fear of it. Most of them afterwards denied that their confessions were true. The Grand Master of the Order and the Preceptor of Normandy repudiated their confessions before being burned alive in Paris in 1314.

The idol which the Templars were accused of worshipping was said to be a human head with curly black hair. It was named Baphomet, possibly a corruption of Mahomet. Some said it was the head of the first Grand Master, 'who made us and has not left us'. Covered with gold and jewels, it was pale and frightening to look at. The girdles which had touched the head were peculiarly sinister, because they suggested a link with the Cathars. The Cathar Perfect originally wore black robes with a cord as a girdle. To escape notice during the persecution, they took to wearing ordinary clothes with the cord concealed beneath them. It was this connection which sent a chill down people's spines at the mention of 'the little cord of the Templars'.

In 1388 the Inquisition tortured a man who revealed the activities of a group of Waldensians near Turin. They worshipped the Great Dragon of Revelation, the creator of the world, who on earth is more powerful than God. They said that Christ was a mere mortal, son of Joseph and not Son of God. They held religious services followed by orgies and on initiation the candidate had to drink a potion, made of toad's excrement, which was so powerful that he could never afterwards leave the sect.

In 1453 a sect of Brethren of the Cross was discovered in Thuringia. They practised flagellation and believed that Satan would regain his lost power and place, and would expel Christ from heaven. They celebrated orgies in secret by night.

Early in the following century it was said that Bohemia was infested with thousands of Luciferans. In Italy Pope Julius II ordered an inquisitor to proceed against 'a certain sect', which renounced the Christian faith, trampled on and dishonoured crosses, abused the sacraments, especially the Eucharist, and took the Devil as their lord and master, offering him obedience and reverence.

By this time the searchlights of persecution were being turned away from the Luciferans and similar heretical sects to be trained on the witches. Many of the sects had been accused of holding secret meetings at night and worshipping the Devil, usually in the form of a man, cat, or goat. Some were specifically charged with believing that the Devil rules this world and will eventually overthrow God. Even when these accusations were lacking, other heretical practices were classed as Satanist because they reversed Christian values—renunciation of Christianity and hostility to the church; condemnation of marriage and procreation; slaughtering of children and cannibalism; orgiastic sexual practices and homosexuality. Most of this pattern of Satanism reappears in the witch trials.

2. Witchcraft

Underneath all the tales there does lie something different from the tales. How different? In this—that the thing which is invoked is a thing of a different nature, however it may put on a human appearance or indulge in its servants their human appetites. It is cold, it is hungry, it is violent, it is illusory. The warm blood of children and the intercourse at the Sabbath do not satisfy it. It wants something more and other; it wants 'obedience', it wants 'souls', and yet it pines for matter. It never was, and yet it always is.

CHARLES WILLIAMS *Witchcraft*

Devil-worship is outside the main body of magical tradition, which is concerned with the magician's domination of all powers, natural and supernatural. It is the preserve of those who surrender themselves to the powers of evil, to become one with them. According to the sixteenth-century *Fausti Höllenzwang* (Faust's Harrowing of Hell), in a preface supposedly written by Faust himself:

> If you wish to become true magi and perform my deeds, you must have knowledge of God as well as of other creatures, but you must not honour him in any fashion but what pleases the Princes of the World . . . he who wishes to practise my art, let him love the spirits of hell and those who reign in the air; for these alone are they who can make us happy in this life; and he who would have wisdom must seek it from the devil.
>
> For what thing in the world is there whose best exponent is not the devil, who is the Prince of the World?
>
> In a word, ask what you will: riches, honour, and glory, you can have them through him, and what you expect of good after your death, in that you deceive yourself.[28]

In one tradition the magician masters evil spirits and makes use of them, in the other he bows down before the Lord of Evil as the fount and provider of his own magical power. It is those who consciously align themselves with the Devil, who 'love the spirits of hell' and spurn the promise of heaven as a snare set by the deceitful Christian God, who delight in the two principal rituals of Satanism, the witches' sabbath and the Black Mass.

The nature and even the existence of the witches' sabbath have been much disputed. Some modern writers dismiss the whole European witch epidemic as a delusion sired by fanaticism out of credulity, others accept the bulk of the witches' confessions as genuine. The truth probably lies between these extremes, but closer to the first of them. The evidence leaves little doubt that many innocent people made up confessions under the pressure of physical and mental torture. Some of those who confessed without torture were clearly deluded. The details of the confessions were usually similar, because they were based on general popular agreement about what witches did and were made in response to leading questions. But to reject all the huge quantities of evidence as illusory, to assume that beneath so much smoke there was no fire at all, seems unduly sceptical. Witches and Satanists exist today and it is likely that they existed in the past, if only in small numbers.

The witch hunts began in France in the early thirteenth century, not long after the crusade against the Cathars, but did not blossom into their full and ugly flower until much later. The first trials which we know of were held in 1245 at Toulouse in the south of France, the principal centre of Catharism. The earliest accounts of the witches' sabbath do not come till a century later, in the same area in 1335, and remain meagre until more than a hundred years later still. The first book to give a detailed account of witchcraft, John Nider's *Formicarius*, was written about 1435. The great majority of the French trials date between 1450 and 1670. There were witch trials in Switzerland, Savoy and Italy in the early fifteenth century and in Germany from 1446, but the bulk of the German trials came after 1570. The first execution for witchcraft in Spain occurred in 1498, but the Spanish Inquisition took a cautious and sceptical attitude to accusations of witchcraft and trials were comparatively rare. The English and Scottish trials date mainly from the sixteenth and seventeenth centuries, from 1566 on. There was a witch scare in Sweden in the later seventeenth century and the trials at Salem, Massachusetts, began in 1692.

The relatively late dates of the trials make it difficult to accept the well-known theory, advanced by Margaret Murray and other writers, that the witch cult was the survival of a pagan religion. 'The evidence proves that underlying the Christian religion was a cult practised by many classes of the community, chiefly, however, by the more ignorant or those in the less thickly inhabited parts of the country. It can be traced back to pre-Christian times and appears to be the ancient religion of western Europe.'[29]

Unfortunately for this enticing theory, the evidence proves nothing of the sort. Not enough is known about the pagan religions of western Europe to connect any of them with the witches and there is a gap in time between the pagan cults and the witch trials. In England, one of the last bastions of paganism in western Europe, there is no evidence that pagan cults survived later than the time of Canute, who died in 1035, and on the Continent they seem to have disappeared long before. The witches were regarded by their Christian antagonists as a new sect and were persecuted as heretics, not as pagans. Pagan ideas and customs did survive in witchcraft, as in Christianity itself, but this is not the same thing as the survival of a particular cult.

Witches existed from very early times and were always thought to be in touch with evil spirits and the powers of the underworld. In medieval Europe the prince of the underworld and the master of demons was Satan and it is probable that the god of the witches was not the supposed 'horned god' of a hypothetical 'Old Religion' but the Devil of Christianity. The principal beliefs and rituals of medieval witches seem to have come from the Cathars, Luciferans and other sects accused of worshipping the Devil, though the witch religion drew on many other sources—magic and sorcery, classical traditions, the Bible, pagan customs and beliefs, and accepted popular notions about the behaviour of witches.

It is also likely that the persecutions of Satanist sects and the witch trials themselves stimulated the activities they were intended to suppress. The righteous were horrified, but some of the unrighteous were probably attracted and the details of ritual and belief brought out and publicised in the confessions could be used as models for imitation. In the same way, modern witches have been strongly influenced by the Murray theory, an interesting example of life conforming itself to fiction.

The Greeks and Romans and the pagan peoples of western Europe believed that witches could work various kinds of harmful magic—blasting crops, bringing storms or drought, sickening cattle, killing or injuring people, helping or hindering love. There is no trace of the later witches' sabbath and its rituals, but it was believed that witches met together on occasion, usually at night. The Norse witches were supposed to meet and hold high revel on the eve of the first of May. The Salic Law of Charlemagne says that if a man is accused of having carried a cauldron 'to the place where witches meet' and it cannot be proved, the slanderer must pay a fine. It was also accepted that witches were cannibals. If a witch is found guilty of eating a man, the Salic Law says, she shall be fined (about three times as much as the slanderer). If witches ate people as often as they were thought to do, which seems unlikely, it may have been the result of the magical theory that a man's life-energy can be acquired by eating him.

Witches were associated by the Greeks and Romans with darkness and death—with night and the moon, the mistress of night, and with the beings who ruled the dead. The divine patron of witchcraft was not a horned god but a goddess—Selene or Hecate or Diana, all of whom were moon-goddesses. Hecate, who came originally from Asia Minor, was the goddess most often invoked by witches and magicians. She was threefold, represented with three heads or three bodies, linked with three phases of the moon—new, full and old—and identified as Luna, the moon, in the sky, Diana on earth, and Proserpine in the underworld. She ruled ghosts, night and darkness, tombs, dogs, blood and terror. She was also the goddess of crossroads. Legions of ghosts were believed to follow her as she roamed grimly through the night and offerings of food used to be left at crossroads for the ghosts. Cynics and unprincipled persons sometimes ate these offerings.

Hecate herself seems to have been forgotten in early Christian times, but memories of her as Diana survived. In the sixth century St. Caesarius of Arles expelled 'the demon whom the peasants call Diana' from a tormented girl. In 1318 Pope John XXII, ordering the investigation of a group of magicians at his court in Avignon, said that they copulated with demonesses called *Dianae*. Tales of the wandering ghosts and their feasts at the crossroads also survived. In the early Middle Ages there were various stories in circulation about hordes of night-flying demons and dead souls. Diana was connected with these and the belief grew up that mortals could ride with her at night.

It is also not to be omitted that some wicked women perverted by the devil, seduced by illusions and phantasms of demons, believe and profess themselves, in the hours of night, to ride upon certain beasts with Diana, the goddess of pagans, and an innumerable multitude of women, and in the silence of the dead of night to traverse great spaces of earth, and to obey her commands as of their mistress, and to be summoned to her service on certain nights.[30]

This passage from an ecclesiastical regulation called the Canon Episcopi, which has been traced back to the ninth century, was quoted by Burchard, Bishop of Worms, about 1020, and was constantly repeated and commented on by later writers. Burchard says that the goddess was also called Herodias, the mortal enemy of John the Baptist, and Holda, a Teutonic goddess. He asks whether his readers believe, as many women do, 'that in bed with your husband at night, you leave the house though all the doors are shut and journey great distances with others similarly deluded and strike men dead with no visible weapon'?[31]

The night-riders were associated with the cannibal vampires and ghosts believed in by the Greeks, Romans and Jews, and the cannibalism ascribed to witches was credited to them. Writing about 1155, John of Salisbury said that a few poor women and ignorant men believed that the Queen of Night or Herodias summoned them to meetings by night, at which there was feasting and celebration. Those who went were rewarded or punished as they deserved, which was later a feature of the sabbath. Children were eaten and then vomited up whole, and the presiding goddess returned them to their cradles.

These stories, based on classical beliefs about Hecate, Diana and demons or ghosts which loved to suck human blood, were repeated and widely believed. They probably lie behind the accusations made against Cathars and witches that they flew to their meetings on animals or broomsticks. The witch's flying ointment also goes back to classical times. In the *Golden Ass* of Apuleius a witch smears her body with ointment and mutters a spell to turn herself into a bird and fly. It was recognised as early as the fifteenth century that the ointment itself might cause delusions. John Nider tells a story in his *Formicarius* about a woman who tested the ointment's efficiency by rubbing herself with it and muttering the appropriate spells in the presence of several trustworthy witnesses. She fell into a disturbed sleep. When she woke up she insisted that she had been with Lady Venus and Diana, but the witnesses testified that she had never left the room. Recipes for the ointment frequently include aconite and belladonna, which are likely to cause delusions, as well as hellebore root, hemlock, baby's fat or soot as a thickener, and bat's blood to aid nocturnal flight. Many witches confessed to flying to the sabbath, but others said they walked there or rode on horseback, and some of the accounts of flying suggest ritual dances rather than real flights.

Witch-hunters found the Canon Episcopi a stumbling-block, because it firmly stated that the ride with Diana, and by implication the flight to the sabbath, was a delusion. In 1458 Nicholas Jacquier, an inquisitor in France and Bohemia, said that the Canon Episcopi did not apply, because the witches were a new sect and not the same as the earlier night-riders. That this was true is suggested by the fact that the classical witches and the night-riders were devotees of a goddess, while the presiding deity of the witches' sabbath was almost always male. Some traces of the goddess did linger on in witchcraft, however. In the early sixteenth century it was said that meetings of Italian witches were presided over by *la Signora*, who wore a golden robe. Basque witches in the early seventeenth century had a Queen of the Sabbath who was the principal bride of the Devil. A Queen of Elfame or Elfin who copulated with male witches was mentioned in some of the Scottish trials. Modern witches have resurrected the goddess, worshipping a Queen of Heaven and All Living.

The goddess and her rout brought into medieval witchcraft the flight to the sabbath, feasting and cannibalism, rewards and punishments, and the significance of crossroads as suitable places for holding sabbaths and making pacts with the Devil. But the night-riders do not account for the major features of the witches' sabbath.

The word 'sabbath' seems to have been applied to the witches' meetings, often held once a week, through hostile association with the Jews, who were also constantly persecuted by Christians. ('Sabbat', which some writers insist on, is simply the Latin and French spelling of sabbath.) Some early writers called the meetings 'synagogues', like the Cathar meetings. Besides the ordinary weekly meetings, special festivals were held on certain evenings each year, but there was not as much general agreement about the dates of these as the Murray school of thought has suggested. In some areas the great feasts were held on February 2 (Candlemas), the eve of May 1 (*Walpurgisnacht*); August 1 (Lammas) and October 31 (the eve of All Saints' or All-Hallows, Hallowe'en). These days point to the survival of pagan customs because they mark the old Celtic division of the year into two halves, beginning on May 1 (Beltane) and November 1 (Samhain), with two subdivisions starting on February 1 and August 1. Beltane, the beginning of summer, and Samhain, the beginning of winter and the day of the powers of darkness, were both celebrated with fire-festivals. In the eighth century All Saints' Day was moved to November 1 or Samhain from its original date, May 13, which in Roman times had been a day dedicated to the *Lemures*, malevolent ghosts which drank human blood.

Another important witch day in some areas was Midsummer Eve, the eve of St. John the Baptist, which had been celebrated as a festival all over pagan Europe. But some witches seem to have concentrated on important Christian festivals for their high sabbaths. The witches of Lyons, about 1460, observed Holy Thursday, Ascension Day, Corpus Christi and the Thursday after Christmas. Basque witches, condemned in 1610, kept the nights before various Christian feasts including Christmas, Easter, Whitsun, Corpus Christi, St. John's Day and All Saints'. In the seventeenth century the Lancashire witches held high revel on Good Friday.

The first accounts of the sabbath were given by Anne Marie de Georgel and Catherine Delort, two elderly witches of Toulouse, tried in 1335. They confessed that they had belonged to Satan's hosts for the past twenty years and had given themselves to him for this life and the next. They had attended many of the weekly sabbaths and had committed 'all manner of excesses' with other men and women there. Both believed that God and the Devil were equal powers, God ruling the sky and the Devil the earth. The struggle between them had gone on since the beginning of time and would continue for all eternity. Souls which the Devil gained were lost to God and lived perpetually on earth or in the air. Catherine Delort believed that Christianity would soon be destroyed. This dualist view of God and the Devil and the belief that the Devil rules the earth, found in an area which had been a hotbed of Catharism, strongly suggests Cathar influence.

Anne Marie de Georgel said that one day outside the town she saw 'a man of huge stature coming towards her across the water'. He was dark-skinned, his eyes were fiery and he was dressed in animal skins. He asked her to give herself to him and she said yes. He blew into her mouth and from the following Saturday on 'she was borne to the sabbath, simply because it was his will'. At the sabbath there was a huge he-goat 'and after greeting him she submitted to his pleasure'. The goat taught her incantations, spells and the secrets of poisonous plants. He told her to honour the Devil and offend God by making sacrilegious communions. She used the secrets the goat taught her and had done all the harm she could.

Catherine Delort, who had also done all the harm she could, had been introduced to witchcraft by her lover, a shepherd. On sabbath nights, she fell into a strange sleep during which she was carried to the sabbath. There she adored the he-goat, served his pleasure and that of all the others present. She said they drank revolting liquids and ate tasteless food. They also feasted on the corpses of new-born children.[32]

About 1375, Pierre Vallin of La Tour du Pin gave himself body and soul to the Devil and did him homage, according to a confession he made as an old man, without torture, in 1438. He gave the Devil his baby sister and the Devil killed her. He rode to the witch meeting on a stick. They ate children and he had intercourse with the Devil, who took the shape of a twenty-year-old girl. Pierre Vallin had been convicted of sorcery in 1430.

According to Nicholas Jacquier (writing in 1458), an old man confessed without torture that as a small child, about 1404, he and his sister and baby brother were taken to the sabbath by their mother and offered to the Devil, who was in the shape of a goat. The children were told that the Devil was their lord and master who would do them much good. They touched the Devil's head and he touched them on the hip with his forefoot, leaving an indelible mark the size of a bean which the old man showed to the investigators.

John Nider says that the Devil appeared at witch meetings in the form of a man. The witches dug up the bodies of unbaptised babies and boiled them in a cauldron. A magic ointment was made from the flesh and the liquid had to be drunk by anyone who joined the sect. A new witch was initiated in a church on Sunday, forswore Christianity and the Eucharist, and did homage to the 'little master'.

Martin le Franc, writing about 1440, said the Devil appeared at the sabbath in the shape of a cat, which all the witches worshipped. He gave them magic powders and ointments. They feasted and then coupled, the women who had no men being served by demons. They flew to and from the meetings on sticks.

A more detailed account of the sabbath and the witches' initiation procedure is given in an anonymous tract, *Errores Gazariorum*, written in Savoy about 1450. A new witch is taken to the 'synagogue' by his sponsor and presented to the Devil, who is in the form of 'an imperfect man' or an animal, usually a black cat. He takes an oath to be faithful to the Devil and society, to come whenever summoned, to bring in new members, to reveal none of the society's secrets and to revenge all injuries done to its members. He also promises to kill children aged three or under, and to do his best to impede marriages by sorcery. After this he adores the Devil and kisses his backside. The Devil gives his new servant a staff and box full of magic ointments and powders. Then they all feast, chewing on roast and broiled babies as delicacies, and they dance. The lights are put out and the Devil cries 'Mestler, mestlet' (*melez, melez*), and there is a promiscuous orgy without regard to sex or family relationships. Afterwards the lights are relit and they eat and drink again. Anyone who has broken a rule of the society is severely beaten. Before leaving they urinate and evacuate in a cask, 'which they say is done in contempt of the sacrament'.[33]

Antoine Rose, a witch of the same area, Savoy, tried in 1477, gave a similar description, varying in detail. Under torture she confessed she had told a neighbour she was in need of money and he promised to help her. One evening he took her to a place where there was a synagogue of people enjoying themselves and dancing backwards. She was frightened, but they persuaded her to do homage to the Devil, a dark man called Robinet, who spoke to her in a hoarse, almost unintelligible voice and promised her plenty of money. She renounced God and the Christian faith, kissed the Devil's foot and agreed to pay him a sum of money each year, which she had done. The Devil gave her a purse full of gold and silver, but when she got home it was empty. He also gave her a stick eighteen inches long and a jar of ointment. She would smear the stick with the ointment, put it between her legs and say, 'Go in the Devil's name, go!' and immediately be carried through the air to the synagogue. There the witches feasted on bread, meat and wine. They danced and the Devil turned into a black dog. They all kissed his hindquarters. The lights were put out and the Devil called 'Mechlet, mechlet', and the men coupled with the women, dog-fashion. The Devil gave them powders and ointments for injuring men and cattle. He told them to do all the harm they could, to worship him in church instead of Christ, and when they took communion to spit out the host. At one meeting a consecrated host was brought, and they trampled on it.[34]

The order of events at the sabbath varied from one area to another. Usually it opened with the witches paying formal homage to the Devil. According to Guazzo's *Compendium Maleficarum* (1626), the witches generally lit a fire and the Devil sat on a throne, in the form of a goat or a dog. '. . . and they approach him to adore him, but not always in the same manner. For sometimes they bend their knees as suppliants, and sometimes they stand with their backs turned, and sometimes they kick their legs high up so that their heads are bent back and their chins point to the sky. They turn their backs and, going backwards like crabs, put out their hands behind them to touch him in supplication. When they speak they turn their faces to the ground; and they do all things in a manner altogether foreign to the use of other men.'[35]

Then came the offering of candles to the Devil and the obscene kiss. New members were initiated, witches' children were presented to the Devil and sometimes baptised by him, and on occasion the Devil would marry a witch couple. Next, the witches sat down to a feast. This was followed by frenzied dancing, which led up to the orgy, in which the Devil himself joined, apparently distributing his favours among as many of the witches as possible. Or sometimes the orgy followed a religious ceremony, a parody of the Catholic Mass. Afterwards the witches reported on the harm they had done since the last meeting and finally the Devil dismissed them.

The descriptions of the sabbath in the confessions reproduce many of the allegations which had been made earlier against devil-worshipping sects—the meeting by night, the Devil's appearance as man, cat, dog or goat, the obscene kiss, the renunciation of Christianity, the slaughtering of children, the feasting and the orgy which followed the putting out of the lights. The witches also shared with the earlier sects a particular hatred for the Eucharist, which was originally rooted in a denial of the Church's claim to be the channel between man and God. The words spoken by the priest in the Mass transformed the bread and wine into the body and blood of Christ, and in eating the body the worshipper became one with Christ. But the heretics believed themselves to be in direct touch with God, without needing the intervention of the Church, the priest and the consecrated host. Disrespect for the Eucharist—expressed, for example, by heretics who said that the host tasted to them like dung—turned in Satanism to positive hatred for the body and blood of the detested Christian Saviour.

Witches had long been accused of cannibalism, but the initiate's oath to impede marriages and the emphasis on child-slaughter suggest that one factor in the early development of the witch cult was the heretical horror of marriage and procreation. From disapproving of childbirth to killing children seems a drastic step, but Clementius of Bucy and his followers had been accused of taking it. Later, one reason for cannibalism was evidently that it bound the witch to the sect, like the toad's excrement of the Turin Waldensians. Some witches said they had eaten small children in the belief that afterwards they would be unable to confess, presumably because they acquired the child's inability to talk.

The obscene kiss appears constantly in the confessions. Some witches said the Devil had a second face, on his rump, which they kissed. Jeannette d'Abadie, a Basque witch, said they kissed the Devil's face, then his navel, phallus and backside, which recalls one of the accusations against the Templars. Witches at Avignon in 1581 said that on initiation the witch cut off a piece of her clothing and gave it to the Devil as a sign of homage. This had earlier been a feature of the Luciferan initiation ceremony. Candles were used to provide light at the sabbath, which was usually held at night, and they also figured in the ritual. In 1564 three men and a woman at Poitiers said they had worshipped a monstrous black goat, kissing it obscenely and offering it candles in fealty. In some cases the Devil lit the candles and gave them to the worshippers, in others they lit them from a candle which he held or which was fixed to one of his horns. This may possibly be another example of a connection between the Devil and the sun, the source of light. The anti-Christian character of the cult is clear from the earliest accounts. The *Malleus Maleficarum* (Hammer of Witches), written by two inquisitors, published in 1486 and regarded in its day as the leading authority on witchcraft, says that renunciation of the Catholic faith was the first of four particular points required of witches (the others being devotion to all evil, the offering of unbaptised children to Satan, and the free indulgence of lust). It also says that many people who asked witches for help complained that in return they had to promise to spit or shut their eyes or mumble offensive words when they saw the host elevated during Mass.[36] The victims of an appalling persecution at Bamberg in the early seventeenth century said that witches renounced Christianity with the words, 'Here I stand on this dung and abjure Jesus Christ.' Four Bamberg witches convicted of keeping the host in their mouths and afterwards defiling it were sentenced to be torn with red-hot pincers as many times as they had defiled it.

Though it does not appear in the early descriptions, later witches confessed to parodying the Mass at the sabbath and this was believed to be, and perhaps became, a stock feature of the ritual. The Jesuit Martin del Rio, writing about 1596, said that witches used holy water and followed the Catholic rite closely. Pierre de Lancre, a lawyer and fanatic witch-hunter, describing his investigations in the French Basque country in 1609, said that the clergy of the area were infected with Satanism. Five priests were identified as having travestied the Mass at sabbaths and one of them had been paid two hundred crowns by the Devil as a reward. On some occasions the Devil himself said Mass. A deposed Presbyterian minister who was one of the Lothian witches, tried in 1678, took the part of the Devil and preached a sermon to the assembled coven, telling them they were happier in him than they could ever be in

God. 'Him they saw, but God they could not see; and in mockery of Christ and his holy ordinance of the sacrament of his supper, he gives the sacrament to them, bidding them eat it and to drink it in remembrance of himself.'[37] The communion bread was like wafers, it was said, and the drink was blood or black moss-water.

Renouncing the God of the Christians, the witches took the Devil for their god. According to de Lancre a newly initiated witch said to the Devil, 'I put myself wholly in thy power and in they hands, recognising no other God, for thou art my God.' Agnes Wobster of Aberdeen, tried in 1596, was accused of calling Satan her god. The Northumberland witches, tried in 1673, called the Devil their blessed saviour and their god. Martin del Rio said that witches hailed the Devil as 'Creator, Giver and Preserver of all', and Silvain Nevillon confessed at Orleans in 1614 that witches recognised the Devil as their god, master and creator.

References to the Devil as creator and master suggest the belief that the world was made and is ruled by the Devil, God being far away. One of the attractions of the witch religion seems to have been the fact that the god was visibly present at the sabbath, incarnate in a man or animal, in contrast to Christ, who had been taken up to heaven. 'Him they saw, but God they could not see', and some said that the idol of the Templars was the head of him 'who made us and has not left us.'

The witches themselves apparently, referred to their god as 'the Devil' in most cases and many of the names given to him imply that he was consciously identified as the Devil of Christianity—Satan, Lucifer, Beelzebub, Belial, Astaroth, Asmodeus, Mammon. In 1595 Jean del Vaux, a monk of the abbey of Stablo in the Netherlands, who confessed without torture, said that the being worshipped at the sabbath was Beelzebub. The witches kissed his footprints and before the feasting began a grace was said, 'In the name of Beelzebub, our Grand Master, Sovereign Commander and Lord'. The Devil sometimes told his flock to revenge themselves, probably because he was the Christian Satan. 'Revenge yourselves or die', the Poitiers witches were told, and at the sabbath's end, according to Martin del Rio, the Devil said, 'Let us take our revenge, so that you may know the law that is opposed to the law of charity; for if we do not, we shall die.' Presumably this meant that unless Christianity was overthrown the Devil and his followers would not gain eternal life.

It seems clear that the Devil who appeared at the sabbath was a man, the leader of the society. He was often a 'black' or 'dark' man, befitting the Devil's role as Prince of Darkness. He was said to be icy cold, like the skeletal man whom the Luciferan initiate had to kiss. Descriptions of his voice sometimes suggest that he was speaking through a mask. The French demonologist Nicholas Remy, writing in 1591, said that demons have voices 'like one speaking in the bunghole of a barrel' and the Devil's voice was frequently said to be thin or hoarse and hard to understand.

When the Devil appeared as an animal he was apparently a man dressed up. Anne Marie de Georgel's 'man of huge stature' was dressed in animal skins. At Poitiers the Devil was a goat who talked like a man, at Brecy in 1616 he was a black dog who stood on his hind legs and talked. In Guernsey in 1617 Isabel Becquet went to the sabbath and saw the Devil as a horned dog, which 'with one of his paws (which seemed to her like hands) took her by the hand: and calling her by her name told her that she was welcome'. Sometimes the disguises were elaborate. The Bamberg witches said that the Devil appeared as a man or a he-goat or a green devil with an owl's head, horns, a black or fiery face, the feet of a goat, a long tail and hands with talons. According to the Scottish witch Agnes Sampson, the Devil's body was hard like iron and he had a nose like an eagle's beak, burning eyes, hairy hands and legs, and claws on his hands and feet.

The Devil's fondness for horns may have come from his link with the number 2, and it is not surprising that he should appear as an animal, since demons had long been believed to show themselves in animal form or in fantastic composite shapes. The early Christian Fathers had described devils appearing as animals or as composite creatures, like Isabel Becquet's dog with horns or the Bamberg green devil. The Devil showed himself most frequently as a goat (though never in this form in England or Scotland, oddly enough) but also as a cat, dog, bull, horse, sheep or, very rarely, as a boar, bear or stag. As a goat, he had horns, a tail, cloven hooves and sometimes a reddish beard. He was usually black and he limped.

The link between the Devil and the goat is probably connected with an essential feature of the sabbath, the copulation of witches with the Devil. In the earliest accounts of the sabbath Anne Marie de Georgel and Catherine Delort both said that they served the pleasure of the he-goat. The belief that devils were capable of intercourse with human beings and desired it came mainly from Jewish traditions—for instance, the story of Adam's connections with Lilith and other demonesses. There were also numerous classical tales of intercourse between human women and the gods, who to Christians were devils, but the principal source was the legend of the Watchers.

A connection between the Watchers, evil and the goat was implied in the Jewish scapegoat ritual. In Leviticus, where this ritual is described, Aaron is told to select a goat 'for Azazel'. He is to place both hands on the head of the goat 'and confess over him all the iniquities of the children of Israel, and all their transgressions in all their sins, putting them upon the head of the goat, and shall send him away by the hand of a fit man into the wilderness'.[38] The Jews performed the ritual down to A.D. 70. The goat was led out into the desert and thrown over a cliff. A scarlet woollen thread was tied to its head, apparently in reference to Isaiah 1.18—'though your sins be as scarlet, they shall be white as snow'. Hundreds of years later a red thread or cord was the mark of a witch.

The ritual was not forgotten. Writing in the thirteen century, Rabbi Moses ben Nahmen explained that 'God has commanded us, however, to send a goat on Yom Kippur to the ruler whose realm is in the places of desolation. From the emanation of his power come destruction and ruin . . . He is associated with the planet Mars . . . and his portion among the animals is the goat. The demons are part of his realm and are called in the Bible *seirim* (he-goats).'[39] This ruler in the wilderness to whom the goat was sent was Azazel, the 'star fallen from heaven' who was the leader of the Watchers in 1 *Enoch*. Associated with Mars, he had taught men to make weapons of war. He had been imprisoned in the desert by God until the day of judgement, when he was to be hurled into the fire.

The scapegoat ritual tended to connect the goat, which bore all the sins of the people, with impurity and evil. Through the link with Azazel, it also connected the goat with the Devil and the fallen angels. In St. Matthew's gospel Jesus says that he will come in glory and divide all the people 'as a shepherd divideth his sheep from the goats'. The goats are the wicked, who will be cast into 'the everlasting fire prepared for the devil and his angels'.[40]

Azazel was the leader of the Watchers, who lusted after the daughters of men, and also the chief of the *seirim* or goat-demons, who are mentioned several times in the Old Testament and were worshipped by some of the Jews. Rehoboam appointed priests for them and Josiah destroyed the places of their worship. Just as the Watchers took mortal women for wives, so the cult of the *seirim* seems to have involved the copulation of women with goats. Leviticus says, 'Neither shall any woman stand before a beast to lie down thereto', and earlier, 'And they shall no more offer their sacrifices unto the *seirim*, after whom they have gone a whoring.'[41] A similar cult existed in Egypt in Plutarch's time. A divine he-goat was worshipped at Mendes, the most beautiful women being chosen to couple with it. This is Eliphas Levi's Goat of Mendes, which he believed to have been the goat of the Witches' sabbath and which he also called the Baphomet of Mendes.

The story of the Watchers and their lust for human women was well known in the Middle Ages. Through this link between the goat, Azazel, the Watchers and the *seirim*, the connection may have developed between devil-worship and the fornication of women with the Devil in the form of a goat. The medieval belief that witches coupled with an animal which was their god was probably strengthened by the passage in Exodus beginning with the terrible verse 'Thou shalt not suffer a witch to live', constantly quoted by witch-hunters. The next verse prohibits lying with a beast and the next the worship of any god but Jehovah.

> Thou shalt not suffer a witch to live.
> Whosoever lieth with a beast shall surely be put to death.
> He that sacrificeth unto any god save the Lord only, he shall be utterly
>   destroyed.[42]

Some modern writers have suggested that memories of the cult of the Greek god Dionysus survived to influence the sabbath. There is no evidence of this, but there are several similarities between Dionysus and the Devil of the witches. Both appealed particularly to women and the rites of both were orgiastic. In animal form Dionysus sometimes appeared as a goat, though more often as a bull. At Eleutherai, the village from which his cult was exported to Athens, he was called Melanaigis, 'he with the black goatskin', and there was a ritual combat between 'the Black One' and 'the Light One', which suggests a parallel with the struggle between the Devil and God. At Delphi, Dionysus ruled the winter months and was apparently linked with the night sun or black sun, leading the dance of the stars, in contrast with the night sun or black sun, leading the dance of the stars, in contrast with the bright sun-god Apollo, who ruled the rest of the year. Dionysus was connected with the underworld, like other gods of fertility and vegetation, because plants and trees grow from beneath the surface of the ground. He was attended by satyrs, lustful goat-spirits like the Jewish *seirim*.

The god Pan, whose cult spread throughout the Greek world, was also a leader of satyrs. Half man and half goat, he was a lustful and energetic god, a giver of fertility. He played on a reed-pipe and the witches of Poitiers said that they danced round the Devil while he played on a pipe with a shrill and hideous note.

According to the Murray theory, the Devil appeared as a goat and in other animal forms because he was the pagan horned god of western Europe. Cernunnos, a stag-god of Gaul, has been selected for this honour, although little is known about him and nothing about the form which his worship took. He was a god of fertility and the underworld, sometimes shown with three heads, like Hecate, and associated with the serpent, like the Devil. Julius Caesar said that the Gauls believed themselves to be descended from Dispater, a Roman god of the underworld. The native name of this god is not known, but if he was Cernunnos this might provide a connection with the Devil as creator of the world and man.

The survival of Cernunnos is unlikely. None of the laws against paganism in western Europe mention a horned god or any god in animal form at all. However, the pagan practice of dressing up in animal masks and costumes on certain occasions did carry over into Christian times. St. Caesarius of Arles, who died in 542, said that 'some dress themselves in the skins of cattle, others put on the heads of beasts, rejoicing and exulting'. Later in the sixth century the Council of Auxerre condemned people who masqueraded as bull-calves or stags on the first of January. Theodore, first Archbishop of Canterbury (668–90), condemned various pagan survivals and also evil-doers, fortune-tellers, poisoners, and 'anyone who goes about as a stag or a bull-calf on the first of January: that is, turning himself into a wild animal and dressing in the skins of cattle and putting on the heads of beasts . . . because this is devilish'.[43]

This type of masked revelry has continued to the present day, but it does not indicate the survival of a cult. Mumming dances in animal costumes are still performed in England, but the dancers are not devotees of a pagan god, any more than American children in Hallowe'en masks. Nor does the first of January seem to have been an important witch festival. But the tradition of dressing up as an animal at times of revelry may have influenced the witches and their Devil. At some sabbaths, the worshippers as well as the god dressed in masks, animal heads and skins, though in most cases they wore their ordinary clothes or went naked.

What seems more likely than the survival of a particular cult—of Cernunnos, Dionysus, Pan or any pagan god—is the survival of an idea. The witches, who were magicians as well as devil-worshippers, apparently shared the magical and pagan sense of the value of the animal side of human nature. Dancing and revelling in animal costumes and the orgiastic worship of an animal god imply the letting loose of the animal in man. In magical theory this is an essential step to the achievement of wholeness, in which man becomes divine, and the Gnostic and heretical belief that experience of all acts and sensations is necessary for salvation expresses the same idea. The witches probably believed that they attained the divine in the sabbath orgy and especially in sexual union with god, who was often in animal form and was said to copulate from the rear, as animals do.

The release of the animal in orgy was frequently approached through wild and frenzied dancing, usually in a circle and moving to the left, the side of evil. A Spanish author, Petrus Valderama, said that witches danced 'in strange fashion: turning their shoulders to each other and taking hold of arms, they rise from the ground and descend, turning around and shaking the head from side to side like fools'. According to Martin del Rio, they danced in couples, back to back and hand in hand, tossing their heads in frenzy. Dancing back to back was considered obscene in the Middle Ages, presumably because it reversed the normal position.

In the orgy itself the witches were accused of committing every conceivable perversion, with other witches and with the Devil, and the sabbath culminated in an animal madness of sensuality, of mingled torment and delight, in which the worshippers attained ecstasy. The union with the Devil was usually described as painful, many witches saying that it was as agonising as childbirth. The Devil's member was scaly, Jeannette d'Abadie said, and she suffered extreme pain. The Devil's phallus was unnaturally large and both it and his emission were cold. The explanation now generally accepted is that an artificial phallus was used. But the experience was also said to be intensely pleasurable. Paulus Grillandus, a judge in which trials at Rome in the early sixteenth century, found that witches enjoyed the Devil 'with the utmost voluptuousness.' A young French witch said, 'I will not be other than I am; I find too much content in my condition; I am always caressed'. In Scotland in 1662 Isobel Gowdie told her accusers that the Devil was 'heavy like a malt-sack; a huge nature, very cold, as ice', but also 'He is abler for us that way than any man can be.'

The same perverse mixture of pleasure and pain appears in accounts of flagellation at the sabbath. Witches were frequently beaten because they had not done enough harm or had displeased the Devil in some other way. Isobel Gowdie said they would tease the Devil and then he would whip them. 'He would be beating and scourging us all up and down with cords and other sharp scourges, like naked ghosts; and we would still be crying: "Pity! pity! mercy! mercy! our Lord!" But he would have neither pity nor mercy.' As one authority commented, 'This sounds much more like a scrimmage of combined sadistic and masochistic pleasure than anything else.'[44]

The ecstatic pleasure of the sabbath had a strong hold on many witches and some of them remained faithful to the Devil to the death. A young Lorraine witch, Jeanne Dibasson, said that the sabbath was 'the true Paradise, where there was more pleasure than it was possible to describe'. Marie de la Ralde, aged 28 and a very beautiful woman, said it was an intense pleasure to go to the sabbath, not so much because of the licence and freedom they enjoyed there, but because the Devil had such an overmastering grip on their hearts and wills that they could scarcely be conscious of any other desire. He made them believe that he was the true God and that the joy of the sabbath was only the beginning of much greater glory. In England, Rebecca West and Rose Hallybread 'died very Stubborn and Refractory without any Remorse or seeming Terror of Conscience for their abominable Witchcraft'. Elinor Shaw and Mary Phillips were asked to say their prayers at their execution, but they laughed loudly, 'calling for the Devil to come and help them in such a Blasphemous manner, as is not fit to Mention . . . and as they lived the Devil's true Factors, so they resolutely Died in his Service'.[45] When Rollande du Vernois was on her way to be burned alive the priests pleaded with her to repent and save her soul by reconciling herself with God, but she would only say that she had had a good master, and so died.

It was widely believed that witches and sorcerers signed a formal contract with the Devil on entering his service. In 1320 an inquisitor in Carcassonne was ordered to proceed against people who sacrificed to demons, worshipped them and paid them homage, or gave them writings and made pacts with them. *Errores Gazariorum*, about 1450, describing the initiation of a witch, says that the Devil draws blood from the witch's left hand and writes with it on paper and keeps the paper. The pact was usually written in the signer's own blood, which carried his life-energy and so bound his life to the Devil.

The pact with the Devil has taken a firm grip on the human imagination and has been the subject of innumerable stories. In return for Satan's favours, the signer pledges his body and soul, at death or after a stated number of years. The Devil lusts for the human body because as a spiritual being he longs for matter, to make himself complete, and for the human soul because it belongs to his enemy, God. His desire to expand the area of Darkness and diminish the regions of Light drives the Devil to accept a bargain in which, according to the stories, he is frequently cheated. Though perhaps the Enemy is not so often swindled. 'He who affirms the Devil', according to Eliphas Levi, 'creates or makes the Devil.' Once the incubus has been conjured up in the magician's imagination, it may not be easy to dispose of it.

In August 1677 a Bavarian painter named Christoph Haizmann was taken to the police, apparently in a convulsion. Panic-stricken, he begged to be sent to a nearby shrine of the Virgin Mary. Nine years before he had made a pact with Satan, written in blood from the palm of his right hand. The term of the pact was now about to run out and he was in terror that the Devil was coming to fetch him. The police believed his story and took him to the shrine. After three days and nights of exorcism there, the repentant Haizmann saw the Virgin in a vision, subduing the Devil and forcing him to give up the pact. It read, 'Christoph Haizmann. I sell myself to this Satan, to be his own bodily son, and belong to him both body and soul in the ninth year.'[46]

A hundred years later, in 1785, two women were broken on the wheel at Hamburg for the murder of a Jew. They had killed him because they needed his blood for writing a pact with the Devil.

Lecturing in Paris in 1929, Maurice Garcon, a lawyer, writer and authority on black magic, described how he had watched a sorcerer invoking Satan in a wood near Fontainebleau. Hidden among the trees, he saw the magician draw a circle on the ground and begin the rites on the stroke of midnight. Two pitch-black candles flickered with a dull blue flame and smoke curled up from herbs burning in a silver censer. The magician stalked about the circle widdershins, reciting incantations until at the peak of the ceremony he offered the Devil a pact scrawled in his own blood. Presenting his soul in payment, he also promised to win Satan a devotee for every wish he was granted, every lust that was satisfied. But the Devil did not appear, 'without question', Montague Summers said, because of the profane watcher's presence.[47]

The idea of the pact seems to have been an offshoot of the early Christian belief that magicians could only perform their arts successfully through the assistance of supernatural beings. As black magicians were obviously not connected with God, they must be receiving help from the Devil. The possibility of making a formal contract with the powers of hell is hinted at as early as the writings of Origen, who died in A.D. 254, but the main impetus to belief in it came from St. Augustine, who said that sorcerers, astrologers and other dabblers in the occult were in league with demons. He condemned 'all arts of this kind . . . arising from the pestiferous association of men with demons, as if formed by a pact of faithless and dishonourable friendship'.[48] The scriptural authority for the pact was Isaiah 28.15. This verse originally had nothing to do with a contract with the Devil but the Vulgate translation suggested that it did—*percurrimus foedus cum morte et cum inferno fecimus pactum*, 'we have signed a treaty with death and with hell we have made a pact'.

Gradually, stories began to circulate about people who had signed themselves over to the Devil. One of the most popular was the story of Theophilus, which has been traced back to the sixth century. Theophilus was an upright Christian who was steward of his local church, but a group of intriguing clergy who disliked him persuaded the bishop to dismiss him. Determined to recover his position, he consulted a Jewish sorcerer, who took him to a crossroads at night. There they met a throng of sinister figures who recall the ghosts and demons which roamed the night with Hecate or Diana—dressed in white robes, carrying candles and uttering loud cries. Their leader, who sat enthroned among them, agreed to help Theophilus if he would renounce Christianity. He did so, writing on parchment 'I deny Christ and his Mother' and sealing it with his ring. The next day he was reappointed steward, but in terror of what he had done, he prayed to the Virgin Mary. She came to him in a vision and although she rebuked him, she gave him back the parchment he had signed.

By the thirteenth century additional details had been added. Theophilus had promised himself body and soul to the Devil, vowing to endure the pains of hell with him to all eternity. He had written the pact in his own blood and the Devil had formally endorsed it. A play called *The Miracle of Theophilus* gives the wording of this endorsement. 'To all who shall see this open letter I, Satan, let know that the fortune of Theophilus is changed indeed and that he has done me homage, so might he have once more his lordship, and that with the ring of his finger he has sealed this letter and with his blood written it, and no other ink has used herein.'[49]

A written pact which is still preserved is the one allegedly signed by Urbain Grandier, a priest of Loudun, who was convicted of bewitching nuns and enslaving them to Satan. He confessed under agonising torture and was burned alive. At his trial in 1634 the pact he had made with Lucifer, written in his own blood, was produced in evidence.

> My lord and master Lucifer, I acknowledge you as my god and prince, and promise to serve and obey you while I live. And I renounce the other God and Jesus Christ, the saints, the church of Rome and all its sacraments, and all prayers that the faithful may offer me; and I promise to do as much evil as I can and to draw all others to evil; and I renounce chrism, baptism, and all the merits of Jesus Christ and his saints; and if I fail to serve and adore you, paying you homage three times a day, I give you my life as your own. Made this year and day.
>
> Signed, Urbain Grandier.

Also produced, and also still preserved, was an endorsement, signed from hell by Satan, Beelzebub, Lucifer, Elimi, Leviathan and Astaroth, accepting the pact. Written from right to left with all the words spelled backwards, it promised Grandier the love of women, the flower of virgins and all worldly honours, riches and pleasure. He was required to pray to the devils instead of to God and to trample underfoot the sacraments of the Church. He was promised a happy life on earth for twenty years, after which he would join the devils in hell to curse God.[50]

The grimoires pay little attention to the pact with the Devil. Their rituals are intended to subject evil spirits to the magician's control and when in need of supernatural assistance they seek it from God. From their point of view, to barter away one's soul in a pact is the desperate resort of the second-rate sorcerer. The *Grand Grimoire* gives an unimpressive process for making a pact, which is really only a method of raising a loan from the Devil and which must be used if the magician is too weak and inefficient to compel the obedience of the demons. The second-rate sorcerer naturally had to deal with a second-rate spirit and the pact is not made with the Devil himself but with one of his subordinates, Lucifuge Rofocale. Lucifuge means 'Fly the light' (and Mephistopheles, the name of the demon with whom Faust signed a pact, may be a faulty Greek rendering of Lucifuge). Rofocale seems to be an anagram of Focalor, the name of a devil in the *Lemegeton* who appears as a man with wings.

To make the pact, the magician goes to an isolated place and draws a triangle on the ground with a bloodstone, preferably a haematite. He places a candle on either side of the triangle and below it writes the name Jesus, an example of the grimoires' persistent tendency to call on God for help even on the most unsuitable occasions. Standing in the triangle and holding a rod of hazel as his wand, the magician chants an incantation calling on Lucifer, Beelzebub and Astaroth to favour and protect him and summoning Lucifuge Rofocale to appear. When the demon comes, he says, 'I am here. What do you want of me? Why do you disturb my rest? Answer me.' The magician explains that he wants to make a pact and be given treasure in return. The demon says, 'I cannot grant your request unless you will agree to give me your body and soul after twenty years, to do with as I please.' Then the magician throws the pact, which he has already prepared, to the demon. Written and signed in blood on parchment it says, 'I promise the great Lucifuge to reward him in twenty years for all treasure which he gives me.'

Not surprisingly, Lucifuge Rofocale may be most unwilling to accept this vague pact with all its obvious loopholes. He is likely to vanish and must be threatened with names of power and recalled. He then appears, complaining that the magician is tormenting him, and grumblingly agrees to lead the magician to 'the nearest treasure' in return for the payment of one coin every month. If the payments are not kept up, he will seize the magician for his own after twenty years. The magician agrees and Lucifuge Rofocale endorses the pact, returns it to the magician and takes him to the treasure.[51]

Modern witches are extremely secretive and very little about their beliefs and practices is known to outsiders. There are said to be as many as six thousand of them in England, with the number steadily increasing. Like other magicians, they insist that they are devoted to good works. Their wax images are intended to heal the sick and far from blasting crops or eating babies, they try to assist the fertility of Nature. A recent report in *Life* describes how they build a fire in the open and draw a magic circle round it with a sword. Then they join hands inside the circle, men and women alternately, and walk round the fire, quickening the pace to a run and chanting a supposedly ancient but bogus-sounding incantation—Eko Eko Azarak, Eko Eko Zomelak, Eko Eko Gananas, Eko Eko Arada.[52]

The witches worship a moon-goddess, whose name is secret, but who is probably Diana, and a sun-god who may be Lucifer. They believe in reincarnation and a Lord of the Underworld who determines when and where the witches will be reborn. This Lord is perhaps Lucifer as black sun and also perhaps Cernunnos, the horned god. The witches say that their goddess, the Queen of Heaven and All Living, went down to the underworld and mated with its Lord, which is a version of the myth of Persephone, the Greek queen of the underworld and a goddess of crops and fertility.

Heavily affected by the Murray theory, the modern witches have gone back beyond the era of the witch trials to the pagan rites from which they believe witchcraft sprang. Some of them claim to have preserved Druid traditions. They are organised in covens of thirteen, each headed by a high priest or high priestess. They celebrate the four great pagan festivals, especially May Eve and All-Hallows Eve, when they leap through bonfires as the pagans did on Beltane and Samhain. This is imitative magic, designed to aid and stimulate the activity of the sun, the source of life on earth. As badges of rank the witches wear garters, sometimes of snakeskin. They usually perform their ceremonies naked and there are hints of flagellatory rituals. Whether they adore the black bulk of the Goat, squatting on its altar, is not known, but they say that their rites bring them a profound sense of security and peace.

3. The Black Mass

Our Father, which *wert* in heaven. . . .

SATANIST PRAYER

The Mass is the central ceremony of the Catholic church, founded by Christ himself and reverenced by his followers for hundreds of years. The Protestant Communion services are based on it, though they differ from it in some important ways. Because of its divine origin and its long traditions of sanctity, the Mass has been frequently copied, not always with blasphemous intent. Alchemists wrote alchemical versions of it. Aleister Crowley wrote his own Mass of the Gnostic Catholic Church and also a Mass of the Phoenix, to be said by the magician daily at sunset. The ceremonial of the Hitler Youth meeting closely resembled the form of the Christian service, with the Nazi flag taking the honoured place of the sacrament and quotations from *Mein Kampf* or from Hitler's speeches replacing the Christian Gospel, Epistle and Creed.

As early as the second century A.D., St. Irenaeus accused the Gnostic teacher Marcus, 'an adept in magical impostures', of what seems to have been a perversion of the Mass to the worship of a deity other than the Christian God. He pretended to consecrate cups of wine and 'protracting to great length the word of invocation, he contrives to give them a purple and reddish colour so that Charis [Grace, a name of the divine Thought], who is one of those that are superior to all things, should be thought to drop her own blood into that cup, through means of his invocation, and that those who are present should be led to rejoice to taste of that cup in order that, by so doing, the Charis who is set forth by the magician may also flow into them'.[53]

Occultists ancient and modern, Christian and non-Christian, have generally accepted that the Mass is a magical ritual of great power. 'High Mass', Cyril Scott says, 'is a form of ceremonial magic which has a very definite effect on the inner planes. . . .' It is 'a channel through which the Master Jesus and the World Teacher can pour their spiritual power'.[54] This high regard for the Mass springs from the fact that the ceremony itself appears to be a magical one. It achieves a magical result through magical methods. Ordinary physical things, the bread and the wine, are changed into the Divine and the worshipper consumes the Divine to become one with God.

The transformation of the bread and wine into the body and blood of Christ depends on the magical use of language, the speaking of words charged with force. The transformation, according to the *Catholic Encyclopedia*, 'is produced in virtue of the words "of consecration", pronounced by the priest assuming the person of Christ and using the same ceremonies that Christ used at the Last Supper'.[55] These words are in Latin—*Hoc est enim corpus meum*, 'For this is my body', and *Hic est enim calix sanguinis mei*, 'For this is the chalice of my blood'. Certain accompanying actions are necessary; the words must be spoken by an ordained priest, and if he spoke them in his own person, instead of in the person of Christ, they would not be effective. Nor are they the words spoken by Jesus himself, who did not speak Latin, but from the magician's point of view their use through the centuries has given them effective magical force. That Catholics take a similar view is suggested by the vote of the Ecumenical Council in 1963 to authorise the saying of Mass in the vernacular provided that the Latin is retained for 'the precise verbal formula which is essential to the sacrament'.

The occult importance of the Mass has been heightened by the fact that Roman Catholics themselves have turned it to all kinds of magical uses. The Gelasian Sacramentary, which contains Roman documents of about the sixth century, includes Masses said to bring good weather, to bring rain, to obtain children, for the protection of someone going on a journey, to ward off diseases of cattle, for a sick person, or to recommend the dead to God's mercy. In 858 Pope Nicholas I condemned the Mass of Judgement, intended to clear or convict a man accused of a crime. The priest would give him communion saying, 'May this Body and Blood of Our Lord Jesus Christ prove thee innocent or guilty this day.' Saying Mass over cattle or farm tools or fishing-boats to bless them and make them productive was common in the Middle Ages and is still practised today.

The superstitious use of the Mass and of objects which were holy because they were blessed by a priest and were used in the Mass or in other church services—especially the consecrated host which was the body of God—sometimes went to remarkable lengths. In the sixteenth century the demonologists John Wier described how a German priest said Mass on the belly of a young nun to cure her of bewitchment. A Dominican tried to expel a demon from a little girl by touching her throat with a vessel full of hosts and attempted to drive a devil out of a possessed cow by burying in the cow's pasture a piece of a stole which had been worn by a priest saying Mass. Wier also mentioned a contemporary method of catching a vampire. Earth from the first three spadefuls of soil thrown into a grave was taken and consecrated by a priest in the Mass and was then trodden under the threshold of the church. If a vampire was in the church she could not get out, because she could not cross this consecrated barrier.

The implication of practices like these was that the Mass contained inherent force which could be put to many uses. This implication was strengthened by Catholic insistence that a priest could say Mass effectively even if he was in a state of sin (because he did not say it in his own person but in the person of Christ). The ceremony and the objects connected with it seemed to have a magical power of their own, regardless of the spiritual condition of those who used them or the purposes for which they were used. From the use of the Mass in white magic came its use in black magic.

The Council of Toledo in 694 condemned priests who said Mass for the dead, naming not a dead man but a living victim whom it was intended to kill. The solemn chant of *Requiem aeternam dona ei, Domine*, 'Give him eternal rest, O Lord', was meant to turn the Mass into a death-blow. The Council ruled that the offending priest and the person who had paid him should both be punished with banishment. Giraldus Cambrensis, who died about 1220, said that some priests in his day would sing Mass for the dead against an enemy ten times, in the hope that he would die on the tenth day or soon after. Other priests would say Mass over a wax image of the victim placed on the altar, cursing him.

In 1500 there was a quarrel between the Bishop of Cambrai and his cathedral chapter. The hostile dean and canons took to including in the Mass a collection of threatening and denunciatory passages from the Old Testament, which were recited by the priest with his back to the altar, the choir singing responses. The bishop appealed to the University of Paris, which ruled that this was a form of incantation against him.

It was not always easy to distinguish black magic from white. The Roman witch judge Paulus Grillandus, writing about 1525, says that it is probably not heretical to say Mass with the intention of finding out whether one person loves another, because this is an appeal to God for knowledge which God has. If Mass is said to provoke love in another, it is probably not heretical, because God commands us to love others. But if in either case Mass is said to enlist the help of the Devil, then it is heretical. He tells a story about a Spanish priest in Rome who composed various prayers asking God to turn the hearts of our nuns so that they would submit to him in love. The priest paid several ignorant monks to include these prayers in the Mass. It was considered a minor sin and he was punished by temporary banishment from Rome. Grillandus also says that it is criminal, though not heretical, to say Mass for the dead against the living and that priests who consecrate the host for use in sorcery would be punished as sorcerers.[56]

In a long ritual for summoning the Spirits of Darkness, the *Grimoire of Honorius* relies heavily on the Mass to strengthen the magician's powers and protect him. The magician, who must presumably be an ordained priest, says a Mass of the Holy Ghost in the middle of the night on the first Monday of the month. This is the Mass for Pentecost, when the disciples received the gift of speaking in tongues, and was perhaps selected to give the magician inspired speech. After he has consecrated the host, he holds it in his left hand, kneels and prays to Christ for help—'. . . give to Thine unworthy servant, holding Thy Living Body in his hands, the strength to use that power which is entrusted to him against the rebellious spirits.'

When the sun rises he takes a black cock, kills it and rips out its eyes, heart and tongue, which are dried in the sun and ground to powder. The rest of the carcass is buried in a secret place. On the next day at dawn the magician chants a Mass of the Angels, which belongs to the feast of the Apparition of St. Michael, the great opponent of Satan, and which therefore strengthens the magician's defences. On the altar he has one of the black cock's feathers. He sharpens it, dips it in the consecrated wine and writes certain magic characters on paper, which he presumably keeps about him for protection. He also keeps part of the consecrated host, wrapping it in violet silk.

Two days later at midnight he lights a candle of yellow wax, made in the form of a cross, and recites Psalm 78, 'Give ear, O my people, to my law.' Then he says Mass for the dead, calling on God to free him from the fear of hell and to make the demons obedient to him. He extinguishes the candle and at sunrise cuts the throat of a young male lamb. The skin of the lamb, on which the powdered organs of the cock are rubbed, is used to make parchment. The carcass is buried with prayers in which the magician identifies the slaughtered lamb with Christ.

> Sacrificed Lamb, be Thou a pillar of strength against the demons! Slain Lamb, give me power over the Powers of Darkness! Sacrificed Lamb, give me strength to subdue the rebellious spirits! So be it.

After drawing complicated magic signs on the parchment and reciting psalms, the magician finally says another Mass for the dead, in which he chants seventy-two great names of power, and then proceeds to the incantation for summoning the spirits to appear.[57] The mixture of piety and sorcery seems extraordinary, but to the writer of the grimoire all these preliminary processes were sources of power which he could turn to his own purposes.

The Mass and the host were used in every kind of sorcery. Priests were constantly ordered to keep the hosts, wine and sacred vessels securely locked up to prevent them from being stolen for use in magic or the making of poisons, and thefts of communion wafers have continued to trouble churches to this day. The *Malleus Maleficarum* says that witches 'make their instruments of witchcraft by means of the Sacraments or sacramental things of the Church, or some holy thing consecrated to God' and they 'sometimes place a waxen image under the Altar-cloth, or draw a thread through the Holy Chrism [oil], or use some other consecrated thing in such a way'. Not only did sacred things carry magical force but the abuse of them was also a source of power. 'And there are some who, in order to accomplish their evil charms and spells, beat and stab the Crucifix, and utter the filthiest words against the Purity of the Most Glorious Virgin Mary, casting the foulest aspersions on the Nativity of Our Saviour from Her inviolate womb.'[58] The perverse excitement of acts of blasphemy generated its own currents of force and sacrilege became one of the essential features of the Black Mass.

When it was known that the Mass was sometimes turned to black magical purposes, it was natural to assume that witches and sorcerers used it in the

Devil's service, and perhaps they did. A witch tried in southern France in 1594 described the saying of Mass at a sabbath held on St. John's Eve, in a field with about sixty people present. The celebrant wore a black cope with no cross on it and had two women as servers. When the host should have been elevated, after the consecration, he held up a slice of turnip stained black and all cried, 'Master, help us.' Louis Gaufridi, strangled and burned for bewitching Madeleine de Demandolx and another nun of Aix, confessed in 1611 that as Prince of the Synagogue, Lucifer's lieutenant, he had celebrated Mass at the sabbath, sprinkling the witches with the consecrated wine, at which they cried out *Sanguis eius super nos et filios nostros*—'His blood be upon us and upon our children'.

There were tales of Masses said with black hosts and black chalices, of mocking screams of 'Beelzebub! Beelzebub!' at the consecration, the wine might be water or urine. The host was triangular or hexagonal, generally black but sometimes blood-red. The priest wore a chasuble—the sleeveless outer robe of the priest saying Mass—which might be brown and embroidered with the figures of a pig and a naked woman, or bright scarlet with a green insert showing a bear and a weasel devouring the host, or deep red with a triangle on the back, in which was a black goat with silver horns. The Goat himself might say Mass, reading from a missal with red, white and black pages, bound in wolfskin.

According to Pierre de Lancre, the Devil said Mass, leaving out the Confiteor, or confession of sins, and the Alleluia. He would mumble words from the Mass until he came to the Offertory, the point in the service at which the collection is taken up. His worshippers presented him with offerings of bread, eggs and money. Then the Devil preached them a sermon and afterwards held up a black host which had his symbol impressed on it instead of the symbol of Christ. He said, 'This is my body', and elevated the host by impaling it on one of his horns, at which they all cried out *Aquerra Goity, Aquerra Beyty, Aquerra Goity, Aquerra Beyty*—'The Goat above, the Goat below; the Goat above the Goat below.' They formed a cross or a semicircle around the altar and prostrated themselves on the ground. Each was given a piece of the host to swallow and 'two mouthfuls of an infernal medicine and brew, of so foul a flavour and smell that they sweated to swallow it, and so cold that it froze them'. After this the Devil coupled with them and the frenzied orgy began.[59]

The witches' Mass was evidently not only a parody of the Christian service but also an adaption of it to the worship of their own god. The black host bearing the Devil's symbol was mystically his flesh—'This is my body'—and when he elevated it they cried out in adoration of him. The witches seem to have preserved the old custom of communion in both kinds, the worshippers receiving the wine as well as the bread, which had been abandoned by Catholics and was later restored by Protestants. They would leave out the confession of sins because they defied the Christian notion of sin and the Alleluis because it was a shout of praise to the Christian God. They became one with their master through the communion of his body and blood and then in sexual union with him, but they probably also felt a fierce sacrilegious thrill in violating the Christian ceremony, which added to the excitement of the orgy.

The same perverse mingling of sacrilege and sensuality is found in the confession of Madeleine Bavent, a nun of Louviers in Normandy. It is impossible to say how much of her autobiography, written in prison, is true, and she herself asked her readers to try to distinguish between the real and the hallucinatory in it. She entered the convent at Louviers when she was 18, in 1625, after she had been seduced by a priest. The chaplain of the convent at this time was Father Pierre David, who believed that God should be worshipped naked in the fashion of Adam, that a believer filled with the Holy Spirit was incapable of sin, and that any act was virtuous if performed in a state of inner devotion. As a sign of humility and poverty, the nuns attended Mass stripped to the skin, and those who were considered holiest, according to Madeleine, were the nuns who went completely naked in church and in the gardens, and danced naked before Father David. She herself was forced to take communion barebreasted and the chaplain caressed her indecently. He also taught the nuns to fondle each other, while he looked on, and to use an artificial phallus.

In 1628 Father Mathurin Picard became chaplain with Father Thomas Boullé as his assistant. They apparently carried Father David's practices to the lengths of positive Satanism. Picard raped Madeleine and other nuns 'committed the most filthy acts with him'. Once or twice a week Madeleine would fall into 'a kind of trance or ecstasy' in which she went to witch meetings at a house near the convent with Picard, Boullé and other priests, three or four of the nuns and a few outsiders. Some of them seem to have worn grotesque animal costumes. The meetings were held in a long narrow room with an altar, on which were candles. The priests recited Mass, using a blood-red host and reading from a blasphemous book full of maledictions against Christianity. The worshippers feasted, twice on roasted human flesh, and afterwards there was a frenzied orgy in which the women submitted to the priests and also, after Father David's death, to his ghost.

The Satanist hatred of Christianity was given full rein. Consecrated hosts were burned and the consecrated wine poured contemptuously on the floor. A small crucifix was brought in at one meeting, hosts were nailed to the figure of Christ and the congregation stabbed at the hosts with knives. Once one of the women brought her own new-born child which was crucified alive on a wooden cross, the hands and feet fastened to the cross with nails stuck through consecrated hosts.

These meetings continued till 1642, when Picard died, and many of the nuns were seized with hysterical paroxysms and convulsions, which were put down to diabolical possession. After long investigations, Boullé was burned alive in 1647. With him was burned the corpse of Picard, which had been exhumed for the purpose. Madeleine Bavent died in prison the same year at the age of 40, after several times trying to commit suicide.

Thirty years later came a fresh outbreak of Satanism in France. Between 1673 and 1680 at least fifty priests were executed for sacrilege and others were imprisoned. Father Davot was convicted of saying the Black Mass over the naked body of a woman, and also of using the Mass in sorcery by placing under the altar-cloth papers bearing the names of those it was hoped either to attract in love or to kill. Father Tournet was convicted of saying Mass on the body of a young girl whom he had made pregnant, with the intention that she would miscarry. She died of fright. Father Lemeignan was imprisoned for life, accused of slaughtering two children and hacking them to pieces during the celebration of Mass. He also said a Mass to discover buried treasure. Father Cotton had baptised a child in holy oil, strangled him and offered his corpse as a sacrifice to the Devil. Father Gerard was convicted of using a girl's body as his altar in saying Mass and copulating with her as part of the ceremony.

Many of the sacrilegious priests were arrested as a result of the activities of a special court, set up by Louis XIV in 1679 to deal with cases of poisoning involving some of the French nobility. The court's sessions were secret and from its verdict there was no appeal. Meeting in a room hung entirely in black and lit with candles, it was called the *Chambre Ardente* or Burning Court. Its investigation, headed by Nicholas de la Reymie, Police Commissioner of Paris, rapidly extended from poisoning into sorcery. The most sceptical modern writers have conceded a strong element of truth in de la Reymie's reports.

The investigations centred round a widow named Catherine Deshayes, known as La Voisin, a fortune-teller and suspected abortionist. It became clear that La Voisin had catered to ladies of high rank as a supplier of poisons, charms and black magical ceremonies. When her house was searched a curious chapel was discovered. Its walls were draped in black and behind the altar was a black curtain with a white cross embroidered on it. A mattress rested on the altar, covered by a black cloth, and on top of this were black candles. A furnace was found in which, apparently, the bodies of children sacrificed in the Black Mass had been destroyed. There were magical books and candles made with human fat, supplied by a public executioner who was one of La Voisin's lovers. La Voisin was burned alive in February 1680 and in October the king suspended the sittings of the Burning Court, probably because his mistress, Madame de Montespan, had been implicated. But de la Reymie continued his enquiries in secret, on the king's instructions, until June 1682.

The beautiful and fascinating Francoise-Athenais, Marquise de Montespan, born in 1641, had become a lady-in-waiting to the queen and had attracted the interest of Louis XIV by 1667, when she first consulted La Voisin. She wanted to alienate the king from both the queen and his current love, the Duchesse de la Vallière, to make herself his mistress and ultimately his wife. La Voisin obtained a priest, Father Mariette, who said a Mass to assist de Montespan in her ambitions. While she knelt, the gospel was read over her bowed head and an incantation chanted—'. . . that the Queen may be barren, that the King leave her bed and board for me, that he give me everything I ask for myself and my relatives . . . that, his affection being redoubled on what has existed in the past, the King may leave la Vallière and look upon her no more; and that, the Queen being repudiated, I may marry the King'. The same ceremony was repeated twice more, the last time in a church. The hearts of two doves were torn out, placed on the altar and consecrated in the names of the king and de Montespan. The dove is a bird of passion, sacred both to Christ and to Venus. In the same year de Montespan became Louis XIV's mistress.

She did not feel secure in his affections and turned again to La Voisin for help. More Masses were said and love-charms were placed under the chalice on the altar and blessed by the priest. They contained powder of dried moles, bat's blood and cantharides. After the service, the favourite took them away and slipped them into the king's food.

In 1673 there was a serious threat that de Montespan might be superseded. To meet the crisis, La Voisin called in the sinister and hideous Abbé Guibourg. Guibourg was in his sixties, a tall, massive old man, disfigured by a squint, blue veins standing out on his bloated, sensual face. He recited three Masses in which his altar was de Montespan's naked body, the chalice resting on her belly. At the Offering of the Elements the priest cut the throat of a child. The blood was drained into the chalice and mixed with flour to make the host. When this wafer was consecrated, de Montespan herself or Guibourg in her name spoke the following incantation.

> Astaroth, Asmodeus, princes of amity, I conjure you to accept the sacrifice of this child, which I offer in return for what I ask: that the King and the Dauphin will continue their friendship towards me, that I may be honoured by the Princes and Princesses of the court, and that the King will refuse nothing I ask of him, both for my relatives and my retainers.

De Montespan took the consecrated wafer and some of the child's blood away with her, to place them in the king's food.

Still the mistress could not feel safe, and in 1676, in which year there was a riot in Paris over the disappearances of children, Guibourg was called in again. The ceremony was repeated three times more in La Voisin's chapel, de Montespan serving as altar on the first occasion and La Voisin taking her place the second and third times. La Voisin's daughter Marguerite described Masses of this type, at which she had been present. The woman for whom the Mass was said lay naked on the mattress on the altar, at right-angles to it, her legs flexed or hanging down over the edge, her head supported on a pillow, her arms stretched out crosswise with black candles on her hands. A napkin bearing a cross was placed on her breasts and the chalice stood on her belly. A child's throat was cut at the Offering of the Elements and the host consecrated over the woman's genitals. 'As often as the priest was to kiss the altar', according to Marguerite, 'he kissed the body, and consecrated the host above the genitals, into which he inserted a small piece of the host. At the end of the Mass, the priest went into (*inibat*) the woman and, dipping his hands in the chalice, washed her genitals.'[60]

The ritual failed to take effect, and in 1679, maddened by the king's passion for another woman, de Montespan resorted to death-magic. Guibourg said a Mass for the dead in the name of the king, mouthing incantations against his life. There was no result and a plot was made to poison the king, which failed when La Voisin was arrested in March 1679. Madame de Montespan was never formally accused and the king, perhaps anxious to avoid scandal, treated her courteously but distantly till her retirement from court in 1691. She became increasingly pious, devoting herself to austerity and good works, though to the end she feared death and the darkness of night. She died in 1707. Guibourg was imprisoned in the castle of Besancon, chained to the wall of his cell for three years till his death.

Whether Guibourg was a conscious Satanist is not clear, though it seems likely. His amatory Mass was apparently an attempt to use the magical force of the orthodox Mass to arouse love and desire, not an adoration of Satan. But the black candles, the chapel hung in black, the incantation to the demons Astaroth and Asmodeus, the offering of a slaughtered child in sacrifice to them, the desecration of the sacrament and the mixture of sacredness and sensuality bring the ceremony close to the Black Mass proper, the turning of the Mass to the Devil's worship.

In eighteenth- and nineteenth-century accounts of the Satanic Mass orgiastic sacrilege and perversion are carried to a point at which the details become unprintable—the worshippers sexually abusing obscene images of Christ and the Virgin or large consecrated hosts split up the middle. The priest follows the Catholic rite closely, but substituting 'Satan' for 'God' and 'evil' for 'good'. Parts of the Mass are read backwards and the Christian prayers are reversed, as in the Satanist version of the Lord's Prayer—'Our Father, which wert in heaven . . . Thy will be done, in heaven as it is on earth. . . . Lead us into temptation, and deliver us not from evil . . .' The purpose is both to degrade the Christian service and to transform it, as a ritual of powerful religious and magical force, to the glorification of the Devil. The same is true of the Devil's hosts and wine, said to be made of excreta, menstrual blood or semen, defecated upon or smeared with semen before being crammed into their mouths by the votaries, for the Devil is lord of the body as opposed to the soul, of fertility as opposed to spirituality. That the 'body and blood' of the god are products of the human body is also possibly connected with the magical doctrine that man is potentially God.

The best authority on Satanist ritual in modern times is J.K. Huysmans. It is not certain that he ever attended a Black Mass, but probable that, as he claimed, he did. He described it in his novel *La Bas*, published in 1891. The hero, Durtal, is taken to a dingy half-dark chapel in a private house, lit by sanctuary lamps hanging from bronze chandeliers with pink pendants of glass. Above the altar is 'an infamous, derisive Christ', its bestial face 'twisted into a mean laugh'. There are black candles on the altar. For incense they burn rue, myrtle, dried nightshade, henbane and the powerfully narcotic thorn-apple. The acolytes and choristers, robed in red, are homosexuals. The Mass is said by an ageing and villainous priest, Canon Docre, wearing a dark red chasuble, beneath which he is naked, and a scarlet cap with two horns of red cloth.

Docre begins the Mass while the choir boys sing the responses and the congregation take the censers and breathe deeply of the intoxicating fumes. Kneeling before the altar, Docre hails Satan as reasonable God, just God, master of slanders, dispenser of the benefits of crime, administrator of luxurious sins and great vices, cordial of the vanquished, suzerain of resentment, accountant of humiliations and treasurer of old hatreds, hope of virility, king of the disinherited, the Son who is to overthrow the inexorable Father. He calls upon the Devil to grant his followers glory, riches and power. Then he curses the execrable Jesus, the impostor and breaker of promises, who was to redeem mankind and has not, who was to appear in glory and has not, who was to intercede for man with the Father and has not. He proclaims that in his quality of priest he will force this do-nothing King and coward God to descend into the host, to be punished by the violation of his body.

While the worshippers writhe and scream hysterically, Docre consecrates and defiles the host in orgasm and hurles it to the floor. The Satanists claw at it, grovelling, tearing off pieces of it and chewing them. Fascinated and appalled, Durtal watches Docre, who, 'frothing with rage, was chewing up sacramental wafers, taking them out of his mouth, wiping himself with them, and distributing them to the women, who ground them underfoot, howling, or fell over each other, struggling to get hold of them and violate them'. Then there is an indiscriminate orgy and Durtal, sickened, creeps away.

This description brings out the Satanist conviction, also found in witchcraft, that Christ is a false god, safely ensconced in heaven, where he cares nothing for humanity, with undertones of the old Gnostic belief that God is far away and has no contact with men, who are under the rule of the Devil. Christianity is a cheat, a quack medicine, and the churches are its hucksters.

The original of Canon Docre was Father Louis Van Haecke, Chaplain of the Holy Blood at Bruges. Huysmans believed that Van Haecke was a Satanist who lured young people into his clutches, corrupted them and initiated them into the mysteries of black magic. He was said to have crosses tattooed on the soles of his feet, so that he continually trod on the symbol of Christ. Sometimes at night fear came upon him and he would scream in panic, recovering himself by lighting all the lamps in the house, yelling diabolical curses and committing horrible blasphemies upon consecrated hosts. The Abbé Boullan, whom Huysmans admired, also appears in *La Bas* in a sympathetic role as Doctor Johannes.

The Black Mass appears more often in fiction than in real life, but there are occasional factual references to it. In 1889 *Le Matin* carried an account by a reporter who had written an article in which doubted the existence of the Satanic Mass, but had then been invited to one. He was taken to it with blindfolds on his eyes and when they were removed found himself in a dark room with erotic murals. On the altar, surrounded by six black candles, was an image of a goat trampling on a crucifix. The priest wore red robes and the congregation of about fifty men and women chanted hymns. Mass was said on the bare body of a woman stretched on the altar. Black hosts were consecrated and eaten by the worshippers and the ceremony culminated in an orgy. *Le Matin* confirmed that the reporter had really been to this meeting, but would give no further details.

In 1895 a Satanic chapel was discovered in the Palazzo Borghese in Rome. The walls were hung in black and scarlet, and behind the altar was a tapestry of *Lucifer Triumphans*. On the altar were candles and a figure of Satan. The chapel was luxuriously fitted out with prayer-desks and chairs in crimson and gold. It was lit by electricity, glaring down from a huge eye in the ceiling.

Writing in 1940, William Seabrook, a collector of occult experiences, said he had seen Black Masses in London, Paris, Lyons, and New York. The Mass is said by an apostate priest, with a prostitute in a scarlet robe as his acolyte. A woman, preferably a virgin, lies naked on the altar before an inverted crucifix. The chalice is placed between her breasts and some of the wine is spilled on her body. After the consecration the host is not elevated but debased and defiled.[61]

A Spanish writer, Julio Caro Baroja, was told about an occurrence in 1942 in the Spanish Basque country. Six men and three women met at a farm, feasted copiously and then stripped themselves naked. They heated up a cauldron of soup and boiled a cat alive in it. They drank the soup, reciting incantations between mouthfuls, and one of them made an altar of planks and parodied the saying of Mass, using slices of sausage as hosts. Through all this, there was much caressing of the woman.[62]

In the 1950s there were reports of Black Masses in Italy and in 1963 there were numerous cases of black magic in England. The altar of a church in Sussex had to be rehallowed after four men had been seen performing a mysterious ritual in the church, apparently attempting to summon up evil spirits. A Black Mass was believed to have been said in the church of St. Mary's, Clophill, in Bedfordshire. Apparently, necromancy was also involved, as the graves of six women had been opened and one skeleton was found inside the church.

* * *

'When anyone invokes the Devil with intentional ceremonies', said Eliphas Levi, 'the devil comes, and is seen.' But Levi's Devil is not a being existing independently of man, but something called into manifestation by the magician's imagination. There are a few convinced Satanists here and there in the world, but for most modern magicians the Enemy of Christendom cannot exist. According to occult theory, there are forces and intelligences, whether inside or outside the magician, which are conventionally condemned as evil, but a god who is entirely evil is as inconceivable as a god who is entirely good. The true God, the One, is the totality of everything, containing all good and all evil, and reconciling all opposites.

To magicians, 'good and evil go round in a wheel that is one thing and not many'. They are two sides of one coin, apparently separate and opposed, but really two aspects of a greater whole. In his attempt to become the whole man, who is God, the magician tries to experience and master all things, whatever their conventional labels. Until he has achieved this by completing the Great Work, it is presumptuous for the magician to speculate on the truth behind the labels, for, as the serpent pointed out in Eden, the knowledge of good and evil belongs to the Divine. Satanism is as harshly rejected by most magicians as it is by Christians. But where the churches, which brought the Devil to life in the first place, condemn his worship as the adoration of evil, magicians despise it as a failure to understand the true nature of the universe.

APPENDIX 1
The Grimoires

1. *Key of Solomon*, the most famous of all magical textbooks, known in versions in various languages, the bulk of them in French or Latin and dating from the eighteenth century, though the grimoire itself is much older. In the first century A.D. Josephus referred to a book of incantations for summoning evil spirits, supposedly written by Solomon. A Greek version in the British Museum may date back to the twelfth or thirteenth century. The *Key* was prohibited as a dangerous work by the Inquisition in 1559.

2. *Lemegeton*, or *Lesser Key of Solomon*, divided into four parts—Goetia, Theurgia Goetia, the Pauline Art and the Almadel. A writer about 1500 mentions the Almadel and Wier drew on the Goetia for his *Pseudomonarchia Daemonum*. The origin and meaning of the word 'Lemegeton' are unknown.

3. *Testament of Solomon*, in Greek, A.D. 100–400.

4. *Grimoire of Honorius*, first published at Rome, 1670. It probably dates from the sixteenth century.

5. *Grimorium Verum*, written in French and supposedly published at Memphis by Alibeck the Egyptian, 1517, but it probably dates from the eighteenth century. It is based on the *Key of Solomon*.

6. *Grand Grimoire*, in French, probably of the eighteenth century.

7. *Red Dragon*, a version of the *Grand Grimoire*.

8. *True Black Magic*, or *The Secret of Secrets*. A French version of the *Key of Solomon*, published in 1750.

9. *Arbatel of Magic*, in Latin, published at Basle, 1575.

10. *The Black Pullet*, supposedly published in Egypt, 1740, but probably dating from the late eighteenth century.

11. *Fourth Book*, added to Agrippa's *Occult Philosophy* after his death. Wier, his pupil, rejected it as forgery.

12. *The Magical Elements*, or *Heptameron*, attributed to Peter of Abano, who died in 1316, but probably written in the sixteenth century as a supplement to the *Fourth Book*.

The 'Hebrew' System in Numerology

The following is a list of the Hebrew letters and their number values. Five of the letters have 'final' forms, used when they appear at the end of a word.

Hebrew Letter	Our Equivalent	Number Value	Hebrew Letter	Our Equivalent	Number Value
Aleph	A	1	Samekh	–	60
Beth	B	2	Ayin	–	70
Gimel	G	3	Pe	P	80
Daleth	D	4	Sade	–	90
He	H	5	Qoph	Q	100
Vau	V, W	6	Resh	R	200
Zayin	Z	7	Shin	S	300
Heth	–	8	Tau	T	400
Teth	–	9	*Final forms*		
Yod	Y	10	Kaph	–	500
Kaph	K	20	Mem	–	600
Lamed	L	30	Nun	–	700
Mem	M	40	Pe	–	800
Nun	N	50	Sade	–	900

This table accounts for eighteen of our letters. Numbers have to be found for C, E, F, I, J, O, U, and X, which do not appear in the Hebrew alphabet. F is numbered 8 from the Hebrew letter *pe* (80) which represents the sound 'ph' as well as 'p'. U is taken to be the same letter as V and numbered 6. C is taken to be the same as G and numbered 3. The rest are filled in from Greek. E is 5 from Greek *epsilon*, which stood for 5. I and J are 1 from *iota* (10), O is 7 from *omicron* (70) and X is 6 from *xi* (60)–though some numerologists count X as 5, presumably because it resembles the dot-symbol for 5, ∴.

Notes

Chapter One/The World of the Black Magician

1. Genesis 3.4–5.
2. Crowley is quoted from his *Magick in Theory and Practice*, 4–5. Agrippa's *Occult Philosophy* is quoted in Yates, *Giordano Bruno*, 136.
3. Levi, *Key of the Mysteries*, 171.
4. Levi, *History of Magic*, 149.
5. Quoted in Kirk and Raven, *Pre-Socratic Philosophers*, 29.
6. See Randolph, *Ozark Superstitions*, 264 f.
7. For Michael Scot on sneezing, see Thorndike, *History of Magic*, ii. 330.
8. Showers, *Fortune Telling*, 324 f.
9. Yates, *Giordano Bruno*, 375–6.
10. Lea, *Materials*, ii. 935.
11. McPherson, *Primitive Beliefs in N.E. Scotland*, 199.
12. Hole, *Witchcraft in England*, 9.
13. Trachtenberg, *Jewish Magic and Superstition*, 124–6.
14. Radford, *Encyclopaedia of Superstitions*, 202.
15. See Seabrook, *Witchcraft*, 19, 72.
16. Bromage, *Occult Arts in Ancient Egypt*, 157.
17. Seabrook, *Witchcraft*, 120 f.
18. James, *Prehistoric Religion*, 20 f.
19. Trachtenberg, *The Devil and the Jews*, 107–8.
20. On this whole subject see Kouwer, *Colors and their Character*, and also Morrish, *Outline of Astro-Psychology*, 110 f.
21. Levi, *Doctrine and Ritual*, 113 f. The 'long and mysterious' incantation is printed in an appendix.
22. Levi, *Key of the Mysteries*, 112–13.
23. See Baldick, *Life of Huysmans*, 154–6.
24. Laver, *The First Decadent*, 139.
25. Huysmans's letters from Lyons are quoted in Baldick, *Life of Huysmans*, 186–9.
26. Boullan's letter to Huysmans is quoted in Rhodes, *Satanic Mass*, 155.

27. Cammell, *Aleister Crowley*, 41–42.
28. See Symonds, *The Great Beast*, 31–32, and Hone, *Yeats*, 106.
29. Symonds, *The Great Beast*, 268.

Chapter Two/Names and Numbers

1. See Clodd, *Magic in Names*, 176–7, and Nilsson, *Greek Folk Religion*, 114–15.
2. The biblical references are Revelation 19.12; Judges 13.18, and Genesis 32.29.
3. 2 Samuel 7.13; Exodus 23.21; Ephesians 1.21.
4. See Budge, *Egyptian Magic*, 137 f.
5. *Cheiro's Book of Numbers*, 71.
6. Campbell, *Your Days Are Numbered*, 71.
7. Montrose, *Numerology for Everybody*, 43.
8. Lopez, *Numerology*, 23.
9. Jones, *Credulities Past and Present*, 287 f.
10. This section is based on *Miracle of the Ages* by an American Pyramid-fancier, Worth Smith.
11. Quotations from Cheasley, *Numerology*, 1, 10, and Montrose, *Numerology for Everybody*, 4.
12. *Metaphysics*, quoted in Kirk and Raven, *Pre-Socratic Philosophers*, 248.
13. *Arithmetic*, quoted in Hopper, *Medieval Number Symbolism*, 38.
14. Curtiss, *Key to the Universe*, 61.
15. *Against Faustus*, quoted in Hopper, *Medieval Number Symbolism*, 78.
16. Thorndike, *History of Magic*, i. 674.
17. Ptolemy, *Tetrabiblos*, I. 2.
18. Adams, *Astrology for Everyone*, 156.
19. Levi, *Doctrine and Ritual*, 45.
20. Thorndike, *History of Magic*, i. 69, 592.
21. Morley, *Agrippa*, i. 150.
22. Thorndike, *History of Magic*, i. 627.

Chapter Three/The Cabala and the Names of Power

1. Ginsburg, *Kabbalah*, 96.
2. Blau, *Christian Interpretation of the Cabala*, 69. My italics.
3. Crowley, *Magick in Theory and Practice*, 196, 230 f.
4. Ezekiel 1.21. *Quia spiritus vitae erat in rotis* (Vulgate).
5. Fortune, *Mystical Qabalah*, 149.
6. Revelation 12.1 and 17.1–6.
7. Ezekiel 1.4.
8. Psalms 68.17.
9. Daniel 10.6.
10. Crowley, *Magick in Theory and Practice*, 370 f., 427–8.

11. Ibid., 143 f., 387 f.
12. Fortune, *Mystical Qabalah*, 76, 99.
13. Gray, *Tarot Revealed*, 3.
14. Case, *Tarot*, 164.
15. Jung, *Mysterium Coniunctionis*, 163.
16. Crowley, *Magick in Theory and Practice*, 430.
17. Ibid., 237.
18. Case, *Tarot*, 52.
19. Rakoczi, *Painted Caravan*, 26.
20. John 3.8.
21. Taylor, *History of Playing Cards*, 468.
22. See Mathers, *Kabbalah Unveiled*, introduction; Trachtenberg, *Jewish Magic and Superstition*, Appendix 1, and Driver, 'Sacred Numbers and Round Figures'.
23. Trachtenberg, *The Devil and the Jews*, 183.
24. Seligmann, *History of Magic*, 350.
25. Matthew 1.17.
26. See Charles, *Revelation of St. John*, i. 364 f., and Torrey, *Apocalypse of John*, 59 f.
27. Crowley, *Magick in Theory and Practice*, 45–49.
28. Matthew 7.22–23, Acts 19.13–15.
29. Nilsson, *Greek Piety*, 175.
30. Butler, *Ritual Magic*, 6.
31. On the 22- and 42-letter names of God, see Trachtenberg, *Jewish Magic and Superstition*, 91 f.
32. Bamberger, *Fallen Angels*, 191.
33. 'Sun, stand thou still'—Joshua 10.12; 'I am Alpha and Omega'—Revelation 1.11; the Comforter—John 14.16; 'But if the Lord make a new thing'—Numbers 16.30.
34. Fortune, *Psychic Self-Defense*, 95.
35. Waite, *Ceremonial Magic*, 295.
36. Crowley, *Magick in Theory and Practice*, 69.
37. Summers, *Witchcraft and Black Magic*, 128.
38. Briggs, *Anatomy of Puck*, Appendix IV.
39. Levi, *Doctrine and Ritual*, 210.
40. Hastings, *Encyclopaedia of Religion and Ethics*, iii. 455.
41. Briggs, *Pale Hecate's Team*, 262.
42. See Crowley, *Magick in Theory and Practice*, 265 f.
43. Symonds, *Magis of Aleister Crowley*, 76 f.

Chapter Four / The Stone and the Elixir

1. Morley, *Agrippa*, ii. 218.
2. Waite, *Secret Tradition in Alchemy*, 315–16.
3. Holmyard, *Alchemy*, 253 f.
4. *Metaphors*, quoted in Thorndike, *History of Magic*, iii. 76.

5. *Scrutinium chymicum*, quoted in Eliade, *The Forge and the Crucible*, 123.

6. Pavitt, *Talismans*, 6.

7. Eliade, *The Forge and the Crucible*, 47.

8. See Toulmin and Goodfield, *Architecture of Matter*, 89–100.

9. Jung, *Psychology and Alchemy*, 409–10.

10. Paracelsus, *Selected Writings*, 88.

11. Jonas, *Gnostic Religion*, 287. My italics.

12. Holmyard, *Alchemy*, 27. Stillman, *Story of Alchemy*, 162–5.

13. Hopkins, *Alchemy Child of Greek Philosophy*, 71.

14. Jung, *Psychology and Alchemy*, 360.

15. For Ripley see Waite, *Secret Tradition in Alchemy*, 207–8. For Quercetanus see Jung, *Psychology and Alchemy*, 228.

16. Aristotle, *Meteorology*, Book III, chapter 6.

17. Jung, *Mysterium Coniunctionis*, 256.

18. I Corinthians 15.36 and 42–44; John 12.24–25.

19. John 3.14.

20. Jung, *Psychology and Alchemy*, 384–5.

21. John 3.3–5.

22. Jung, *Mysterium Coniunctionis*, 266–8.

23. Holmyard, *Alchemy*, 143.

24. Stillman, *Story of Alchemy*, 178–9.

25. Jung, *Mysterium Coniunctionis*, xv.

26. Crowley, *Magick in Theory and Practice*, 22–23.

27. Ibid., 263.

28. Levi, *Doctrine and Ritual*, 17.

29. Jung, *Psychology and Alchemy*, 256.

30. Paracelsus, *Selected Writings*, 291 f., Morley, *Agrippa*, i. 203–4.

31. Jones, *Occult Philosophy*, 111–12.

32. Scott, *Outline of Modern Occultism*, 79–82.

33. Hall, *Most Holy Trinosophia*, xxv.

34. Taylor, *Alchemists*, 117–18.

35. Leyel, *Magic of Herbs*, 186–7.

36. Wootton, *Chronicles of Pharmacy*, i. 389–92.

37. Bacon, *Sylva Sylvarum*, section 928.

38. Hartmann, *Paracelsus*, 185 f.

39. Janet, *Psychological Healing*, i. 30–32.

Chapter Five/Astrology

1. Chatelherault, *You and Your Stars*, 1.

2. Lewinsohn, *Science, Prophecy and Prediction*, 107 f.

3. Kingsley, *Outrageous Fortune*, 5.

4. Hall, *Philosophy of Astrology*, 17.

5. Ptolemy, *Tetrabiblos*, I. 17.
6. Thorndike, *History of Magic*, ii. 417.
7. Robson, *Fixed Stars and Constellations*, 23.
8. Adams, *Astrology for Everyone*, xix–xx, 181.
9. See Reid, *Towards Aquarius*, and Hone, *Modern Textbook*, 276 f.
10. Thorndike, *History of Magic*, iv. 370–1.
11. Ibid., v. 202 f., and Mackay, *Extraordinary Popular Delusions*, 265–6.
12. Kingsley, *Outrageous Fortune*, 62.
13. Quoted in an article by Ellic Howe in *American Astrology* magazine, October 1962.
14. Summers, *Witchcraft and Black Magic*, 125.
15. Waite, *Ceremonial Magic*, 304–5, Idries Shah, *Secret Lore of Magic*, 107–8.
16. Waite, *Ceremonial Magic*, 26 f.
17. See Yates, *Giordano Bruno*, 62 f., 331 f.
18. Waite, *Ceremonial Magic*, 84 f.

Chapter Six / Ritual Magic

1. Butler, *Ritual Magic*, 10.
2. Crowley, *Magick in Theory and Practice*, 72.
3. Waite, *Ceremonial Magic*, 159–60.
4. Isaiah 29.1.
5. Gardner, *Witchcraft Today*, 20.
6. Mathers, *Sacred Magic of Abramelin*, introduction.
7. Givry, *Pictorial Anthology*, 105.
8. Butler, *Ritual Magic*, 200–1.
9. Levi, *Doctrine and Ritual*, 298–300.
10. Waite, *Ceremonial Magic*, 280–2; Idries Shah, *Secret Lore of Magic*, 269.
11. Fortune, *Psychic Self-Defense*, 183–4.
12. Holmyard, *Alchemy* 141.
13. Butler, *Ritual Magic*, 218–25.
14. Kittredge, *Witchcraft*, 206.
15. Crowley, *Magick in Theory and Practice*, 95–97.
16. For varying versions of these incantations see Waite, *Ceremonial Magic*, 227 f.; Idries Shah, *Secret Lore of Magic*, 183 f., and Appendices; Butler, *Ritual Magic*, 73–76.
17. Crowley, *Magick in Theory and Practice*, 265 f.
18. Symonds, *Magic of Aleister Crowley*, 196 f.
19. Mark 3.22.
20. Jeremiah 19.5.
21. Gaster, *Dead Sea Scriptures*, 298.
22. Matthew 6.24.
23. 2 Peter 2.15; Revelation 2.14.
24. Mathers, *Kabbalah Unveiled*, introduction.
25. Waite, *Ceremonial Magic*, 325 f.

26. Butler, *Ritual Magic*, 12–13.
27. Gardner, *Witchcraft Today*, 104.
28. Rahner, *Greek Myths and Christian Mystery*, 223 f.
29. Idries Shah, *Secret Lore of Magic*, 112.
30. Waite, *Ceremonial Magic*, 311–12.
31. Thorndike, *History of Magic*, iv. 300.

Chapter Seven / The Worship of the Devil

1. Amos 3.6; Isaiah 45.7; Ecclesiasticus 11.14.
2. 2 Samuel 24.1; 1 Samuel 16.14; Judges 9.23; Isaiah 19.14; 1 Kings 22.19–22.
3. Numbers 22.22; 1 Samuel 29.4.
4. Zechariah 3.1–2.
5. *1 Enoch* 40.7 and 53.3–5 (Charles edn.).
6. 1 Chronicles 21.1, and cf. 2 Samuel 24.1.
7. Genesis 6.1–5.
8. *1 Enoch* 6.1–2. Biblical references are Psalm 82; Isaiah 24.21; Job 4.18.
9. *1 Enoch* 7.3–5; 10.5–6.
10. *1 Enoch* 15.3–7.
11. Isaiah 14.12–15.
12. Graves and Patai, *Hebrew Myths*, 57–59.
13. *1 Enoch* 54.5–6; 86.1.
14. *Vita Adea et Evae* 12–16, in Charles, *Apocrypha and Pseudepigrapha*.
15. 1 Corinthians 15.22.
16. Matthew 4.8–9; Luke 4.6; John 12.31; 14.30; 16.11; 2 Corinthians 4.3.
17. Isaiah 27.1.
18. Driver, *Canaanite Myths*, 103.
19. Revelation 12.3–12.
20. Grant, *Gnosticism and Early Christianity*, 150.
21. Irenaeus, *Against Heresies*, I. 24.
22. Ibid., I. 6, and I. 23.
23. Ibid., I. 25.
24. See Runciman, *Medieval Manichee*.
25. Lea, *History of the Inquisition*, ii. 335.
26. Summers, *Geography of Witchcraft*, 457–8.
27. See Martin, *Trial of the Templars*.
28. Butler, *Ritual Magic*, 204.
29. Murray, *Witch-Cult in Western Europe*, 11–12.
30. Lea, *Materials*, i. 178–9.
31. Baroja, *World of the Witches*, 61–62.
32. Ibid., 84.
33. Lea, *Materials*, i. 273–5.
34. Ibid., i. 238–40.

35. Robbins, *Encyclopedia of Witchcraft*, 420.
36. *Malleus*, Part I, Question 2, and Part II, Question 1, chapter 1.
37. Law's *Memorialls*, quoted in Davidson, *Rowan Tree and Red Thread*, 16.
38. Leviticus 16.7 f. The Authorised Version translates 'for Azazel' as 'for the scapegoat'.
39. Bamberger, *Fallen Angels*, 154–5.
40. Matthew 25.31 f.
41. 2 Chronicles 11.15, 2 Kings 23.8, Leviticus 17.7; 18.23. The Authorised Version translates *seirim* as 'devils' or 'satyrs'.
42. Exodus 22.18–20.
43. Summers, *Geography of Witchcraft*, 65–71.
44. Williams, *Witchcraft*, 161–2.
45. Murray, *Witch-Cult in Western Europe*, 25–26.
46. Robbins, *Encyclopedia of Witchcraft*, 239.
47. Summers, *Witchcraft and Black Magic*, 35–40.
48. *De Doctrina Christiana*, quoted in Lea, *Materials*, i. 199–200.
49. Givry, *Pictorial Anthology*, 177.
50. Both documents are reproduced in Robbins, *Encyclopedia of Witchcraft*, 377–9.
51. Waite, *Ceremonial Magic*, 254–62; Idries Shah, *Secret Lore of Magic*, 64–67.
52. 'Real Witches at Work', *Life*, November 13, 1964.
53. Irenaeus, *Against Heresies*, I. 13.
54. Scott, *Outline of Modern Occultism*, 115, 126.
55. *Catholic Encyclopedia*, iv. 277.
56. Lea, *Materials*, i. 409–12.
57. Waite, *Ceremonial Magic*, 265 f.; Idries Shah, *Secret Lore of Magic*, 256 f.
58. *Malleus*, Part II, Question 1, chapters 5 and 12.
59. Murray, *Witch-Cult in Western Europe*, 148–9.
60. Rhodes, *Satanic Mass*, Appendix 3.
61. Seabrook, *Witchcraft*, 84.
62. Baroja, *World of the Witches*, 229–30.

Bibliography and Suggestions for Further Reading

Anything approaching a complete bibliography of works on magic and occultism, even restricted to those available in English, would fill a book or more by itself. The following list includes the books mentioned in the text and notes, except for standard reference works, and also other books which I have found helpful. A few brief notes on some of them may be of use to readers not familiar with the subject who want to read further.

There is no good history of magic in English. The great work on medieval magical theory and practice is Professor Thorndike's massive and monumentally learned *History of Magic and Experimental Science*, covering the period from Pliny to the seventeenth century. For the history of ceremonial magic see Professor Butler's admirable and highly readable *Ritual Magic*. Selections from the grimoires will be found in *Ceremonial Magic* by A. E. Waite and *The Secret Lore of Magic* by Idries Shah, the two books covering much the same ground.

The only way to approach modern magical theory is through the books of magicians themselves, especially Crowley, Levi and Mathers. The works of Dion Fortune and Franz Hartmann are also helpful. I have found no biography of Mathers, or of Levi in English, but there is a brilliant life of Crowley, *The Great Beast* by John Symonds, with additional information in the same author's *The Magic of Aleister Crowley*. For Huysmans, the Abbé Boullan and the battle of bewitchment, see the biographies of Huysmans by Robert Baldick and James Laver. Mr. Baldick has also written an introduction to Keene Wallis's translation of *La Bas*.

For the early history of numerology see Hopper's *Medieval Number Symbolism* and for Pythagoras the books by Burnet and by Kirk and Raven. The Curtisses are perhaps the clearest and most interesting of modern numerologists.

The classic work on the Cabala is Ginsburg's *The Kabbalah*. The leading modern authority on the subject is Professor Scholem, whose *Major Trends in Jewish Mysticism* is essential and fascinating reading. I also recommend J. L. Blau's short book. There is an old edition of the *Sepher Yetzirah* by W. W. Westcott, a founder of the Golden Dawn.

There is no really good book on the Tarot, occult or scholarly. The standard work is Waite's *Pictorial Key*, which is abrupt and contemptuous in tone, but contains a good many helpful hints. Mathers's booklet *The Tarot* is very brief and relies heavily on Eliphas Levi.

On the names of power, and on Jewish magic in general, Trachtenberg's *Jewish Magic and Superstition* is essential. *The Devil and the Jews* by the same author, a study in anti-Semitism, contains interesting material on magic. The Mathers edition of *The Sacred Magic of Abramelin the Mage* is available in a modern reprint.

Alchemy has been more written about than cast light on. From the chemical points of view, the books by E. J. Holmyard and F. Sherwood Taylor are helpful. From the mystical point of view, I recommend Silberer and Jung.

The nearest approach to a history of astrology is Eisler's *Royal Art of Astrology*, written from an anti-astrological standpoint. Innumerable books by modern astrologers are available. Margaret E. Hone's *Modern Text Book* is clear and comprehensive. Lyndoe's *Astrology for Everyone* is also useful.

On Gnosticism, see the books by Jonas and Grant, and for the medieval heretical sects Runciman's *Medieval Manichee* and Lea's *History of the Inquisition*. For the history of the Devil, and demonology in general, Bamberger and Langton are both excellent. There is a good book on the Black Mass, *The Satanic Mass* by H. T. F. Rhodes.

The best brief introduction to witchcraft is by Charles Williams. Professor Lea's *Materials Towards a History of Witchcraft* is a collection of notes for a projected book on the subject, which was never written. Much of it is in Latin and it suffers from poor arrangement and the absence of an index, but it is an essential source-book. Among more popular books, the works of Montague Summers suffer from excessive credulity but contain much valuable material. Margaret Murray's theory is expounded in *The Witch-Cult in Western Europe* and in the more easily available *God of the Witches*. *A Razor for a Goat* by Elliot Rose is a corrective to Murray and Summers. On sex in witchcraft and in the Black Mass, see R. E. L. Masters, *Eros and Evil*.

ADAMS, E., *Astrology for Everyone*, Dodd Mead, N.Y., 1960 (reprint of 1931 edn.).
APULEIUS, *The Golden Ass*, trans. R. Graves, Pocket Books, N.Y., 1954. Paperback.
ARISTOTLE, *Meteorologica*, trans. H. D. P. Lee, Loeb, 1952.

BACON, F., *Sylva Sylvarum* (in vol. 2 of *Works*, Longmans, London, 1870).
BALDICK, R., *The Life of J.-K. Huysmans*, Clarendon Press, Oxford, 1955.
BAMBERGER, B. J., *Fallen Angels*, Jewish Pub. Soc. of America, Philadelphia, 1952.
BAROJA, J. C., *The World of the Witches*, trans. N. Glendinning, Weidenfeld & Nicholson, London, 1964.
BELL, E. T., *The Magic of Numbers*, McGraw-Hill, N.Y., 1946.
BERKELEY, G., *Siris* (in vol. 3 of *Works*, Clarendon Press, Oxford, 1901).
BLAU, J. L., *The Christian Interpretation of the Cabala in the Renaissance*, Columbia Univ. Press, N.Y., 1944.
BOSMAN, L., *The Meaning and Philosophy of Numbers*, Rider, London, 1932.

BOUISSON, M., *Magic: Its History and Principal Rites*, trans. G. Almayrac, Dutton, N.Y., 1961.

BRIFFAULT, R., *The Mothers*, Macmillan, N.Y., 1927. 3 vols.

BRIGGS, K. M., *The Anatomy of Puck*, Routledge & Kegan Paul, London, 1959.

—*Pale Hecate's Team*, Routledge & Kegan Paul, London, 1962.

BROMAGE, B., *The Occult Arts of Ancient Egypt*, Aquarian Press, London, 1953.

BUDGE, E. A. W., *Amulets and Talismans*, University Books, N.Y., 1961 (reprint of *Amulets and Superstitions*).

—*Egyptian Magic*, Kegan Paul, London, 1899.

BURNET, J., *Early Greek Philosophy*, Black, London, 4th edn., 1930.

BUTLER, E. M., *Ritual Magic*, Noonday Press, N.Y., 1959. Paperback.

CAMMELL, C. R., *Aleister Crowley*, Richards Press, London, 1951.

CAMPBELL, F., *Your Days are Numbered*, Gateway, N.Y., 1931.

CASE, P. F., *The Tarot*, Macoy, N.Y., 1947.

CATO, *On Agriculture*, trans. W. D. Hooper, Loeb, 1960.

CHARLES, R. H., *The Apocrypha and Pseudepigrapha of the Old Testament*, Clarendon Press, Oxford, 1913. 2 vols.

—*The Book of Enoch, or 1 Enoch*, Clarendon Press, Oxford, 1912.

—*The Revelation of St. John*, Scribner's, N.Y., 1920. 2 vols.

CHATELHERAULT, E., *You and Your Stars*, Pearson, London, 1960.

CHEASLEY, C. W., *Numerology*, Rider, London, 1926.

CHEIRO, *Cheiro's Book of Numbers*, Herbert Jenkins, London, n.d.

CIRLOT, J. E., *A Dictionary of Symbols*, trans. J. Sage, Routledge & Kegan Paul, London, 1962.

CLODD, E., *Magic in Names*, Dutton, N.Y., 1921.

crowley, a., *Magick in Theory and Practice*, Castle Books, N.Y., n.d. (originally published in 1929).

—*Moonchild*, Mandrake Press, London, 1929.

CUMONT, F., *Astrology and Religion Among the Greeks and Romans*, trans. J. B. Baker, Dover, N.Y., 1960 (reprint of 1912 edn.).

—*The Oriental Religions in Roman Paganism*, Open Court, London, 1911.

CURTISS, H. A. and f. h., *The Key of Destiny*, Curtiss, San Francisco, 1923.

—*The Key to the Universe*, Curtiss, Washington, 1917.

DAVIDSON, T., *Rowan Tree and Red Thread*, Oliver & Boyd, Edinburgh, 1949.

DRIVER, G. R., *Canaanite Myths and Legends*, Clark, Edinburgh, 1956.

—'Sacred Numbers and Round Figures', in *Promise and Fulfilment, Essays Presented to S. H. Hooke*, Clark, Edinburgh, 1963.

The Egyptian Secrets of Albertus Magnus, no publisher, n.d. Paperback.

EISLER, R., *The Royal Art of Astrology*, Herbert Joseph, London, 1946.

ELIADE, M., *The Forge and the Crucible*, trans. S. Corvin, Harper, N.Y., n.d.

—*Patterns in Comparative Religion*, trans. R. Sheed, Sheed & Ward, N.Y., 1958.

FORTUNE, D., *The Mystical Qabalah*, Williams & Norgate, London, 1935.
—*Psychic Self-Defence*, Aquarian Press, London, 1959 (reprint of 1930 edn.).

GARDNER, G. B., *Witchcraft Today*, Citadel Press, N.Y., 1955.
GASTER, T. H., *The Dead Sea Scriptures*, Doubleday, N.Y., 1956.
GIBSON, W. B., *The Science of Numerology*, Burt, N.Y., 1927.
GINSBURG, C. D., *The Kabbalah*, Routledge & Kegan Paul, Ondon, 1955 (reprint of 1863 edn.).
GIVRY, G. DE, *A Pictorial Anthology of Witchcraft, Magic and Alchemy*, University Books, N.Y., 1958 (reprint of 1931 edn.).
GRANT, R. M., *Gnosticism and Early Christianity*, Columbia University Press, N.Y., 1959.
GRAVES, R., *The White Goddess*, Farrar, Strauss & Cudahy, 1948.
—and patai, r., *Hebrew Myths: The Book of Genesis*, Doubleday, N.Y., 1964.
GRAY, E., *The Tarot Revealed*, Inspiration House, N.Y., 1960.

HALL, M. P., *The Most Holy Trinosophia of the Comte de St.-Germain*, Philosophers Press, Los Angeles, 3rd edn., 1949.
—*The Philosophy of Astrology*, Philosophical Research Soc., Los Angeles, 1943.
HARGRAVE, C. P. A., *A History of Playing Cards*, Houghton Mifflin, N.Y., 1930.
HARTMANN, F., *Magic White and Black*, Kegan Paul, London, 1893.
—*Paracelsus*, Kegan Paul, London, n.d.
HEINDEL, M., *Simplified Scientific Astrology*, Rosicrucian Fellowship, Oceanside, 1928.
HOLE, C., *Witchcraft in England*, Scribner's, N.Y., 1947.
HOLMYARD, E. J., *Alchemy*, Penguin, 1957. Paperback.
HONE, J., *W. B. Yeats, 1865–1939*, St. Martin's Press, N.Y., 1962.
HONE, M. E., *The Modern Text Book of Astrology*, Fowler, London, revised edn., 1955.
HOOKE, S. H., *Babylonian and Assyrian Religion*, Hutchinson, London, 1953.
HOPKINS, A. J., *Alchemy Child of Greek Philosophy*, Columbia Univ. Press, N.Y., 1934.
HOPPER, V. F., *Medieval Number Symbolism*, Columbia Univ. Press, N.Y., 1938.
HUGH OF ST.-VICTOR, ST., *Selected Spiritual Writings*, Harper & Row, N.Y., 1962.
HUYSMANS, J.-K., *Down There (La Bas)*, trans. K. Wallis, intro. R. Baldick, University Books, N.Y., 1958.

IDRIES SHAH, S., *The Secret Lore of Magic*, Muller, London, 1957.
IRENAEUS, ST., *Against Heresies* (in *Writings*, Clark, Edinburgh, 1884. 2 vols.).

JAMES, E. O., *Prehistoric Religion*, Praeger, N.Y., 1957.
JANET, P., *Psychological Healing*, trans. E. and C. Paul, Macmillan, N.Y., 1925. 2 vols.
JONAS, H., *The Gnostic Religion*, Beacon Press, Boston, 1958.
JONES, M. E., *Occult Philosophy*, McKay, Philadelphia, 1947.
JONES, W., *Credulities Past and Present*, Chatto & Windus, London, 1880.
JUNG, C. G., *Mysterium Coniunctionis*, trans. R. F. C. Hull, Routledge & Kegan Paul, London, 1963.
—*Psychology and Alchemy*, R. F. C. Hull, Routledge & Kegan Paul, London, 1953.
JUNGMANN, J. A., *The Early Liturgy*, trans. F. A. Brunner, Univ. of Notre Dame Press, 1959.

KING, H. C., *The Background of Astronomy*, Braziller, N.Y., 1958.

KINGSLEY, M., *Outrageous Fortune*, Duell, Sloan & Pearce, N.Y., 1951.

KIRK, G. S., and RAVEN, J. E., *The PreSocratic Philosophers*, Cambridge Univ. Press, 1960.

KIRKCONNELL, W., *The Celestial Cycle*, Univ. of Toronto Press, 1952 (on the *Paradise Lost* theme).

KITTREDGE, G. L., *Witchcraft in Old and New England*, Harvard Univ. Press, 1929.

KOUWER, B. J., *Colors and Their Character*, Martinus Nijhoff, The Hague, 1949.

KRAMER, S. N., *The Sumerians*, Univ. of Chicago Press, 1963.

KUNZ, G. F., *The Magic of Jewels and Charms*, Lippincott, Philadelphia, 1915.

LANGTON, E., *Essentials of Demonology*, Epworth Press, London, 1949.

LAVER, J., *The First Decadent*, Faber, London, 1954.

LEA, H. C., *A History of the Inquisition of the Middle Ages*, Harper, N.Y., 1888. 3 vols.

—*Materials Towards a History of Witchcraft*, ed. A. C. Howland, Yoseloff, N.Y., 1957 (originally published in 1939). 3 vols.

LENORMANT, F., *Chaldean Magic*, Bagster, London, 1877.

LETHBRIDGE, T. C., *Witches: Investigating an Ancient Religion*, Routledge & Kegan Paul, London, 1962.

LEVI, E., *The History of Magic*, trans. A. E. Waite, Dutton, N.Y., 3rd edn., n.d.

—*The Key of the Mysteries*, trans. A. Crowley, Rider, London, 1959.

—*Transcendental Magic, Its Doctrine and Ritual*, trans. A. E. Waite, Redway, London, 1896 (referred to in the text and notes as *Doctrine and Ritual of Magic*).

LEWINSOHN, R., *Science, Prophecy and Prediction*, Premier Books, N.Y., 1962. Paperback.

LEYEL, C. F., *The Magic of Herbs*, Harcourt Brace, N.Y., 1926.

LOPEZ, V., *Numerology*, Citadel Press, N.Y., 1961.

LOWE, J. E., *Magic in Greek and Latin Literature*, Blackwell, Oxford, 1929.

LUCAN, *Pharsalia*, trans. R. Graves, Penguin, 1957.

LYNDOE, E., *Astrology for Everyone*, Dutton, N.Y., 1960.

MACCULLOCH, J. A., *The Celtic and Scandinavian Religions*, Hutchinson, London, n.d.

MACKAY, C., *Extraordinary Popular Delusions and the Madness of Crowds*, Page, 1932 (reprint of 1852 edn.).

Malleus Maleficarum, trans. M. Summers, Pushkin Press, London, 1951.

MARTIN, E. J., *The Trial of the Templars*, Allen & Unwin, London, 1928.

MASTERS, R. E. L., *Eros and Evil*, Julian Press, N.Y., 1962.

MATHERS, S. L., *The Book of the Sacred Magic of Abramelin the Mage*, De Laurence, Chicago, 1932.

—*The Kabbalah Unveiled*, Kegan Paul, London, 1938 (first published in 1887).

—*The Tarot*, Occult Research Press, N.Y., n.d. Paperback. (First published in 1888.)

MCPHERSON, J. M., *Primitive Beliefs in the North-East of Scotland*, Longmans, Green, London, 1929.

MIALL, A. M., *Complete Fortune Telling*, Greenberg, N.Y., 1950.

MONTROSE, *Numerology for Everybody*, Blue Ribbon Books, N.Y., 1940.

MORLEY, H., *Life of Agrippa*, Chapman & Hall, London, 1856. 2 vols.

MORRISH, F., *Outline of Astro-Psychology*, Rider, London, 1952.

MURRAY, M. A., *The God of the Witches*, Anchor Books, N.Y., 1960. Paperback. (First published in 1933.)

—*The Witch-Cult in Western Europe*, Clarendon Press, Oxford, 1921.

NILSSON, M. P., *Greek Folk Religion*, Harper Torchbooks, N.Y., 1961 (reprint of 1940 edn.).

—*Greek Piety*, trans. H. J. Rose, Clarendon Press, Oxford, 1948.

NORTON, T., *The Ordinall of Alchimy*, intro. E. J. Holmyard, Williams & Wilkins, Baltimore, 1929.

OVID, *Fasti*, trans. J. G. Frazer, Loeb, 1931.

PAPINI, G., *The Devil*, trans. A. Foulke, Dutton, N.Y., 1954.

PARACELSUS, *Selected Writings*, trans. N. Guterman, Routledge & Kegan Paul, London, 1951.

PAVITT, W. T. and K., *The Book of Talismans, Amulets and Zodiacal Gems*, Rider, London, 1922.

Pistis Sophia, trans. G. Horner, S.P.C.K., London, 1924.

PLUTARCH, *Isis and Osiris*, trans. F. C. Babbitt (in vol. 5 of *Moralia*, Loeb, 1936).

PTOLEMY, *Tetrabiblos*, trans. F. E. Robbins, Loeb, 1940.

RADFORD, E. and M. A., *Encyclopaedia of Superstitions*, ed. C. Hole, Hutchinson, London, 1961.

RAHNER, H., *Greek Myths and Christian Mystery*, trans. B. Battershaw, Burns & Oates, London, 1963.

RAKOCZI, B. I., *The Painted Caravan*, Brucher, The Hague, 1954 (on the gipsy Tarot).

RANDOLPH, V., *Ozark Superstitions*, Columbia Univ. Press, N.Y., 1947.

READ, J., *Through Alchemy to Chemistry*, Bell, London, 1957.

REDGROVE, H. S., *Bygone Beliefs*, Rider, London, 1920.

REID, V. W., *Towards Aquarius*, Rider, London, n.d.

RHODES, H. T. F., *The Satanic Mass*, Citadel Press, N.Y., 1955.

RIGHTER, C., *Astrology and You*, Fleet, N.Y., 1956.

ROBBINS, R. H., *The Encyclopaedia of Witchcraft and Demonology*, Crown, N.Y., 1959.

ROBSON, V. E., *The Fixed Stars and Constellations in Astrology*, Lippincott, N.Y., 1923.

ROSE, E., *A Razor for a Goat*, Univ. of Toronto Press, 1962.

RUNCIMAN, S., *The Medieval Manichee*, Cambridge Univ. Press, 1955.

SCHMIDT, P., *Superstition and Magic*, Newman Press, Westminster, 1963.

SCHOLEM, G. G., *Major Trends in Jewish Mysticism*, Schocken Books, Jerusalem, 1941; N.Y., 1946.

SCOTT, C., *An Outline of Modern Occultism*, Dutton, N.Y., 2nd edn., 1950.

SEABROOK, W., *Witchcraft: Its Power in the World Today*, Harcourt Brace, N.Y., 1940.

SELIGMANN, K., *History of Magic*, Pantheon Books, N.Y., 1948.

Sepher Yetzirah, trans. W. W. Westcott, Occult Research Press, N.Y., n.d. Paperback.

SHOWERS, P., *Fortune Telling for Fun and Popularity*, Blakiston, Philadelphia, 1945.

SILBERER, H., *Problems of Mysticism and Its Symbolism*, trans. S. E. Jelliffe, Moffat, Yard, N.Y., 1917.

SMITH, D. E., *History of Mathematics*, Dover, N.Y., 1958 (reprint of 1923 edn.). 2 vols.

SMITH, W., *Miracle of the Ages*, Fowler, London, 1934.

STILLMAN, J. M., *The Story of Alchemy and Early Chemistry*, Dover, N.Y., 1960 (reprint of *The Story of Early Chemistry*, 1924).

SUMMERS, M., *The Geography of Witchcraft*, Kegan Paul, London, 1927.

—*Witchcraft and Black Magic*, Rider, London, 1946.

SWIFT, J., *Predictions for the Year 1708 by Isaac Bickerstaff, Esq.*

SYMONDS, J., *The Great Beast*, Roy Publishers, N.Y., 1952.

—*The Magic of Aleister Crowley*, Muller, London, 1958.

TAYLOR, E. S., *History of Playing Cards*, Hotten, London, 1865.

TAYLOR, F. S., *The Alchemists*, Schuman, N.Y., 1949.

THEOCRITUS, *Idylls*, trans. C. S. Calverly, Bell, London, 1913.

THEOPHRASTUS, *Enquiry into Plants*, trans. A. Hort, Loeb, 1916. 2 vols.

THOMPSON, C. J. S., *The Mystery and Lure of Perfumes*, Lippincott, Philadelphia, 1927.

THORNDIKE, L., *A History of Magic and Experimental Science*, Macmillan and Columbia Univ. Press, 1923–58. 8 vols.

TORREY, C. C., *The Apocalypse of John*, Yale Univ. Press, 1958.

TOULMIN, S., and GOODFIELD, J., *The Architecture of Matter*, Harper & Row, N.Y., 1962.

TRACHTENBERG, J., *The Devil and the Jews*, Meridian Books, N.Y., 1961 (first published in 1943).

—*Jewish Magic and Superstition*, Behrman's, N.Y., 1939.

VIRGIL, *Eclogues*, trans. C. S. Calverly, Bell, London, 1913.

WAITE, A. E., *The Book of Ceremonial Magic*, University Books, N.Y., 1961 (reprint of the author's revised version of his *Book of Black Magic and of Pacts*, 1898).

—*The Holy Kabbalah*, University Books, N.Y., n.d.

—*The Pictorial Key to the Tarot*, Rider, London, 1922 (first published in 1910).

—*The Secret Tradition in Alchemy*, Knopf, N.Y., 1926.

WALTON-JORDAN, J., *Your Number and Destiny*, Rowny Press, Santa Barbara, 1936.

WILLIAMS, C., *Witchcraft*, Meridian Books, N.Y., 1959. Paperback. (First published in 1941.)

WOOTTON, A. C., *Chronicles of Pharmacy*, Macmillan, London, 1910. 2 vols.

YATES, F. A., *Giordano Bruno and the Hermetic Tradition*, Routledge & Kegan Paul, London, 1964.

ZAIN, *Predicting Events*, Church of Light, Los Angeles, 1934.

Index

About the Author

Richard Cavendish (1930–2016) was a highly regarded and widely published British historian of magic, myth, and the occult. Educated at Oxford, Cavendish also wrote on British history. He is best remembered for *The Black Arts* (1967), and for editing the acclaimed and influential 24-volume *Man, Myth & Magic: An Illustrated Encyclopedia of the Supernatural*, published from 1970 to 1972.